THE JOURNEY OF CHRISTIANITY TO INDIA IN LATE ANTIQUITY

How did Christianity make its remarkable voyage from the Roman Mediterranean to the Indian subcontinent? By examining the social networks that connected the ancient and late antique Mediterranean to the Indian Ocean, central Asia, and Iran, this book contemplates the social relations that made such movement possible. It also analyzes how the narrative tradition regarding the apostle Judas Thomas, which originated in Upper Mesopotamia and accredited him with evangelizing India, traveled among the social networks of an interconnected late antique world. In this way, the book probes how the Thomas narrative shaped Mediterranean Christian beliefs regarding coreligionists in central Asia and India, impacted local Christian cultures, took shape in a variety of languages, and experienced transformation as it traveled from the Mediterranean to India and back again.

NATHANAEL J. ANDRADE is an associate professor in the Department of History at Binghamton University (SUNY). His previous book was *Syrian Identity in the Greco-Roman World* (Cambridge, 2013).

THE JOURNEY OF CHRISTIANITY TO INDIA IN LATE ANTIQUITY

Networks and the Movement of Culture

NATHANAEL J. ANDRADE

Binghamton University (SUNY)

CAMBRIDGE
UNIVERSITY PRESS

University Printing House, Cambridge CB2 8BS, United Kingdom

One Liberty Plaza, 20th Floor, New York, NY 10006, USA

477 Williamstown Road, Port Melbourne, VIC 3207, Australia

314-321, 3rd Floor, Plot 3, Splendor Forum, Jasola District Centre, New Delhi - 110025, India

103 Penang Road, #05-06/07, Visioncrest Commercial, Singapore 238467

Cambridge University Press is part of the University of Cambridge.

It furthers the University's mission by disseminating knowledge in the pursuit of education, learning and research at the highest international levels of excellence.

www.cambridge.org
Information on this title: www.cambridge.org/9781108409551
DOI: 10.1017/9781108296953

© Nathanael J. Andrade 2018

This publication is in copyright. Subject to statutory exception and to the provisions of relevant collective licensing agreements, no reproduction of any part may take place without the written permission of Cambridge University Press.

First published 2018
First paperback edition 2021

A catalogue record for this publication is available from the British Library

Library of Congress Cataloging in Publication data
NAMES: Andrade, Nathanael J., author.
TITLE: The journey of Christianity to India in late antiquity : networks and the movement of culture / Nathanael J. Andrade, State University of New York, Binghamton.
DESCRIPTION: New York : Cambridge University Press, 2018. | Includes bibliographical references and index.
IDENTIFIERS: LCCN 2017051167 | ISBN 9781108419123
SUBJECTS: LCSH: Missions – India – History. | Church history – Primitive and early church, ca. 30-600. | Acts of Thomas. | Thomas, Apostle, Saint, active 1st century.
CLASSIFICATION: LCC BV3265.3 .A53 2018 | DDC 275.4/01–dc23
LC record available at https://lccn.loc.gov/2017051167

ISBN 978-1-108-41912-3 Hardback
ISBN 978-1-108-40955-1 Paperback

Cambridge University Press has no responsibility for the persistence or accuracy of URLs for external or third-party internet websites referred to in this publication, and does not guarantee that any content on such websites is, or will remain, accurate or appropriate.

Contents

List of Maps	*page* vii
Preface	ix
Acknowledgments	xii
List of Abbreviations	xv
Introduction	1

PART I THE ACTS OF THOMAS — 25

1 The *Acts of Thomas* and Its Impact — 27

PART II CHRISTIANITY, NETWORKS, AND THE RED SEA — 67

2 Early Christianity and Its Many Indias: Complexities of the Sources — 69

3 The Roman Egyptian Network, the Red Sea, and the Indian Ocean — 94

PART III CHRISTIANITY, NETWORKS, AND THE MIDDLE EAST — 137

4 The Movement of Christianity into Sasanian Persia: Perspectives and Sources — 139

5 Social Connectivity between the Roman Levant, Persian Gulf, and Central Asia — 164

6 The Late Antique Impact of the *Acts of Thomas* and Christian Communities in India — 207

Conclusion — 233

Appendix 1: Beginning of Syriac *Acts of Thomas* (Wright's Text)   238
Appendix 2: Beginning of Greek *Acts of Thomas* (Bonnet's Text)   240
Bibliography   242
Index   292

Maps

1. Trade routes of Afro-Eurasia. *page* 17
2. Trade routes and monsoons of the Indian Ocean. 70
3. Trade and communication routes of Asia. 71

Preface

This book examines how the religion of Christianity traveled from the Mediterranean to India. As such, it may seem obvious what one means by "Christianity" at a glance. But the term itself can be quite vexing. Several factors make it so. First, what defines "religion" (and thus Christian religion) and whether it existed among various premodern societies are increasingly issues of debate.[1] While acknowledging the complications and possibilities for anachronism, I will nonetheless employ terms like "religion," "religious culture," and "Christianity" (with its religious implications) throughout this work. Whatever problems they may raise, they do serve the present purpose of defining the type of culture (or cultures) whose movement this book aims to trace.

Second, it is not always easy to distinguish between Christianity and Judaism as two stable and separate religions. Scholars vary in their perspectives regarding when they became distinct, and even then, some have argued that certain Jews were in practice Christians and certain Christians were in practice Jews throughout antiquity. Further difficulties are posed by the widely recognized premises that Christianity and Judaism are blanket terms for multiple, distinct strands of Christian or Jewish belief, practice, and culture. Ancient Jews and Christians often differed regarding what the normative practices or beliefs that constituted the proper bases of their religion were. Given that Christianity and Judaism were characterized by multiplicity and underwent internal transformations, it has been difficult to create universal criteria by which to define or classify them.[2] Even religions that have been deemed beyond the boundaries of Christianity in

---

[1] For example, Nongbri, *Before Religion*; Barton and Boyarin, *Imagine No Religion*; Boyarin, *Border Lines*; BeDuhn, "Mani and Crystallization."

[2] For the challenges of defining Judaism, Christianity, and their divergences and intersections, see, for instance, Boccaccini, *Middle Judaism*; Boyarin, *Border Lines*; Becker and Reed, *Ways That Never Parted*; Shanks, *Partings*; and King, "Which Early Christianity?" This list is by no means comprehensive.

the past have therefore received reevaluation as forms of Christianity. Manichaeism has increasingly been recognized as one such form, even if it may be best to conceive of it as an eclectic and cosmopolitan religion that interwove Christian, Zoroastrian, Jain, and Buddhist religious strands.[3]

When this book uses the term "Christianity," it is in the most inclusive sense possible. The term integrates the various religious communities that scholars have typically labeled "Judaeo-Christian," "baptist," or Manichaean to distinguish them from what have arbitrarily been defined as more "normative" forms of Christianity. But this is primarily for the purpose of making it easier for readers to navigate general trends in the movement of Christian cultural strands over vast distances. When this book makes references to "baptists," "Judaeo-Christians," and Manichaeans, it is not with the intent of taking a particular position on whether they were or were not Christians. Recognizing how porous and unstable religious boundaries were, it simply stresses how such figures too embodied, carried, and moved threads of what can be defined as Christian culture. Similarly, when this book employs the phrasing "Christian culture," it is not to imply that a single, monolithic Christianity or Christian culture inhabited ancient Afro-Eurasia. One can speak of many "Christianities" or "Christian cultures." But for purposes of clarity, references to Christianity or "Christian" denote any practice, cultural life, or person within a vast and diverse array that can be qualified as Christian in context. Christian culture was very heterogeneous indeed; Christians assumed many shapes and sizes. Such points are relevant to the second consideration.

This book examines sources depicting the movement of Christianity to India, and it includes Manichaeism as a religion that both shaped and intersected with the categorical frame of Christianity.[4] As such, it analyzes the early movement of Manichaeism and the sources that describe it. But it does not recount the entire history of its movement throughout Afro-Eurasia. It instead explores how it traveled on the first legs of its journey to the Roman empire and central Asia from its lower Mesopotamian regional

---

[3] Scholars have traditionally construed Manichaeism as a religion entirely distinct from Christianity, but it has more recently been conceived of as a culturally pluralistic strand of Christianity that earned a reputation for heterodoxy over late antiquity. See, for example, BeDuhn and Mirecki, *Frontiers of Faith*, in which BeDuhn and Mirecki, "Placing the *Acts of Archelaus*"; Van Oort, *Augustine and Manichaean Christianity*; BeDuhn, "'Not to Depart from Christ'"; and Pederson, "Manichaean Self-Designations in the Western Tradition." But more recently, see BeDuhn, "Mani and Crystallization"; and De Jong, "*Cologne Mani Codex*," 132-34 for critiques of premises that Manichaeism was a form of Christianity or derived from any dominant religious strand. Other works on Manichaeism are referenced in this book as appropriate.

[4] See, for example, BeDuhn, "Mani and Crystallization."

origins. This is in part because the study of Manichaeism has increasingly constituted its own unique field of analysis, and the nature of its movement throughout Eurasia and north Africa, attested by sources in a dazzling array of languages, has received the examination of specialists. But it is also due to the fact that such a study of Manichaeism would extend beyond the geographic and chronological parameters of this study.

Place names can be vexing too. Given the trans-regional and, indeed, trans-imperial nature of this work, it is not unusual to encounter cities, sites, and regions that bear different names in diverse languages. This tendency is amplified by the fact that vast empires governed by different language groups rose, underwent consolidation, and receded, often leaving a legacy of place names if nothing else. Classical Babylonia, for instance, could be represented by different terms in Greek, Aramaic, or Iranian languages. It is noteworthy that for the connected territories between the Levant and China, scholars have been assembling a polyglot database of place names.[5] This work will often (but not always) use Greek names or terms for sites in the Middle East, Red Sea, or Indian Ocean, for the following reasons. First, many of the sources cited in this work were composed in Latin or Greek, and even if many sources are in Syriac too, they sometimes represent a tradition informed by Greek precursors. Second, with the obvious exception of Indian Ocean and east African locations, many regions treated in this work were at some point governed by successor empires of Alexander the Great or by the Roman empire, in which Greek toponyms proliferated. Third, many names of ports in coastal India are known primarily from Greek or Latin texts. Muziris and Barbarikon are some key examples. The use of Greek and Latin toponyms will not be universal, however, and certain occasions justify using other languages. In direct quotations of ancient sources in Syriac or Asian languages, the toponym typically will be cited according to the language used. In Chapter 4, the consolidation of Christianity in Sasanian Persia is examined through the prism of Syriac texts. Aramaic or Iranian toponyms will thus be rendered as they normally appear in Syriac sources.

---

[5] Lieu and Mikkelsen, "Places and Peoples," with Lieu, "Da Qin." See *Serica*: bighistoryinstitute.org/pubstatic/research/centres_and_groups/ancient_cultures_research_centre/research/cultural_ex_silkroad/serica/. The various place names for sites (when known) in the Indian Ocean can be synthesized by consulting the scholarly literature cited in this book.

Acknowledgments

The research and composition of this book have been a rewarding odyssey. I cannot thank enough people, and I cannot thank many people enough. But here I will try, however insufficient it may be. The Department of History at the University of Oregon and its faculty were marvelous in their support for much of the book's research and writing. The Department of History at Binghamton University (SUNY) helped me bring it to a satisfying close. At crucial junctures, an Andrew Mellon Foundation Fellowship for Assistant Professors at the Institute for Advanced Study at Princeton (2012–2013) and a Solmsen Fellowship at the Institute for Research in the Humanities at the University of Wisconsin (2015–2016) provided me with immense resources, wonderful colleagues, and a priceless commodity: time. I do not think that I could have completed the book without them. A Loeb Classical Library Foundation Fellowship generously supported my research travel overseas. With a Faculty Research Award from the Office of the Vice President for Research and Innovation at the University of Oregon, and a Brush Fellowship from the History Department, I did a great deal of research, writing, and travel. The Institute for African Studies at Columbia University also deserves mention and gratitude for extending to me an affiliation that also made much of my research possible.

The gratitude that I owe others is limitless. Many drafts of chapters have been circulated. Numerous presentations have been given. A host of conversations has enriched me. So I have many people to thank for their advice and input. David Potter and Emma Dench deserve special mention for years of unwavering support for all my research endeavors. Raymond Van Dam has long inspired my deepest reflections on late antiquity. Michael Sharp imparted invaluable contributions to the project at every critical stage and in every conceivable form. Sarah Starkey, Rogini Rajendiran, and Jay Boggis enabled me to bring it to a successful close. I cannot imagine having finished the book without them. The anonymous referees provided vital guidance for new conceptualization and rewriting; I thank them for their thoughtfulness and insight. Angelos Chaniotis, Susan Friedman, Ariel Lewin, A. E. T. McLaughlin, Ali Akhtar, Hamish Cameron, Edward Watts, Rubina Raja, Katell Berthelot, Joseph Reed, Jennifer Baird, and Ted Kaizer gave me the opportunities to present my work at various stages. Glen Bowersock, Susan Ashbrook Harvey, Christopher Jones, Stephen Shoemaker, Steven Sidebotham, Jeremy Simmons, Roberta Tomber, and Joel Walker enriched me with their conversations and correspondence. The staff of the IAS (Princeton), IRH (Wisconsin–Madison), and the History Departments of the University of Oregon and Binghamton University (SUNY) deserve special mention: Marian Zelazny, Maria Tuya, Terrie Bramley, Ann Harris, Megan Falater, Hari Jost, Daniel Kim, Martina Armstrong, Kathleen Brenner, Sharon Fipps, Nicholas Mahlum, Colleen Marshall, Keith Limbach, and Kathleen Fedorchak exceeded every need. There is a long list of people who have shaped my work and narrative: Derick Alexandre, Alexander Angelov, Sean Anthony, Jonathan Arnold, Bryan Averbuch, Lindsay Braun, Howard Brown, Sam Caldis, Elizabeth Casteen, Giuseppe Castellano, John Chaffee, Aquila Chase, Rob Chenault, John-Henry Clay, Kathleen Coleman, Patricia Crone, Edward Dabrowa, Davaleena Das, Arnab Dey, Nicola di Cosmo, Sean Dry, Jennifer Finn, Gil Gambash, Patrick Geary, David Graf, Max Harris, Heather DeHaan, Jeremy Hutton, Young Kim, Dimitri Krallis, Derek Kreuger, Stephen Lambert, Meg Leja, Vincent Lloyd, David Luebke, Rachel Mairs, Randall McGowen, Richard McKenney, Jonathan McLaughlin, Ian Mladjov, Ian Moyer, Jason Neelis, John Nicols, Lynn Nyhart, Elizabeth Platte, Ruben Post, Talia Prussen, Xiaoyan Qi, Joe Ricker, Rubina Raja, Samuele Rocca, Emily Rush, Ortal-Paz Saar, Adam Schor, Kent Schull, Andreas Schwab, Jared Secord, Eivind Seland, Paul Taylor, Sarah Trevisan, Peter Van Alfen, Ute Wartenberg, Leigh Ann Wheeler, Elsbeth van der Wilt, Bob Wolenksy, Lisa Wolverton, George Wright, and Marta Żuchowska. As always, my parents, brothers, and extended family were ceaseless in their help, and they handled parts of the manuscript too. I owe special heartfelt thanks to my wife Jinny, my mother Marcia, and my father Paul in this respect.

Many parts of Chapter 5 appeared in *Mediterraneo Antico*. Substantial portions of Chapter 3 were published in the *Journal of Hellenic Studies*. With the kind permission of the journals' editors and the Society for the Promotion of Hellenic Studies, such material has been reproduced.

The book is dedicated to my son Oliver, whose patience and playful smile have helped me weather long hours of work. I hope that he can someday understand why I have done it. I also wish to remember my grandfather Joseph and my aunt Jennifer. Treasuring the best of the apostolic teachings, they could not witness the book's completion.

Abbreviations

AB	*Analecta Bollandiana*
AE	*L'Année épigraphique*
AJA	*American Journal of Archaeology*
AMSS	*Acta Martyrum et Sanctorum Syriace.* Ed. Paul Bedjan. 7 vols. Paris and Leipzig: Harrassowitz, 1890–1897
BNJ	*Brill's New Jacoby.* Ed. Ian Worthington (Leiden: Brill: 2007–). See also *FGrH*
CCSL	Corpus Christianorum. Series Latina
CSCO	Corpus Scriptorum Christianorum Orientalium
CSEL	Corpus Scriptorum Ecclesiasticorum Latinorum
CIIP	*Corpus Inscriptionum Iudaeae/Palaestinae*
CIS	*Corpus Inscriptionum Semiticarum* (1881–)
CRAI	*Comptes rendus des séances de l'Académie des Inscriptions et Belles-Lettres*
FGrH	*Die Fragmente der griechischen Historiker* (including *BNJ*). Ed. Felix Jacoby et al. Leiden: Brill, 1923–
GCS	Die griechischen christlichen Schriftsteller der ersten Jahrhunderte
GRBS	*Greek, Roman, and Byzantine Studies*
IGSK 65	*Inschriften griechischer Städte aus Kleinasien.* Vol. 65: *Iscrizioni dello estremo oriente greco: un repertorio.* Ed. Filippo Canali de Rossi. Bonn: Habelt, 2004
IGLS 17.1	*Inscriptions grecques et latines de la Syrie*, Vol. 17, fasc. 1: *Palmyre.* Ed. J.-B. Yon. Beirut: IFPO, 2012
IHatra	*Inventaire des inscriptions hatréennes.* Ed. Basile Aggoula. Paris: Geuthner, 1991; Klaus Beyer, *Die aramäischen Inschriften aus Assur, Hatra und dem übrigen Ostmesopotamien: (datiert 44 v. Chr. bis 238 n. Chr.).* Gottingen: Vandenhoeck & Ruprecht, 1998;

	Roberto Bertolino, *Manuel d'épigraphie hatréenne*. Paris: Geuthner, 2008
JAOS	*Journal of the American Oriental Society*
JECS	*Journal of Early Christian Studies*
JHS	*Journal of Hellenic Studies*
JRS	*Journal of Roman Studies*
JThS	*Journal of Theological Studies*
JWH	*Journal of World History*
OCP	*Orientalia Christiana Periodica*
ODB	*Oxford Dictionary of Byzantium*. Ed. Alexander Kazhdan. 3 vols. New York: Oxford University Press, 1991
OGIS	*Orientis graeci inscriptiones selectae*. Ed. Wilhelm Dittenberger. Leipzig: Hirzel, 1903–1905
O. Kell.	*Greek Ostraka from Kellis*. Ed. K. A. Worp. Oxford: Oxford University Press, 2004
O. Petr.	*Greek Ostraca in the Bodleian Library at Oxford and Various Other Collections*. Ed. Jon Gavin Tait and Claire Préaux. 3 vols. London: Egypt Exploration Society, 1930–1964; *Ostraca greci e bilingui del Petrie Museum of Egyptian Archaeology*. Ed. Maria Serena Funghi, Gabriella Messeri, and Cornelia Römer. 3 vols. Florence: Gonnelli
P. Cair. Isid.	*The Archive of Aurelius Isidorus in the Egyptian Museum, Cairo, and the University of Michigan*. Ed. A. E. R. Boak and H. C. Youtie. Ann Arbor: University of Michigan Press, 1960
P. Col.	*Fourth Century Documents from Karanis*. Ed. Roger Bagnall and Naphtali Lewis. Missoula, MT: Scholars Press, 1979; and *Columbia Papyri*. Vol. 8. Ed. Roger Bagnall, T. T. Renner, and K. A. Worp. Atlanta, GA: Scholars Press, 1990
P. Dura	*The Excavations at Dura Europos, Final Report*, Vol. 5, Pt. 1. *The Parchments and Papyri*. Ed. C. Bradford Welles, Robert Fink, and J. Frank Gilliam. New Haven, CT: Yale University Press, 1959
P. Harr.	*The Rendel Harris Papyri of Woodbrooke College, Birmingham*, Vol. 1. Ed. J. E. Powell. Cambridge: Cambridge University Press, 1936

P. Lond.	Greek Papyri in the British Museum. Ed. F. G. Kenyon et al. 7 vols. London: British Museum, 1893–1974
P. Oxf.	Some Oxford Papyri. Ed. E. P. Wegener. 2 vols. Leiden: Brill, 1942–1948
P. Oxy.	The Oxyrhynchus Papyri (1898–)
P. Panop. Beatty	Papyri from Panopolis in the Chester Beatty Library. Ed. T. C. Skeat. Dublin: Hodges and Figgis, 1964
P. Rylands	Catalogue of the Greek and Latin Papyri in the John Rylands Library, Manchester. Ed. A. S. Hunt et al. 4 vols. Manchester: Manchester University Press, 1911–1952
P. Sakaon	The Archive of Aurelius Sakaon: Papers of an Egyptian Farmer in the Last Century of Theadelphia. Ed. G. M. Parássoglou. Bonn: Habelt, 1978
PAT	Palmyrene Aramaic Texts. Ed. Delbert Hillers and Eleonora Cussini. Baltimore: Johns Hopkins University Press, 1996
PO	Patrologia Orientalis
SB	Sammelbuch griechischer Urkunden aus Ägypten. Strasbourg: Trübner, 1915–
SC	Sources chrétiennes
SEG	Supplementum Epigraphicum Graecum
TEAD	The Excavations at Dura-Europos: Preliminary Reports. New Haven, CT: Yale University Press, 1929–1952; The Excavations at Dura Europos: Final Reports. New Haven: Yale University Press, 1946–
TLG	Thesaurus Linguae Graecae (2001–)
ZPE	Zeitschrift für Papyrologie und Epigraphik

Introduction

In the city of Jerusalem, a follower of the recently crucified Jesus confronts one of the greatest challenges that he has faced. Having cast lots with the rest of Jesus' apostles, he discovers that he is to trek to India to preach. But he refuses due to the enormity of the task. As he wavers, the likeness of Jesus appears to him in a vision and exhorts him to complete his mission. But he again refuses. It just so happens that an Indian merchant is in Jerusalem, and Jesus, recently resurrected, approaches him in the marketplace. Offering his recalcitrant apostle as a slave, he quickly composes a contract with the merchant, and the transaction is sealed. The Indian merchant, named Habban, sails from Jerusalem with his slave, and by doing so, he ensures the evangelization of India.[1] Thus begins the surviving *Acts of the Apostle Thomas*, one of the most oft-cited sources for the movement of Christianity from the Roman empire throughout the ancient Asian landmass.

Historians are invariably at the mercy of their sources, and this is certainly so for historians endeavoring to narrate the voyage of early Christianity to the Indian subcontinent and how it traveled across Asia to reach it. This book accordingly examines the movement of Christianity to various parts of the ancient Afro-Eurasian world system and its anchorage in them through the analytical lenses offered by recent trends in world history. As it does, it also raises the question of what exactly constitutes an historical source for the arrival of Christianity in India or, for that matter, in the Iranian plateau or central Asia. As ancient historians increasingly craft narratives of the transimperial and intercrossed webs of ancient societies, their expanded scope necessitates that they consult sources that have been generated by diverse unfamiliar contexts or that possess epistemologically complicated backgrounds. But such sources are not always placed in proper context, and the

---

[1] *Acts of Thomas* 1–3 in the Greek (ed. Bonnet); ܚܒܢ ܩ in the Syriac (ed. Wright). On slavery in the *Acts of Thomas*, see Glancy, "Slavery."

epistemological issues that they raise are not always adequately recognized. As a result, many of the texts that scholars from diverse fields have treated as historical sources for Christianity's early movement to India and central Asia are perhaps not sources for this phenomenon at all. They instead reflect historical experiences of a literary tradition, not the fact of Christianity's movement. No source is perhaps more vulnerable to this critique than the apocryphal *Acts of Thomas* (or hereafter the *Acts*).[2]

According to the *Acts of Thomas*, an apostle named Judas evangelized all of India. Because this apostle bore the Aramaic epithet of "twin" (ܬܐܘܡܐ, *tāmā*), he quickly became known as "Thomas" (ܬܐܘܡܐ, *tāwma* or a similar variation). Far from being a sterile narrative known only to enthusiasts of antiquity, this text is part of the living tradition of Thomas Christians in south India. Many of these in fact trace their communal origins to the activity of this very apostle and accordingly value the testimony offered by his *Acts*, alongside certain orally transmitted narratives linked intimately to their sacred topographies. As the chapters of this book outline, the *Acts of Thomas* has been cited by Thomas Christians as evidence for the antiquity of Christian traditions in south India and for missions that the apostle Thomas conducted there in the decades after the death of Jesus of Nazareth. It has also served as fodder for historians of ancient and late antique Christianity or of the connectivity of the Mediterranean, Red Sea, and Indian Ocean worlds, even when they deem the events or people of the *Acts* to be invented.[3] In fact, the *Acts*' fundamental ambiguity and empirical weaknesses often constitute the greatest assets for the scholars who treat it as evidence for the phenomena that they seek to evaluate. While probably composed in Syriac in Upper Mesopotamia during the mid-to-late third century (as discussed in Chapter 1), the text is by most reckonings unclear regarding whether Judas Thomas traveled from the Levant to India by way of the Red Sea or via Mesopotamia and the Persian Gulf. In its apparent lack of clarity, and due to the existence of known trade routes in both instances, it is often surmised that early Christianity could have followed either route at an early date and probably did so. Whether scholars believe the account, deem it invented, think it contrived in its specifics but representative of a broader phenomenon, or proclaim uncertainty, they have repeatedly cited the *Acts* in support of the premise that it could be a source for Christianity's arrival and anchorage in India before 400 CE.

---

[2] *Acts of Thomas* (ed. Bonnet) for Greek and (ed. Wright) for Syriac.
[3] For connectivity within the Mediterranean, see Horden and Purcell, *Corrupting Sea*.

In light of such issues, this book analyzes how Christianity traveled from the Roman Mediterranean to central and south Asia. But it does so in ways that rely as little as possible on the dubious testimony of apostolic apocrypha and late antique hagiographies. By examining the dispositions of the social networks that connected the various regions of the ancient Afro-Eurasian world system, it probes how and when traders and travelers carried their embodied Christian cultures to new places, transferred them to converts, and thereby enabled these cultures to find regional anchorage and enjoy movement farther afield. The book is in this regard part of a recent fruitful trend in intercrossed or connected histories that examine the interactions of various populations inhabiting the world system of ancient Afro-Eurasia.[4] It does not analyze the totality of dynastic interactions, objects exchanged, or ideas transmitted by such populations, and it does not provide a historical description of the populations, kingdoms, or empires of Afro-Eurasia involved. But it does focus on the movement of Christianity and the networks that carried its culture, and it thereby reconstructs the social connectivity by which Christian subjects transported their Christian culture in its various forms from the Mediterranean basin to the Indian Ocean world.

As the book maintains, what can be known about ancient socio-commercial networks is of immense value for those who aim to reconstruct the movement of Christianity throughout the ancient Afro-Eurasian world system. The textual and archaeological evidence for such networks between the Mediterranean and the Indian subcontinent provides valid alternatives to dubious literary narratives. By contemplating the networks, one can craft a new lens of interpretation regarding when and how Christianity arrived and became anchored in central Asia and the Indian subcontinent, and one can trace the social pathways that it followed. The networks also illuminate how the remarkable narrative tradition regarding the deeds of the apostle Judas Thomas traveled from its origins in Upper Mesopotamia

---

[4] Werner and Zimmermann, *De la comparaison à l'histoire croisée* and "Beyond Comparison" (for the approach); Lieberman, *Beyond Binary Histories*; Subrahmanyam, *Explorations in Connected History* (for early modern periods); and Pollock, *Language of the Gods*. I borrow the concept of "world system" from Frank and Gills, *World System* and "5000 Year World System" and Beaujard, "World-Systems." For the ancient world specifically, see Reed, "Beyond the Land of Nod"; Dilley, "Religious Intercrossing"; Pollard, "Indian Spices and Roman 'Magic'"; Fitzpatrick, "Provincializing Rome"; McLaughlin, *Rome and the Distant East*; Beaujard, *Mondes*; Fowden, *Before and After Muhammad*; Hansen, *Silk Road*; Wilken, *First Thousand Years*; Canepa, *Theorizing Cross-Cultural Interaction*; Beckwith, *Greek Buddha*; Lieu and Mikkelson, *Between Rome and China*; Scott, *Ancient Worlds*; Frankopan, *Silk Roads*; Nickel, "First Emperor."

to south India, where Thomas Christians would continue to reanimate it well over a thousand years later.

Socio-Commercial Networks and Christian Culture: Dispositions and Significance

According to the *Acts*, an Indian merchant named Habban purchased the apostle Judas Thomas in Jerusalem and transported him to India. He did so at the prompting of his king, who wanted a craftsman to build him a palace. As we will see in various parts of the book, certain features of the narrative correspond with contemporary evidence for commercial practices in the ancient world. But for the most part, the narrative misrepresents or occludes many of the practices and relationships that enabled commodities and even traders to travel throughout the geographic span between the Roman Levant and India. What made such movement possible therefore merits clarification.

In 157 CE, Palmyrene merchants who had recently returned from a commercial trip to "Scythia" (north India) arranged for certain notables to be commemorated by honorific statues and inscriptions at their ancestral city of Palmyra, a site located in the dry Syrian steppe. The inscriptions, written in Greek and Palmyrenean Aramaic, have suffered damage and possess certain lacunae, but their general message is clear.[5] In these inscriptions, the merchants identified themselves by the names of the ship captains or owners who had transported them to and from north India, and they celebrated conspicuous individuals who had aided them in their journey as patrons. At least one of these patrons was a certain Marcus Ulpius Iaraios, whose benefactions to caravans, merchants, or expatriates are among the most commemorated in Palmyrene epigraphy and whose son on one occasion led a caravan from the Persian Gulf to Palmyra.[6] While the specific inscriptions do not pinpoint where these patrons or merchants resided, a host of other documents from Palmyra constitute honorific inscriptions that caravans traveling between Palmyra and the Persian Gulf or expatriate communities residing near the gulf, especially at Charax Spasinou, Phorat, and Vologasias, raised for notables who had

---

[5] *IGLS* 17.1.250, with perhaps 17.1.26. The name of the patron and date from 17.1.26 has been effaced, but some suggest that it was the famous Marcus Ulpius Iaraios, the prominent Palmyrene identified in 17.1.250 and who is recognized for his patronage in a number of Palmyrene inscriptions. See *IGLS* 17.1.26 for commentary.

[6] *IGLS* 17.1.202, 248–50, [251], 255–56, [313]; *PAT* 1411.

helped them.⁷ The merchants who traveled to "Scythia" were accordingly among expatriate Palmyrenes who dwelled near the Persian Gulf. While some of their patrons may have been Palmyrenes who served in the royal administration of Mesene at places such as Bahrain⁸ or south Mesopotamia,⁹ their patrons predominantly dwelled at Palmyra.

The inscriptions commissioned by the Palmyrene merchants who had sailed to India are important documents for Palmyrene commercial networks.¹⁰ As texts, they illustrate the movements of merchants and their connections to patrons at Palmyra. But the value of these inscriptions is not limited to their status as texts. As material and physical objects, they were the products of the social networks that Palmyrenes maintained over the vast distance between the Roman Levant and north India. They in fact both expressed and perpetuated relationships of reciprocity and social pathways that enabled the movement and transfer of commodities from south Asia to the Roman Mediterranean. Such commodities brought immense wealth.¹¹ Despite being expatriates who resided in cities of lower Mesopotamia and the Persian Gulf, the Palmyrenes who trekked to India from Persian Gulf sites maintained business connections in their home city. The notables for whom they raised statues and honorific inscriptions were in fact financial patrons, investors, creditors, commercial contacts, and brokers of protection from brigands.¹² These in many ways facilitated the activities of the caravans that moved goods from Palmyra, across the desert, and to the Persian Gulf. They also enabled the seaward voyages of merchants who received these products. In exchange, grateful merchants commissioned honorific inscriptions and statues to commemorate such acts and to confer honor upon their patrons.

Through such commemoration, Palmyrene investors and patrons built reputations as upright citizens and benefactors, even as they pursued their

---

⁷ *IGLS* 17.1.16, 23–25, 87, 127, 150, 241, 243, and 245; *PAT* 1062=Milik, *Dédicaces*, 13=*SEG* 7.135=Delplace and Yon, "Inscriptions," 284, An 30 (residential communities) and *IGLS* 17.1.67, 74, 87–89 and 240–51 (caravans/merchants).
⁸ *IGLS* 17.1.245.
⁹ *IGLS* 127 and 150; *PAT* 1062=Milik, *Dédicaces*, 13=*SEG* 7.135=Delplace and Yon, "Inscriptions," 284, An 30 reflects a patron with an orientation at Vologasias. *IGLS* 17.1.246 apparently commemorates a figure at Phorat.
¹⁰ My analysis of Palmyrene trade and networks is informed by Gorea, "Sea and Inland Trade"; Seland, "Organisation," "Palmyrene Long-Distance Trade," and *Ships of the Desert*; and Gregoratti, "Palmyrenes" and "Palmyra," with Ruffing, "Trade with India," 200 and 208; and Young, *Rome's Eastern Trade*, 123–68 (esp. 151–56).
¹¹ A tomb inscription of Palmyra documents a caravan's haul or the tariff on it. See *PAT* 2634; de Romanis, "*Aurei*," 63–69; Tchernia, *Romans and Trade*, 8.
¹² The key work on Palmyra's notables is Yon, *Notables*, with 100–18 especially treating their links to caravans and their protection. My views differ somewhat from those of Young, *Rome's Eastern Trade*, 123–68 (esp. 151–56), who sees synodiarchs and not patrons as primary investors.

own financial interests. A notable named Soados, son of Boliades, who probably resided at Vologasias in lower Mesopotamia during part of his career, was in this vein commemorated by caravans, Palmyra's civic council, and Roman magistrates for his support of merchants, caravans, and the expatriate community at Vologasias. On at least one occasion, he organized an armed forced that protected caravans from the imminent threat of brigands.[13] Some such figures could even serve as *synodiarch*, a civic official responsible for organizing the actual caravans to the Persian Gulf. Just as often, they received honors from a caravan through the activity of its *synodiarchs*, or from Palmyrenes linked to the residential communities at Charax Spasinou, Phorat, and Vologasias. These inscriptions are remarkable for their emphasis on the altruism of commercial investors and patrons. Strictly speaking, they were being celebrated for civic benefactions that aided caravans, the merchants on a ship, or a group of traders, whether these benefactions assumed the form of money, intervention with foreign governments, or the actual organization of protection.[14]

But the generosity and protection of such patrons should not disguise the personal stake that they had in the enterprises of those whom they aided. Despite the inscriptions' emphasis on altruism, it is reasonable to infer that their good deeds were motivated by their investment in the cargos that certain members of a caravan, ship, or port community transported. Such patrons could lend money to certain individual merchants for the acquisition of a cargo or even a ship, and by protecting or facilitating the movements of an entire caravan or vessel, they were probably protecting individuals to whom they were financially connected. In this sense, Palmyrene patrons constituted players within a commercial network that ultimately linked them to the Palmyrene merchants of the Persian Gulf who sailed to India. Despite the vagaries of distance, they supplied credit, financial resources, commodities, or protection to expatriate or itinerant merchants; in return, they received information, different commodities, profits, and admiration. As a result, investors and merchants established trust in one another and nourished beliefs that contacts would fulfill their obligations even if they were far away.[15]

---

[13] *IGLS* 17.1.127 and 150; *PAT* 1062=Milik, *Dédicaces*, 13=*SEG* 7.135=Delplace and Yon, "Inscriptions," 284, An 30; *IGLS* 17.1.29. See Andrade, "Inscribing the Citizen."

[14] *IGLS* 17.1.16, 23–25, 127, 150, 241, 243, and 245; *PAT* 1062=Milik, *Dédicaces*, 13=*SEG* 7.135=Delplace and Yon, "Inscriptions," 284, An 30 (residential communities) and *IGLS* 17.1.67, 74, 87–89, 240–51 (caravans/merchants).

[15] My views are especially informed by the studies of Aslanian, *From the Indian Ocean* on early modern Armenian merchants and Terpstra, *Trading Communities* on Roman traders, along with Terpstra, "Palmyrene Temple" (esp. 44–46), Ruffing, "Trade with India," and Tchernia, *Romans and Trade*, 28–50.

The form of social relations that characterized Roman-era Palmyra finds a striking parallel in a fascinating Greek inscription perhaps originating from the vicinity of Kandahar (Alexandria Arachosia) in central Asia during the second century BCE. An epitaph, it contains the testimony of a merchant named Sophytus, whose father bore the Indian name of Narates (Nārada in Sanskrit), and it describes how he funded his commercial enterprises on the Silk Road by borrowing money and then traveling to "many cities."[16] Sophytus was undoubtedly enmeshed in his own social network that facilitated the movement of credit, information, and commodities over long distances, but the specific components of his network remain obscure. It is therefore fortunate that Palmyrenes inscriptions more adequately illuminate such social connectivity.

The physical bodies of Palmyrenes were ultimately responsible for carrying products, information, credit, and culture over long distances. After all, such articles could only travel as far and as fast as the bodies that bore them. But social relations were the sinews that made possible the movement of such bodies and the articles that they carried, and they facilitated the transfer of culture from one mobile body to another. They ultimately enabled wealthy patrons at Palmyra to forward credit and protection over vast geographic spaces. They facilitated the movement of merchants who trafficked goods in caravans across dry steppe wilderness and perhaps on rafts down the Euphrates to Palmyrene expatriates on the Persian Gulf. They empowered Palmyrene expatriates, who received such goods, to transfer them to ships, to contract sea-captains and sailors (and perhaps even acquire a vessel), to move such commodities to India, and to bring back eastern products for caravans to carry from the Persian Gulf to Palmyra.[17] However hierarchical or uneven they may have been, the bonds of reciprocity, mutual obligation, and information transmission that connected all these players created social pathways that were essential to the movement and transfer of the commodities that they sought. These relationships constituted a social network.

The Palmyrene socio-commercial network is only one of many that contributed to an interconnected antiquity. Its social dispositions were

---

[16] Merkelbach and Stauber, *Jenseits des Euphrat*, no. 105=Bernard, Pinault, and Rougemont, "Deux nouvelles inscriptions," 227–356. Recently, Mairs, "*Sopha gramma*" and *Hellenistic Far East*, 106–17; Neelis, *Early Buddhist Transmission*, 100–1 and 108. The inscription's provenance, however, has not been established.

[17] Seland, "Persian Gulf or the Red Sea?," "Organisation," "Palmyrene Long-Distance Trade," and *Ships of the Desert*; and Gorea, "Sea and Inland Trade" provide details regarding the forms of travel that the Palmyrenes undertook.

standard in premodern and even early modern times. Consisting of a core group that shared regional origins, and even civic, ethnic, or religious affiliations as well, it extended over vast spaces and intermingled with other networks that had their own unique compositions. It also established residential settlements in foreign places, especially on the Persian Gulf. These maintained contact with compatriots at Palmyra through caravans and mobile players, but they also facilitated meaningful social interactions between Palmyrenes and the residents of lower Mesopotamia, Mesene, and the Persian Gulf. The Palmyrene network also moved culture. It brought a cursive script abroad, and this may even have been adopted by the Manichaeans at the Persian Gulf.[18] Its activity is presumably one of the reasons why Palmyrene and north Indian art apparently came to share some common features.[19]

In antiquity, networks like that of the Palmyrenes created social pathways along which culture traveled. This was not the only phenomenon on which networks had an impact. In recent years, scholars have yoked the explanatory power of social networks in a variety of ways.[20] Their work has illuminated the formation of trans-Mediterranean Greek ethnicity,[21] the cohesion of late antique doctrinal factions,[22] rabbinic social relations and practices,[23] and the effectiveness of communication and informed decision-making in the ancient Athenian democracy.[24] They have also been the focus of archaeologists who have harnessed their explanatory potency to illustrate regional connections and the economic and social significance of sites.[25] On the basis of the *Periplus of the Erythraean Sea*, a recent study has employed the approach to visualize the connectivity of ports and sites of

---

[18] Pederson and Larsen, *Manichaean Texts*, 3–5 and 113–85 (esp. 132–37 and 164).

[19] Ingholt, *Palmyrene and Gandharan Sculpture*; Schlumberger, *L'Occident*, 226–390; Long, "Facing the Evidence," 138–39.

[20] Some key introductions are Watts, *Six Degrees*; Scott, *Social Network Analysis*, and *What Is Social Network Analysis?*; Wasserman and Faust, *Social Network Analysis*; Carrington, Scott, and Wasserman, *Models and Methods in Social Network Analysis*; Barabási, *Linked*, and *How Everything Is Connected to Everything*; Newman, Barabási, and Watts, *Structure and Dynamics of Networks*.

[21] Malkin, Constantakopoulou, and Panagopoulou, *Greek and Roman Networks*; Malkin, *Small Greek World*.

[22] Schor, *Theodoret's People*.   [23] Hezser, *Social Structure of the Rabbinic Movement*.

[24] Ober, *Democracy and Knowledge*.

[25] Knappett, *Network Analysis in Archaeology*, in which "Introduction: Why Networks?" 4–6 (diffusionism); and Rivers, Knappett, and Evans, "What Makes a Site Important," 125–50. Also, Knappett, *Archaeology of Interaction*; Bentley, "Introduction to Complex Systems" and "Scale-Free Network Growth." The volume of Fenn and Römer-Strehl, *Networks in the Mediterranean World* contains articles that analyze the circulation of pottery (which suggests the existence of broader social networks even if the identities of their participants are still obscure).

the Indian Ocean and the demand and circulation of products.[26] Network approaches are the main analytic focus of a new volume on the Roman East and Parthia.[27]

Despite their different focuses, all these studies have demonstrated the importance of social networks for transmitting knowledge and organizing human activity. They all point to a significant social fact of the premodern world, which did not know telegraphs, telephones, or email. In such a world, ideas and culture, like material objects and letters, only traveled when human bodies carried them. For ideas and culture to traverse geographic expanses, the people that embodied them had to move and transfer them to other human bodies that could carry them elsewhere. Known details about the individual players in the socio-commercial networks of the Red Sea, Indian Ocean, and Middle East are seemingly insufficient to do serious social network analysis on them or represent them visually beyond a general scheme, even if one can implement such analysis regarding sites and commodities.[28] But the ability of Christian culture to travel from the Mediterranean to India in late antiquity means that social networks connected these regions and enabled Christianity's movement. Without them, Christianity would have gone nowhere.

A notable point of comparison is the movement of the cult of Jupiter Dolichenus. Jupiter Dolichenus was by origins a north Syrian divinity that was worshipped throughout the Roman empire in the second and third centuries ce. While scholars had long noticed that Roman soldiers often worshipped him, it was not entirely clear how the cult of Jupiter Dolichenus had traveled. But recent scholarship, informed by social network theory, has now addressed this question. Putting it simply, north Syrian soldiers stationed in Dacia brought the cult from the Near East to eastern Europe. From there, military logistics transferred soldiers who worshipped Jupiter Dolichenus from eastern Europe to other places in the empire. They then formed social bonds with other soldiers and transferred the culture of their cult to them. These other soldiers subsequently traveled and formed new social bonds.[29] Thus did social networks

---

[26] Seland, "*Periplus of the Erythraean Sea.*"
[27] Teigen and Seland, *Sinews of Empire*. I regret that this was published too recently to be factored into my narrative.
[28] Seland, "*Periplus of the Erythraean Sea.*"
[29] Collar, "Military Networks," 217–46, "Commagene, Communication, and Cult"; *Religious Networks*, 79–146. The last of these also explores the transmission of other cults and of ideas among rabbinic Jewish networks.

established by the Roman military and its deployment of soldiers enable the movement of people and culture in antiquity.

The fact that culture depended on social networks for its movement means that networks must have enabled Christianity to travel from the Mediterranean to India. Simply put, Christianity could not have traveled to India without them. In the paragraphs to follow, we will explain why these networks, like the Palmyrene one, were predominantly commercial in nature. The evidence for them is limited, but studies done on the social and commercial activity of merchants in other periods yield insight into the typical dispositions that such commercial networks bore.[30] They consisted of merchants with common regional origins (Palmyrene, Maghribī, Sephardic, Armenian, north Indian), and their regional basis could receive further religious refinement (Jewish, Christian, Muslim, Buddhist). They usually maintained a core point of logistical organization, or hub, in their place of regional origin. The Palmyrenes had theirs at Palmyra. But merchants and investors could also establish their hubs in places to which their ancestors had migrated. Early modern Armenians had theirs in Iran (at Julfa), and the medieval Maghribī Jews maintained one in north Egypt.[31] From their hubs, investors and merchants forwarded money or credit and coordinated their activity with overseas connections. But their primary overseas contacts were compatriots who had formed residential communities in foreign ports or cities. These created nodes to which hubs were connected. They harvested local knowledge, acquired products, and made sales for investors and contacts at the hubs. Connecting the hubs and nodes were mobile people. Acting as links, they moved information, products, money, and credit between them. The Palmyrene network

---

[30] The recent scholarly literature that illuminates the dispositions of commercial networks in antiquity and that informs my analysis of them is Aubet, *Commerce and Colonization*: ancient Assyrians; Terpstra, *Trading Communities*: Roman Mediterranean; Terpstra, "Roman Trade": Nabataeans; Gorea, "Sea and Inland Trade" and Seland, "Organisation," "Palmyrene Long-Distance Trade," and *Ships of the Desert* (esp. 75–88): Palmyrenes; de la Vaissière, *Sogdian Traders*; and Hansen, *Silk Road*, 113–40: Sogdians of central Asia, east Iran, and west China (key Sogdians letters are now accessible, in translation by Nicholas Sims-Williams, available at http://depts.washington.edu/silk road/texts/sogdlet.html); Goldberg, *Trade and Institutions* and "Choosing and Enforcing Business," 3–40: Maghribī Jews; Ho, *Graves of Tarim*: Yemenis; Trivellato, *Familiarity of Strangers*: Sephardic Jews; Aslanian, *From the Indian Ocean*: early modern Armenians; Neelis, *Early Buddhist Transmission*: south Asian Buddhists. The analysis of Goitein, *Letters of Medieval Jewish Traders* and Goitein and Friedman, *India Traders* is also illuminating. The material that directly treats Indo-Mediterranean trade and commerce between Rome and Iran is cited in this book as appropriate. Markovits, *Global World of Indian Merchants*, 24–31 and 176–84 provides key formulation for early modern Indian networks.

[31] Aslanian, *From the Indian Ocean*; Goldberg, *Trade and Institutions* and "Choosing and Enforcing Business," 3–40.

described above also bore the standard features of premodern ones. The networks that enabled Christianity to travel to India did so as well.

The primary reason that premodern networks had such a regional basis, oftentimes with further ethnic, civic, or religious nuancing, had to do with vetting. Merchants or investors who often worked with limited judicial means to enforce agreements selected business contacts based on reputation. But in a world that did not know telegraphs, telephones, or email, one could only measure the reputations of people living overseas by having physical contact with them or having intermediaries who did. Merchants therefore often selected as their overseas associates their own compatriots, who were known to them or their other compatriot contacts in some way.[32] As we will see, the evidence for networks between the ancient Mediterranean and India has many gaps. But it still indicates that these networks conformed to the standard dispositions exhibited by premodern commercial networks generally. We should thus accept that the ancient networks had the same basic features and that these structured the movement, activities, and relationships of the merchants and travelers who transported Christian culture, in its varied forms, over vast distances as they moved and fulfilled their obligations of reciprocity.

In ancient Afro-Eurasia, people's mobile bodies were responsible for transporting the cultural idioms that marked the identities of religious communities or differences among them. In other words, human bodies carried religious culture over vast geographic landscapes and transmitted it to other human bodies to which they were linked by social networks. But the primary means by which the religious culture of Christianity was transferred from one body to another was conversion. Such a statement, of course, merits some qualification. The transfer of religious culture can occur without conversion; distinct religious groups of ancient Afro-Eurasia shared and transmitted religious ideas to one another.[33] Religious cultures also often transformed amid conversion or transmission.

Moreover, how one defines conversion is not a simple matter, as it occupies a vast spectrum of social activity. For some, it can entail drastic renunciation of a former subjectivity and social life in favor of a new

---

[32] Terpstra, *Trading Communities*, esp. 65–70 and 95–125, with "Palmyrene Temple," 44–46.
[33] For examples of scholarship focusing on Manichaeism and other religions in contact with it, see Gardner, "Comments on Mani"; Klein, "Epic Buddhasarita"; Dilley, "Religious Intercrossing," 58–70, "Mani's Wisdom," "Also Schrieb Zarathustra?" and "'Hell Exists'"; BeDuhn, "Iranian Epic" and "Mani and Crystallization"; Jones, "Things Mani Learned." On Buddhist transmission to the Mediterranean, see Beckwith, *Greek Buddha*; and McLaughlin, *Rome and the Distant East*, esp. 47. Dognini, "Nascita" and "Primi contatti" notes similarities between Christian and Indian narratives, but see Sidebotham, *Berenike*, 257.

religious credo and novel relationships. For others, it can be a gradual realignment that involves social continuities and the navigation of different contexts and expectations that prompt situational shifts in behavior.[34] People do not always agree on what conversion is, and in antiquity Christians differed regarding whether conversion required one to disassociate from pagans or Jews or always to place ecclesiastical or ascetic interests before secular ones.[35] During his career, Augustine of Hippo experienced conversion to Manichaeism and pro-Nicene Christianity, and thereby the Christian encounter with civic institutions and practices, in different ways at different times.[36]

Despite such complications, one defensible way to conceive of conversion is as the adoption of new social alignments, network affiliations, and practices in ways that facilitated the transfer of religious culture among bodies and, by extension, discrete social networks. Defined in such terms, religious conversion was a vital facet of how Christian culture, even as it transformed itself, came to permeate certain socio-commercial networks so that these could transfer it to other networks.[37] This does not mean that conversion and other forms of cultural transfer are the inevitable results of commerce. But in the ancient world, members of socio-commercial networks often forged social relationships with external parties other than those of a strictly commercial nature, whether these were friendships, intermarriage, or participation in common residential institutions. Over time, these relationships eventually facilitated both conversion (however exactly it was precipitated) and other forms of cultural transfer. Likewise, as socio-commercial networks integrated new members, they transferred

---

[34] Rothman, *Brokering Empire*, esp. 87–164; BeDuhn, *Augustine's Manichaean Dilemma*, esp. 1.8–10, 23–25, 63–71, 96–105, 130–31, 166–70, and 193–217; Cameron, "Christian Conversion," esp. 10–14. In late antique Egypt, Christian converts frequently maintained cultural practices and social relations that offended more radical or militant Christian authorities. Frankfurter, *Religion in Roman Egypt*, esp. 263–84. Sizgorich, *Violence and Belief*, 20–55 and 108–43 contains important discussion and examples from late antiquity.

[35] Witness the different definitions of Christian conversion set in sixth-century upper Mesopotamia by John of Ephesus, *Lives of the Eastern Saints*, in *PO* 17 (ed. Brooks): 229–47. For key treatment of this episode, Sizgorich, *Violence and Belief*, 135–37. For parallels in the early modern Mediterranean, Rothman, *Brokering Empire*, esp. 87–164. For such issues in late antique North Africa, Rebillard, *Christians and Their Many Identities*; and BeDuhn, *Augustine's Manichaean Dilemma*.

[36] BeDuhn, *Augustine's Manichaean Dilemma*. Key passages are Augustine, *Conf.* (ed. Verheijen) 5.14.24–25, 6.4.5–11.20, 8.2.3–7.18, and 8.12.28–30; *Civ. Dei* (ed. Dombart and Kalb) 1.32–35. Key discussion is BeDuhn, *Augustine's Manichaean Dilemma* 1.8–10, 23–25, 63–71, 96–105, 130–31, 166–70, and 193–217 and, for Augustine and his contemporaries, Rebillard, *Christians and Their Many Identities*, 61–91.

[37] Urban, *Metaculture*, esp. 60–62. Likewise, Knappett, *Archaeology of Interaction*, 136–45.

their culture to them.[38] Thus firm foundations were laid for conversion and its transmission of Christian culture in places to which socio-commercial networks extended. Moreover, as we will see, the most adamant evangelizers among Christians and Manichaeans (including Mani) followed the well-laid social pathways of the socio-commercial networks embedded in their regions of origin.

But Christian culture did not travel through and among socio-commercial networks at a fast or even a steady and diffuse pace. Instead, it traveled in fits and starts. It laid deep roots before moving farther afield. In this vein, it should be stressed that the speed with which first-century Christianity and third-century Manichaeism traveled is deceptively exceptional and not paradigmatic.[39] In fact, Christianity often experienced lengthy periods of localized gestation. These periods of anchorage and deep rootedness are not surprising. Once Christianity reached many coastal cities of the Mediterranean basin during its first-century circulation, Christian adherents with evangelical dispositions were arguably more focused on amplifying the local potency of Christian culture than transmitting it to new places. The normative practices of the congregations, controversies and conflicts within and among communities regarding doctrine, and at various times the persecution suffered from imperial officials, are just a few of the issues that Christian authorities and laypersons confronted.[40] When they did exercise ambitions to convert new Christians, they were foremost intent to root their religion thoroughly in the localities and regions in which they lived.[41] As Christian authorities and laypersons worked to recruit local converts, competed to define normative

---

[38] It is perhaps impossible to explain in functionalist terms why people convert to new religions or why the "innovation" of Christian culture "cascaded" through socio-commercial networks. Rogers, *Diffusion of Innovations*; Burt, "Social Capital," 37–54; Collar, *Religious Networks*, 18–19 discuss this issue. For "cascade" and "innovation," see Watts, *Six Degrees*, 220–89. For works on conversion or early Christianity rooted in social science or anthropology, see Hefner, *Conversion to Christianity*; Gooren, *Religious Conversion and Disaffiliation*; Blasi, Duhaime, and Turcotte, *Handbook of Early Christianity*.

[39] The bibliography and approaches on this matter are vast, and the following is not meant to be comprehensive: Freyne, *Jesus Movement*; Rothschild and Schröter, *Rise and Expansion*, especially Meeks, "From Jerusalem to Illyricum," 167–82; and Dunn, "Rise and Expansion," 183–204; Meeks, *First Urban Christians*; Still and Horrell, *After the First Urban Christians*; White and Yarbrough, *Social World of the First Christians*; Esler, *Modeling Early Christianity*; Stark, *Rise of Christianity*, esp. 49–71 (importance of networks).

[40] See Harris, *Spread of Christianity* in which especially Drake, "Models of Christian Expansion," 1–14; the articles of Green and MacDonald, *World of the New Testament* discuss the primary issues that early Christians faced, describe Christian texts and their foremost concerns, and outline the geography that early Christians inhabited.

[41] Apologetic and didactic texts convey central concerns. See, e.g., Jacobsen, Ulrich, and Brakke, *Critique and Apologetics*; Nasrallah, *Christian Responses*; Freyne, *Jesus Movement*, 313–50.

Christian values and practices, or endeavored to exert hegemony over civil or religious communities in a given place, they did usually did not seek converts abroad. Christians in both the Roman and Sasanian empires exhibited such tendencies before the fourth century. Subsequently, when Christian preachers did establish Christianity in remote regions abroad, they were following well-established networks and social pathways to accomplish their task.

Such an understanding of Christianity's movement, however, often contrasts with how its circulation is represented by literature. Ancient apocrypha, hagiographies, church histories, and chronicles often ascribe the evangelization of a city or region to the preaching of a radical itinerant figure, not to the cumulative cultural impact of socio-commercial networks. They also depict the sudden integration of converts into a new social community and their radical renunciation of the communities and networks to which they formally belonged. By the fourth century, such forms of literature were widespread. Some associated the evangelization of remote regions with apostles or their early converts, and they therefore ascribed India to Judas Thomas; Edessa and Upper Mesopotamia to Addai; lowland Sasanian territory to Mari; and the Iranian plateau to Aggai, to name a few examples. Even the activity of figures with firmer historical grounding, like Frumentius in Aksumite Ethiopia, were couched in layers of romance that likened them to early apostolic preachers. Significantly, such narratives were determined by various literary motifs, potent symbolisms, and tropes offered by the Christian gospels, The Acts of the Apostles, ancient novels,[42] and Manichaean accounts of Mani (who was himself modeled on Zarathustra and Buddha).[43]

Due to their literary emulations, it must be stressed that such narratives often do not reflect the actual social dispositions or practices of the Christians who read them or held their protagonists in awe.[44] Idealized narratives that described sudden conversions, miracles, and radical breaks with previous social traditions or that celebrated the goals of ambitious evangelizers did not necessarily reflect the practices and perspectives of many Christians. They simply stabilized recognizable boundaries amid dynamic contexts of quotidian or amicable social interaction. Through such narratives, Christians conceptualized the nature of putatively ideal

---

[42] Saint-Laurent, *Missionary Stories*, is a key treatment.
[43] Poirier, "*Actes de Thomas*"; Drijvers, "Addai und Mani," 171–85; and De Jong, "*Cologne Mani Codex*," esp. 145–47 note relationships. See also Gardner, "Comments on Mani"; Klein, "Epic Buddhasarita"; Deeg and Gardner, "Indian Influence"; and Jones "Things Mani Learned."
[44] Sizgorich, *Violence and Belief* (esp. 1–20 and 108–43) is a valuable treatment in this regard.

Christian behaviors, even if they fell short of them in practice. Even when such narratives depict preachers as being abetted by the movements of merchants, they often distort how Christian culture actually moved and what conversion entailed.

But socio-commercial networks provide alternative ways to gauge how Christianity traveled. As this book argues, an analysis of their dispositions, linkages, and residential presences facilitates a more accurate reconstruction of how Christianity moved throughout the ancient Afro-Eurasian world system than the invented traditions of the *Acts of Thomas*, the testimony derived from them, and similarly dubious narratives. For in truth, preachers often did not dislodge themselves from regional social networks, expatriate from their home regions, or travel to the remote ends of the earth. When they did evangelize foreign places, they often followed the well laid social pathways blazed by socio-commercial networks and then conducted evangelizing efforts at their residential settlements. The ability of certain cultural forms to permeate a network, to become rooted in a locality, and to be transferred to new networks therefore often required substantial time, even centuries. But even if the process was gradual, it was made possible by socio-commercial networks, whose residential settlements provided a basis for evangelic efforts. Socio-commercial networks in such ways shaped how culture traveled, and the pace at which it did so.

Social Networks and the State of the Question

Reflection on social networks has not yet shaped how scholars understand Christianity's movement across Asia or the Indian Ocean. For well over a century, the spate of scholarly viewpoints has assumed many forms. Various parts of this book will address them as appropriate, and we need not summarize them in detail here. But the standard viewpoints can be distilled to a few basic premises. In the past, scholars have ascribed a certain validity to the *Acts of Thomas* and similar apostolic apocrypha, hagiographies, and ecclesiastical histories from late antiquity regarding Christianity's movement. They also have found corroboration in undated oral traditions, objects, and documents in India that pertain to the apostle Thomas or Christians but that are void of an established context. Scholars either detect what they understand to be an historical kernel in these sources or deem their composition to reflect the broader social phenomenon of Christianity's movement. Due to their understanding of such sources, scholars thus perceive Christianity to have arrived in India at various times between the apostolic era and the mid-third century CE (or they at least surmise that such an arrival was probable). They also regard the known trade routes that stretched from Roman territory deep into Asia and the Indian Ocean to strengthen this premise. (Map 1) After all, ancient people and culture moved quickly and far among trade routes, and diverse forms of social contact occurred throughout them. By this reasoning, their existence seems to support the assumption that the various sources, however invented, fanciful, or late they might be, were documenting the general phenomenon of Christianity's movement across Asia or the Indian Ocean.

In the scholarly literature, an array of ungrounded assumptions regarding the late antique literary sources, undated oral traditions and material objects, and ancient trade are thus invoked to support Christianity's early presence in India. Their permutations are many. Such assumptions are in various instances marginal or central to an argument, and scholarly works may cite some of them while omitting others. But sometimes a synthesis that argues for Christianity's early arrival in India virtually embraces them all. A chapter from Frykenberg's *Christianity in India* in fact does precisely that.[45] Since it is emblematic of widespread scholarly viewpoints on the early movement of Christianity to India, we will cite it accordingly while outlining some of the most recurring premises in the following discussion.

One series of assumptions pertains to the Thomas narrative itself. First, the fact that the *Acts* places Judas Thomas at the court of a king named Gudnaphar/Goundaphores is often cited to support the veracity or value of the narrative for Christianity's historical movement. After all, Indo-Parthian kings of the first century CE (and perhaps first century BCE) who bore the personal name or royal title of Gondophares are documented by coins and inscriptions.[46] But one could just as easily argue that the text's version of Goundaphores and his encounter with Judas Thomas is essentially an invented literary representation (although perhaps experienced by readers as historical). The *Acts* could have simply imposed the name or title of historical kings on a largely contrived character who plays a key role in a contrived narrative.[47] Another common assumption is that the *Acts'* treatment of Christianity's early arrival in India receives support from oral traditions, customs, or undated inscriptions and documents that Thomas Christians of contemporary south India maintain and ascribe to

---

[45] Frykenberg, *Christianity in India*, 91–110. Similarly, Frykenberg, "India," 142–55, and "Christians in India"; and McDowell, *Fate of the Apostles*, 157–74.
[46] Frykenberg, *Christianity in India*, 94–95 and 97–98. On Gondophares and Indo-Parthian kings, see Chapter 1, p. 43, n. 57.
[47] As noted by Van den Bosch, "India and the Apostolate," 132–35.

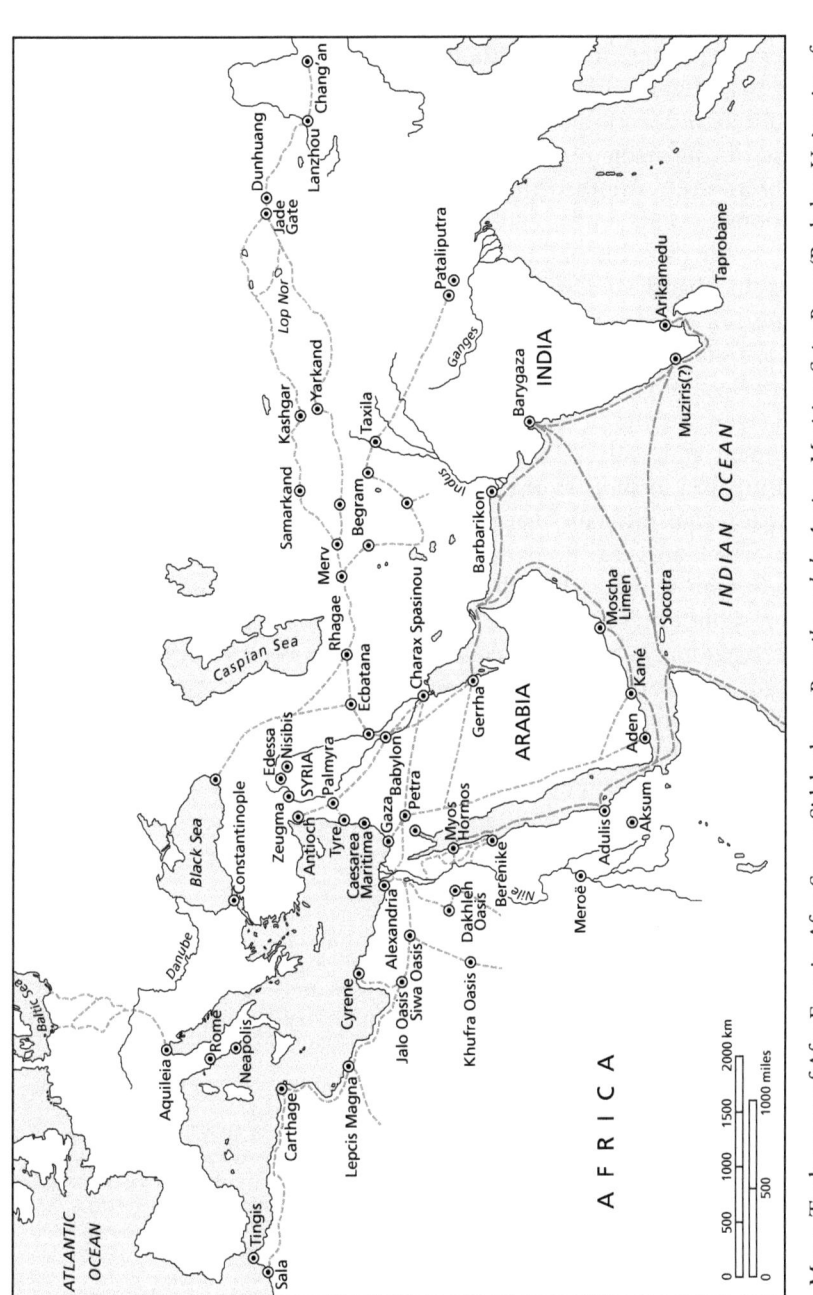

Map 1 Trade routes of Afro-Eurasia. After Steven Sidebotham, *Berenike and the Ancient Maritime Spice Route* (Berkeley: University of California Press, 2011), Fig. 11.1, drawn by M. Hense.

remote antiquity. In keeping with this assumption, the oral traditions or undated objects are treated as though they were actually ancient or originated in antiquity and have been largely preserved unchanged.[48] But none of these have secure dates, and they in fact bear signs of having been produced in medieval or modern times, in part because of their anachronisms.[49] Another problematic belief is that the *Acts* and the oral traditions contain similar episodes because they constitute independent, corroborating sources for Christianity's early arrival in India.[50] But it is just as possible that the oral traditions have been derived and adapted from the narrative of the *Acts* itself and therefore do not constitute truly independent testimony.[51] If this is the case, the oral traditions do not support the historical validity of the *Acts*, for the text is ultimately their source.

Likewise, a series of assumptions pertaining to the broader context of movement and social contact between the Mediterranean and India is often invoked in support of the Thomas tradition's historical value. One of them is that the trade that flourished between the Mediterranean and India, which attracted Roman merchants to the subcontinent, must have brought Christian preachers there (and even Roman cohorts).[52] Whatever the possibilities may have been, no rigorous analysis at all has yet been made regarding when Christians in particular became involved in the dynamics of this trade and thus began traveling to India. Another dubious premise is that when late Roman ecclesiastical historians and patristic authors described how missionaries traveled to a place called "India" and sometimes even encountered Brahmins there, they were referring to the subcontinent. But as we will see, such authors more often used the term

---

[48] Frykenberg, *Christianity in India*, 92–93 and 101–102.
[49] We will treat these issues in Chapters 1 and 6, especially p. 65, n.132 and pp. 207–213, n. 1–17. One famous oral tradition claims that Thomas arrived in "December of the year 50 of the Messiah." Translated by T. K. Josephus and published by Henry Hosten, it can be found in Menachery, *Nazranies*, 520. The use of *anno domini* dating is clearly anachronistic, as is what appears to be the use of the Gregorian calendar.
[50] Frykenberg, *Christianity in India*, 103.
[51] This possibility has been noted as early as Brown, *Indian Christians*, 51–52. See Chapter 6, pp. 208–212 (with n.6) and 228–32.
[52] Frykenberg, *Christianity in India*, 102–3, with n. 19. Frykenberg repeats the widespread but tenuous and now largely dismissed premise that two Roman cohorts were stationed at Muziris (although his chapter mistakenly places these non-existent cohorts at Arikamedu). The theory of the two cohorts was based on what scholars during the nineteenth and early twentieth centuries interpreted as their appearance in the Peutinger map next to the temple of Augustus at Muziris. But this was before a reliable edition of the Peutinger map had been made and was probably encouraged by a faulty copy or scholarly error. No one working directly with the Peutinger map or a reliable edition since the early twentieth century has asserted the presence of cohorts. Fauconnier, "Graeco-Roman Merchants," 88–91. Also see p. 105, n. 42 on the Peutinger map.

"India" for Ethiopia and Arabia and even placed Brahmins within them.[53] In a similar vein, one can also cite the claim that the bricks of Thomas' tomb at Mylapore are similar to those of a "warehouse" at Arikamedu that scholars sometimes associate with Roman traders (and occasionally even call a "Roman warehouse").[54] This would suggest that the apostle Thomas or Christians had arrived on the Coromandel coast in the first century amid the throes of Indo-Mediterranean trade. The problem is that the "warehouse" and other buildings at Arikamedu have no distinctly Roman or Mediterranean features. The premise that Thomas' tomb or its bricks demonstrate links to the Roman Mediterranean has not been supported by rigorous archaeological analysis.[55]

Finally, oral traditions and undated (or problematically dated) texts associated with figures other than the apostle Thomas are often cited to support the premise of Christianity's early arrival in the subcontinent. These include oral traditions and a (now lost) copper plate grant for Thomas Kinayi, who reputedly came to south India in 345;[56] the oral traditions of the Jews of Cochin regarding their migration to India after the Babylonian conquest (597 BCE) and their revolts against Rome (66–74 and 132–35 CE) and a copper plate grant that they date to 379;[57] and an undated text on palm leaves from Quilon that describes how a Chola king

---

[53] Frykenberg, *Christianity in India*, 103. We will discuss this in Chapter 2. Key studies are Schneider, *L'Ethiopie et l'Inde* and now "So-Called Confusion."

[54] Schurhammer, "New Light," 99–101; Nedungatt, *Quest for the Historical Thomas*, 308–12. I thank Stephen Shoemaker for helpful discussion on the topic.

[55] Begley, "Changing Perceptions of Arikamedu," 23, with Suresh, *Arikamedu*, 51. See Chapter 3, p. 122, n. 120–21.

[56] Frykenberg, *Christianity in India*, 104 and 107–10. His views summarize the arguments of Kollaparambil, *Babylonian Origins*. We will discuss Thomas Kinayi in Chapter 6, but note that the oral poems for him use *anno domini* dates for 345 CE. Intriguingly, Frykenberg seems to conflate the date of 345 CE that appears as an alphabetical chronogram in a key song with the actual date for the song's composition, thus stating that "solid historical evidence of formal church life in India, albeit tenuous, dates from the year AD 345" (107). The oral traditions are in Kollaparambil, "Historical Sources" (oral traditions at v–xiii), with Joseph, "Thomas Cana," 56.161–66 and 57.103–6.

[57] Frykenberg, *Christianity in India*, 103 mentions the Jews of southwestern India and links to the "first Exile" (but not the copper plates of Cochin). Such claims about Jews circulate in secondary literature (and are sometimes ascribed to local Jewish traditions), but they have no basis in ancient sources. See, e.g., Pothan, *Syrian Christians*, 6–9 and 33; Brown, *Indian Christians*, 59–63; Menon, *Historia of Kerala*, 2.504–6. To a certain extent, these unsubstantiated views regarding Jewish migration are derived from tenuous interpretations of toponyms mentioned in the Hebrew Bible, very late traditions, or loan words for commodities or animals in Hebrew texts. For example, Puthiakunnel, "Jewish Colonies"; and Gurukkal, *Rethinking Classical Indo-Roman Trade*, 108. Some oral traditions date to 379 CE certain copper plates that document how a Chera king conferred privileges upon a Jewish community at Cochin. These plates, however, were issued by a king who lived in the tenth or eleventh century. See Menon, *Survey of Kerala History*, 102–3 and 124–25; Fischel, "Exploration," esp. 230–31, n. 6; Katz, *Jews of India*, 13–15; Narayanan, *Perumals of Kerala*, 68–70 for discussion, with pp. 219–220, n. 46. On Jews in India, see also Wink, *Al-Hind*, 99–100.

persecuted Christians in 293 CE.[58] But again, nothing securely situates the oral traditions, copper plates, or palm-leaf text in remote antiquity. If anything, the copper plates bear signs of having been produced in the ninth–tenth centuries CE.[59] The view that relentlessly violent Persian persecutions against Christians (including laypersons) induced waves of exiles to India is also problematic.[60] The premise of such unrelenting violence has been challenged by recent scholarship.[61]

As this book proceeds, it will often return to the assumptions just described. But for now, it should simply be noted that scholars only arrive at more reliable documentation during the medieval Islamic period of the eighth–tenth centuries CE. At this time kings in the Kerala coast bestowed privileges upon Persian Christians (*tarisapalli*), Jewish trade guilds (*anjuvannam*), and guilds that included Christians (*manigrammam*). Such privileges, dated according to the reigns of current monarchs, were inscribed on copper plates near Quilon for leading Christian figures like Sapir Iso and Iravi Korttha,[62] and as we will see, the lost plates for Thomas Kinayi probably date from this period. In general, scholarship on medieval Christians in south India is on more stable ground in terms of the available and reliable sources. But scholarly beliefs regarding ancient Christianity in India rely on a litany of widespread but tenuous claims. Altogether they ascribe the early presence of Christianity in India to sources that have not been properly contextualized.

Plates are translated in Gundert, "Translations and Analysis," 134–42; Dikshitar, *South Indian Inscriptions*, 345–48 (mistitled).

[58] Frykenberg, *Christianity in India*, 107. Also Neill, *History of Christianity in India*, 42, who notes that the narrative is in Malayalam. Nedungatt, *Quest for the Historical Thomas*, 351, describes the source as "an ancient book on palm leaves." He does not state what specifically supports an ancient dating. But the legend seems to use *anno domini* dating to situate the event in 293 CE, which suggests a later or modern date. This tradition would appear to have been put in writing c. 1800 CE (Farquhar, *Apostle Thomas in India*, 62, n. 4). For other late texts, see Mundadan, *Sixteenth Century Traditions*, 60–67 and *History of Christianity*, 30.

[59] See previous note and Chapter 6, pp. 209–211 (with n. 9–13) and 219–20.

[60] Frykenberg, *Christianity in India*, 104–5 and 108–9.

[61] In various ways, the recent work of Payne, *State of Mixture* and Smith, *Constantine and the Captive Christians* challenges the premises of relentless Sasanian Persian persecution, and it is problematic to conceive of "refugees" who were escaping it. See Chapter 4, p. 158.

[62] Frykenberg, *Christianity in India*, 111–14 (111 specifies Christian/Jewish communities and guilds); and Malekandathil, *Maritime India*, 38–61 (38–41 for key figures and guilds); Narayanan, *Perumals of Kerala*, 277–94 (with guild names). Also see Wink, *Al-Hind*, 71 and 101. We will discuss these plates in Chapter 6, but for translations, see Dikshitar, *South Indian Inscriptions*, 350–55 and 357–63, with additional key plates at 348–50, 355–57, and 363–77; Gundert, "Translations and Analysis," 126–34, with additional key plates at 117–25; and Pothan, *Syrian Christians*, 32–33 and 102–5, with Cereti, "Pahlavi Signatures" for signatures on the plates. For a recent collaborative and international project on the Quilon copper plates, see "The Copper Plates from Kollam," http://849ce.org.uk/, with new translation and studies forthcoming in Lambourn, Veluthat, and Tomber, *Copper Plates from Kollam*.

As stated previously, the problem with such perspectives is that they are based on literary sources, oral traditions, and material objects of highly dubious historical value, at least in respect to ancient Christianity's movement. We will return to this complication continually. But another issue is that they do not ask of social networks the questions that they should. Trade routes do not exist without social networks, and people and culture do not simply move indiscriminately along them. In antiquity, social networks shaped and structured where people and culture traveled, and it is thus important to explore the beginning and end points between which networks facilitated actual movement. But social networks could not carry culture if the people who formed them had not yet embodied it so that they could move it. If none of the Syrian or Egyptian merchants who traveled into the hinterland of Asia or the Indian Ocean had yet become Christian, then their networks were arguably not yet carrying Christianity anywhere. Similarly, if a network of Christians only extended part of the way to India, it could not bring Christianity there by itself. It had to transfer Christian culture to the inhabitants of places in which it had forged residential settlements or to members of other networks, thereby ensuring that Christian culture could travel through an interconnected geography of Afro-Eurasia. Such transfers often occurred slowly or required substantial time.

In such respects this book confronts issues beyond the exact date when Christianity became firmly anchored in India. Broader questions are at stake. The relationship between creative literary genres and historical phenomena; the crafting of historical experiences from literary and oral inventions; and the connection (and distance) between social practices and their representations are among them. One cannot meaningfully measure how and when Christianity arrived in India without explicitly or implicitly taking a position on these issues. How they are understood will inevitably shape how Christianity is perceived to have traveled. This book parts ways from most previous scholarship principally by maintaining that knowledge of socio-commercial networks and other social factors should provide context for the *Acts of Thomas* and problematic literary narratives, not vice versa. The regional dispositions of socio-commercial networks in fact shaped how most forms of Christian culture were transported throughout the ancient world system. They were vital in structuring how Christianity traveled from the Mediterranean world to the Red Sea, Iran, central Asia, and the Indian Ocean world between the first and fifth centuries CE.

Chapter 1 provides a general analysis of the *Acts of Thomas* and the narratives of Thomas' preaching that preceded the *Acts*. While exploring textual issues that offer challenges to the historical validity of the *Acts*, it also demonstrates how the *Acts* shaped Christians' understanding of their religious geographies and history.

Chapters 2 and 3 shift focus to the Red Sea and Indian Ocean. As they argue, a Roman Egyptian network extended into the Red Sea and Arabian Sea, and it therefore transmitted Christianity to Aksumite Ethiopia, south Arabia, and perhaps Nubian Ethiopia during the fourth century CE. But it did not carry Christian culture to India. The principal reasons for this are as follows. First, from the first century to the late third century, the network extended directly to India and fostered direct contact between the Roman Mediterranean and the Indian subcontinent. But Christianity had not yet penetrated it in any substantive form, and it therefore did not carry Christian culture to new places and transfer it to new bodies and new locations. After the late third century CE, the Roman Egyptian network suffered disruption. Its reach into the Red Sea was restored by the early fourth century, and it was thereby able to anchor Christianity in Red Sea regions. But its direct contact with India was not restored until c. 500 CE, and by that time, the lowland Sasanian network and a counterpart anchored in coastal Fars had firmly rooted Christian culture in south Indian ports, as well as Sri Lanka.

Chapters 4–6 treat the interconnections of the Levant, Mesopotamia, Iran, the Persian Gulf, and India. They explore how Christianity first arrived and took root in these regions. They also comment on the relevance of Mani and the early movement of Manichaeism. As these chapters argue, Christian merchants who were members of a Levantine socio-commercial network carried Christian beliefs and practices to lowland Parthian/Sasanian territory over the first through fourth centuries CE. As they formed meaningful social bonds and relationships with residents of lower Mesopotamia, Khuzistan, Maišan, classical Assyria, and the Zab River region, they transmitted their Christian culture to them in ways that enabled a lowland Sasanian network to move such culture to new regions. But this process of conversion, transfer, rootedness, and further movement did not happen immediately; it actually lasted for centuries and occurred much more slowly than the rapid movement of Manichaeism across Asia. It was only after the lowland Sasanian network had sufficiently cultivated Christian beliefs and practices that travelers moved them across the Iranian plateau, into central Asia, deep into the Persian Gulf, and to India. This process began during the late fourth century CE and persisted throughout the fifth.

The social pathways and time by which Christianity traveled to India were foremost determined by the interconnected socio-commercial networks that carried it. Such networks both enabled its movement and imposed the limits within which it happened. How such networks cohered, created the pathways by which Christianity traveled, and related to the late antique literature on Christianity's movement is truly remarkable. To their remarkable dispositions, and their bearing on how we understand the *Acts of Thomas*, we now turn.

PART I

The Acts of Thomas

CHAPTER I

The Acts of Thomas *and Its Impact*

According to the *Acts of the Apostle Thomas,* when the apostles were in Jerusalem, Judas Thomas was apportioned by lot the land of India for preaching. But he refused to go. He was, as he claimed, Hebrew and weak, and he wondered aloud how he could teach the Indians. Approached by the resurrected Jesus to undertake this mission, he remained recalcitrant. He was willing to go anywhere; only to India he would not go. It was only after Jesus, his twin, sold him to the Indian merchant Habban in Jerusalem that Judas Thomas fulfilled his apportioned task of preaching to the Indians. The pair sailed from Jerusalem to India and reached the court of King Gudnaphar. With this intriguing episode, the *Acts of the Apostle Thomas* (hereafter the *Acts*) begins its narrative.

The date and location of composition for the *Acts* are matters of some debate, and as this chapter argues, its surviving form was composed in Syriac by a writer of the mid-to-late third century with links to the Upper Mesopotamian city of Edessa. But its narrative has enjoyed a marvelous afterlife. In antiquity, the *Acts* and its variants traveled far beyond the geographical confines of the Roman Levant, and the unlikely journey of Judas Thomas has been celebrated in a host of different languages. After its initial composition, the *Acts* exerted an overwhelming impact on how Christians experienced the history and geography of their religion. Due to this text, late antique Christians marveled at the religious brethren in India that they would never see or meet. Nearly two millennia after it was written, Thomas Christians of south India still trace the origins of their religious community to the sojourning apostle who arrived at its shores. In so many ways, the text has even shaped how modern scholars of antiquity have envisioned the topography of early Christianity. Such enduring legacies of the *Acts* constitute a principal theme of this book.

But before exploring the wondrous life, afterlife, and impact of the *Acts,* it is important to establish how the text itself was born. As this chapter stresses, the *Acts* has a complicated genealogy, and its inception was not the brainchild of a single author. It came into being through numerous layers of storytelling and the intervention of many different contributors. Due to the dynamic process through which it was created, the text bears the hallmarks of the earlier traditions from which it was derived, and the creative process that produced the text has bearing on its historical value.

Outline of the *Acts of Thomas*

The surviving version of the *Acts* is immensely complicated.[1] Strictly speaking, it is not even the account of an apostle named Thomas. The most preeminent complete Syriac manuscript names him Judas Thomas, but earlier Syriac fragments at Sinai simply call him Judas. Similarly, the Greek text refers to him as Judas Thomas or Thomas, but as it progresses, it tends simply to call him the apostle Judas.[2] It therefore appears that the earliest Syriac and Greek traditions, following the list of apostles in Luke and the Acts of the Apostles, treated Judas (ܝܗܘܕܐ; Ἰούδας) as the protagonist's proper name. But at various points, it described him as "twin" (ܬܐܡܐ, *tāmā*) to denote his status as Jesus' twin and, it would appear, his visual double.[3] Nonetheless, because this apostle bore the Aramaic epithet of "twin" (ܬܐܡܐ, *tāmā*), he became known as "Thomas" (ܬܐܘܡܐ, *tāwma* or a similar variation; Θωμᾶς) and sometimes "Didymos" (Greek for twin) in external literature almost immediately after the *Acts* began to circulate. Later copyists even inserted the name "Thomas" into the *Acts'* Syriac manuscripts.[4] While the link between the *Acts* and other so-called Thomasine literature is still unclear, the *Acts* nonetheless coheres with the Coptic *Gospel of Thomas* and *Thomas the Contender* by indicating that its holy figure properly named Judas could be called "Thomas,"

---

[1] Drijvers, "Acts of Thomas," 321–39 provides a useful introduction to the text and the scholarship up to c. 1990.

[2] This book will generally call the protagonist of the *Acts* Judas Thomas, for sake of consistency. See Klijn, *Acts of Thomas*, 6–7 regarding the name of the apostle and its appearance in the London manuscript edited by Wright and the early fragments from the Sinai palimpsest. For manuscripts, see n. 7.

[3] Luke (ed. Nestle-Aland) 6:13–16 and Acts (ed. Nestle-Aland) 1:13. Also, it is worth mentioning that the same apostle who was known in the Gospel of John as "Judas, not the Iscariot" (14:22) and was thereby distinguished from the figure called "Thomas, who is also Didymos" (11:16, 20:24, and 21.1) received the appellation of "Judas Thomas" in the Old Syriac version of John (ed. Lewis; ed. Burkitt; and ed. Kiraz) 14:22. Athikalam, "St. Thomas the Apostle," 339–41. Klijn, *Acts of Thomas*, 6–7 discusses the apostle as Jesus' twin and instances in which they bear the same likeness.

[4] In certain instances, the copyists of the London manuscript published by Wright or antecedents from which it was derived endeavored to replace "twin" (ܬܐܡܐ) with "flood" (ܛܘܦܢܐ), but the Greek supports that "twin" was in the original. See ܝܡ and ܢܚ of the Syriac (ed. Wright), with Wright's comments on 170 and 180, and the Greek text (ed. Bonnet) 31 and 39. See Klijn, *Acts of Thomas*, 6–7.

Outline of the Acts of Thomas

whether as an epithet or as a proper name. Some have even associated it with a distinctive "Thomasine" form of Christian belief and practice, even if some recent scholarship has also criticized the view that a "Thomasine" Christian movement existed.[5]

As an article of Christian culture, the narrative of Judas Thomas' feats traveled along social networks that moved it both westward and eastward from its probable Upper Mesopotamian point of origin. But as the narrative traveled, those who encountered it reconstituted it in various ways or endowed it with new significance. Many scholars have surmised that the text's original language was Syriac, but doubts persist.[6] Either way, it certainly appeared in its basic Greek form at such an early stage that the Greek and Syriac versions are somewhat autonomous of each other and were perhaps even cross-pollinating. Known Greek manuscripts vastly outnumber the Syriac ones. It also seems that the surviving Greek version often preserves readings closer to the original composition (whatever its language) than the surviving Syriac tradition, which readers altered in various ways over time so that it aligned with their normative views.[7]

---

[5] For references, see *Gospel According to Thomas* (ed. Layton) 53–54: (Didymos Judas Thomas) and *Thomas the Contender* (ed. Layton) 180–81 (Judas Thomas). What link (if any) that connects these various texts featuring Judas Thomas is still, however, extremely unclear. Drijvers, "*Acts of Thomas*," 324–25 and Van Rompay, "East: Syria and Mesopotamia," 369–70 discuss scholarship on this matter. For discussion or criticism of the notion of "Thomasine" Christianity and meaningful literary or social links among the various works of "Thomasine" literature, see Poirier, *Évangile*; Sellew, "Thomas Christianity," 11–35; Luttikhuizen, "Hymn of Judas Thomas," and Piovanelli, "Thomas in Edessa?" 443–62. For the layered figure of the apostle Thomas in early Christian literature, see Most, *Doubting Thomas*. Amid the lack of consensus regarding the date and origins of the *Gospel of Thomas*' composition, the links among the various works of early Thomasine literature, and whether there was a discrete "Thomasine" Christianity, these other texts will not be factors of the present analysis of the *Acts*.

[6] Attridge, "Original Language" and *Acts of Thomas*, 3–4; Klijn, *Acts of Thomas*, 1; Myers, *Spiritual Epicleses*, 1–2. For doubts, Roig Lanzillotta, "Syriac Original?" with Klauck, *Apocryphal Acts*, 142.

[7] See Klauck, *Apocryphal Acts*, 142. The Syriac only exists in two manuscripts that predate the tenth (or indeed the fifteenth) century, and one of these is very fragmentary. Otherwise, the Greek manuscripts exist in greater abundance, and twenty-one have been collated into Bonnet's critical edition; about eighty that contain at least parts of the text are now known. Two early Greek manuscripts of particular importance are complete or nearly so. Myers, *Spiritual Epicleses*, 15–17; Klijn, *Acts of Thomas*, 1–4; Klauck, *Apocryphal Acts*, 142; and Attridge, *Acts of Thomas*, 2–4, treat technical matters regarding the Greek and Syriac manuscripts. Roig Lanzillotta, "Syriac Original?" explores the relationships between the Greek and Syriac versions and much of the prior scholarship. The text of Wright is based on a tenth-century manuscript BM Add. 14645 (936 CE), but fragments of a fifth/sixth-century text have been found in a palimpsest from Sinai (published in Lewis, *Acta*). Otherwise, Syriac manuscripts from between the fifteenth and nineteenth centuries exist, with one (Sachau 222 of Berlin, which is available digitally through the Staatsbibliothek zu Berlin) being heavily edited in *AMSS* 3.3–119 and being quite similar to an unedited manuscript from Cambridge (Cambridge Syr. 2822), and one from Harvard University (MS Syriac 38), which is available digitally through the Harvard University Library system (*Hollis*) at the time of this book's composition. Vat. Syr. 597 contains a large fragment of the *Acts*, but only from the middle to the end. See Van Lantschoot,

After its initial stages of composition, many different Christian groups and movements read the text and translated it into numerous languages (including Latin, Coptic, Ethiopic, Armenian, and Arabic).[8] As the *Acts* circulated among diverse religious communities, however, Christians did more than merely alter it or its language. They also endowed its narrative with significances that aligned with their doctrinal visions. Because the *Acts* exhibits certain elements that perhaps reflect Gnostic trends in late antique strands of Christianity, it was valued by Manichaeans and Priscillians.[9] In the late fourth and early fifth centuries, Epiphanius of Salamis, Augustine of Hippo, and Turribius of Asturica associated the narrative with Manichaeans, Priscillians, and other "heretical" groups while nonetheless being familiar with its contents.[10] In such ways, the narrative traveled, transformed, and assumed varied value and significance in the eyes and hands of late antique Christians.

The *Acts*' composition was just as complex as its subsequent travels and transformations. In its surviving state, the basic plot of the *Acts* narrates how Judas Thomas arrived in India, evangelized local populations, and eventually suffered martyrdom. But the plot also lacks a continuous narrative thread and contains an assortment of random miracles that could easily have been derived from previous works and that are not set in India in any obvious way.[11] A brief description of its contents provides some clarification.

In the existing complete manuscripts (especially the Greek ones), the *Acts* is organized into thirteen "Acts" of the apostle, with a brief narrative of his martyrdom at the end. Act I (as numbered in the Greek text), with

---

Inventaire, 128. An additional manuscript has been discovered recently in Kerala, India. Briquel-Chatonnet, Desreumeux, and Thekeparampil, "Découverte d'un manuscrit." For the complex Greek manuscripts and recensions (as known c. 1900), see Bonnet, *Acta*, xv–xxvii. Unless otherwise indicated, my references to the Syriac text are from Wright's edition of BM Add. 14645 and to the Greek from Bonnet. One can detect the complicated entanglement of the Greek and Syriac traditions in the learned English translations and commentaries of Klijn, *Acts of Thomas* and Attridge, *Acts of Thomas*.

[8] Myers, *Spiritual Epicleses*, 6; Klijn, *Acts of Thomas*; and Jullien and Jullien, *Apôtres des confins*, 82–87, discuss the various translations of the Greek and Syriac and present bibliography on publications, editions, or translations thereof; Schneider, *L'Ethiopie et l'Inde*, 138, represents authors and texts that cite or engage with the Greek tradition. For Thomas in the Coptic and Georgian tradition, see Poirier, *Version Copte*, and Vashalomidze, "Apostle Thomas." Myers, *Spiritual Epicleses*, 57–111, treats the redaction of the basic text after its composition.

[9] Aug., *Sermon on the Mount* (ed. Mutzenbecher) 1.20.65, *Against Adimantus* (ed. Zycha) 17, *Against Faust* (ed. Zycha) 22.79; Turribius, *Letter to Leo* (PL 54, col. 694). Poirier, "Actes de Thomas" discusses Manichaean reception. Note, however, that Luttikhuizen, "Hymn of Judas Thomas," casts doubt on the Gnostic inclinations of the *Acts* and the *Hymn of the Pearl*.

[10] Aug., *Sermon on the Mount* (ed. Mutzenbecher) 1.20.65, *Against Adimantus* (ed. Zycha) 17, *Against Faustus* (ed. Zycha) 22.79; Turribius, *Letter to Leo* (PL 54, col. 694).

[11] See Myers, *Spiritual Epicleses*, 29–34.

which this chapter is chiefly concerned, describes how Judas Thomas is acquired by the Indian merchant Habban and evangelizes his first followers at their first port of call.[12] When the *Acts* begins, the apostles are in Jerusalem, and they are allotting among themselves the regions in which they are to preach. India falls by lot to Judas Thomas, but he objects. He claims that he is weak, and being Hebrew, he is not able to teach the Indians. Judas Thomas remains obstinate even after Jesus appears to him in a vision. Amid the reluctance of Judas Thomas to go to India, an Indian merchant named Habban happens to be present. The Syriac text (from the London manuscript) introduces Habban by stating that he "happened to be in the south land," which is often taken to be a corruption. The Greek claims that he came "there (i.e., Jerusalem) from India."[13] Habban had been sent by King Gudnaphar to find a craftsman, and Jesus appears to Habban and sells Judas Thomas to him. The next day, Judas Thomas finds Habban while he is loading goods onto his ship, and when they both have boarded, a favorable wind then takes Habban and Judas Thomas to their first port of call. In the Syriac tradition, it is called "Sandarūk" or "Sanadrūk" (ܣܢܕܪܘܟ) and qualified by a term that can refer to a city, town, or fortress (ܟܪܟܐ). In the Greek version of the text, the site is principally called Andrapolis, though several variations exist in the manuscripts.

Over the course of Act II, Judas Thomas remains in this port city, where he and Habban attend a feast thrown by the local dynast to celebrate his daughter's marriage. When a servant strikes him, Judas Thomas informs him that he will see the hand that struck him dragged by a dog. The same night, a lion dismembers the servant, and a dog carries his hand to the wedding party. After this miraculous event, Judas Thomas, with the help of his resurrected twin Jesus, succeeds in converting the participants at the banquet and the newly wedded couple. But when the king discovers this, he accuses Judas Thomas of sorcery. Accordingly, he and Habban depart for India.

In Act II, Habban and Judas Thomas arrive at the court of king Gudnaphar/Goundaphores. The name or title of Gondophares was borne by historically attested Indo-Parthian (Pahlava) kings who ruled the Indus river valley and parts of central Asia during the early first century CE,[14] but the text does not state where exactly Judas Thomas encountered Gudnaphar/Goundaphores. The king confers upon Judas Thomas a sum

---

[12] *Acts of Thomas* 1–3 in the Greek (ed. Bonnet); ܣܢܕܪܘܟ in the Syriac (ed. Wright).
[13] Greek from 2 (ed. Bonnet); Syriac from ܟܪܟܐ (ed. Wright).   [14] See next section, pp. 43, n. 57.

of money with which to build a palace, and Judas Thomas meanwhile preaches and evangelizes the various cities and villages of India. When the king discovers this, he questions Judas Thomas about his progress, and Judas Thomas informs him that he is building a palace in heaven. The king imprisons Judas Thomas and deliberates a punishment. The same night, the king's brother Gad becomes ill and dies, and the king decides to execute Judas Thomas as a sorcerer. But Gad, recently deceased, has an encounter with angels, who show him the heavenly palace of his brother. After being revived, Gad informs Gudnaphar of the heavenly palace, and the king releases Judas Thomas from prison and converts to his faith.

After this episode, the narrative consists of a series of "Acts" that focus on an assortment of miracles and acts of preaching. These "Acts" do not pursue any noticeable plot progression or connection to the previous narrative, and nothing about them reflects an explicitly Indian setting. Instead, they are a random assortment of relatively short episodes that probably circulated previously in various sources without being set in India specifically.[15] In these "Acts," Judas Thomas most notably resurrects a youth killed by a talking serpent or dragon; converses with a talking colt; expels a demon from a woman; resurrects a murdered woman who then proceeds to describe hell; revives the deceased wife and daughter of an unnamed general (who is later identified as Siphor); and tames wild asses with his voice. By contrast, the *Acts'* second half, namely Acts IX to XIII, treats Thomas' encounter with the Indian monarch Mazdai, and it has a clearer plot progression.[16] Over the course of these Acts, Judas Thomas converts members of Mazdai's family and court, and persuades them to renounce intercourse (including marital intercourse) until he is imprisoned and eventually stabbed to death by Mazdai's soldiers at an unnamed location. The martyr scene may have been written autonomously and added to the main narrative.[17] Thus ends the *Acts of Thomas*.

The *Acts of Thomas*: Reflections on Date, Language, and Location

Due to the intricacies and apparent randomness of its narrative, the date of the *Acts'* composition is not yet firmly established by scholarship. A composition in the early third century, most probably at Edessa, is often

---

[15] Myers, *Spiritual Epicleses*, 29. [16] Myers, *Spiritual Epicleses*, 30–34.
[17] Myers, *Spiritual Epicleses*, 33.

surmised for various reasons.[18] The text includes Latin terms and names that could reflect the recent integration of Upper Mesopotamia into the Roman provincial system, and its Syriac terminology, or at least that of the controversial *Hymn of the Pearl*, bears continuity with Syriac civil documents of Edessa and its environs from the 240s.[19] The later insertion of *The Hymn of the Pearl* by Manichaeans, which is commonly but not universally surmised, and the text's depiction of Judas Thomas and Jesus as a twin dyad suggest that the text served as inspiration for the Manichaeans to treat Mani as Jesus' twin. If so, the text anteceded the third-century rise of Manichaeism.[20] Finally, Eusebius indicates that Origen cited a text or a basic tradition regarding Thomas' activity in Parthia in his *Commentaries on Genesis* (begun c. 225 CE).[21]

While the factors just described seem to establish that the text was written after 200 CE, they do not anchor the text in the early third century specifically. A more recent and preferable position is that the text, as it survives, was composed in the middle or late third century CE.[22] This viewpoint better explains the text's characterization of the king Mazdai in "Acts" IX to XIII. While in many ways a generic pagan, Mazdai possesses certain Zoroastrian traits, including a name akin to the god Ahura Mazda. He even has Judas Thomas endure a trial by fire.[23] His antagonism to the preaching of Judas

---

[18] The information just described constitutes the observations of Bremmer, "*Acts of Thomas*," 76–79, with some additions that also support a third-century date generally. Also see Attridge, *Acts of Thomas*, 14–15.

[19] The Syriac papyrus/parchment documents are P1-3 in Drijvers and Healey, *Old Syriac Inscriptions*, Appendix 1, 232–48.

[20] Edited texts of the *Hymn of the Pearl* are in Poirier, *Hymne de la Perle*, 330–36 and 350–56; Ferreira, *Hymn of the Pearl*, 39–65 and 82–95. The *Hymn of the Pearl* is 108–13 of the Greek text (ed. Bonnet), of the Syriac ܡܕܐ-ܡܐ (ed. Wright), but it varies significantly in the Syriac and Greek traditions and does not appear in most manuscripts for the *Acts of Thomas*. Poirier, *Hymne de la Perle*, 171–84 and 310–17, discusses the manuscripts and dates the insertion as early as the third century based on similarities in how the *Hymn* and the *Cologne Mani Codex* (ed. Koenen and Römer) 17–24 characterize their respective protagonists (the crown prince and Mani). This suggests that the insertion of the *Hymn* and the narrative of the *Cologne Mani Codex* are roughly contemporary. For potential influences of the *Acts* on Manichaean thought, see Drijvers, "*Acts of Thomas*," 337–39, and now Tardieu, *Manichaeism*, 9–10. Ferreira, *Hymn of the Pearl*, 4–6, discusses various theories on the date of the *Hymn of the Pearl*. But note Roig Lanzillotta, "Syriac Original?" 121–22, who doubts the later insertion of the *Hymn of the Pearl* into the *Acts of Thomas* and sees it as a part of the original text.

[21] Eusebius, *HE* (ed. Schwartz and Mommsen) 3.1.1–3. For dating of the commentary on Genesis, see McGuckin, "Life of Origen," 12. This tradition also appears in Rufinus, *HE* 3.1 (ed. Schwartz and Mommsen) and Socrates, *HE* 1.19 (ed. Hansen).

[22] The following largely recounts the detailed discussion of Myers, *Spiritual Epicleses*, 29–55, who locates the composition of the text at Nisibis, not Edessa (34–44).

[23] Myers, *Spiritual Epicleses*, 41–42 and 51–52, and bibliography. Daryaee, *Sasanian Persia*, 85–86, discusses the texts that describe ordeals by fire or heated metal (such as molten metal poured on one's

Thomas at his court and the Persian names of his family members suggest that the composition of Acts IX to XIII was influenced by the transition from Parthian to Sasanian rule in Mesopotamia and the intensifying competition between Christians and Zoroastrians there during the middle of the third century CE. It could even coincide with the aggressive efforts of the Sasanian Persian court (and the priest Kirdir) to promote Zoroastrianism as Iran's supreme religion between 273 and 293, while preceding the violent confrontations of the mid-fourth.[24] Other factors are noteworthy too. For example, the tradition for Thomas' preaching that Origen cited in fact rendered him the evangelizer of Parthia, not India. Some treat the Parthian and Indian traditions as complementary, and later we will explore how narratives about Thomas' travels in Parthia may have involved a visit to north India. But Origen was probably not referring to the surviving text of the *Acts* but to an earlier tradition focusing on Thomas' preaching in Parthian territory.[25] The *Acts'* treatment of Judas Thomas and Jesus as a twin dyad also could have emulated Manichaean treatments of Mani. Likewise, the later insertion of the *Hymn of the Pearl* into the *Acts* by Manichaeans (if this occurred) does not necessarily have bearing on its date of composition. As we will see, the lack of secure independent witnesses to the surviving *Acts* or Thomas' Indian travels before the fourth century also makes a middle or late third-century date seem likely too.

Moreover, the *Acts* exhibits various signs of being the redaction of prior textual traditions, and these help determine when it was produced.[26]

---

chest). Mazdai makes Judas Thomas stand on fire-scorched iron plates in order to verify the truth of his self-identification in ܒܪܐ - ܐܚܐ of the Syriac (ed. Wright) and 104 of the Greek (ed. Bonnet). Mazdai is introduced by name at 87 of the Greek (ed. Bonnet), ܐܘܢ of the Syriac (ed. Wright). Tubach, "Historische Elemente," 98–103, discusses the Iranian background to the name and figure, who nonetheless represents no known king in India.

[24] *Acts of Thomas*: ܟܠܗ, ܟܠܗ, ܐܚܐ - ܐܚ of the Syriac (ed. Wright) and 87, 100, 139–40 of the Greek (ed. Bonnet), with Myers, *Spiritual Epicleses*, 51–52. For Iranian origins, see Gignoux, *Iranisches Personennamenbuch* 2.2, 161, and 181–82 and Gignoux, Jullien, and Jullien, *Iranisches Personennamenbuch* 7.5, 99, and 126. Not all the names in Syriac are taken straight from Iranian languages. In this case, for instance, Siphur apparently is the Syriac rendering of a Greek version of the Iranian name Shapur. For late-third century hostility to Christianity, see Daryaee, *Sasanian Persia*, 69–72 and 75–77, and Kreyenbroek, "How Pious?" 7–15. The boasts of the priest Kirdir from the edition/translation of Gignoux, *Quatre inscriptions du mage Kirdir*, 60 and 69–70, are relevant. Payne, *State of Mixture*, 23–24, argues that Kirdir sought to subordinate, not eliminate Christians. The rivalry depicted in the *Acts* could have aligned with this social context.

[25] See Myers, *Spiritual Epicleses*, 47–48. For treatments as complementary, see McGrath, "History and Fiction," 302; and Nedungatt, *Quest for the Historical Thomas*, 113–18.

[26] What follows in this paragraph are mostly the observations of Myers, *Spiritual Epicleses*, 29–34. For a full examination that supports the premise of a heavy initial redaction of assembled episodes, as well as the redactions of subsequent copyists, see Myers, *Spiritual Epicleses*, 57–111. The issue of redaction is also examined by Tissot, "Actes de Thomas," 223–32, Klauck, *Apocryphal Acts*, 143–44, Saint-Laurent, *Missionary Stories*, 22–23.

As noted previously, the *Acts* (particularly the Greek version) is organized into thirteen "Acts" of the apostle, with a brief narrative of his martyrdom at the end. These "Acts" can be meaningfully divided into two parts. Acts I–VIII are largely discrete independent units whose internal narratives have little connection to those of the other "Acts." Acts III–VIII scarcely even reflect the text's putatively Indian setting. By contrast, the *Acts*' second half, namely Acts IX–XIII, treats Thomas' encounter with the Indian monarch Mazdai, a pagan who nonetheless has certain Zoroastrian resonances and antagonism to Judas Thomas' preaching. This is also the only part of the text that features a coherent narrative thread and that emphasizes ascetic celibacy throughout (in the middle Acts, marriage and martial intercourse are not condemned, even if extramarital sex is). Accordingly, the author of the surviving *Acts* apparently wrote this sequence during the mid-to-late third century in light of the increased rivalries between Christians and Zoroastrians in Persia. Significantly, Acts VII and VIII constitute a bridge between the two parts. In these Acts, Judas Thomas encounters and aids an anonymous general, but in Acts IX to XIII, this general has the name of Siphor. This indicates that the author had integrated the material on the initially anonymous general and had then accordingly tailored Acts IX–XIII, in which the general bears a name. In other words, the same author who wrote Acts IX–XIII also organized and redacted Acts I–VIII, which consisted of an assemblage of earlier material that constitutes the first half of the surviving work. While assuming its basic form, it seems, in the mid-to-late third century, the resulting narrative thus integrated traditions and perhaps even textual passages from earlier periods. It also interwove an array of themes from the gospels, Acts of the Apostles, ancient novels, and, it would appear, Manichaean (and Zoroastrian) narrative traditions.[27]

Another vein of thought, however, situates the *Acts* in an earlier period and distances the composition from both a Syriac original and a provenance in Upper Mesopotamia. A recent preliminary study, which promises more detailed (and welcome) publications to follow, has argued for conceiving of the *Acts* as a Greek composition of the second century produced by the cosmopolitan Mediterranean milieu in which other apostolic apocrypha can be situated. This theory is worth due consideration. But more work needs to be done before this can be a convincing interpretation.[28] A putative second-century date would be based on a certain consistency

---

[27] Saint-Laurent, *Missionary Stories*, 21–23; Poirier, "*Actes de Thomas*"; Drijvers, "Addai und Mani," 171–85; De Jong, "*Cologne Mani Codex*," esp. 145–47.

[28] Roig Lanzillotta, "Syriac Original?" makes such arguments. The article is by its author's admission (127–28) a preliminary study and a critique of what scholars have in the past treated as Syriac

with the cultural, religious, and intellectual currents of the second century, similarities and parallels with other apostolic apocrypha, and the premise that "orientalist" views have encouraged waves of scholars to locate the text in the Syriac literary environment of third-century Edessa.[29] But the *Acts*' disposition as a heavily composite text that integrated earlier invented traditions and even textual material could explain in part how ideas and idioms appropriate to the second century could persist in the third-century narrative. As we will see, the surviving text of the *Acts* may even have been engaging with late second-century textual traditions that had located Thomas in Parthia.[30] Moreover, if the surviving form of the *Acts* was composed in the second century, it is odd that no secure literary witnesses to it or Thomas' Indian travels (as opposed to Thomas' travels in Parthia) date before the mid-fourth century and that the text seems to contain a variation on a passage from the third-century Syriac *Book of the Laws of the Countries*.[31]

In regards to location of composition, the preliminary study argues against Edessene origins on account of the possibility that the "oriental" proper names that appear in the *Acts* and the *Hymn of the Pearl* reflect how Christians of the eastern Mediterranean were portraying an eastern environment. They do not necessarily point to the place where the *Acts* originates. After all, the author could have simply used what Greeks and Romans understood to be standard eastern names like Mygdonia or Mazdai for the text's characters. The study also tends to ascribe (with some validity) the associations that scholars have made between the *Acts* and Edessene or Manichaean literature with a uniform "orientalism," whereby unexplained phenomena could simply be ascribed to eastern inspirations.[32]

But such views seem to downplay some serious factors that suggest an Upper Mesopotamian provenance and Syriac priority, or at least parity, with Greek. Legitimate correspondences do appear to exist between the *Acts* and Manichaean literature, not least the treatment of Judas Thomas as Jesus' twin and (it would seem) visual double that we have mentioned above. Premises of the Syriac text's dependence on a prior Greek version

---

influences on the Greek text. It thus focuses mostly on the Greek tradition (and not the Syriac one) and raises serious concerns about many traditional arguments for a Syriac original. But his suggestions about dating and location do not engage substantively with the treatment of Myer, *Spiritual Epicleses*, 29–55 (even while citing it) and her focus on the text as the product of layers of redaction. I raise other considerations in the discussion to follow.

[29] Roig Lanzillotta, "Syriac Original?" 120–27. [30] See discussion at pp. 50–54.
[31] See discussion at pp. 62–63, n. 123–125 for attestations. See following paragraphs and pp. 37, n. 33, and 52–53 for the Syriac *Book*.
[32] Roig Lanzillotta, "Syriac Original?" 120–27.

Acts of Thomas: Date, Language, and Location 37

and a provenance outside the Roman Near East, as currently formulated, do not adequately account for the following features of the text. One is the appearance of an "Indian" king bearing the historical Indo-Parthian title Gondophares (which was probably known to Palmyrenes through contact with north India). Another is the presence of an "Indian" merchant with a fairly uncommon Aramaic name attested in the Near East (Habban) but largely unknown elsewhere. Other notable features are the seeming reference to an obscure port site on either the island of Kharg or the island of Bahrain and what appears to be an explicit variation on a statement from the Syriac *Book of the Laws of the Countries*.[33] These all suggest that the text was written in a Levantine or Mesopotamian place whose inhabitants had some direct contact with the Persian Gulf (but not necessarily India). One can comment further on factors that link the text to Edessa or Upper Mesopotamia. The earliest certain witnesses to the surviving text of the *Acts* and its narrative of Judas Thomas' ministry in India (as opposed to Parthia) are the Syriac *Teaching of the Apostles* (*Doctrina Apostolorum*, c. 325–350 CE) and the Syriac poet Ephrem, both with meaningful Edessene connections.[34] Likewise, Syriac and Greek texts informed by Edessene traditions have a marked tendency, like the *Acts*, to use the apostle's "primitive" name and call him Judas or Judas Thomas, not just Thomas.[35] Even if the original text of the surviving *Acts* was composed in Greek (and not Syriac), it would not eliminate the possibility that the cosmopolitan and bilingual city of Edessa was the site of composition. We will return to the issue of Edessene provenance in this chapter.

But one final and perhaps decisive factor does, in my view, support Syriac priority for the *Acts*, or at least relative parity and mutual dependence between the Syriac and Greek traditions (and by implication, an Upper Mesopotamian origin). It also situates the basic Syriac version of the surviving text in the mid-to-late third century or so, with the Greek version taking form in the late third or even early fourth. This factor is the tendency for the surviving Greek text to treat silver as uncoined bullion (ἄσημον) measured by weight (like *litrai*).[36] In the first two "Acts," the

---

[33] See discussion at pp. 43–48, with n. 57 for Gondophares, Habban, and the port site. For the passage, see Ramelli, *Bardesane di Edessa*, 252–57, and *Bardaisan of Edessa*, 111–15; Klijn, *Acts of Thomas*, 162–63 on 83–84 of the Greek text (ed. Bonnet) and ܐܣܝܡܐ of the Syriac (ed. Wright), with Lewis, *Acta*, ܀·܀ for the Sinai fragments; and Syriac *Book* (ed. Drijvers) 14–16 and (ed. Ramelli) 146. For the Syriac *Book* and its date, see p. 52, n. 92.
[34] See discussion at pp. 57–58.
[35] See, e.g., the Addai tradition represented by Eusebius, *HE* (ed. Schwartz and Mommsen) 1.13.11; *Teaching of Addai* (ed. Phillips) ܗ : Judas Thomas.
[36] I thank Angelos Chaniotis for steering me to this promising line of inquiry.

Syriac text on certain occasions depicts financial exchanges in silver as involving coins. For example, Habban purchases Judas Thomas from Jesus for "twenty (pieces) of silver (*kespā*)." Although no explicit word for "pieces" or "coins" appears, it is clearly implied and consistent with the reading of at least one manuscript of the Greek version that refers to twenty silver coins (*nomismata*).[37] Certainly not reflecting the actual costs of a slave in silver denarii during the second or third century, this aspect of the text calls to mind the thirty silver pieces for which Judas Iscariot betrayed Jesus in the canonical gospels.[38] Significantly, it also treats exchanges in silver coinage as normative. But most edited manuscripts of the Greek tradition (that is, the selection in Bonnet's volume) describe the price for Judas Thomas as "three pounds of bullion" (τριῶν λιτρῶν ἀσήμου), with silver being implied, not specified. As we will see in the following paragraphs, the term ἄσημον often referred to silver bullion in late antiquity. But since the word literally meant "unmarked" or "unstamped," in earlier periods it strictly described uncoined bullion and was usually qualified by a reference to a specific metal. Yet, as we have seen, at least one Greek manuscript (ἀργυρίου νομίσματα εἴκοσι) is consistent with the Syriac, and some others specify pounds of "silver" (ἀργυρίου).[39] These aspects suggest that the Greek version is in some ways dependent on the Syriac tradition and has ultimately transformed its portrayal of a financial exchange in silver coins into one involving weighed bullion.

Likewise, in India king Gudnaphar pays Judas Thomas in silver and gold (*kespā w-dahbā*) according to a passage from the Syriac version, which survives in both the London manuscript and the Sinai fragments.[40] Most edited manuscripts (in Bonnet's volume) of the two main Greek recensions for the passage describe the king as sending to Judas Thomas "gold and (silver) bullion" (χρυσίον καὶ ἄσημον). Only a few specify silver (ἀργύριον) by name. Again, the two Greek recensions of the passage generally seem to have represented the Syriac term for silver (*kespā*) with

---

[37] *Acts of Thomas* (ed. Wright) ܟܣܦܐ of the Syriac: ܥܣܪܝܢ ܟܣܦܐ; *Acts of Thomas* (ed. Bonnet) 2, with apparatus criticus.
[38] Particularly in Matthew (ed. Nestle-Aland) 26:15. Klijn, *Acts of Thomas*, 21–22, for further discussion. The slave named "Abban" from *AE* 1896, no. 21 is sold for two hundred silver denarii; the slave in Drijvers and Healey, *Old Syriac Inscriptions*, 232–35, is 700 denarii, the one in Feissel, Gascou, and Teixidor, "Documents," 6–16 (*P. Euphrat.* 6–7) is 600 denarii.
[39] *Acts of Thomas* (ed. Bonnet) 2 of the Greek, with apparatus criticus for variations in the twenty-one manuscripts that he edited. Eighty containing at least parts of the narrative are now known; Klauck, *Apocryphal Acts*, 142. All comments on the Greek version in the following paragraphs are based on Bonnet's manuscripts, which are now admittedly a fraction of the total discovered.
[40] *Acts of Thomas* (ed. Wright) ܟܣܦܐ- ܘܕܗܒܐ of the Syriac, with Lewis, *Acta*, ܡܓ: ܟܣܦܐ ܘܕܗܒܐ.

a word that strictly meant bullion (ἄσημον) before the late antique period (see the following paragraphs). The more literal rendering of "silver" (ἀργύριον) that sometimes appears in manuscripts for the passages explored so far might reflect early stages of translation and textual transmission (or perhaps they were added much later). The surviving Greek tradition thus mostly appears to invite the reader to understand that the term for uncoined bullion (ἄσημον) refers to silver even without an explicit reference to silver.[41] It also apparently reflects a contemporary society in which people were accustomed to financial transactions that consisted of gold coinage and silver bullion and in which the term bullion (ἄσημον) specified silver bullion or simply silver. As we will see momentarily, these were later Roman social phenomena that took shape after 275 CE.

Intriguingly, the *Hymn of the Pearl,* whatever its origins and relationship to the *Acts,* exhibits similar tendencies. The Syriac text refers to gold (*dahbā*) of the *Gelāyē* and silver (*sīmā* or *sēmā*) from Ganzak. The corresponding Greek passage renders these as χρυσός and ἄσημος.[42] The appearance of *sīmā* (or otherwise *sēmā*) poses a unique complexity. Attested in Middle Persian (*asēm*), it is clearly a cognate of ἄσημον, and it is commonly surmised that the term passed from Middle Persian to Syriac through Greek.[43] The problem is that the term is not attested in Old Persian or Parthian (that is, before the third century CE), and as we will learn below, ἄσημον, meaning bullion, was not used for silver generically until after 275 CE. It is best to conceive of *sīmā* or *sēmā* as a word of Greek origin (ἄσημον) that passed into Syriac and Middle Persian during the late third century or thereafter and that referred to silver bullion, whereas *kespā* tended to denote silver coinage in Syriac. Since the Greek of the *Hymn of the Pearl* otherwise bears signs of being dependent on the Syriac,[44] the Syriac reference to silver (*sīmā* or *sēmā*) was probably a Greek loan. But it governed the appearance of ἄσημος in the Greek version of the *Hymn.*

By contrast, the only instances in which both the Greek and Syriac *Acts* refer to silver coins in corresponding passages can be explained by New Testament influences. These involve moments in which the women of Mazdai's court bribe jailors who have detained Judas Thomas. In Act XIII

---

[41] *Acts of Thomas* (ed. Bonnet) 19 of the Greek. The translation of Attridge, *Acts of Thomas,* 30, rightly specifies bullion.
[42] *Hymn of the Pearl* (ed. Poirier and ed. Ferreira) line 6 of the Greek and Syriac. For more on the *Hymn* and its peoples/places, see Chapter 5, pp. 191–194, n. 75–86.
[43] For the Middle Persian origin, Brockelmann-Sokoloff, *Syriac Lexicon,* 958–59 and Ciancaglini, *Iranian Loanwords in Syriac,* 218.
[44] See pp. 191–192, n. 75.

of the Syriac version, they pay 360 *zuzes* in the Syriac, with "zuz" referring to a Jewish denomination of the Roman period that was sometimes analogous to a Roman denarius in Syriac literature. In the corresponding Greek passage, they pay 363 staters of silver. Both zuzes and staters appear as terms for units of Jewish currency in the Greek New Testament and its Syriac versions, and this surely informs their appearance in the *Acts*.[45] Likewise, in Act IX the Syriac refers to twenty *zuzes* and the Greek to ten denarii. These references also have New Testament antecedents.[46]

Altogether, the tendencies just described support Syriac priority or parity between the Syriac and Greek, especially for Acts I–II. The Greek tradition has seemingly transformed the Syriac's references to silver coins or simply to silver into references to silver bullion specifically. These tendencies also have implications for dating the *Acts*. For various reasons, the period after 275 CE (and certainly the fourth century CE) witnessed the marginalization of silver currency. Due to the reforms of Aurelian (273 CE), Diocletian (293 CE), and Constantine (312 CE),[47] gold increasingly became the basis of financial exchanges involving coins. By contrast, silver coinage ceased to play a central role, and exchanges in uncoined silver bullion valued by weight, which had occurred previously to a lesser extent, took increasingly visible precedence. Since silver was now usually traded in bullion, the term for unstamped or uncoined bullion (ἄσημον) came to be used frequently in papyrus documents for silver or employed to draw a distinction between gold and silver ("gold and bullion"; χρυσὸς/χρυσιὸν καὶ ἄσημον). By contrast, in previous periods the metallic composition of bullion (ἄσημον) would usually have been specified by name (like ἀργύριον).[48] As we have seen, in most edited manuscripts (of Bonnet's

---

[45] *Acts of Thomas* (ed. Bonnet) 151 of the Greek text and (ed. Wright) ܙܘܙܐ. Matthew (ed. Nestle and Aland for Greek; ed. Kiraz for Syriac) 17:24–27 arguably informs both narratives. A search through the standard Syriac lexica (Payne Smith, *Thesaurus*, 1097–1098; Brockelmann-Sokoloff, *Syriac Lexicon*, 371) yields numerous attestations of "zuz" and its appearance in Syriac literature.

[46] *Acts of Thomas* (ed. Bonnet) 118 of the Greek text and (ed. Wright) ܙܘܙܐ. For denarii in the gospels, see (ed. Nestle-Aland) Matthew 18: 20:1–16, 22:19; Mark 6:37, 12:15, 14:5; Luke 7:41, 10:35, 20:24; and John 6:7, 12:5.

[47] Discussed by Bambourg, "Later Roman Empire," 258–74; Banaji, *Agrarian Change*, 39–44; Potter, *Roman Empire at Bay*, 268–71 and 385–87; Corbier, "Coinage and Taxation," 329–46, 352–53, and 358–59; Bagnall, *Currency and Inflation*, 49–56; Estiot, "Later Third Century" and Abdy, "Tetrarchy."

[48] *P. Oxy.* 12.1524 (301–324 CE), 14.1653 (307 CE), 27.2474 (275–299 CE), and 33.2673 (304 CE), with 46.3307 and 54.3756 (301–325 CE): here "neither gold, nor un-coined bullion, nor silver" distinguishes gold coins, silver bullion, and coined silver folles, as in *P. Panop. Beatty* 2 (300 CE), esp. lines 300–5; *SB* XVI 12566 (275–325)=Youtie, "*P. Mich. Inv.* 1759," 276–78; *P. Cair. Isid.* 69–70 (310 CE), 89, (308 CE), and 127 (310 CE); *O. Kell.* 25 (327–38 CE); *P. Col.* 138–39 (308 CE); *P. Harr.* 1.97 (fourth century CE); *P. Oxf.* 15 (late third century CE); *P. Sakaon* 57 (312–29 CE); *SB* XIV.12215 (301–350 CE).

volume) the Greek *Acts* exhibits the same intriguing habit of using ἄσημον without any qualification for silver, and this implies a presumption that silver was, by convention, bullion in form. In fact, Greek papyri from Egypt produced after 275 CE and containing references to pounds (λίτραι) of silver (ἀργύριον), uncoined silver bullion (ἄσημον), the phrasing of "gold and (silver) bullion" (χρυσός/χρυσιὸν καὶ ἄσημον), or transactions involving them represent the best textual parallels for how the Greek *Acts*, and even the Syriac and Greek of the *Hymn of the Pearl*, portrays transactions in precious metals.[49]

Accordingly, the tendency for manuscripts of the Greek *Acts* to specify unstamped bullion where corresponding passages of the Syriac text refer to silver or silver coins situates the surviving Greek *Acts* to a period shortly after 275 but presumably before the mid-fourth century (when Greek authors certainly start to cite it). The basic surviving Syriac text, by contrast, can be situated somewhat earlier, even if it underwent the subsequent layers of redaction for which it is known. Although it does not capture actual third-century prices, it depicts a society in which exchanges in silver coins (even if heavily debased), not bullion, were standard. On this basis, the Syriac text can best be placed in the mid-to-late third century, before or during the initial stages of the vast fiscal shifts of 275–325. We can surmise that the surviving Greek text, following shortly after, took shape near the end of the third century even if it had roots in prior decades. A composition in Syriac also would indicate that the text in its basic surviving form was composed in Upper Mesopotamia, a site of Syriac and Greek bilingualism.

In a similar vein, one last comment can be made regarding the treatment of the general Siphor as a *stratelatēs* instead of *stratēgos* in the Greek text of the *Acts*.[50] While Greek authors preceding the third century CE sometimes used the term *stratelatēs* to denote a general, this was quite uncommon. *Stratēgos* was overwhelmingly preferred. But during the late-third and fourth centuries, *stratelatēs* became a common Greek translation for the *magister militum* and other key military posts in the imperial administration. *Stratelatēs* thus became much more popular as a term for a military commander among Greek authors and even became a loan word in Syriac

---

Texts and dates are accessible online through papyri.info. Note that even in transactions involving gold bullion and silver bullion, the gold bullion tends to be called "gold" (χρυσός) and the silver "bullion" (ἄσημον). So prevalent is the association between silver and uncoined bullion after 275 CE.

[49] See previous footnote and *P. Oxy.* 10.1288 (319–24 CE) and 51.3624 (359 CE); *P. Col.* 7.160 (354 CE) and 9.244 (mid-fourth century CE). Texts and dates are accessible online through papyri.info.

[50] *Acts of Thomas* (ed. Bonnet) 62, 69–70, 81, 93, 100, 102, 105, 136, and 138.

by the fifth century.⁵¹ This too would situate the Greek *Acts* closer to c. 300 CE than to earlier periods. The corresponding Syriac simply describes Siphor as *rab ḥaylā*.⁵² This is a standard Syriac term for a military leader during late antiquity and probably in itself has little implication for dating the text. But the correspondence of *rab ḥaylā* and *stratelatēs* has an epigraphic parallel from late third-century Palmyra, itself a seat of bilingualism in Greek and Aramaic. In 271 CE, two generals of the famous dynast Zenobia identified themselves by the title of *rb ḥyl'* and *stratelatēs* in an inscription that honored her.⁵³ By this time, both the Palmyrenes and Edessenes had noticeably begun to use the term *strategoi* for the *duumviri* of their home cities, which now had the status of *colonia*, but not for military commanders.⁵⁴ In fact, the last inscriptions in which Palmyrenes called a domestic general *strategos* date to c. 200 CE. They started to use *stratelatēs* for military leaders only some time after earning colonial status under the emperor Septimius Severus or, more likely, Caracalla.⁵⁵ Overall, Siphor's stature as *rab ḥaylā* and *stratelatēs* locates the text, or at least the Greek tradition, to later in the third century.

Altogether, the apparent mid-to-late third-century composition of the Syriac text and its integration of an assemblage of existing material have bearing on the issue of whether the *Acts* is a reliable historical source. The opening sequence of the *Acts*, in which Habban transports Judas Thomas from Jerusalem to India by sea, in fact bears signs of having been part of a previous textual tradition that was redacted and integrated into the surviving text. If such is the case, then the text has limited value as a source for the contemporary movement of Christianity or for direct contact between the Roman Levant (including Palestine and Upper Mesopotamia) and India. To the anomalies of the opening sequence, we now turn.

Geographic Anomalies of the Opening Sequence

In its surviving form, the *Acts* narrates how Judas Thomas arrived in India to preach. But it intriguingly reflects little real knowledge of India's

---

[51] My observations on the Greek are based on searches in *TLG*, with Mason, *Greek Terms for Roman Institutions*, 13 and 155–62. For *stratelatēs* as a term for *magister militum*, see *ODB* (entries: *magister militum* and *stratelatēs*). The word recurs in the Syriac of the *Chronicle of ps.–Joshua Stylite* (ed. Chabot), which is easily accessible in translation with commentary in Trombley and Watt, *Chronicle*.

[52] He is introduced at *Acts of Thomas* (ed. Wright) ܪܒ of the Syriac, with various references in ܪܒ ܚܝܠܐ - ܪܒ ܚܝܠܗ, and ܪܒܗ.

[53] *IGLS* 17.1.57.

[54] *IGLS* 17.1.61 and 65; P1 in Drijvers and Healey, *Old Syriac Inscriptions*, 232.

[55] *IGLS* 17.1.222 and 307; *Dig.* (ed. Mommsen and Krueger) 50.15.5.

topography or internal history. Despite various theories regarding exactly where in India the *Acts* depicts Judas Thomas as traveling and efforts to identify distinct Indian practices in its narrative, the fact remains that its version of India bears no toponyms, with one possible exception, and does not specify any distinctively Indian landmarks and customs.[56] It does describe Judas Thomas' encounter with a king identified as Gudnaphar (Syriac) or Goundaphores (Greek), whose name (Gondophares) is of Iranian origin and was borne as a name or title by Indo-Parthian (or Pahlava) kings in north India during the first century CE.[57] The name of Gudnaphar's brother Gad may also be based on an Indo-Parthian figure.[58] Knowledge of such names or titles, however, was probably transmitted to the Roman Near East through the Palmyrene commercial network that maintained active contact with north India between the late-first and late-third centuries CE.[59] It need not reflect the activity of Christians in India or direct contact between Upper Mesopotamia and the subcontinent. Otherwise the royals that it depicts and identifies by Iranian names, such as Mazdai, Vizan, and Siphor, seem to be completely invented.[60] As later parts of this chapter argue, the lack of specific knowledge in the surviving text reflects a mid-to-late third-century Edessene literary agenda that

---

[56] Useful observations and references are provided by McGrath, "History and Fiction," esp. 304–6; Van den Bosch, "India and the Apostolate," 125–48 (esp. 128–29). Despite efforts to see Indian customs in the text (like bathing before a meal), these typically are not uniquely or distinctly Indian and are attested among Greeks and Romans too.

[57] Luke, "Gondopharnes," 433–50; Tubach, "Historische Elemente," 72–98; and Bivar, "Gondophares," 26–36 discuss Gondophares I, traditionally associated with the *Acts of Thomas* and the Takht-i-Bahi inscription. Some numismatists support this association. See Cribb, "New Evidence" and "Western Satraps and Satavahanas"; Errington and Curtis, *From Persia to Punjab*, 50–71; and Rezakhani, *ReOrienting the Sasanians*, 34–40. But others now link Sases Gondophares to the king portrayed by the *Acts* while dating him to the early to mid-first century CE and the period of the Takht-i-Bahi inscription. See Senior, *Indo-Scythian Coins*, 1.124–26. For the coins (with images), Bopearchchi, *Indo-Greek*, 55–60 and 106–11, nos. 118–202; and Senior, *Indo-Scythian Coins*, 1.108–26 and 2.148–58 and 167–74; Rienjang, "Indo-Parthian Coins." For the etymology of Gudnaphar/Vindafarna(h), see Gignoux, Jullien, and Jullien, *Iranisches Personennamenbuch* 7.5, 76; and Luke, "Gondopharnes," 438–39. For the Indo-Parthian (or Pahlava) kingdom, see Puri, "Sakas and the Indo-Parthians"; and Bopearachchi, "Indo-Parthians." Note that "Gudnaphar," the Syriac version in the surviving *Acts*, switches the "d" and "n" (as Gignoux, Jullien, and Jullien comment). Some tenuous interpretations try to associate the figure, as well as king Mazdai, with south Indian kings. See McGrath, "History and Fiction," 300, n. 5; Mundadan, *History of Christianity*, 26; and Van den Bosch, "India and the Apostolate," 126–27, n. 4 and 135.

[58] On Gadavhara Gadana (or Gudavhara Gadana), see Cribb, "New Evidence," 294–98; and Senior, *Indo-Scythian Coins*, 1.111–21 and 2.178–81; Reed, "Beyond the Land of Nod," 64, n. 66; McGrath, "History and Fiction," 301–02; Van den Bosch, "India and the Apostolate," 133–35.

[59] See discussion in pp. 4–8, 16, and 37. I elaborate on this view in a more robust way in forthcoming work.

[60] Van den Bosch, "India and the Apostolate," 126–27, n. 4 and 135; McGrath, "History and Fiction," 300.

distances Judas Thomas from the evangelization of Parthia, with which he had been previously credited. The author of the text, knowing virtually nothing about India (other than a king named Gudnaphar/Goundaphores), simply interwove existing traditions about the apostle with new material pertaining to his interactions with King Mazdai.

But Judas Thomas' movement to India in the opening episode in the *Acts* is also vexing,[61] and it too bears signs of redaction indicating that the text has little historical value as a source for movement between the Roman Levant and India. Because it depicts Habban and Judas Thomas as sailing directly from Jerusalem to India without encountering a landmass, it deviates from any realistic portrayal of movement in the ancient world. Jerusalem is an inland city. Even if it had been located on the Mediterranean coast, one would not have been able to sail to India from it.[62] This lack of realism can be explained by various factors. Space and geography are not necessarily informed by the strictly material elements of physical terrains, and how Romans and Christians experienced and understood landscapes and movement across them did not necessarily correspond with their actual physical features.[63] Moreover, a primary goal of ancient apocryphal literature and hagiography is to convey a higher truth through the marvelous, unbelievable deeds of apostles or saints. In such instances, composition was often construed as an act of piety, and geographic realism and close attention to empirical details are not necessarily essential in such narratives.[64] The debt that the *Acts* owes to its engagement with the conventions of the ancient novel and other apostolic apocrypha, in which protagonists routinely wandered or relocated far from home, also may have had an impact.[65] Finally, it is not unusual for ancient authors to conflate inland cities with the ports

---

[61] *Acts of Thomas* (ed. Wright) ܡܚܕ - ܡܚܕ of the Syriac; (ed. Bonnet) 1–3 of the Greek.
[62] This problem is noted, for instance, by Huxley, "Geography in the *Acts*," 72; and Glancy, "Slavery," 6–7.
[63] Some examples with such a focus are Brodersen, *Terra cognita*; Nasrallah, *Christian Responses*; Shepardson, "Controlling Contested Spaces," 483–516; and *Controlling Contested Places*; and Parker, *Making of Roman India*.
[64] See, for instance, the emphasis of Burrus, *Sex Lives*. Harvey, "Martyr Passions and Hagiography," provides a helpful introduction to the complex, multiform genre of hagiography, the various cultural or literary *topoi* that shaped the formation of its narratives, and their link to historicity, contemporary social issues, gender, and power. In the same volume, Shoemaker, "Early Christian Apocryphal Literature," provides a useful examination of early Christian apocryphal literature, within which the *Acts of Thomas* is normally classified, its intersections with the (later) genre of hagiography and contemporary novels, and debates regarding classification. For hagiography, writing, and piety, see Krueger, *Writing and Holiness*.
[65] Treatment of the various issues pertaining to the ancient novel can be found in Whitmarsh, *Cambridge Companion*. For novelistic and antinovelistic tendencies, see König, "Novelistic and Anti-Novelistic Narrative."

that gave access to them, and ships could be described as sailing from Rome (and not literally from Ostia) or from Aksum (and not literally from Adulis).[66]

Still, it is worth noting that apostolic apocrypha or hagiographies oftentimes described trips from Jerusalem with an eye for realistic travel. A Syriac text entitled the *History of Philip, Evangelist and Martyr* is careful to specify that Philip traveled from Jerusalem to Carthage by moving overland from Samaria and then to Caesarea Maritima before boarding a ship.[67] Moreover, it is evident that the voyage of Habban and Judas Thomas, as depicted in the *Acts*, troubled certain Christian readers. For this reason, a shorter fourth-century variation of the *Acts* that survives in Latin transfers the setting of the apostle's purchase by Habban from Jerusalem to Caesarea Maritima.[68] This did not resolve how one could sail from the Roman Levant to India, but it did at least represent Thomas and Habban as sailing from a port city. As we will learn later, the sixth- or seventh-century *Acts of Mar Mari* provides a detailed and roughly realistic representation of its saint's itinerary through Mesopotamia, Assyria, the Zab River region, Khuzistan, and Fars. In light of this inclination toward geographic realism in ancient Christian narratives, the topography of the *Acts* is in many respects eccentric.

Along with Jerusalem's depiction as a port city that gives access to India, other eccentricities from the opening sequence can be summarized briefly here.[69] Judas Thomas himself, for example, is described as being a master craftsman of both river craft and ships' masts. Despite the nearby presence of the Dead Sea, the Sea of Galilee, and the Jordan river, these skills more befit the inhabitant of a town located near where a river lets into a large body of water known for being a commercial crossroads, like the Mediterranean or the Persian Gulf.[70] It is worth noting that Habban's name is not a traditional Sanskrit or Prakrit one. It is instead attested at Palmyra and also, it would seem, in a Latin and Greek papyrus describing the purchase of a slave originating from somewhere in Mesopotamia at

---

[66] *The Old Man of Edessa* (ed. Amiaud), and the *Life of Alexius* (ed. Rösler) 509: Rome to Seleucia in Pieria; the *Peoples of India and the Brahmins* (ed. Berghoff and ed. Derrett) 7: Aksum to "India."
[67] *History of Philip* (ed. Wright) ܓܠܝ : to be distinguished (probably) from the *Acts of Philip* (ed. Bovon, Bouvier, and Amsler).
[68] The Latin *Passion of the Holy Apostle Thomas* (*Passio sancti Thomae apostoli*) (ed. Zelzer) 1–3 shifts this episode to Caesarea, an actual port. Zelzer dates the text to the fourth century (xxiv–xxvi).
[69] *Acts of Thomas* (ed. Wright) ܩܡܕ – ܩܡܚ of the Syriac; (ed. Bonnet) 1–3 of the Greek.
[70] *Acts of Thomas* (ed. Wright) ܩܡܚ and ܩܡܛ of the Syriac; (ed. Bonnet) 3 of the Greek. Repeated at ܩܢܒ of the Syriac (ed. Wright), with the Sinai fragments of Lewis, *Acta*, ١٩٢, and 17 of the Greek (ed. Bonnet).

46 The *Acts of Thomas* and Its Impact

Seleucia in Pieria in 166 CE. But it appears to be a fairly uncommon name with an uncertain meaning, and it would seem to reflect the text's Upper Mesopotamian provenance (as opposed to being a "standard" eastern name used by a Mediterranean author).[71]

Another oddity is that the Syriac text describes Judas Thomas and Habban as sailing to the "city," "town," or "fortress" (ܟܪܟܐ) called "Sanadrūk" (or Sandarūk/Sandrūk) (ܣܢܕܪܘܟ) after encountering a favorable wind.[72] They travel to India thereafter. Here, the Syriac reading seems better than that of the Greek version, whose manuscripts name "Andrapolis" and certain variations resembling "Sanadrūk/Sandarūk/Sandrūk."[73] Despite many efforts to locate the place in the Middle East or India (whether as Sanadrūk/Sandarūk/Sandrūk or Andrapolis) and to posit a trip through either the Persian Gulf or the Red Sea,[74] no convincing explanation has materialized. One possibility, though tenuous, is that the text is referring to a site in Bahrain where Islamic Arabic sources claim that the Sasanian king Ardashir I (224–242 CE) killed a king named Sanatruk/Sanatruq. His fortress could have borne an eponymous name.[75] Bahrain (often called Tylos/Thilos) was also a key stopover point between Mesene and the Indian Ocean.[76]

---

[71] *AE* (1896) 21=*P. Lond.* 2.229, with Klijn, *Acts of Thomas*, 21, though various Semitic names could in theory explain the Latin and Greek forms; *PAT* 0932. Attested in Aramaic, the name appears to be of Arabic origin. Variously interpreted as linked to dropsy or monkey (Harding, *Index*, 177–75; Stark, *Personal Names*, 87), it also may be linked to a root suggesting a "dear" or "beloved" quality and whose permutations are much more common. Harding, *Index*, 172–75, with *IHatra* 153, 159, 169, and 411 (of Beyer): *Habba* or *Habbay*.

[72] As stated in *Acts of Thomas* (ed. Wright) ܣܢܕܪܘܟ of the Syriac; Gignoux, Jullien; and Jullien, *Iranisches Personennamenbuch* 7.5, 121 on the name and its various renderings in Syriac.

[73] *Acts of Thomas* (ed. Bonnet) 3 of the Greek, with xxi of Bonnet's volume. Based on the apparently contrived name of Andrapolis (Man-City) and textual variations like Enadroch and Enadoch, it seems that the toponyms that appear in the Greek manuscripts were the product of scribal difficulties with what had originally been the Syriac rendering of "Sanadruk (or Sandarūk/Sandrūk), the city/town/fortress." Nothing suggests a link to the Andhra of south India. Klijn, *Acts of Thomas*, 24.

[74] Huxley, "Geography in the *Acts*," 72–73, presents the theory that Hatra is the port of "Andrapolis" due to kings named Sanatruq there. For the kings, see *IHatra* 28, 36–37, 79, 82, 112, 120, 124, 139, 144, 194–99, 202–3, 229, 231–32, 287, 333–34, 341–42, 345, 347, 353, 367, 370, 375–80, and 384c–385. For other theories, Kurikilamkatt, *First Voyage*, 41–65 and "First Port," 3–20; Farquhar, *Apostle Thomas in India*, 12–19; Klijn, *Acts of Thomas*, 24; Van den Bosch, "India and the Apostolate," 129–31; Jullien and Jullien, *Apôtres des confins*, 82–87 and 95; Attridge, *Acts of Thomas*, 13.

[75] Salles, "Bahrain," 134–35, "Travelling to India," 162–63, "Towards a Geography," 152, makes this intriguing suggestion. Hoyland, *Arabs*, 27–28; Kervran, *Qal'at al-Bahrain*, 249–52; and Potts, *Arabian Gulf*, 2.229–32 and "Archaeology and Early History," 42, describe the episode and discuss sources. Kervran, *Qal'at al-Bahrain* and "Siècle obscure," 284–303, treats the site.

[76] *IGLS* 17.1.26 (north India), 245 (Tylos) and 250 (north India). See Young, *Rome's Eastern Trade*, 139–43; McLaughlin, *Rome and the Distant East*, 96–106; Gorea, "Palmyrene Tablette" and "Sea and

But it is perhaps better to surmise that Sanadrūk/Sandarūk/Sandrūk (ܣܢܕܪܘܟ) refers to the island of Kharg or even a specific port site on it, even if doing so in a confusing way. Greek-speaking Romans, most notably Claudius Ptolemy, called Kharg by the alternate names of "the island of Alexander" (*Alexandrou*) and *Arakia*. Later Persian and Arab authors identified it as *Kharak* or *Harak*. It was a stopover for merchants sailing from Charax Spasinou, and a port settlement known by the same name as the island reasonably found a home there, even if it is obscure.[77] Sanadrūk/Sandarūk/Sandrūk (ܣܢܕܪܘܟ) intriguingly contains many letters of Alexander's name in Syriac (ܐܠܟܣܢܕܪܘܣ).[78] It is also notable that Roman geographers circulated diverse permutations of the names for Kharg and varied in their understanding of whether these referred to the same or different islands. So Pliny claims that in the Persian Gulf, near Persis, were the islands of Psilos, Cassandra, and Aracha.[79] Kassandra (as it is in Greek) here seems to be an alternative, distorted, or vernacular rendering of the name *Alexandrou*. As such, Pliny was probably treating what were (according to Ptolemy) two names for the same island (*Alexandrou* and *Arakia*) as two distinct islands (*Kassandra* and *Aracha*). Altogether it is conceivable that the author of the third-century Syriac text of the *Acts* was engaging with a tradition of Judas Thomas' travels that involved a port site on Kharg, which was known to have the Greek name *Alexandrou* or *Kassandra*. The port "town" or "city" that the apostle visited may have simply shared the island's name. But the author, either rearranging the name from confusion or using a variant form, rendered it as Sanadrūk/Sandarūk/Sandrūk (ܣܢܕܪܘܟ). From there, the Greek tradition provided additional variations on this obscure and confusing toponym. Intriguingly, a later reference to a monastery at a "city" or "town" (ܡܕܝܢܬܐ) called "Sanadrūn" (or Sandarūn/Sandrūn) (ܣܢܕܪܘܢ) has similarly been linked to the name "Alexandria."[80] It is however hard to tell whether it refers to the same place as the site mentioned in the *Acts*, though it is possible.

Inland Trade"; Smith, *Roman Palmyra*, 74–80. Tylos was a significant transit and administrative point in the Seleucid Persian Gulf too, as shown by Kosmin, "Rethinking the Hellenistic Gulf."

[77] Steve, *Ile de Khārg*, 6–11 and 65–68; Cohen, *Hellenistic Settlements in the East*, 211. The main Greek sources are Ptolemy (second century), *Geog.* (ed. Stückelberger and Graßhoff) 6.4.8 (Ἀλεξάνδρου ἡ καὶ Ἀρακία); and Marcian of Heraclea (fifth century), *Periplus maris exteri* (ed. Müller) 1.24 (νῆσος Ἀλεξάνδρου), at 1.530 (of 515–61).

[78] See, e.g., *Martyrs of Karka d-beth Slok*, in Bedjan, *AMSS* 2.510.

[79] Pliny, *NH* (ed. Jahn and Mayhoff) 6.111. Ammianus (ed. Seyfarth) 23.6.41 calls it *Alexandria*.

[80] *Julian Romance* (ed. Hoffmann) 241 and (ed. Sokoloff) 489, with Klijn, *Acts of Thomas*, 24. Muraviev, "Reconstructed Colophon," 402–3 discusses "Alexandria," though he connects it to the Egyptian one. The date and original language of the *Julian Romance* is debated. See Sokoloff, *Julian Romance*, vii–viii.

What "Sanadrūk" (or Sandarūk/Sandrūk) describes remains mysterious and obscure. But it still makes sense to conceive of it as a stopover location in the Persian Gulf, probably Bahrain or Kharg. This has certain implications for how we understand the textual genealogy of the *Acts*. One cannot sail directly and rapidly from Jerusalem to the Persian Gulf, even if one encounters a favorable wind (as the *Acts* describes). So the episode in general seems to have been excerpted from a previous textual tradition in which the transaction between Jesus and Habban happened near the Persian Gulf and the mouths of the Tigris and Euphrates rivers.[81]

Likewise, the beginning of the *Acts* further consists of a darkly humorous episode that plays upon the status of Judas Thomas as Jesus' twin. It describes how Jesus advertises Judas Thomas to Habban from a distance; Habban as a result does not get a close look at him. It is only after Jesus and Habban draft a contract that he allows Judas Thomas to approach. Habban, confronted by a master and a slave who are visually identical, then seeks and receives confirmation from Judas Thomas that he is actually Jesus' slave.[82] The dark humor of the passage is based on the fact that it was illegal in the Roman empire to sell free people into slavery, and if Jesus was free, one would assume that his twin was too.[83] Moreover, Jesus neither has legal ownership over Judas Thomas nor the civil authority to compose a bill of sale. Jesus basically forges a civil document to give ostensible legitimacy to an illegal slave transaction. But Jesus and Judas Thomas also cleverly exploit a legal technicality. A free man who willingly colluded in his sale in order to profit from his price could be legitimately enslaved.[84] So Judas Thomas falsely identifies Jesus as his legal owner, and Jesus then gives him the silver with which Habban had paid for him. But a key element of the dark humor seems to be missing. Nowhere in the opening episode is Judas Thomas introduced as Jesus' twin; this is only established later in the *Acts*.[85] As a result, it appears that the episode was extracted from a prior text in which the twin relationship between Jesus and Judas Thomas had been well established before the episode occurred. But in the surviving text, it is not.

---

[81] Huxley, "Geography in the *Acts*," 72 likewise suggests an earlier tradition in which Judas Thomas encounters Habban in Mesopotamia.

[82] *Acts of Thomas* (ed. Wright) ܩ-ܩܚܕ of the Syriac; (ed. Bonnet) 1–3 of the Greek.

[83] Harper, *Slavery in the Roman World*, 392–98.   [84] Harper, *Slavery in the Roman World*, 395.

[85] *Acts of Thomas* 31, 34 (not in Syriac), 39, 45, 54–57, 151–56 of the Greek text (ed. Bonnet), and ܚܒܪ-ܐܚܝ, ܐܚܐ-ܕܗܘ of the Syriac text (ed. Wright), with ܩܡܝ and ܐܚܝ of the Syriac (see Wright's comments on 170 and 180), describes Judas as having a double form (his and Jesus'), as having the likeness of Jesus, or as Jesus' twin. For a compelling instance early in the narrative, see *Acts of Thomas* (ed. Bonnet) 11–12 of the Greek and (ed. Wright) ܩܗ-ܩܘ of the Syriac.

Geographic Anomalies of the Opening Sequence 49

Finally, when Habban is first introduced by the Syriac narrative of the London manuscript, the texts reads "a certain merchant, an Indian, happened [to be] in the south land from [something illegible]; his name was Habban."[86] A lacuna unfortunately obscures the name of the place from which the merchant traveled. The text is often deemed corrupt here, as it would make sense to describe India, not Jerusalem, as "the south land." The Greek omits any reference to the "south land" and describes Habban as being "there (Jerusalem), having come from India" (ἐκεῖ ἀπὸ τῆς Ἰνδίας ἐλθόντα). Later manuscripts in Syriac variously modify the passage to indicate that Habban came to Jerusalem from India, from the south land, or both.[87] But it is possible that the Syriac of the London manuscript has the correct reading. Other texts produced in Upper Mesopotamia describe various southward points, including lower Mesopotamia, as the "land of the south."[88] So it could be surmised, if one accepts Syriac priority for the passage and an Edessene place of composition, that its wording is confusing because the opening episode was excerpted from a prior textual tradition in which it made more sense.

All such anomalies suggest that the opening episode of the *Acts* was taken from an earlier textual tradition in which the transaction between Jesus and Habban occurred at a site in Mesene, at the confluence of the Persian Gulf and Tigris/Euphrates rivers. There key transit points for commerce, like Charax Spasinou, existed.[89] From an Edessene perspective, this would have constituted "the south land" to which Habban had arrived from India, and Habban and Judas Thomas could have then sailed to the "town" (ܟܪܟܐ) called "Sanadrūk (or Sandarūk/Sandrūk) (ܣܢܕܪܘܟ) somewhere in the Persian Gulf. But the author of the *Acts*, while assembling and redacting stories from various sources, simply transferred the sequence to Jerusalem and opened the entire narrative with it. As a result, Habban and

---

[86] *Acts of Thomas* (ed. Wright) ܒܪ of the Syriac.
[87] See the reading of MS Syriac 38, at the Houghton Library of Harvard University (available digitally through *Hollis*), 123r and of the Sachau manuscript 222 of Berlin (2v) in Bedjan, *AMSS* 3.4 (and available digitally through the Staatsbibliothek zu Berlin). Similarly, Cambridge Syr. 2822, 3r, omitting any reference to India or to Habban's being Indian, claims that "a certain merchant came from the land of the south."
[88] *Teaching of the Apostles* (ed. Cureton) ܠ and (ed. Vööbus) 1.210 on the missionary fields of Addai and Aggai; Witakowski, "Origin of the 'Teaching of the Apostles,'" 161–71 discusses date. John of Ephesus, *Lives of the Eastern Saints* in *PO* 17 (ed. Brooks) 109 and *PO* 18 (ed. Brooks) 621.
[89] Gregoratti, "Parthian Port" and Yon, "Ports" provide coverage of trade in the Persian Gulf, including the material finds. Also, Bab. Talmud, *Bab. Bath.* (ed./trans. Epstein) 73a and *Shabb.* (ed./trans Epstein) 101a. See Oppenheimer, *Babylonia Judaica*, 243; Pliny, *NH* (ed. Jahn and Mayhoff) 6.145; Bowersock, Review of *IGLS*; Steve, *Ile de Khārg*, 13–68.

Judas Thomas made their improbable voyage from Jerusalem to the Persian Gulf (and India) entirely by sea, and the dark humor associated with Jesus' selling his visual duplicate into slavery was obscured.

The Parthian and Indian *Acts of Thomas* and Their Impact

This chapter has so far stressed that the *Acts* is a heavily redacted composite text. It also suggests that the episode of the *Acts* that portrays a sea voyage from Jerusalem to India was excerpted from a precursor that described a nautical voyage from the Persian Gulf to Bahrain or Kharg and then the subcontinent. Due to these features, the *Acts'* has little value as a testament for the actual travels of Judas Thomas, for Christianity's early movement, or for social relationships between inhabitants of the Roman Levant and of the Indian subcontinent. It largely contains an assortment of preexisting invented traditions. Some of them (Acts III–VIII) may not have even been originally set in India at all.

But other factors shed light on the *Acts'* limited historical value. One is the fact that various conflicting traditions regarding Thomas' ministry and martyrdom existed in antiquity. Before the Indian *Acts* was composed, it was widely believed that Judas Thomas had not suffered martyrdom, and early Christian witnesses usually did not associate him with an overseas ministry. When they first began to accredit him with worldly travels, they conceived of Thomas as the evangelist of Parthian territory, not India. Moreover, by the late third century, Edessene Christians vaunted the apostle Addai and his Edessene disciples as the evangelists of Parthian territories. Since the surviving text of the *Acts* was most probably written in Syriac in an Edessene context, its composition was in many ways shaped by the increased importance of the Addai tradition among Edessenes themselves. An Edessene apparently rewrote the tradition regarding the missionary travels of Thomas so that it situated him in India and ceded Parthian territory to Addai and his Edessene converts. In this way, the surviving text is consistent with the rise of the Addai tradition and Edessene claims of primacy during the mid-to-late third century.

If the separate traditions regarding Thomas' Parthian and Indian travels were unreliable as historical sources, late antique Christians certainly did not interpret them in this way. Under their profound influence, it was believed that Christian brethren inhabited the Iranian plateau, central Asia, and the Indian subcontinent. But their beliefs were based on two separate invented traditions, not on the presence of actual Christians in remote parts of Eurasia. As articles of Christian culture, the narratives of both the Parthian and Indian exploits of Judas Thomas circulated among the social networks of Mediterranean Christians. They accordingly exerted immense impact on how Christians in the Roman world envisioned the topography of Christianity. This observation is worth emphasis. Despite being a composite accretion of invented layers, the traditions of Thomas' Parthian and Indian ministries were nonetheless endowed with substantive historical value by the late antique Christians who learned of them. In this sense, these traditions reflect the actual historical experiences of early Christians and how they conceived of their religious geographies. But since so many Christians in late antiquity believed that Christian brethren resided in Iran, central Asia, and India, their statements run the risk of being construed as independent testimony for the history of Christianity's actual movement. They are not. In fact, various shifts and transformations in late antique Christian conceptions of the travels and death of Thomas reveal how various contributors shaped the literary legacy of his career to fulfill their own needs. The new layers of invention that they added to the traditions of Thomas' travels and martyrdom in fact may help secure the date for the birth of these traditions and for the composition of the Indian *Acts*. But such layers also diminish the value of these narratives as historical sources for the movement of Christians or for trans-imperial connections between the Mediterranean and Indian Ocean worlds, even if late antique Christians endowed them with historical value.

The surviving text of the Indian *Acts* did not constitute the oldest tradition regarding the apostle Judas Thomas. As previously noted, Eusebius claims that Origen had cited a "tradition" (*paradosis*) regarding Thomas' evangelization of Parthia in his *Commentaries on Genesis*, which he began c. 225. While this *paradosis* could be deemed an oral tradition, in another statement Eusebius indicates that several apocryphal *Acts* that Origen mentioned were certainly circulating as written texts. Origen was therefore most probably referring to a text that had been circulating under anonymous authorship and had generally been deemed of oral origin.[90] Yet, even Thomas' evangelization of Parthia was arguably not the oldest tradition that circulated regarding his career. At the end of the second century, Clement of Alexandria, citing the earlier testimony of Heracleon, lists Thomas among the apostles who did not suffer martyrdom.[91] This

---

[90] Eusebius, *HE* (ed. Schwartz and Mommsen) 3.1.1–3, with 3.25.1–7 (which verifies that Eusebius conceived of apocryphal *Acts* to be written documents). Bremmer," *Acts of Thomas*, 17; Myers, *Spiritual Epicleses*, 47–48, on Origen having referred to a text that described Thomas' work in Parthia.

[91] Clement of Alexandria, *Strom.* (ed. Stählin and Früchtel) 4.9.71.3–4.

could mean that Thomas was not martyred in the tradition of his Parthian ministry, but since Clement never refers to this tradition in his corpus, he probably did not know of it. Similarly, the Acts of the Apostles, the *Gospel of Thomas*, and *Thomas the Contender* are silent on any issues of overseas travel or martyrdom. Accordingly, when Origen encountered the text celebrating Thomas' Parthian mission, the tradition that it conveyed was a relatively recent innovation. This Parthian *Acts of Thomas* was probably produced roughly between 150 CE and 200 CE, or slightly later.

Intriguingly, the Parthian *Acts* had a substantial impact on how Christians conceived of their religious geography in the third and fourth centuries.[92] It affected the perspective offered by the Syriac *Book of the Laws of the Countries*, a Platonic-style dialogic composed at Edessa by a follower of the notable Christian philosopher Bardaisan c. 200–225 CE. In a famous passage, the text placed Christians in Bactria, Parthia, Media, and Persis.[93] This same passage later appeared, with some variation or distortion, in the Greek text of Eusebius' *Ecclesiastical History* and in Rufinus' Latin translation of the *Clementine Recognitions*. Rufinus' *Clementine Recognitions* even accredits letters of the apostle Thomas for imparting such information on the presence of Christians in Parthia, a vital indication that the Parthian *Acts of Thomas* was the source.[94] The references to female promiscuity among the Kushans/Bactrians that appear in these passages could perhaps reflect forms of polyandry attested in Bactrian documents.[95] Still, the views of third-century Christians regarding the existence of coreligionists in Iran, central Asia, and parts of north India had most probably been shaped by an engagement with the invented literary tradition of Judas Thomas' Parthian travels. The Syriac *Book* therefore assumes that Christian brethren resided among the Kushans or Bactrians, who during the early third century ruled the portions of central Asia and north India that first-century Indo-Parthians

---

[92] The following summarizes the arguments of Andrade, "Syriac *Book*" but adds some additional material on Bactrian polyandry. The reader should consult the article for more detailed elaboration about the Syriac *Book* and further references. A different interpretation of the passage is provided by Jullien and Jullien, *Apôtres des confins*, 130–32, also Debié, Perrin, and Mahé, "L'Orient," 616.

[93] *The Book of the Laws of the Countries* (ed. Drijvers) 46 and 60 and (ed. Ramelli) 182 and 196–98.

[94] Eusebius cites the excerpt in *Preparation for the Gospel (Praeparatio Evangelica)* (ed. Mras and des Places) 6.10.46, with *FGrH/BNJ* 719, F. 3; *Clementine Recognitions* (ed. Rehm and Streker) 9.29.1–2. Rufinus' translation noticeably associates Susian women with a custom by which they were permitted to engage in polyandry while married. This is analogous to the same custom that the Syriac *Book* ascribes to woman among the Kushans/Bactrians. For discussion of the *Clementine Recognitions*, date, and relation to the Syriac *Book*, see Jones, *Pseudoclementina Elchasaiticaque*, 3–5, 8, 21–22, and 68–71.

[95] Crone, *Nativist Prophets*, 400–8 discusses polyandry in Iran. For document, Sims-Williams, *Bactrian Documents*, 32–35.

had governed.[96] Given the influence of the Parthian *Acts* on authors and works from third- and fourth-century Syria, it probably originated in the vicinity. The fact that Clement of Alexandria does not associate Thomas with Parthia (as noted previously) suggests that it did not originate at Alexandria.[97]

The Parthian *Acts* also arguably shaped how Origen conceived of the movement of Christianity. In a passage written c. 240, he understood its progression to have stopped among the Seres (of west China) and the region of *Ariake*, which corresponds to Āryāvarta (heartland of the Aryas).[98] Intriguingly, Origen's testimony indicates that he believed that Christians lived in the Kushan empire, namely in the parts of central Asia and north India once ruled by Indo-Parthian (Pahlava) kings. Accordingly, the Parthian *Acts* may have contained a narrative of Judas Thomas' trip to Gudnaphar's court, and the author of the Indian *Acts* may have used its material for the opening sequences of the surviving text. This would explain why third-century texts placed Christianity in Kushan central Asia and north India. If so, the origins for the tradition that Judas Thomas visited Gudnaphar can be situated to the latter half of the second century CE or so. No evidence indicates that it existed long before.

Although the Indian *Acts* displaced the Parthian *Acts* during the fourth century, the tradition persisted. As we will see, the ecclesiastical historians Rufinus and Socrates, along with the apocryphal *Acts of Philip*, refer to it. Significantly, Thomas' activities among Parthians, Medes, Persians, Karmanians, Hyrcanians, Bactrians, and Margians are often invoked by late antique and early medieval apostolic itineraries, which eventually combined and conflated the Parthian and Indian traditions. These are mostly anonymous, though some have circulated spuriously under the names of the third- and fourth-century authors Hippolytus, Epiphanius,

---

[96] The Kushan empire is treated in numerous articles of Harmatta, *History of the Civilizations of Central Asia* (Vol. 2), especially Puri, "Kushans," and Jayaswal, *Glory of the Kushans*. Also, Sims-Williams and Cribb, "New Bactrian Inscription" (focusing on the Rabatak inscription); Thapar, *Early India*, 217–24; Neelis, *Early Buddhist Transmission*, 132–45; Burstein, "New Light," 188–90; Rezakhani, *ReOrienting the Sasanians*, 46–72. IGSK 65.314–19 represent Bactrian inscriptions of central Asia (with 318 being the Rabatak inscription). For coins, Jongeward, Cribb, and Donovan, *Kushan, Kushano-Sasanian, and Kidarite Coins*. For chronologies (which are debated), see Cribb, "Western Satraps and Satavahanas" and "The Early Kushan Kings"; and Falk, "Kaniska Era."

[97] Debié, Perrin, and Mahé, "L'Orient," 613–14 suggest Alexandrian origins for the tradition.

[98] Origen, *Comm. Matt.* (ed. Klostermann) 24.9–14, with Andrade, "Syriac Book," 165. For date, see McGuckin, "Scholarly Works of Origen," 30. For *Ariake*, *PME* (ed. Casson) 6, 41, and 54; Ptolemy, *Geog.* (Stückelberger and Graßhoff) 7.1.6; and Neelis, *Early Buddhist Transmission*, 193–96, with Casson, *Periplus*, 197. The "Seres" are discussed at length in Chapter 5. See Nedungatt, *Quest for the Historical Thomas*, 107–11 and "Christian Origins," 418–20, for discussion about Origen's passage and its importance.

and Dorotheus or were inserted into later Greek translations of Jerome's writings. The apostle Thomas' putative visit to such peoples noticeably coincides with the Christian geographies envisioned by the Syriac *Book of the Laws of the Countries* and by Origen, as described previously. Isidore of Seville, writing c. 600 CE, and a fifth- or sixth-century manuscript fragment are not least among those that provide commentary in this vein.[99] We will return to these itineraries in detail in Chapter 6, as they constitute important evidence for the arrival of Christianity and the Thomas narrative in India. But presently, it is worth discussing how Thomas' itinerary in Parthia was shifted to India by the surviving *Acts*.

The Shift in the Itinerary of Judas Thomas

If the tradition of Thomas' Parthian activity was widely cited by Christians of Syria, Upper Mesopotamia, and the broader Mediterranean during the third and fourth centuries, it is worth exploring how a later third-century author came to realign Thomas' itinerary so that he exclusively evangelized India, as the surviving *Acts* describes. As this section maintains, such a realignment in fact reflects the religious needs of Edessenes of the period.[100] These were developing their own local tradition regarding the evangelization of Parthian territory, and as they did so they variously begin to situate the missionary activity of Judas Thomas elsewhere.

By the fifth century, the Edessene narrative of Addai's conversion of King Abgar the Black had assumed the form of the surviving Syriac text. In this form, it reflects many of the broader imperial and doctrinal issues of the period. Its noticeable anti-Judaic bent shows that it was certainly concerned with the relationship of Christians and Jews and on proper imperial governance in regards to this issue during the fifth century CE.[101] But by 315 CE, and perhaps as early as c. 300 CE, Eusebius recorded how Edessenes had set in motion the tradition that Jesus of Nazareth had

---

[99] Isidore of Seville, *Births and Deaths of the Fathers* (ed. Gómez) 73 claims that Thomas preached among Parthians, Medes, Persians, Hyrcanians, and Bactrians before dying at "Calaminia, a city of India." Dolbeau, "Listes d'apôtres," 458–63 (reproduced and updated in *Prophètes*, 173–79), includes discussion of the significance of the Verona fragment, for which Turner, "Primitive Edition," 63–64, contains the passage. Recent key work on the apostolic itineraries (a genre that begins in the fourth/fifth century) is Guignard, "Greek Lists." For the tradition reflected by the Verona fragment (*Anonymus* I), see Guignard, "Tradition grecque," and "Greek Lists," 480–87. For fuller discussion, see pp. 222–25, n. 58–65.

[100] Myers, *Spiritual Epicleses*, 34–44, by contrast, locates the place of composition at Nisibis.

[101] Griffith, "*Doctrina Addai*"; and Wood, "We Have No King but Christ," 101–10. Also see Saint-Laurent, *Missionary Stories*, 36–55.

engaged in epistolary correspondence with the contemporary Abgar king of Edessa and that the apostle Judas Thomas had therefore sent "Thaddaeus" or Addai to convert Edessa. Eusebius even claims that the narrative, written in the Syriac language, was housed in the archives of Edessa. This was the version that he cited.[102] Eusebius' testimony indicates that stories of Addai had been circulating for at least a generation or so by the time that he composed his *Ecclesiastical History*.[103] The Addai tradition can therefore be securely situated in the late third century, and maybe even before.[104]

Accordingly, the initial narrative regarding the correspondence between Abgar and Jesus and Addai's ministry at Edessa was roughly contemporary to the Indian *Acts*' composition and redaction. Such Edessene narratives were significantly creating memories of Upper Mesopotamia's Christian conversion in ways that highlighted the primacy of Edessa. They maintained that Edessa's conversion did not merely begin with the Pentecostal moment but from King Abgar's personal relationship with Jesus and his efforts to save Jesus from the plots against him. The rise of the Addai narrative at Edessa during the middle or late third century provides an explanation for how the surviving Indian *Acts* came to be composed at this time. As we have seen, the existing text bears the hallmarks of a composition in the mid-to-late third century. The need to shift Thomas' zone of evangelization so that Parthian territory could be allotted to Addai is the best explanation for this shift. The author of the surviving text accordingly produced a narrative of Judas Thomas' Indian travels that interwove new material and invented traditions that had previously existed. As such the text displays no actual historical, geographic, or ethnographic knowledge of the Indian subcontinent. Its only remotely historical reference is to a king named Gudnaphar/Goundaphores. But since the earliest sources on Thomas do not associate him with an overseas ministry, Judas Thomas' encounter with him was an invented tradition that was perhaps derived

---

[102] Eusebius, *HE* (ed. Schwartz and Mommsen) 1.13 and 2.1.6–8. Eusebius produced several editions of the *Ecclesiastical History* during his lifetime. Most of the extant version of Eusebius' *Ecclesiastical History* was completed by c. 315 (with the tenth book being produced in an update of c. 325), but the first seven books were perhaps composed before the tetrarchic persecutions of 303–311. See Barnes, "Editions" and *Constantine and Eusebius*, 126–63; Louth, "Date"; and Burgess, "Dates and Editions." The late third-century Christian narrative of Addai, who significantly shares his name with a notable disciple of Mani, is examined by Drijvers, "Addai und Mani," 171–85; Ramelli, "Addai-Abgar Narrative," 213–25.

[103] As also noted by Van Rompay, "East: Syria and Mesopotamia," 371; and explored by Brock, "Eusebius and Syriac Christianity."

[104] Ramelli, "Addai-Abgar Narrative," 213–21, has recently argued for roots in the early third century.

from an episode in the narrative of the Parthian *Acts*. Despite its contrived qualities, the Indian narrative quickly exerted a substantial impact, and over the fourth century it displaced the earlier tradition regarding the travels of Judas Thomas in Parthia and the Iranian plateau.

Altogether, the evidence supports the idea that under the influence of the Edessene narrative of Addai, first attested by Eusebius, the Indian *Acts* was composed in the middle or late third century and implicitly reserved Mesopotamia for Addai. But one can find additional reasons why certain writers would have removed Judas Thomas from all Parthian territory, including the Iranian plateau. These reasons are closely linked to narratives pertaining to Addai's disciple Aggai, which had much currency at Edessa but did not receive the same external attention as those of Addai/Thaddaeus. By the time of the fifth-century composition of *The Teaching of Addai*, Aggai was being depicted in variations of the Addai narrative as an Edessene responsible for processing and refining silk for the king. The tradition held that Addai had appointed him his successor at the time of this death, and Aggai had in turned appointed priests and leaders in "all the land of *bēt nahrīn*" (that is, Mesopotamia). He was eventually murdered by one of Abgar's rebellious pagan sons.[105] But other narratives of apparent Edessene origin had ministries of both Addai and Aggai extending well beyond Upper Mesopotamia. According to the Syriac *Teaching of the Apostles* (*Doctrina apostolorum*), which was composed at Edessa around 325–350 CE or so,[106] Judas Thomas had preached in India and had sent letters to Edessa from there. But Addai had converted Edessa and Mesopotamia, and Aggai had converted the territories of Sasanian Persia that were outside Mesopotamia, such as Assyria, Armenia, Media, Khuzistan (Elymais), and points farther east.[107]

In other words, certain Edessenes of the middle or late third century were accrediting an apostle technically sent by Jesus himself with converting Edessa and Parthian Mesopotamia. They were also maintaining that an Edessene native who was a disciple of this apostle had proceeded to evangelize Parthian Iran and the remote eastern regions of the world. But accounts of Thomas' Parthian ministry were problematic for

---

[105] *Teaching of Addai* (ed. Phillips) ܠܗ, ܡܢ, ܠܒܪ, ܐ–ܒܐ.
[106] Witakowski, "Origin of the 'Teaching of the Apostles,'" 161–71 provides illuminating discussion of the internal evidence for the dating and provenance of the *Doctrina apostolorum*. On the tradition of Aggai, see Jullien and Jullien, *Apôtres des confins*, 73–75.
[107] *Teaching of the Apostles* (ed. Cureton), ܠܐ–ܠܗ and (ed. Vööbus) 1.209–10. Despite scholarly claims to the contrary (Farquhar, *Apostle Thomas in India*, 28–32, and Nedungatt, *Quest for the Historical Thomas*, 180–85), the references to the alleged letters of Judas Thomas should be understood to be based on the tradition of the *Acts* (not actual letters sent from India).

Edessenes who valued the Addai and Aggai tradition and its implications for Edessa's religious primacy, and third-century Edessenes therefore began to place the ministry of Judas Thomas in Indian regions that Addai and Aggai had not reached. It was within such a context that an Edessene rewrote the *Acts* of Judas Thomas so as to shift his region of activity from Parthia to India. Otherwise, Edessenes treated Judas Thomas as the apostle who dispatched Addai into Parthian territory. The *Teaching of Addai* and Eusebius' citation of its basic tradition maintain that Judas Thomas was responsible for sending Addai to Edessa after Jesus' death, presumably before embarking for India.[108] Likewise, a late antique Latin variation on the Thomas narrative similarly claims that Thomas had sent "Tatheus" from Jerusalem to Abgar at Edessa before being sold to the merchant "Abban" and transported to India. These texts, which emphatically separate the itineraries of Thaddaeus/Addai and Thomas, reflect the impact that third-century Edessenes exerted by allotting Parthia to Addai and his disciples and India to Thomas.[109]

It is certainly clear that the basic Addai tradition, as reflected in the *Ecclesiastical History* of Eusebius and in the *Teaching of the Apostles* (*Doctrina apostolorum*), had emerged at Edessa by the middle or late third century, precisely when the surviving text of *Acts* was redacted and composed. In such a context, an Edessene author was inclined to compile, redact, and write a narrative that stressed Judas Thomas' conversion of India but that removed him from Parthia, a place whose conversion was now being attributed to apostles or disciples linked especially to Edessa, namely Addai and Aggai. This narrative integrated material from the Parthian *Acts* and other existing traditions regarding Thomas that had not been set in India but which the narrative's author shifted to the imagined "India" represented in the Indian *Acts*. But the surviving *Acts'* representation of India was not based on any reliable historical, geographic, or ethnographic knowledge of the Indian subcontinent, and as we will see in subsequent chapters, it certainly did not reflect any direct contact between Upper Mesopotamians and Indians of south Asia. It nonetheless generated the belief among Upper Mesopotamians that Judas Thomas had evangelized India and had died there. In fact, even the relic cult for Judas

---

[108] Eusebius, *HE* (ed. Schwartz and Mommsen) 1.13.11; *Teaching of Addai* (ed. Phillips) ∞.
[109] *Miracles of the Blessed Apostle Thomas* (*De miraculis beati Thomae apostoli*) (ed. Zelzer) 1–3. This is perhaps sixth-century (Zelzer, xxvi–xxxii) and part of the "ps.-Abdias'" collection (for the material of "ps.-Abdias," see Fabricius, *Codex* 2.687–736); Klauck, *Apocryphal Acts*, 176. *Liber Responsalis*, PL 78, col. 819, *de sancto Thoma, in matutinibus laudibus* cites a quotation of Jesus from *Miracles* verbatim in its first line.

Thomas at Edessa, attested in the fourth century, can perhaps be linked to this trend.[110] In a famous passage from the *Nisibene Hymns*, Ephrem echoes the claim of Edessenes that Thomas' remains had been transported to Edessa from India by a merchant.[111] By acquiring and transferring Thomas' putative remains from India, Edessenes created yet another narrative of Thomas that kept him clear of Parthia, whether dead or alive.

But it is also worth noting that Edessenes did not merely shift the activity of Judas Thomas to India during the mid-to-late third century. Certain articles of evidence indicate that they also located him in an entirely imagined representation of China. The tradition behind this material is complicated. Perhaps originating as a third-century CE pseudepigraphon narrated from the perspective of the Magi in the Gospel of Matthew, the narrative was apparently redacted in the late third or fourth century to include the activity of Judas Thomas, as told from his perspective.[112] The narrative was then subsequently integrated into the eighth-century Syriac chronicle of ps.-Dionysius (the *Chronicle of Zuqnin*). According to the chronicle, the apostle, who is significantly called "Judas Thomas" in keeping with Edessene fashion, converted the Magi to Christianity during his eastern itinerary. Intriguingly, Judas Thomas had encountered the Magi as they dwelled in the land of "Shir." By this the text appears to refer to the land of the "Seres," which was in reality the Tarim Basin or even interior China but nonetheless a place that many people in antiquity located near what they deemed to be the world's easternmost sea.[113] While it is difficult to discern the source of the chronicle's conversation between the Magi and Judas Thomas, it is perhaps significant that the chronicle in this episode retains the name Judas, the distinctly early form of the apostle's name in Edessene Syriac texts and in Eusebius' citation of them. This would suggest that the

---

[110] Ephrem, *CN* (ed. Beck) 42.1–3; *Itinerary of Egeria* (ed. Maraval) 17.1 and 19.2–3. The later *Passio Thomae* dates the translation of Thomas' relics to the 230s, but as argued in Chapter 6, p. 226, n. 69, this account is not reliable.

[111] Ephrem, *CN* (ed. Beck) 42.1–3.

[112] Landau, *Revelation of the Magi*, 18–26, treats the complex genealogy of this episode. Note that Landau, *Sages and the Star Child*, 22–136, has produced a critical edition and translation. Also see Andrade, "Syriac Book," 160, for a briefer version of what follows. The dating is nonetheless a difficult issue; see Reed, "Beyond the Land of Nod," 79–80.

[113] *Chronicle of Pseudo-Dionysius* (also known as *Zuqnin*) (ed. Chabot) 1.86–90 (with 1.162–63 and 186 referring simply to the travels of "Thomas" and his relics at Edessa). Also see Landau, *Revelation of the Magi*, 82–86 (English) and *Sages and the Star Child* (Syriac) 67–71. Ramelli, "Tradizione su Tommaso," 74–75; Jullien and Jullien, *Apôtres des confins*, 111–12, discuss the sources. Tubach, "Der Apostel Thomas in China," 71–74, treats "Shir." For "Seres" as being the inhabitants of the Tarim Basin and interior China in Roman imperial thought, see Ptolemy, *Geog.* (Stückelberger and Graßhoff) 1.11–12, 6.13–17; de la Vaissière, "Triple System," 527–36.

origin of this tradition was Edessa, where Thomas retained his original name of Judas most prominently throughout late antiquity.

A similar abbreviated episode regarding the Magi also appears in a Latin sermon regarding the Gospel of Matthew, and it briefly touches upon Thomas' visit with the Magi. As typical in Greek and Latin patristic sources, the apostle is simply called Thomas; the name Judas is not retained. It is generally accepted that the narrative from the eighth-century Syriac chronicle and the Latin sermon on Matthew derive from a common source tradition that ultimately had an origin in Syria and circulated in Syriac, even if the Latin sermon seems to have obtained its information from a Greek witness. The pseudepigraphon of the Magi described above, which had been redacted to include an encounter with Thomas, is the likely candidate.[114] Because the chronicle retains the name of "Judas," it can be surmised that this common source tradition preceded the fourth century and circulated in north Syria or Upper Mesopotamia.

As we have seen, the Parthian *Acts* was circulating as early as the late second century and left late antique and early medieval traces, but it began to be overshadowed by the Indian *Acts* in the fourth century, when references to Thomas' Indian travels first appear in Syriac, Greek, or Latin sources.[115] In fact, the testimony of Arnobius of Sicca, active shortly after 300 CE, maintains that the Christian message had arrived in India and among the Persians, Medians, and Parthians (along with the Seres).[116] This may reflect a misunderstanding of where the Syriac *Book of the Laws of the Countries* had located Christian communities, if one assumes that Arnobius had access to a Greek or Latin iteration. But if his statement regarding the presence of Christians in India does in fact refer to the subcontinent (as opposed to Ethiopia), it would suggest that he was ultimately informed by the traditions of the lost Parthian *Acts* (Persians, Medians, and Parthians), the surviving Indian *Acts* (Indians), and possibly the aforementioned pseudepigraphon that celebrated Thomas' encounter with Magi in "Shir" (China). In such

---

[114] Landau, *Revelation of the Magi*, 18–26, provides treatment. Also see Ramelli, "Tradizione su Tommaso," 74–75; Jullien and Jullien, *Apôtres des confins*, 111–12. The *Incomplete Work on Matthew* 2.2.2 is in PG 56, col. 637–38. This episode is also repeated in Bayan, "Synaxaire Arménien," 420–21. For introductions to the chronicle and translations of its later parts, see Witakowski, *Chronicle* and Harrak, *Chronicle*.

[115] Some examples from the fourth century that link Judas Thomas or Thomas to India are Ephrem, (ed. Beck) *CN* 42.1–3; Cyrillona, *On the Scourges* (ed. Griffin), lines 610–620, with Griffin, *Critical Study*; Ambrose, *in Ps.* (ed. Petschenig) 45.21; Gaudentius, *Tract.* (ed. Glück) 17.11; Greg. Naz., *Or.* (ed. Moreschini) 33.11; John Chry. *That Christ Is God*, 5–6 (PG 48, col. 822), *Act. Apost.* 4.4 (PG 60, col. 47), *Ioan.* 65.1 (PG 59, col. 361); Jerome, *Ep.* (ed. Hilberg) 59.5; *Manichaean Psalms* (ed. and trans. Allberry and ed. Richter) 192.15, 193.2, and 194.13.

[116] Arnobius, *Against the Pagans* (ed. Reifferscheid) 2.12. Simmons, *Arnobius*, 47–94 establishes date.

a case, Arnobius' testimony would constitute another article of evidence that the Indian *Acts* could not have been written later than c. 300 CE. Arnobius also would have been writing just as the Indian *Acts* had begun to displace the Parthian *Acts* in terms of its impact on Christian perceptions. Whether Arnobius was referring to the Indian *Acts* is, however, by no means certain.

Despite the general shift of Thomas' itinerary from Parthia to India in late antiquity, the tradition that Judas Thomas or Thomas converted Parthia persisted, and eventually some Edessenes apparently resolved this issue not by creating geographical distance between Addai and Thomas but by conflating the two figures. A Greek inscription from the vicinity of Edessa, dating to the fifth or sixth century, contains a segment of a letter or statement that Jesus allegedly sent to King Abgar, in which he promises to send him an apostle. It is a variant on a nearly identical and very famous segment of Jesus' letter found in the lengthy citation of the Addai narrative that Eusebius claimed to have existed in Syriac at Edessa and that he incorporated in his early fourth-century *Ecclesiastical History*. It also replicates a verbal statement that Jesus had intermediates convey to Abgar in the surviving fifth-century Syriac *Teaching of Addai*. But in the *Ecclesiastical History* and the *Teaching of Addai*, Jesus' statement does not name his apostle, and it is directly after this statement that both accounts claim that Judas, also called Thomas, had dispatched Addai to Edessa. By contrast, in this Edessene inscription, Jesus himself promises to send an apostle named "Thaddaeus, also called Thomas."[117]

Influence on Christians of Antiquity

As described so far, the Indian *Acts* consists largely of redacted material from previous written traditions. It also reflects the critical intervention of a third-century Edessene perspective that transformed the Parthian ministry of Thomas into an Indian one. But these were not the only dramatic shifts that the reputation of the apostle Judas Thomas experienced. Written and oral traditions regarding the apostle Thomas, his evangelizing mission, and his fate underwent layers of transformation and rewriting over the course of late antiquity. Amid their transformations, these traditions also provide grounding for establishing the dates of composition for

---

[117] *IGSK* 65.29; Eusebius, *HE* (ed. Schwartz and Mommsen) 1.13.10 (letter) and 1.13.11 (name); *The Teaching of Addai* (ed. Phillips) ܐ (letter)–ܗ (name). In the very late *Armenian Synaxarium*, the tension between the figures Thomas and Addai is reconciled by having Thomas preach in Mesopotamia and dispatch Addai to Edessa specifically. Bayan, "Synaxaire Arménien," 420–21.

the Parthian and Indian *Acts* and, by extension, their impact on Christian perspectives for Christianity's movement throughout Afro-Eurasia.

None of the early sources that provide information on a putative Thomas or Judas Thomas figure make any statement regarding far-flung evangelizing activity or death. As noted previously, at least one source from the later second century describes Thomas as not having suffered martyrdom.[118] This suggests that the Parthian *Acts*, if it in fact included a segment on the martyrdom of Judas Thomas, had not been composed earlier than that time. Yet, it also preceded the *Book of the Laws of the Countries* and a commentary of Origen in ways that situate it before c. 225 CE. All other sources that refer to Thomas' Parthian adventures or the arrival of Christianity in the Iranian plateau or central Asia were composed in the third or fourth centuries CE, or later. Aside from Origen, the Syriac *Book*, and Eusebius, the earliest testimony comes from Rufinus, Socrates, and the *Acts of Philip*.[119] The fact that Origen and the Syriac *Book* are the earliest witnesses to the Parthian *Acts* and that Clement of Alexandria apparently did not know of it has bearing on the narrative's place and date of composition. The Parthian *Acts* was apparently written somewhere in north Syria or Upper Mesopotamia, and either in Greek or Syriac, at roughly 150–200 CE or slightly later. Subsequently, the narrative traveled to Alexandria and Caesarea, in one of which locations Origen learned of it c. 225 CE or thereafter.

During the mid-to-late third century, an Edessene contravened the tradition of Judas Thomas' Parthian travels by producing the surviving text of the *Acts*, which shifted his preaching to India. Over the fourth century, this text and its basic narrative superseded the Parthian tradition of Judas Thomas' travels.[120] In fact, all the sources that refer to the Indian *Acts* date to the fourth century or thereafter, and Eusebius, writing in the early fourth century, apparently did not know about it (even if he knew of the Parthian *Acts*). As we have seen, the Christian author Arnobius (c. 303 CE), who claimed that preachers had ensured that the Christian message had been narrated among the Indians, Seres, Persians, Medes, and various other peoples, may have known both the Parthian and Indian

---

[118] Clement of Alexandria, *Strom.* (ed. Stählin and Früchtel) 4.9.71.3–4.
[119] *The Book of the Laws of the Countries* (ed. Drijvers) 60 and (ed. Ramelli) 196–98; Eusebius, *HE* (ed. Schwartz and Mommsen) 3.1.1–3. Rufinus, *HE* (ed. Schwartz and Mommsen) 3.1.1–3; Socrates, *HE* (ed. Hansen) 1.19.2; *Clementine Recognitions* (ed. Rehm and Streker) 9.29.2; *Acts of Philip* (ed. Bovon, Bouvier, and Amsler) 3.2 and 8.1, which refers to the Parthian and Indian ministries.
[120] As noted by Myers, *Spiritual Epicleses*, 48–49.

narratives.[121] While cultivating a typical trope of early Christian literature informed by the Acts of the Apostles and the apostolic "apocrypha," his account regarding the Christian presence among the Persians, Medians, and Parthians was apparently informed by the Parthian *Acts*, perhaps along with the *Book of the Laws of the Countries*. His inclusion of India, if not referring to Ethiopia or being informed by Thomas' activity in north India in the Parthian *Acts*, could have been dictated by the Indian *Acts*. If so, it would suggest that the text was circulating in the Mediterranean by the early fourth century. His omission of the Bactrians/Kushans and his claim that Christianity had reached the Seres can be explained by the fact that Roman-era authors sometimes conflated the Bactrians/Kushans with the "Seres," whom geographers located to the east of the Kushan empire in the Tarim Basin.[122] But it also may have been shaped by the recent circulation of the previously discussed pseudepigraphon that celebrated the encounter of Thomas with Magi in "Shir." As previously stated, however, it is unclear whether Arnobius had access to the Indian *Acts*. He could even have simply misunderstood where the Syriac *Book of the Laws of the Countries* (through a Greek or Latin iteration) claimed Christians to live.

Otherwise, more secure citations of Thomas' Indian ministry among late antique authors only begin in the mid-fourth century, as does their assumption that Indians of the subcontinent had converted to Christianity. Such citations reflect how the narrative tradition of the Indian *Acts* was carried from its Upper Mesopotamian context by networks of Christians that spanned the Mediterranean. For India, statements preceding c. 500 CE have been made by *The Teaching of the Apostles* (as we have seen), Ephrem, Cyrillona, Ambrose, Epiphanius, Augustine, various Coptic Manichaean Psalms, John Chrysostom, Gaudentius of Brescia, Jerome, Paulinus of Nola, ps.-Gelasius, Turribius of Asturica, and Jacob of Sarug.[123] But it should be

---

[121] Arnobius, *Against the Pagans* (ed. Reifferscheid) 2.12. Simmons, *Arnobius*, 47–94, for date.

[122] For similar conflation of "Seres" and central Asia, see *Refutation of All Heresies* (ed. Marcovich/ed. Litwa) 9.13.1. For "Seres," see Ptolemy, *Geog.* (Stückelberger and Graßhoff) 1.11–12; 6.13–17; de la Vaissière, "Triple System," 527–36.

[123] Ephrem, *CN* (ed. Beck) 42.1–3; Cyrillona, *On the Scourges* (ed. Griffin), lines 610–620, with Griffin, *Critical Study*; Ambrose, *in Ps.* (ed. Petschenig) 45.21; Gaudentius, *Tract.* (ed. Glück) 17.11; Greg. Naz., *Or.* 33.11 (ed. Moreschini); John Chry. *That Christ Is God*, 5–6 (PG 48, col. 822), *Act. Apost.* 4.4 (PG 60, col. 47), *Ioan.* 65.1 (PG 59, col. 361); Jerome, *Ep.* (ed. Hilberg) 59.5; *Acts of Philip* (ed. Bovon, Bouvier, and Amsler) 3.2 and 8.1; *Manichaean Psalms* (ed. and trans. Allberry and ed. Richter) 192.15, 193.2, 194.13; Paulinus. *Carmina* (ed. de Hartel) 19.80–82; ps.-Gelasius, *HE* (ed. Hansen) 2.28.2–3 and 2.38.2–5; Jacob of Sarug, *Homilies on Thomas* (ed. Strothmann); Epiphanius, *Pan.* (ed. Holl) 47.1.5 and 61.1.5; Aug., *Sermon on the Mount* (Mutzenbecher) 1.20.65, *Contra Adimantum* (ed. Zycha) 17, *Against Faustus* (ed. Zycha) 22.79; Turribius, *Letter to Leo*, (PL 54, col. 694). Nedungatt, *Quest for the Historical Thomas*, 177–200 discusses.

stressed here that these sources have no bearing on the actual historical situation of Christianity in the Iranian plateau, central Asia, or India. Instead, on the basis of the Parthian or Indian *Acts* and their core narratives, which circulated as complete texts, abridgements, oral communications, or skeletal outlines in apostolic itineraries, the authors of such testimony believed that Thomas had evangelized these regions. The early medieval *Liber responsalis* accordingly described how Jesus appeared to Thomas at night in a vision and told him not to fear going to India.[124] The work was paraphrasing the opening scene of the surviving *Acts*, if perhaps from one of the late antique Latin variations. The same can be said, for instance, regarding a later emulator of Isidore of Seville and, farther east, for an Armenian synaxary that describes how Habban transported Thomas to India.[125] It is worth noting that synaxaries often integrate oral traditions and are composed for recitation, and they embody the dynamic interplay of written and oral that can make a narrative transform.[126] But the narrative of the Armenian synaxary ultimately originates in the Parthian and Indian *Acts*.

The testimony of such authors also indicates in general terms how the Parthian and Indian narratives of Thomas' deeds traveled during the course of late antiquity. As we have noted in the Introduction, socio-commercial networks and their residential settlements provided the well-laid social pathways that churchmen and preachers could exploit. In fact, north Syria and Upper Mesopotamia contained well-established Christian populations during the second century and thereafter (Chapter 4), and north Syrians avidly participated in a Levantine socio-commercial network that extended westward throughout the Mediterranean littoral (Chapter 5).[127] Because its various segments included pagans, Jews, and Christians of the Roman Near East, this network played a key role in Christianity's early

---

[124] *Liber Responsalis*, PL 78, col. 819, *de sancto Thoma, in matutinibus laudibus*. This has been attributed to Gregory the Great, but this attribution is generally in doubt. Hiley, *Western Plainchant*, 602–14, does not treat it as a legitimate work of Gregory on music. Its first line cites nearly verbatim the probably sixth-century *Miracles of the Blessed Apostle Thomas* (*De miraculis beati Thomae apostoli*) (ed. Zelzer) 3 (xxvi–xxxii for discussion of date). Gregory associates Thomas with India in *Hom. in Evang.* (ed. Étaix, Morel, and Judic) 17.17. Nedungatt, *Quest for the Historical Thomas*, 200–211 discusses, along with later examples not mentioned here.

[125] *Births and Deaths of the Patriarchs* (ed. Fraga) 49.1–3 and 57.2; Bayan, "Synaxaire Arménien," 415–17 and 420–21. Also see Isidore of Seville, *Births and Deaths of the Fathers* (ed. Gómez) 73 and 80.

[126] See Watts, "Theodosius II," 279–83.

[127] For the network and its extension in late antiquity, see Decker, "Export Wine Trade" and *Tilling the Hateful Earth*; Pieri, *Commerce du vin*; Humphries, "Trading Gods" (with emphasis on religion). For some examples of Syrians abroad: *P. Oxy.* 52.3053–3054 document Syrian and Upper Mesopotamian traders and slaves in Egypt. *IGF* nos. 141 and 143 place Syrians in Gaul. Noy, *Foreigners at Rome*, 234–45 and 318–21, provides evidence for Syrians in Rome. Solin, "Juden und Syrer" treats Syrians in the western provinces.

movement and anchorage throughout the Mediterranean basin.[128] It also provided the social pathways along which Christians carried the culture of the Parthian and Indian narratives of Judas Thomas' preaching to various sites of the Roman Mediterranean, including Caesarea Maritima, Alexandria, North Africa, and Italy. The cultures of these narratives traveled rapidly after their respective compositions, and the narrative of the Indian *Acts* therefore soon came to enjoy wide popularity among speakers and writers of Latin, Greek, Syriac, and Coptic (and later of Armenian, Ethiopic, Arabic, and Georgian). As Christians throughout the Mediterranean and Upper Mesopotamia engaged with the tradition, modified it, or rendered it in new languages, they reshaped its culture. But its culture had a profound impact on them too, for it framed how they conceived of the history and geography of Christianity in Asia.

Conclusion

In modern times, scholarly positions on the *Acts* have varied tremendously. The interpretations regarding this oft-revisited text have even recently occupied the spectrum from that of complete fiction to complete historical accuracy, and everything in between.[129] While acknowledging its many invented or inaccurate qualities, scholars in certain instances maintain that the *Acts*' existence still points to an actual mission that the apostle Thomas conducted in India or at least acknowledge the possibility.[130] In other instances, they have treated the text as reflecting normalized travel from the Levant or Upper Mesopotamia to India, some accurate historical

---

[128] Some articles of the vast bibliography for Christianity's early Mediterranean movement are Freyne, *Jesus Movement*; Rothschild and Schröter, *Rise and Expansion*, especially Meeks, "From Jerusalem to Illyricum," 167–82, and Dunn, "Rise and Expansion," 183–204; Meeks, *First Urban Christians*; Still and Horrell, *After the First Urban Christians*; White and Yarbrough, *Social World of the First Christians*; Esler, *Modeling Early Christianity*; Stark, *Rise of Christianity*, esp. 49–71 (importance of networks); Harris, *Spread of Christianity* in which especially Drake, "Models of Christian Expansion," 1–14; the articles of Green and MacDonald, *World of the New Testament*.

[129] To select a few examples, Van den Bosch, "India and the Apostolate," 125–48 (emphasizes unreliability as a representation of India, even if contemporary Christians may have been in India); McGrath, "History and Fiction," esp. 307–10 (moderate position, in which the text is "historical fiction" and perhaps indicative of Thomas' mission to India); Kurikilamkatt, *First Voyage* (historical and geographical accuracy).

[130] McGrath, "History and Fiction," esp. 307–10; Kurikilamkatt, *First Voyage*; Baumer, *Church of the East*, 15–19 and 235–36; Jullien and Jullien, *Apôtres des confins*, 19–20: Nedungatt, *Quest for the Historical Thomas*, 81–96, and "Apocryphal *Acts of Thomas*"; Hage, *Orientalische Christentum*, 315–17; Frykenberg, *Christianity in India*, 92–110. Further examples supporting its historicity or related traditions are Kolangadan, "Historicity," 305–27; Menachery, "Veracity," 21–27; Athikalam, "St. Thomas the Apostle," 333–51; Vashalomdize, "Apostle Thomas," 79; Vadakkekara, *Origins of India's St. Thomas Christians* and *Origin of Christianity in India*; McDowell, *Fate of the Apostles*, 157–74.

and geographical knowledge of India by the author or among Upper Mesopotamians, or the possible existence of Christianity in India by the fourth century.[131] On this score, the testimony of various patristic authors, who cited Thomas' ministry or expressed their belief that Christian brethren inhabited India, has been treated as corroborating evidence for the historical validity of the *Acts*' narrative. Given its importance for the Thomas Christians inhabiting the Kerala coast of India, whose oral traditions in many ways cohere with its narrative, it is no surprise that it has been frequently cited in modern scholarship on early Christianity in India. But even in such scholarship, the *Acts*' historical validity is a topic of debate, and it is still uncertain whether the Indian oral traditions constitute independent witnesses or were ultimately derived from the *Acts*' narrative.[132]

Indeed, the surviving *Acts* has left an indelible imprint on the scholarship of early Christianity and its possible arrival in ancient India. But the issues discussed thus far indicate that its narrative has no historical validity in this regard. A mid-to-late third-century innovation, it reflects the intervention of an Edessene author who interwove, redacted, and amalgamated previous invented traditions with newly produced material. Whereas the earliest tradition held that Judas Thomas did not preach outside the Roman empire or suffer martyrdom, an unknown figure of the late second century or so generated a narrative that located his ministry in Parthian territory, and perhaps Indo-Parthian north India.

---

[131] Ramelli, "Tradizione su Tommaso," 59–82, esp. 65; Seland, "Trade and Christianity," 78–79, and "Networks and Social Cohesion," 385–86; Tubach, "Historische Elemente," 49–116; Ellerbrock and Winkelmann, *Die Parther*, 273–75; Jullien and Jullien, *Apôtres des confins*, 109; Vashalomdize, "Apostle Thomas," 79; Debié, Perrin, and Mahé, "L'Orient," 614–15.

[132] For varied perspectives on the relationship between the *Acts*, the oral traditions, and the formation of Christianity in India, see Medlycott, *India and the Apostle Thomas*; Mackenzie, *Christianity in Travancore*; Dahlmann, *Thomaslegende*; Zaleski, *Apostle St. Thomas in India* and *Origines du christianisme aux Indes*; Smith, *Early History of India*; Mingana, "Spread of Early Christianity," 435–515; Farquhar, "Apostle Thomas in North India," 80–111, *Apostle Thomas in North India*, and "Apostle Thomas in South India," 20–50; D'Crux, *St. Thomas the Apostle in India*; Tisserant, "Syro-Malabar Église," cols. 3089–3162; Brown, *Indian Christians of St. Thomas*; Tisserant, *Eastern Christianity in India*; Keay, *History of the Syrian Church in India*; Neill, *History of Christianity*, esp. 26–40; Perumalil, *Apostles in India*; Farquhar, *Apostle Thomas in India*; Gielen, *St. Thomas the Apostle of India*; Mundadan, *History of Christianity*, esp. 9–60; Podipara, *Thomas Christians and Thomas Christians and Their Syriac Treasures*; Samuel, Santiago, and Thiagarajan, *Early Christianity in India*; Samuel, *Heritage of Early Christian Communities in India: Some Landmarks*; Vadakkekara, *Origins of St. Thomas Christians* and *Origin of Christianity in India*; Kurikilamkatt, *First Voyage*; Frykenberg, *Christianity in India*; Yacoub and Moussa, *History of the Syrian Church of India*; Fenwick, *Forgotten Bishops*. For a useful survey of the literature until the last few years, see Nedungatt, *Quest for the Historical Thomas*, xvii–xxxiv and 3–33.

Subsequently, the surviving text of the *Acts* shifted the activity of Judas Thomas to India in ways that enabled Addai and his disciples to become the supreme evangelists of Parthian territory. This shift accommodated the primacy of Edessa in bringing Christianity to its various regions and negated the impact of the Parthian *Acts*, even as it perhaps reused material from it. In fact, the opening sequence of the Indian *Acts*, in which Habban transports Judas Thomas from Jerusalem to India, bears the hallmarks of having been redacted from a previous textual tradition in which this sequence happened at a site on the Persian Gulf. It may even have been derived from an episode in the Parthian *Acts* itself.

But despite their contrived contents and the literary agendas responsible for creating them, the narratives of both the Parthian and Indian *Acts* shaped the views of late antique Christians. These believed that Thomas evangelized Parthia or India or that Christian brethren inhabited these regions. As a result, their testimony bears little historical value beyond establishing how they experienced the late antique topography of Christianity due to the influence of the various traditions regarding Thomas. The problematic nature of the Indian *Acts* and its Parthian antecedent, along with their vast impact on late antique Christian beliefs, makes it desirable to explore alternative ways to create historical narratives for the movement of Christianity to central Asia and India. The remainder of the book examines how analyses of socio-commercial networks can enable us to do this. To the world of the Red Sea and Indian Ocean we now turn.

PART II

Christianity, Networks, and the Red Sea

CHAPTER 2

Early Christianity and Its Many Indias
Complexities of the Sources

According to various late antique authors, a second-century Alexandrian named Pantaenus traveled from Roman Egypt to India to preach the Christian message. When he arrived, he discovered that the apostle Bartholomew had been there, and he had circulated among the Indians a version of the gospel of Matthew written in Hebrew. While it is a fascinating narrative, its historical value is not particularly easy to assess. In this regard, it embodies many of the epistemic complexities featured by the Indian *Acts of Thomas*, which narrates an unlikely voyage from the Roman Levant to India. But encapsulated in these narrative traditions are two distinct geographic and social pathways by which Christianity could have traveled to the Indian subcontinent. One pathway led from the Roman Levant across Mesopotamia, Mesene, and the Persian Gulf (Map 3). Chapters 5–6 explore it in detail. The other extended from Alexandria across Roman Egypt, the Red Sea, and the broader Indian Ocean (Map 2). We will explore it in Chapter 3.

The movement of Christianity along the pathway across Egypt and the Red Sea is in fact ostensibly described by many late antique ecclesiastical historians and authors. The preaching of Pantaenus among Indians is just one example. Other texts invoke the fourth-century missionary work of figures named Frumentius and Theophilus the "Indian." Composed primarily during the fourth and fifth centuries, all such narratives linked the movement of Christianity to charismatic individuals who traveled to "India" from Roman Egypt. As the next two chapters maintain, these narratives bear some historical value. Epigraphic and archaeological evidence shows that Christianity was in fact transported by a Roman Egyptian socio-commercial network from Alexandria and the Egyptian hinterland to various parts of the Red Sea and the Indian Ocean world (Chapter 3). This network could have even transported Christian culture to Indian locations and anchored it among the peoples who lived in them.

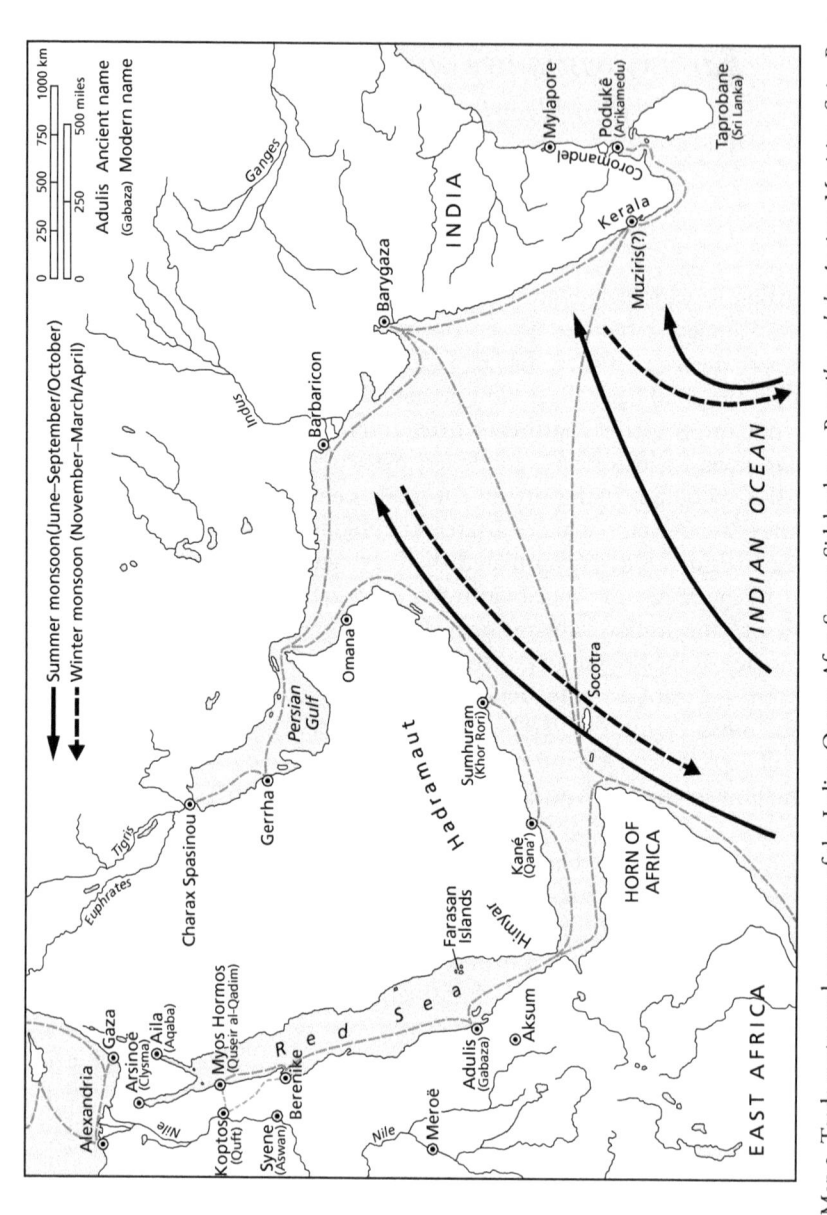

Map 2 Trade routes and monsoons of the Indian Ocean. After Steven Sidebotham, *Berenike and the Ancient Maritime Spice Route* (Berkeley: University of California Press, 2011), Fig. 4.2, drawn by M. Hense.

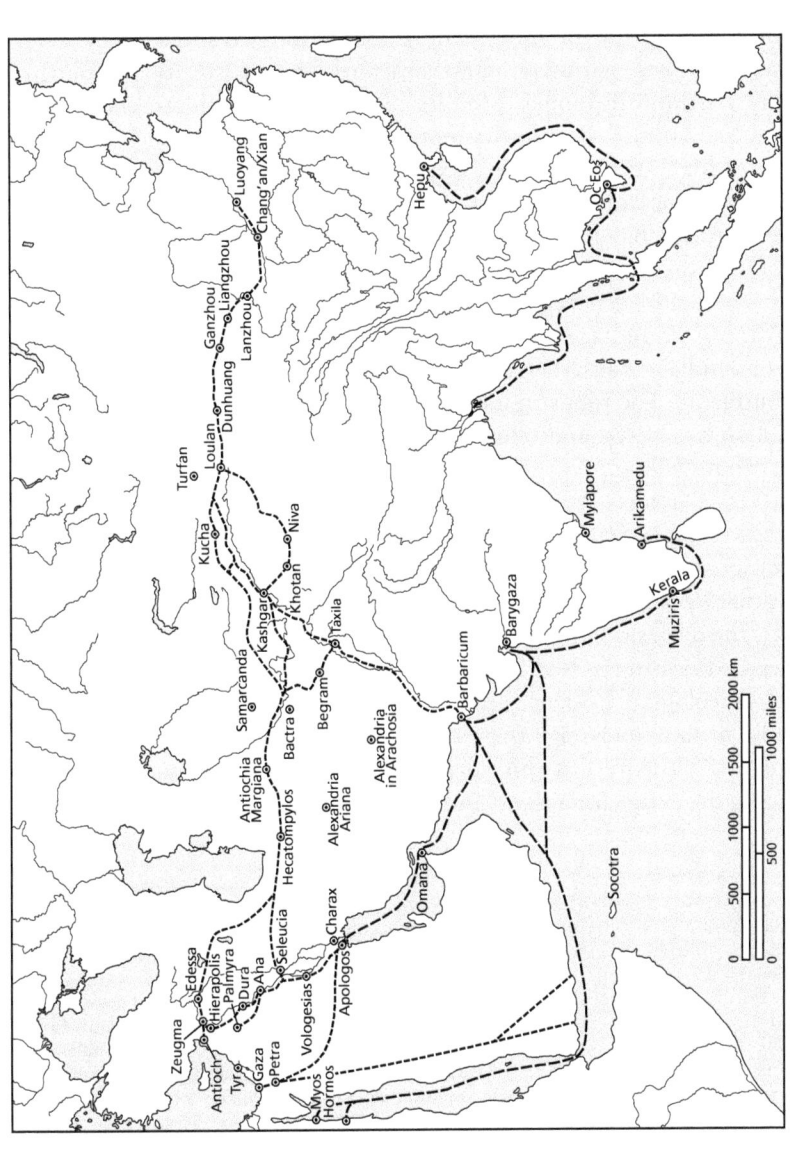

Map 3 Trade and communication routes of Asia. After Marta Żuchowska, "Palmyra and the Chinese Silk Trade," in Jørgen Christian Meyer, Eivind Seland, and Nils Anfinset (eds.). 29–38, *Palmyrena: City, Hinterland, and Caravan Trade between Orient and Occident* (Oxford: Archaeopress, 2016), Fig. 1, drawn by R. Zukowski after Paul Bernard, "De l'Euphrate à la Chine avec la caravane de Maès Titianos (c. 100 ap. n. è)," *CRAI* 149.3, Fig. 2. Converted to grayscale by N. Andrade.

This chapter accordingly probes the various sources composed by late antique Roman Christian authors that describe the evangelization of places called "India." But as it argues, most of these texts are of little value as historical sources for the movement of Christianity to India. They were instead providing narratives for the arrival of Christianity in fourth-century Aksumite Ethiopia, Meroitic Ethiopia, or south Arabia, which they labeled "India." But this has not curbed the belief that such texts are testimony for Christianity's early arrival in the Indian subcontinent. While the tendency for late antique Christian sources to confuse or conflate India and east Africa has long been noted,[1] a recent vein of scholarship has maintained that late antique Roman authors, much like certain classical Greek and Latin geographers that preceded them, often distinguished east Africa from India geographically. Such descriptions of the evangelization of "India" could therefore be referring to activity on the Indian subcontinent.[2] The robust trade between Roman Egypt and India, which moved objects, ideas, and religious tropes between the two places, would appear to provide support for such testimony.

But as Chapter 3 maintains, the "global" circulation of objects and the trans-imperial transmission of religious ideas (as opposed to religious conversions) that commercial networks facilitated do not constitute evidence that Roman Christians were evangelizing in India before c. 400 CE. In fact, the disposition of the Roman Egyptian socio-commercial network that extended into the Red Sea, as represented by the textual, epigraphic, and archaeological evidence, indicates that Christianity did not travel to India or find anchorage there due to the activity of Roman Egyptian merchants. Moreover, as this chapter argues, all late antique narratives regarding the evangelization of "Indians" were almost certainly referring to

---

[1] Schneider, *L'Ethiopie et l'Inde* is the seminal work on the conflation of India, Ethiopia, and Arabia. Also see Schneider, "So-Called Confusion"; Mayerson, "Confusion of Indias," 169–74; and (for Jews) Van der Horst, "'India'," 574–79. Nedungatt, "India Confused?" 315–37 and *Quest for the Historical Thomas*, 63–80 understates the conflation and argues that patristic sources distinguished the subcontinent from other places.

[2] Nedungatt, "India Confused?" 315–37, *Quest for the Historical Thomas*, 63–80 and 119–36, and "Christian Origins," 399–422; Ramelli, "Missione di Panteno," "Cristianesimo," and "Early Christian Missions," 221–31. Tomber, "Bishops and Traders," 225 and Seland, "Trade and Christianity," 79–80, and "Networks and Social Cohesion," 385–86 note the frequency of confusion but accept that the Indian subcontinent could be the referent of "India." Herodotus, 3.17–22, 3.98–105 and 7.65 and 7.69–70 distinguishes India and Ethiopia. Ctesias, Megasthenes, Strabo, Pliny, and Claudius Ptolemy distinguished the regions geographically even if they sometimes conflated their characteristics. The *Periplus of the Erythraean Sea* and the author known as "Cosmas Indicopleustes" also distinguish the subcontinent from other places. Nedungatt, "India Confused?" 320–22 and 325–29 and "Christian Origins," 401–2, but see Schneider, *L'Ethiopie et l'Inde* and now "So-Called Confusion." For Ctesias and Megasthenes, see *FGrH/BNJ* 688 and 715.

peoples of east Africa and south Arabia. Even if such sources distinguished east Africa from the Indian subcontinent geographically, other factors prompted them to describe the peoples of east Africa and south Arabia as "Indians." The sections to follow outline what these intimately related factors are.

The Impact of Indo-Mediterranean Trade and the Shifting Category of "Indian"

One key factor shaping how late antique Christian authors conceived of east Africans and Arabians as "Indians" was the historical transformation that the Roman Egyptian socio-commercial network experienced during the late third and early fourth centuries CE. While Chapter 3 examines the textual, epigraphic, and archaeological evidence for the phenomenon, it can be stated briefly here that a Roman Egyptian trade network maintained direct contact with India from the first century BCE to the late third century CE. While it did so, it facilitated knowledge about geography and society in the Indian Ocean world that enabled writers and geographers like the author of the *Periplus of the Erythraean Sea*, Strabo, Pliny, and Claudius Ptolemy to differentiate among the inhabitants of east Africa, south Arabia, and India with a certain degree of precision, even if other authors of the period could still conflate them and their putative characteristics.[3] But during the late third century, the Roman Egyptian trade network suffered a substantial disruption. The network was revitalized by the mid-fourth century, but it no longer extended directly to India. Instead, it extended to Aksumite Ethiopia, south Arabia, and Socotra, to which it carried Christian culture, and it also facilitated the period's intensive diplomatic ties between Rome and Aksumite Ethiopia and south Arabia. Yet, it only reestablished direct contact with India during the early sixth century.[4] As Roman Egyptians lost direct contact with the Indian subcontinent for roughly two hundred years, they increasingly relied on intermediaries who actually did sail to India for transit products from the subcontinent, and these included Indians, Ethiopians, and Arabians alike.

Amid such shrinking horizons and a reliance on members of various Red Sea and Indian Ocean populations as intermediaries, Romans increasingly used the term "Indian" for any population whose merchants were involved

---

[3] *PME* (ed. Casson); Strabo (ed. Radt), 16.3–4 generally; Pliny, *NH* (ed. Jahn and Mayhoff) 6, esp. 102–4; Ptolemy (ed. Stückelberger and Graßhoff) 7.1–3. For conflation, Schneider, *L'Ethiopie et l'Inde* and now "So-Called Confusion."

[4] Chapter 3 analyzes this network, its extension, and its retraction.

in trade in the Red Sea and Indian Ocean or that inhabited territory south of Egypt. As they did so, they conceived of the regions that these "Indians" inhabited as different "Indias," just as geographers consciously linked putative "Arabians" to various distinct regions of southwest Asia called "Arabia" in antiquity.[5] Some of them began to confuse east Africa, south Arabia, and India geographically; others distinguished among these places but deemed them to be inhabited by different *ethnē* of Indians. This explains how late antique ecclesiastical histories increasingly conceived of east African and Arabian peoples as "Indians" in ways that exceeded the tendencies of classical Latin and Greek authors and geographers, who sometimes did so as well. For instance, some late antique Roman Christians described Arabia or Aksumite Ethiopia as "farther India" or "inner India." In this way, they distinguished Arabia or Aksumite India from Meroitic Ethiopian lands to the northwest, which they called "nearer India," "the India adjoining Ethiopia," or simply Ethiopia. A certain number conflated the Meroitic and the Aksumite "Indias" by calling either or both of them collectively Ethiopia or India. Finally, others ascribed the terms "Ethiopia" and "nearer" India to the stretch of territory between Egypt and Aksumite Ethiopia, with both terms referring to the same place (Meroitic Ethiopia) or to two putatively distinct regions within that territory.[6]

In his discussion of the Himyarites of Arabia, the ecclesiastical historian Philostorgius (cited by Photius) perhaps put it best. While situating them among "the innermost Indians" (τοὺς ἐνδοτάτω Ἰνδούς), he states: "and this *ethnos* of Indians (τὸ δὲ τῶν Ἰνδῶν ἔθνος τοῦτο) had the name of

---

[5] MacDonald, "Arabi," "Arabes," and "Arabs" on these Arabias, along with MacDonald et al., "Arabs."
[6] Sozomen, *HE* (ed. Bidez and Hansen) 2.24.1: "the inner of those called Indians by us"=Aksumite Ethiopia; Socrates, *HE* (ed. Hansen) 1.19.1–2: Ethiopia=Meroitic Ethiopia, India adjoining Ethiopia=Meroitic Ethiopia, inner India=Aksumite Ethiopia; Rufinus (ed. Schwartz and Mommsen) 5.10.2 and 10.9: Ethiopia=Meroitic Ethiopia, nearer India=Meroitic Ethiopia, farther India=Aksumite Ethiopia and Arabia; Theodoret, *HE* (ed. Parmentier and Hansen) 1.23.2: farthest India=Aksumite Ethiopia; Philostorgius, *HE* (ed. Bidez and Winkelmann) 3.5–6: Ethiopia=Aksum; India=Greater Arabia; *The Peoples of India and the Brahmins* (ed. Berghoff and ed. Derrett) 4: king of the Indians=king of Aksum. These labels will be explained and justified in the remainder of this textual section; what must be stressed is that the evangelizer Frumentius clearly became bishop of Aksum (which Sozomen, Socrates, and Rufinus called "inner India" or "farther India") under Athanasius of Alexandria. Athanasius, *Apology to Constantius* (ed. Brennecke, Heil, and von Stockhausen) 29–31. On Nubian Kush and Aksum, see now Hatke, *Aksum and Nubia*. For clarification, it must be stressed that Greek sources referred to places like Aksum as "inner India" because they conceived of it as an interior India, with regions such as Meroitic Ethiopia being on the "outer" edge of the various Indias. Latin sources, having a different orientation, described places like Aksum as "farther India" in reference to its distance from the Roman Mediterranean and Egypt in comparison to Meroitic Ethiopia, an "India" that was nearer to these locations. For helpful comments, see Johnson, *Literary Territories*, 133–34.

Sabaeans ... but now has the name of Homerites."[7] Philostorgius was clearly conceiving of south Arabians as "the innermost Indians," and he defined the Himyarites as one among many Indian *ethnē* that populated the Indian Ocean world. John Malalas too reckoned the Himyarites of Arabia and the Aksumites of Ethiopia to be "*Indoi*," and he therefore deemed their famous conflict in the 520s CE to have been waged by "Indians" on different continents separated by water.[8] The *Martyr Act of Saint Arethas* similarly locates "India" at an orientation and distance from southwest Arabia more befitting the horn of Africa or easterly points of Arabia than the Indian subcontinent.[9]

As noted above, Philostorgius explicitly construed the Himyarites to be "this *ethnos* of Indians" (τὸ ... τῶν Ἰνδῶν ἔθνος τοῦτο) and among "the innermost Indians" (τοὺς ἐνδοτάτω Ἰνδούς). But his treatment of Arabians as "Indians" was in fact so emphatic that he described Theophilus, a native of Socotra, as an "Indian" who evangelized "Indians" of Arabia who reportedly had already been visited by the apostle Bartholomew (otherwise famous for his work in Ethiopia).[10] An epitome of his treatment, which is contained in the works of the Byzantine author Photius, claims that Theophilus, who originated from the island of "Dibous," had been sent by his countrymen to Rome as a hostage while young. When Theophilus was an adult, the emperor Constantius II dispatched him on embassy to south Arabia, where Jews by then noticeably lived, to build churches for Roman merchants.[11] While there, Theophilus converted the leader of the

---

[7] Philostorgius, *HE* (ed. Bidez and Winkelmann) 2.6: τὸ δὲ τῶν Ἰνδῶν ἔθνος τοῦτο Σάβας ..., τὰ νῦν δὲ Ὁμηρίτας καλεῖσθαι. For additional examples, with bibliography, see Goldenberg, *Curse of Ham*, 211 and 377–78; and Van der Horst, "'India'," 575–76.

[8] John Malalas (ed. Thurn) 18.9, 15, and 56.

[9] *Martyr Act of Saint Arethas* (ed. Detoraki) 2 (with 29) indicates that Roman territory in Egypt or Arabia is farther (60 *monai*) from southwest Arabia than "India" (50 *monai*). By this logic, "India" is not much farther from southwest Arabia than Ethiopia (30 *monai*). Also, the text assumes that travelers along the Arabian Sea first bypass "India" before reaching Persian territory. "India" in this case must represent an east African or south Arabian location.

[10] Philostorgius, *HE* (ed. Bidez and Winkelmann) 3.4–6, with 2.6. For late antique and Byzantine references to this figure, see Fiaccadori, "Teofilo I," 295, n. 2. Gregory of Nyssa believed that Theophilus was from east Africa: *Eun.* (ed. Jaeger) 1.47. Theophilus apparently settled in Antioch after his journey. See Amidon, *Philostorgius*, 43–44 (based on the Suda, Θ 197); and Elm, *Sons of Hellenism*, 243–44 and 281, with Philostorgius, *HE* (ed. Bidez and Winkelmann) 7.6, 8.2, and 9.1. For reasons described in the following paragraphs, I disagree with the conclusions of the learned articles of Fiaccadori, "Teofilo I" and "Teofilo II," and Ramelli, "Cristianesimo," 114–16 regarding Theophilus' origins and arrival in the subcontinent.

[11] On Jews and the statement of the *Martyr Act of Saint Arethas* apparently derived from Philostorgius, see Bowersock, "New Greek Inscription from South Yemen," 393–96. For Jews in south Arabia, see Bowersock, *Throne of Adulis*, 78–92; and Tobi, "Jews of Yemen." Whether Photius or a predecessor was the epitomizer is an issue. See Amidon, *Philostorgius*, xxi–xxiii.

"Sabaeans" or Himyarites and built churches in three different cities across south Arabia. One was at Aden on the Red Sea; the other was at the shore of the Persian Gulf.[12]

From this point, however, Philostorgius' text poses complications. It first describes Theophilus as having crossed from Arabia to "Dibous," his homeland and an island of the "Indians." Judging from the geography of Philostorgius' account, "Dibous" (apparently derived from *dibba*, a Prakrit word for island) was the island of Socotra, not Sri Lanka or the Maldives.[13] Socotra was an island located at a roughly equidistant position between Yemen and the horn of Africa, and as we will see, it was a common point of exchange for sailors moving from Roman Egypt, India, and south Arabia who left a substantial corpus of graffiti in a grotto there.[14] From "Dibous," Philostorgius claims that Theophilus traveled to "the rest of India" and corrected the flawed practices of Christian inhabitants who had reportedly been converted by the apostle Bartholomew.[15] But directly after stating this, Philostorgius describes how Theophilus had crossed to Ethiopia from "this Arabia Magna," by which the text is clearly referring to the "India" in which he had been conducting his ministry.[16] Some scholars attribute the sudden shift from "India" to "Arabia Magna" to an omission in Philostorgius' account introduced by Photius. They thus claim that the "India" to which Theophilus (and Bartholomew) had traveled was the subcontinent and that the lost material described Theophilus' travel from India to Arabia.[17] But nothing indicates that Photius omitted anything substantial from Philostorgius' narrative here, and it makes little sense to surmise that Photius decidedly omitted material that would have been of obvious interest for an audience seeking to learn about Theophilus' ministry in the Indian Ocean. Philostorgius is simply using both "(innermost) India" and "Arabia Magna" for Arabia. In his narrative, Theophilus had traveled there from "Dibous" (Socotra) and then had proceeded from there to Aksum.

---

[12] Philostorgius, *HE* (ed. Bidez and Winkelmann) 3.4.
[13] For "Dibous" as Socotra, see Bukharin, "Greeks on Socotra, 522–26 and Schneider, *L'Ethiopie et l'Inde*, 31–32. But also (contra) Strauch, "Socotra and the 'Indian Connection'," 398–99; Amidon, *Philostorgius*, 40, n. 8; Fiaccadori, "Teofilo I." Later in this section, we discuss how the *Exposition of the Entire World (Expositio totius mundi)*, the Greek *Itinerary from Eden (Hodoiporia apo Edem)*, and Ammianus use the same name for Socotra.
[14] *PME* (ed. Casson) 20–33. Strauch et al., "Catalogue," for the inscriptions, graffiti, and drawings from travelers in the cave of Hoq.
[15] Philostorgius, *HE* (ed. Bidez and Winkelmann) 3.5, with 2.6.
[16] Philostorgius, *HE* (ed. Bidez and Winkelmann) 3.6.
[17] Amidon, *Philostorgius*, 22, n. 18 and 42–43, n. 13 and 16, with Fiaccadori, "Teofilo II," 290–91.

It is clear, then, that Philostorgius considered "India" to be a legitimate name for Arabia and that he was using "India" and "greater Arabia" (Arabia Magna) interchangeably to describe the portion of south Arabia beyond the immediate territory controlled by the Himyarites.[18] This interpretation is strengthened by the fact that previously in his history, as we have already noted, Philostorgius described how Bartholomew preceded Theophilus in preaching among the Sabaeans of Arabia, and he defined the Sabaeans as "innermost Indians" and "this *ethnos* of Indians" which is currently called the "Homerites."[19] Likewise, when he described Socotra (Dibous) as an island of "Indians," he was conceiving of it as an island off Arabia where "Indian" Arabians dwelled and not denoting islands farther afield. Travelers with clear links to Roman Egypt have in fact left Greek epigraphic traces in these regions.[20] It is therefore no surprise that late antique sources indicate that Christianity had arrived in south Arabia and Socotra through Roman activity by the fourth century.

Similar issues plague the Latin *Exposition of the Entire World (Expositio totius mundi)* and the Greek *Itinerary from Eden (Hodoiporia apo Edem)*, whose treatments of the Red and Arabian Sea regions are based on a common source. The *Exposition* is generally deemed a mid-to late fourth-century text. It provides a description of the putatively known world from its easternmost point to the Roman empire, with some discussion of the various peoples inhabiting it. The *Itinerary* was composed some time between the mid-fourth and mid-sixth centuries.[21] It too relates an itinerary that starts from the world's easternmost points and proceeds westward. But while providing ostensible measurements of distances, it provides only skeletal information about lands and societies. One of the key differences between the two texts is that the *Itinerary* adds references to Christians that do not appear in the *Exposition*. But overall they both constitute confusing and confused accounts. Their common confusion resides in the fact that they purport to describe a linearly east-to-west itinerary from Eden (treated as the world's farthest point east) to the Roman empire, but in so doing,

---

[18] Schneider, *L'Ethiopie et l'Inde*, 31–32. Also, Goldenberg, *Curse of Ham*, 211 and 377–78; Van der Horst, "'India'," 575–76; Debié, Perrin, and Mahé, "L'Orient," 614.
[19] Philostorgius, *HE* (ed. Bidez and Winkelmann) 2.6–8.
[20] Bukharin, "Greek Inscriptions at Hoq," and "Greeks on Socotra" provides commentary and treats the Greek inscriptions of Socotra and south Arabia.
[21] *Itinerary* (ed. Rougé) 350–55, with 57–69 for date. The *Itinerary* appears to share a common fourth-century source with the beginning of the *Exposition of the Entire World*, which noticeably does not place Christians in any "India." The *Exposition* perhaps dates to the mid-fourth century (9–27 of Rougé's edition). Bukharin, "Greeks on Socotra," 523–24 provides useful discussion of date (probably fifth century, and certainly before 540).

they virtually locate the entirety of the Red Sea, east Africa, and Arabia east of the Sasanian Persian empire. The best explanation for this confusion is that as Romans increasingly conceived of south Arabia, Meroitic Ethiopia, Aksumite Ethiopia, and Socotra as lands inhabited by "Indians," the authors of the texts conflated them with the Indian subcontinent and situated them geographically where the Indian subcontinent roughly was (east-southeast of Sasanian Persia and the Iranian plateau).

Starting with the easternmost point of Eden, both the *Itinerary* and the *Exposition* ostensibly proceed to describe territories in a progression that moves directly westward toward the Roman empire.[22] Most of their initial references, unfortunately, cannot be understood with confidence. Confusingly, most of them, often informed by biblical toponyms or people, involve the taking of names with links to Arabia, Ethiopia, or the Red Sea and placing them deep in the hinterland of Asia. Emer/Iemar may denote Himyar. Likewise, Evilat/Ebelat, a biblical location near Eden, was by late antiquity associated with a putative people of Arabia or east Africa. Choneum/Chonai or Chonaioi (as they appear) too may be derived from the name for what was commonly understood to be people of east Africa (*Chousaioi*, that is, the Kushites), though some see this as describing Huns.[23] After mentioning these allegedly far-eastern places, the *Exposition* and *Itinerary*, again with the pretension of proceeding east to west, describe how one reaches "Diva/Diaba," "Greater India," Aksum, and then "lesser India." Noticeably, the *Exposition* describes "greater India" and Aksum as virtually adjacent, and the *Itinerary* locates "lesser India" in the Red Sea. But both texts omit Arabia by name. It is accordingly clear that "Diva/Diaba" is Socotra, whose name was derived from the Prakrit *dibba* (island) and appears in Philostorgius' discussion of Theophilus the "Indian" as Dibous. Likewise, Arabia is the landmass that the *Exposition* and *Itinerary* describe as "greater India," which they locate beside the island of "Diva/Diaba" (Socotra).[24] The "lesser India" of the Red Sea was Meroitic Ethiopia. In this respect, the texts describe in serial fashion the locations that one would encounter while sailing from Socotra and south Arabia ("India") to Aksum and north along the Red Sea coast. It is worth emphasizing that the *Itinerary* claims that

---

[22] *Exposition* (ed. Rougé) 8–21, with previous note.
[23] The biblically based links to south Arabia and Ethiopia are made by Josephus, *AJ* (ed. Niese) 1.130–35 and 220–21; Gen. 2.11–12 in the Septuagint (ed. Rahlfs-Hanhart); Cosmas Indicopleustes (ed. Wolska-Conus) 2.27, who does however distinguish the sons of Chous, as Ethiopians or Arabians, from *Ouvvoi* (Huns) of inner Asia. Bukharin, "Greeks on Socotra," 523–24; Atwood, "Huns and Xiongnu," 36–37 discuss the possibilities for the place names.
[24] As argued by Bukharin, "Greeks on Socotra," 522–26. Schneider, *L'Ethiopie et l'Inde*, 29–30.

Christians inhabited these very regions, whereas the earlier *Exposition* is silent on the matter.

After describing such east African and Arabian areas, the texts intriguingly appear to locate the Red Sea, Aksum, Arabia, and Meroitic Ethiopia east of the Iranian plateau. So they continue to proceed "westward" to describe Persia and the nearby land of the Saracens. Both texts accordingly treat Persia as adjacent to "lesser India" (Meroitic Ethiopia) for a traveler moving west; the *Exposition* even claims that the Persians accepted elephants from lesser India. It is similarly near the land of the Saracens that the *Itinerary* places the Sinai port of Aila, which it strangely treats as the harbor of "Persia, India (meaning Arabia), and Egypt." Accordingly, the only geographically intelligible part of these itineraries is their depictions of a trip from south Arabia and Socotra to Aksumite and Meroitic Ethiopia. But even then, the authors of the texts situated all these locations east of Persia.

As Chapter 3 emphasizes, Roman Egyptians had lost direct contact with the Indian subcontinent from the late third to the early sixth centuries CE. As this occurred, Romans began to describe commercial middlemen in Indian Ocean trade, including Ethiopians and Arabians, as Indians and referred to their home regions as "Indian." The *Exposition* and *Itinerary* are very much convoluted products of this period. Like Philostorgius in his more lucid treatment of Theophilus the "Indian," they therefore describe Arabia as "India" and the island of Socotra as "Diva/Diaba," all while situating "lesser India" (Meroitic Ethiopia) between Egypt and Aksum. Their geography is noticeably limited to south Arabia, the Red Sea, and east Africa, and does not extend deeply into the Indian Ocean. The *Itinerary* therefore and quite significantly situates Christians in south Arabia, Socotra, Aksumite Ethiopia, and Meroitic Ethiopia, and in the next chapter, we will see how these regions did in fact harbor Christians by the mid-fourth century CE. But it bears no mention of Christians in the Indian subcontinent or Sri Lanka, and the emphatic treatment that both the *Exposition* and *Itinerary* give to the "Indias" in east Africa and Arabia reflects the restricted horizons of Roman Egyptians in this period. Because it had become fashionable to describe east Africa and Arabia as "India," the authors of these texts (and apparently their common fourth-century CE source) did not merely refer to Arabia and east Africa as "India." In their confusion, they had situated the entire Red Sea littoral and Arabia (as "India") east of Iran.

If the *Exposition* and *Itinerary* simply conflated Arabia and the Indian subcontinent, the *Letter Regarding the Peoples of India and the Brahmins* did so too.[25] Written some time between 350 and 500 CE and typically attributed in the past to Palladius of Helenopolis, the first part of the *Letter* describes the alleged travels of an unnamed *scholastikos* (a lawyer or jurist) from Aksum and into the Indian Ocean world. The second part, putatively based on the work of the Roman author Arrian on India, provides a variation on an oft-told dialogue between Alexander the Great and Indian Brahmins. It is clearly not the original work of Palladius or the author of the general text.[26] Moreover, this text survives in several Latin recensions of varied reliability,[27] with the most heavily modified, redacted, and problematic (as well as popular) being the "Sistine edition."[28] It is now surmised that the "Sistine edition," despite being the best known of the Latin recensions, is the "literary fraud" of an early modern humanist, but it nonetheless has been sometimes treated as an ancient witness.[29] While the Latin version(s) is often attributed to Ambrose, such an association is problematic, especially if the Greek version was not composed before c. 400 CE.[30] Due to doubts raised about the antiquity and authenticity of the "Sistine" Latin recension, it will not be discussed further.

Whatever its authorship, the *Letter* indicates that its writer, his colleague Moses of Adulis (or Museus of the Doleni in the Latin versions), and the *scholastikos* had not reached Taprobene (normally Sri Lanka) or the Indian subcontinent.[31] At the beginning of the Greek text, the author claims that he and his episcopal colleague Moses had only reached the "outermost parts" (*ta akroteria*) of "India" a few years before the text's composition.

---

[25] *The Peoples of India and the Brahmins* (ed. Berghoff; ed. Derrett).

[26] For discussion of the text, its structure, and its antecedents, see Derrett, "Theban Scholasticus," 22–23; Weerakkody, *Taprobane*, 119–31; Faller, *Taprobane*, 142–51; and now Johnson, "Real and Imagined Geography," 412 and *Literary Territories*, 134–35.

[27] Cracco Ruggini, "Cristianizzazione," for discussion (65–69), textual excerpt from the later "Bamberg" recension (70–71), and textual edition (72–79). Weerakkody, *Taprobane*, 119.

[28] Cracco Ruggini, "Cristianizzazione," 65–69 for treatment and 72–79 for text (as compared with the edition from more reliable Latin manuscripts); Weerakkody, *Taprobane*, 119–20 discusses. This spurious version can also be found in various editions of Ambrose of Milan's corpus. The Latin version(s) renames Moses, the bishop of Adulis, so that he is Museus, bishop of the Doleni. Parroting the Greek text, it does not independently attest the activity of churchmen in India.

[29] Weerakkody, *Taprobane*, 119–20; Cracco Ruggini, "Cristianizzazione," 66–67. The issues outlined so far do not prevent scholars from attributing the problematic Latin text to Ambrose and treating it as accurate and reflecting a real voyage. Nedungatt, *Quest for the Historical Thomas*, 76 and "India Confused?" 330–31, for instance, discusses "Ambrose" but does not mention the previous Greek version on which it is based or recognize that the spurious Latin version is probably not very ancient.

[30] Derrett, "Theban Scholasticus," 23 and Weerakkody, *Taprobane*, 120 cast doubt on the attribution to Ambrose.

[31] *The Peoples of India and the Brahmins* (ed. Berghoff; ed. Derrett) 1.1–14 is the focus here. The text and its significance for the relations between "Ethiopian India" and the subcontinent are discussed in Schneider, *L'Ethiopie et l'Inde*, 357–59; and Bowersock, *Throne of Adulis*, 23–24. For *Taprobane*, see Weerakkody, *Taprobane*; and Faller, *Taprobane*.

This phrase may refer, as some have argued, to a promontory on the horn of Africa described by Pliny as *promunturium Indorum*.³² But it could simply denote a location in Arabia or east Africa. The author, however, claims that he had learned about the Brahmins from the Theban *scholastikos*, who had apparently traveled to India itself (but not Taprobene). This *scholastikos* had visited Aksum, whose king the text classifies as an Indian.³³ From there, he had boarded the boats (*ploiaria*) of "Indians" involved in trade, or in other words the boats of Aksumite Ethiopians, and he had then departed. Having arrived in what the Greek text calls the region of the Bisades, a pepper-producing people, the *scholastikos* was taken hostage until the nearby king of Taprobene (normally Sri Lanka) secured his release due to his respect for the Romans.³⁴

In various ways, it is evident that the description of the Brahmins in these texts was not based on a real encounter between Romans and Brahmins; it simply reflects how the text maps philosophical and monastic values that circulated in the Roman empire onto what are basically contrived representations of Brahmins.³⁵ But just as significant is how the text reflects the shrinking horizons of the period and therefore operates within the same geographic and social frame as the *Exposition* and the *Itinerary*. The text's description of diplomatic relations between the Roman empire and the king of Taprobene is revealing in this regard. Although Roman Egyptians did not extend their commercial network to India during the fourth and fifth centuries CE, diplomatic contacts between Rome and Arabia and Socotra were frequent. An edict of Constantius II from the Theodosian Code even apparently regulates how long ambassadors to Aksum and Himyar could linger at Alexandria,³⁶ and the activity undertaken by Theophilus "the Indian" of Socotra at the behest of Constantius

---

³² *The Peoples of India and the Brahmins* (ed. Berghoff; ed. Derrett) 1.1. Muckensturm-Poulle, "Palladius' Brahmans," 157–58 discusses the reference to the Horn of Africa. Pliny, *NH* (ed. Jahn and Mayhoff) 6.175.
³³ *The Peoples of India and the Brahmins* (ed. Berghoff; ed. Derrett) 1.4.
³⁴ *The Peoples of India and the Brahmins* (ed. Berghoff; ed. Derrett) 1.3–10. Derrett, "Theban Scholasticus," 26–30 provides a useful summary of the text, while accepting the historicity of a trip to "Malabar" and not realizing that the author may be referring to Aksumite Ethiopians as "Indians." Weerakkody, *Taprobane*, 119–31; and Faller, *Taprobane*, 142–51 likewise treat as an historical trip to India.
³⁵ Such issues are raised by Schneider, *L'Ethiopie et l'Inde*, 357–59; Bowersock, *Throne of Adulis*, 23–24. Also Muckensturm-Poulle, "Palladius' Brahmans," while not doubting the travels of the Theban *scholastikos*, asserts that Palladius' depiction of Brahmanic philosophy does not cohere with the reality. It is worth observing that Brahmins were not key players in south Indian society until the eighth century. See Chapter 6, p. 210, n. 10–11.
³⁶ *CT* (ed. Mommsen) 12.12.2; Munro-Hay, *Aksum*, 80.

II reflects the intensifying relations between Romans and Socotra and south Arabia during the fourth and fifth centuries.

As a result, the *Letter*'s treatment of Rome's diplomatic relations with the Indian Ocean world strongly suggest that it was imposing the labels of India and Taprobene (Sri Lanka) onto Arabia and Socotra and conflating certain characteristics of those who inhabited south Arabia and the Indian subcontinent (like pepper production). If its later (and spurious) Latin variation, the "Sistine" recension, claims that the *scholastikos* visited Muziris, "the emporium of India this side of the Ganges," it reflects how the deeply problematic Latin text, apparently doctored by an early modern humanist, was simply trying to improve on its misleading Greek original. Since the original described the putative voyage that a *scholastikos* had made to south Arabia, and almost Socotra, but had labeled these places India and Taprobene (Sri Lanka), the humanist "fixed" the tradition by citing a city of India named in classical sources.[37]

Yet, the *Letter* was not the only fourth- or fifth-century CE document that conflated diplomatic relations between the Roman empire and the Arabian "India" with those between Rome and the subcontinent. In the late fourth century CE, Ammianus claimed that Indian peoples (*nationes Indicae*) from as far away as the *Divi* and *Serendivi* competed to send embassies and gifts to the emperor Julian.[38] As noted previously, the *Divi* were the inhabitants of Socotra (*Diva* or *Dibous*). The *Serendivi* would normally be a term for the inhabitants of Sri Lanka (*siṃhaladvīpa*), and it is possible that kings on the island maintained an interest in Roman affairs despite the general disruption in its direct contact with Roman merchants.[39] But Ammianus' statement probably reflects a tendency among later Roman authors to call Socotra by names traditionally used for Sri Lanka, and he is likely misconstruing an embassy from Socotra as embassies from two different island peoples. This possibility for the conflation of Socotra and Sri Lanka (or the division of Socotra into two islands) is strengthened by the fact that in his excursus of Persia and its adjacent territories (including Arabia Felix), Ammianus refers to Socotra by its Greek name of *Dioscurides* while apparently being unaware that he had elsewhere referred to its inhabitants as *Divi*.[40] Moreover, in the Latin, Coptic, Armenian, and Georgian versions of a text attributed to Epiphanius of Salamis, the *Divi* and *Serendivi* are both

---

[37] Weerakkody, *Taprobane*, 119–20; Cracco Ruggini, "Cristianizzazione," 66–67.
[38] Ammianus (ed. Seyfarth) 22.7.10. [39] Bukharin, "Greeks on Socotra," 523.
[40] Ammianus (ed. Seyfarth) 23.6.47. As used in *PME* (ed. Casson) 30.

associated with "Indian" peoples of Arabia.[41] This suggests that Ammianus was referring to putative peoples from Socotra, not Sri Lanka.[42]

It can thus be surmised that Ammianus' *Divi* and *Serendivi* were "Indians" of Socotra or south Arabia and that Ammianus misconstrued *Dioscurides* and *Diva*, both being names for Socotra, as two different islands. Ammianus' confusion reflects a general loss of geographic knowledge of the Arabian Sea that prompted many late antique authors to engage in the two following paradoxical formulations. First, they treated the different names for Socotra (*Dioscourides, Diva*) as if they referred to separate places. Second, they conflated the various islands of the Indian Ocean in ways that prompted them to apply traditional names for Sri Lanka (Taprobene, *Serendiva*) to Socotra. The end result was an onomastic instability whereby the traditional names for certain islands of the Indian Ocean circulated promiscuously as references to other islands. In the same manner that the *Letter* describes Socotra as Taprobene, Ammianus thus construes an embassy from Socotra as being from two different putative island peoples (the *Divi* and *Serendivi*) presumably because his contemporaries were using different names for Socotra's inhabitants.[43]

As discussed in Chapter 3, it was only during the sixth century that the Roman Egyptian socio-commercial network re-established direct contact with India. Such direct contact with the subcontinent sharpened the ability of certain Romans to distinguish among the regions and societies of the Indian Ocean. But it did not prevent late antique Roman Christians from continuing the trend of calling various places in east Africa and Arabia "India." The work of the anonymous figure known by modern scholars as Cosmas Indicopleustes, arguably the most reliable late antique witness to the Red Sea and Indian Ocean worlds, provides key evidence. "Cosmas" had traveled to various parts of the Red Sea and Indian Ocean in the late 510s and 520s CE, including Aksumite Ethiopia, the Horn of Africa, and Sri Lanka.[44] Decades later he described what he had learned about these regions in a lengthy work on the geography and topographies of Christian peoples.

---

[41] Epiphanius, *De gemmis* (ed. Günther) 748–49 (passage absent from the Greek in *PG* 43, 293–304); Windstedt, "Coptic Legends," 218–22, with translation on 219; (ed. Blake and De Vis), 11, 109, 242–43; (ed. Albrecht and Manukyan) 9–10 and 52–53, with Weerakkody, *Taprobane*, 180; Faller, *Taprobane*, 135–41.

[42] Ammianus' treatment has bearing on how we understand Basset, "Synaxaire arabe," 277, which describes an embassy from "India" to Honorius and Arcadius.

[43] Similarly, Weerakkody, *Taprobane*, 125 and 179–81; Faller, *Taprobane*, 137–41.

[44] For "Cosmas'" personal observations, see Cosmas Indicopleustes (Wolska-Conus) 2.30, 2.54, and 3.64–65. For dating his activity at Adulis (perhaps 518–520), see Robin, "Nagrān," 77–79; and Speidel, "Wars, Trade, and Treaties," 83.

Significantly, "Cosmas" variously described Aksumite Ethiopia, the Horn of Africa (Barbaria), or Arabia as "inner India" while otherwise expressing full awareness that these were geographically different from the Indian subcontinent, which his text also called "inner India."[45] In reference to a seaward voyage from the Red Sea into the Gulf of Aden, he even notes how he had "sailed upon inner India and nearly passed by to Barbaria (the Horn of Africa)." In this case, "inner India" certainly refers either to Aksumite Ethiopia, the Horn of Africa, Arabia, or a place in between.[46] As such, this "inner India" was distinct from the subcontinent, which he would elsewhere call "inner India" or "the innermost India of all."[47] "Cosmas" had visited the Aksumite kingdom, the Horn of Africa, and, it seems, Sri Lanka (*Taprobane*) if not the Indian mainland, and he certainly could distinguish them geographically. But he persisted in the conventional wisdom that while east Africa, Arabia, and the Indian subcontinent were distinct, they still were the homes of varied "Indian" peoples. Being so, they constituted different "Indias," and even the name "inner India" could be used for east Africa, Arabia, or the subcontinent.

Narratives of Apostolic and Late Antique Evangelization and Their Impact

Late antique traditions regarding the travels and preaching of the first-century CE apostles also had a strong impact on the tendency of Roman Christians to describe various regions of Arabia and east Africa as "India." Whatever their knowledge of the geography and society of the Indian Ocean may have been, various writers who treated the travels of early apostles could wittingly ascribe the label "India" to Meroitic Ethiopia, Aksumite Ethiopia, and Arabia to fulfill various literary or evangelical needs. After it had become typical to conceive of east Africans and south Arabians as certain types of Indians, many late antique ecclesiastical historians endeavored to discern where the original apostles had preached and how their zones of evangelization were different from those of more recent preachers. This feat was not particularly easy. Clearly, the tradition that Matthew had preached among Ethiopians and Bartholomew among

---

[45] Cosmas Indicopleustes (ed. Wolska-Conus) 2.30 and 49 and 3.65; Bowersock, *Throne of Adulis*, 22–33 treats Cosmas and his text (23 for observation regarding "Cosmas" and India).
[46] Cosmas Indicopleustes (ed. Wolska-Conus) 2.30. The text indicates that the author had sailed ἐπὶ τὴν ἐσωτέραν Ἰνδίαν, which is best understood to mean that he had arrived "upon" or "at" inner India while heading toward Barbaria (πρὸς τὴν Βαρβαρίαν). Also, Schneider, *L'Ethiopie et l'Inde*, 34.
[47] Cosmas Indicopleustes (ed. Wolska-Conus) 2.45 and 3.65.

"nearer Indians" was well established by the fourth century.⁴⁸ But by this time, Ethiopia, "nearer India," and "India adjoining Ethiopia" were being used synonymously for the same place, namely Meroitic or Nubian Ethiopia. In their efforts to differentiate the regions in which Matthew and Bartholomew had allegedly preached from one another, and from those of more recent evangelizers, various ecclesiastical historians began to treat "Ethiopia" and "nearer India" (or "India adjoining Ethiopia") as two distinct regions that they located narrowly between Roman Egypt, the Red Sea, and Aksumite Ethiopia, which they labeled "inner/farther India."

The endeavors of Rufinus, Socrates, Sozomen, and Theodoret to map the missionary zones of Matthew, Bartholomew, and the fourth-century CE preacher Frumentius all reflect this trend.⁴⁹ As Chapter 3 illustrates, the Roman Egyptian socio-commercial network into the Red Sea provided Frumentius and other preachers with the social pathways and residential settlements that made their evangelization of the Aksumite monarchy possible. Frumentius, in fact, emerges as a bishop of Aksum in an apology that Athanasius of Alexandria wrote in the late 350s; Athanasius was his metropolitan, and he conceived of the Christians of Aksum that Frumentius governed as "Indians."⁵⁰ Whatever his role may have been in bringing Christianity to the region, the historical figure Frumentius was certainly an agent of Christianity in Aksumite Ethiopia. While possessing many romantic traits, late antique ecclesiastical histories were therefore describing how Frumentius preached in Aksumite Ethiopia when they gave him credit for evangelizing "inner/farther India." They were not referring to the Indian subcontinent.⁵¹ Accordingly, when Sozomen associates Frumentius with the evangelization of "the inner of those called Indians by us" (τοὺς ἔνδον τῶν καθ' ἡμᾶς Ἰνδῶν), he is describing the Aksumites. When Socrates, Rufinus, and Theodoret similarly link Frumentius to "the innermost Indians," "farther India,"⁵² and "farthest

---

⁴⁸ As seen in the traditions about Pantaenus, discussed on pp. 88–90.
⁴⁹ Sozomen, *HE* (ed. Bidez) 2.24.1; Socrates, *HE* (ed. Hansen) 1.19.1–2; Rufinus, *HE* (ed. Schwartz and Mommsen) 5.10.2 and 10.9; Theodoret, *HE* (ed. Parmentier and Hansen) 1.23.2. Also, *Chronicle of Pseudo-Dionysius* (also known as *Zuqnin*) (ed. Chabot) 1.162–63. Schneider, *L'Ethiopie et l'Inde*, 30.
⁵⁰ Athanasius, *Apology to Constantius* (ed. Brennecke, Heil, and von Stockhausen) 29–31. On this episode (with comparison to ancient narratives of the arrival of Christianity in Iberia), see Haas, "Mountain Constantines"; and Robin, "Arabia and Ethiopia," 273–76. Athanasius, *Ep. ad Afros* (ed. Brennecke, Heil, and von Stockhausen) 1.2.2–3 contains the reference to "Indians." Nedungatt, "Christian Origins," 421 interprets Frumentius' activity differently.
⁵¹ Ramelli, "Cristianesimo," 104–10, and "Early Christian Missions," 228–30 argues in favor of the Indian subcontinent. For correct observation, Johnson, *Literary Territories*, 133–34.
⁵² Sozomen, *HE* (ed. Bidez and Hansen) 2.24.1; Socrates, *HE* (ed. Hansen) 1.19.1–2; Rufinus, *HE* (ed. Schwartz and Mommsen) 5.10.2 and 10.9.

India,"⁵³ the implications are the same. Rufinus even states that "farther/inner India lies in the middle, between it (nearer India) and Parthia, but deeper in the interior by a long expanse (*longo tractu*)."⁵⁴ His text in this sense seems to conflate Aksumite Ethiopia and Arabia as a single "India." But since he places farther/inner India between nearer India (Meroitic Ethiopia) and Parthia, he clearly is not referring to the subcontinent.

Still, the fact that the "inner/farther" India in which Frumentius preached was Aksumite Ethiopia posed a problem for the authors just described. Meroitic Ethiopia had previously been ascribed to both Matthew and Bartholomew, with certain traditions linking Matthew to "Ethiopia" and others associating Bartholomew with "nearer India" or "India adjoining Ethiopia." As late antique authors endeavored to confer upon Matthew and Bartholomew their own unique fields of preaching between Egypt and Aksum, they created space by treating "Ethiopia" and "nearer India" as referring to separate but adjoining geographic regions located between Egypt and the region of "inner/farther India," that is Aksumite Ethiopia.⁵⁵ But it is clear that they were using both "Ethiopia" and "nearer India" in reference to Meroitic Ethiopia and its vicinity. In fact, while deeming Aksumite Ethiopia to be "inner India," Socrates and Rufinus even specify that "nearer India" was the "India adjoining Ethiopia," that is, adjoining Meroitic Ethiopia.⁵⁶

The late fifth-century CE anonymous history traditionally attributed to Gelasius of Cyzicus resolved this issue in a different way, and this difference is significant for establishing the "India" to which Frumentius traveled. First, the text, instead of using the different names Ethiopia and "nearer India" or "India adjoining Ethiopia" for the same place (Meroitic Ethiopia), shifts the missionary region of Matthew from Ethiopia to Parthia and places Bartholomew in "Ethiopia" instead of its synonym "India."⁵⁷ While doing so, it emphasizes that the bishop of Alexandria was the metropolitan bishop of Egypt and additional territory stretching as far as "the districts of India," a clear reference to both Meroitic and Aksumite Ethiopia, which represented by the late fifth century *eparchiai* of "Indian" peoples adjoining Egypt.⁵⁸

---

⁵³ Theodoret, *HE* (ed. Parmentier and Hansen) 1.23.2.
⁵⁴ Rufinus, *HE* (ed. Schwartz and Mommsen) 10.9.
⁵⁵ Sozomen, *HE* (ed. Bidez and Hansen) 2.24.1; Socrates, *HE* (ed. Hansen) 1.19.1–2; Rufinus, *HE* (ed. Schwartz and Mommsen) 5.10.2 and 10.9.
⁵⁶ Socrates, *HE* (ed. Hansen) 1.19.2; Rufinus, *HE* (ed. Schwartz and Mommsen) 10.9.
⁵⁷ Ps.-Gelasius, *HE* (ed. Hansen) 3.9.2–3.
⁵⁸ Ps.-Gelasius, *HE* (ed. Hansen) 2.28.2–3 and 2.38.2–5.

Second, whereas the ecclesiastical historians who described Frumentius' activity had not associated the apostle Thomas with an India, the anonymous author was certainly familiar with the Indian *Acts of Thomas*. He therefore claims that Thomas evangelized "the Indians of greater India" (τοῖς τῆς μεγάλης Ἰνδίας Ἰνδοῖς). In this instance, "greater India" refers to the subcontinent, a region that the text ascribes to the oversight of the late fifth-century Sasanian Persian Church of the East (as Chapter 4 discusses).[59] By describing the Indian subcontinent as "greater India," the author distinguishes it from what the text calls the *eparchiai* of "India" that were within the orbit of the bishop of Alexandria, that is Meroitic and Aksumite Ethiopia.

Third, when the text describes the "India" that had not yet been evangelized by apostles and therefore needed the arrival of Frumentius, its language is quite explicit. It in fact labels the inhabitants of Aksumite Ethiopia as "the Indians far away from the Parthians" (τοῖς πόρρω Ἰνδοῖς Πάρθων) and as "innermost India" (τὴν ἐνδοτάτην Ἰνδίαν).[60] By using such terminology, the text distinguishes Aksumite "India," which was indeed quite far from Parthia, from the Indian subcontinent, which was closer to it. Yet, the text also replicates the phrase that ecclesiastical predecessors had used for the region of Aksum (inner India), thereby leaving no doubt regarding the India to which Frumentius was envisioned as traveling. Not only does the anonymous historian demonstrate again that "inner" India typically referred to the Aksumite kingdom or Arabia, but the author also shows that individual writers could conceive of many different regions of Africa, Arabia, and the Indian subcontinent as "Indias."

The Polyvalence of "India" and Difficulties with the Transmission of Information

Yet another factor that determined how late antique authors could ascribe the label "India" to various east African and Arabian locations is the polyvalence of the word "India" and the difficulty of establishing its meaning within written or oral sources. Even authors who associated "India" and "Indian" exclusively with the subcontinent, and who therefore

---

[59] Ps.-Gelasius, *HE* (ed. Hansen) 3.9.2. Ps.-Gelasius, *HE* (ed. Hansen) 2.28.4 and 2.38.5 lists the following as a signatory bishop of the council of Nicaea: Ἰωάννης Πέρσης ταῖς ἐν Περσίδι πάσῃ καὶ τῇ μεγάλῃ Ἰνδίᾳ. See Schneider, *L'Éthiopie et L'Inde*, 32–33.

[60] Ps.-Gelasius, *HE* (ed. Hansen) 3.9.2–4. Nedungatt, *Quest for the Historical Thomas*, 219 interprets differently.

did not habitually use the terms for peoples or places in east Africa or Arabia, could fall victim to it. Namely, when such authors learned of the evangelization of an "India" from written texts or heard of the existence of "Indian" Christians from oral informants, they assumed that these were references to the subcontinent. Their sources and informants, however, were actually describing the Christian conversion or religiosity of Ethiopians or Arabians. But amid the transmission of information and knowledge, such semantic value for the term "Indian" had been lost due to its fundamental polyvalence.

Many early Christian authors understood that the Indian subcontinent, as "India," was distinct from east Africa and Arabia. Tertullian, Clement of Alexandria, Bardaisan, Ambrose of Milan, John Chrysostom, Jerome, Orosius, and Theodoret are just a few that predate the sixth century CE.[61] But when such authors encountered sources that described east Africa or Arabia as "India," they could misconstrue such unqualified labels as being references to the Indian subcontinent. The fourth-century testimonies of the Christian authors Eusebius and Jerome regarding an Alexandrian named Pantaenus is one key example. According to them, Pantaenus, the head of a catechetical school in Alexandria, traveled to "India," where he discovered that the apostle Bartholomew had already circulated the gospel of Matthew in "Hebrew."[62] This trek putatively occurred in the later second century. Pantaenus' connections to the Indian subcontinent are suggested by the fact that his student Clement, a notable figure of Alexandria, apparently knew the Sanskrit/Prakrit word for Buddhists or ascetics (*sramanas/samanas*), in addition to his knowledge about the Brahmins and a venerable figure called Buddha.[63] Jerome even adds that Pantaenus had preached to Brahmins. Variations on the activity of Bartholomew or Pantaenus appear in many

---

[61] Nedungatt, "India Confused?" 329–35 and *Quest for the Historical Thomas*, 75–79 provides the specifics.

[62] Eusebius, *HE* (ed. Schwartz and Mommsen) 5.10; Jerome, *Illustrious Men* (ed. Ceresa-Gastaldo) 36 and *Ep.* (ed. Hilberg) 70.4. Ramelli, "Missione di Panteno," 45–58 and "Early Christian Missions"; Seland, "Trade and Christianity," 79–80 and "Networks and Social Cohesion," 365–86; McLaughlin, *Roman Empire*, 174. Eusebius, *HE* (ed. Schwartz and Mommsen) 3.39.16 attributes the view that the gospel was written in Hebrew to Papias, who flourished in the first half of the second century. For the Hebrew gospel attributed to Matthew in antiquity, see Edward, *Hebrew Gospel*. Turner, *Matthew*, 15–16 also discusses the late antique tradition that the gospel of Matthew was written in Hebrew.

[63] Schneider, *Die grossen Felsen-Edikte Aśokas*, 76–77 and 118–19 (13Q-R); Clement, *Strom.* (ed. Stählin and Früchtel) 1.15.71.3–6. Eusebius, *HE* (Schwartz and Mommsen) 5.11 claims that Pantaenus was Clement's teacher. Note, however, that Clement knew of the work of Megasthenes and could have gotten information from his tradition. *BNJ/FGrH* 715, T1 and F3a. Reed, "Beyond the Land of Nod," 66–67, n. 78 discusses sramanas/samanas.

other late antique accounts,[64] and the tendency for Jerome elsewhere to distinguish between Ethiopians/Ethiopia and Indians/India could suggest that the sources were describing a trek to the subcontinent.[65] But these accounts were probably just replicating the references to "India" made by the sources that they were consulting, even if their sources were in fact calling Meroitic Ethiopia "India."

Significantly, Eusebius provides no distinguishing information regarding the "India" to which Pantaenus traveled; he merely indicates that Pantaenus had intended to evangelize nations of the "east." It is possible that Eusebius thought that Pantaenus had reached the subcontinental India. But he could very well have been misconstruing a trip to Ethiopia that his sources had described as "India" as a trek to the subcontinent. In either case, Rufinus' translation of Eusebius' passage is more specific in regard to what sort of trip to "India" he deemed Pantaenus to have undertaken. It specifies that Pantaenus had traveled to *India citerior* ("nearer India"), and as we have seen previously, Rufinus uses this term to describe Meroitic Ethiopia while generating a notional distinction between "Ethiopia" and its putatively adjacent "nearer India."[66] Socrates even describes this same India as the "India adjoining Ethiopia" (that is, Meroitic Ethiopia).[67] It is therefore reasonable to surmise that Eusebius, whether he knew it or not, was recounting a mission that allegedly went to Meroitic Ethiopia. But because Jerome was consulting Eusebius or other sources that described Pantaenus' putative ministry in Meroitic Ethiopia as occurring among "Indians," he assumed that Pantaenus had traveled to the subcontinent. He therefore claimed that Pantaenus had preached among the Brahmins.

According to the accounts of both Eusebius and Jerome, Pantaenus discovered that "Indians" possessed a Hebrew gospel of Matthew anteceding the Greek version. It had been brought to them by the apostle Bartholomew. This tradition further suggests that the accounts of Eusebius and Jerome reflect the circulation of a narrative that endowed

---

[64] Schneider, *L'Ethiopie et l'Inde*, 139–41.
[65] Jerome, *Illustrious Men* (ed. Ceresa-Gastaldo) 36; *Ep.* (ed. Hilberg) 70.4. For clear differentiation, *Ep.* (ed. Hilberg) 53.1 and 125.3, for example. Jullien and Jullien, *Apôtres des confins*, 43–53; Ramelli, "Missione de Panteno," 52–58, "Cristianesimo," 104–10 and "Early Christian Missions," 221–31; Tomber, "Bishops and Traders," 225 (but noting the difficulties); Seland, "Trade and Christianity," 79–80 and "Networks, and Social Cohesion," 385–86; Nedungatt, *Quest for the Historical Thomas*, 119–36 and "Christian Origins," 399–422 regard the Indian subcontinent to be the probable referent.
[66] Eusebius, *HE* (ed. Schwartz and Mommsen) 5.10.2; Sozomen, *HE* (ed. Bidez and Hansen) 2.24.1 and Socrates, *HE* (ed. Hansen) 1.19.2; Rufinus, *HE* (ed. Schwartz and Mommsen) 5.10.2 and 10.9. Schneider, *L'Ethiopie et l'Inde*, 140–41.
[67] Socrates, *HE* (ed. Hansen) 1.19.2.

Christianity in Meroitic Ethiopia with a spurious apostolic origin.[68] Whatever the historicity of Pantaenus' trip may have been, the traditions regarding Bartholomew's circulation of the Hebrew gospel written by Matthew reflect how late antique Christians were reconciling the different traditions that had attributed the evangelization of Meroitic Ethiopia to both apostles.[69] In this instance, Bartholomew could receive credit as the first evangelist of Meroitic Ethiopia; Matthew could earn renown as the writer of the text that Bartholomew circulated there. But because the sources for the tradition had described Pantaenus' activity as being in "India," Jerome construed his zone of activity as the subcontinent. Remarkably, a later Greek translator of Jerome transferred Bartholomew's (and thus Pantaenus') activity to Arabia Felix, where it claims that the apostle had conversed with the Indians "called the fortunate."[70] Another late text would shift him to the most remote of three "Indias."[71]

The instability that the terms "Indian" and "India" endured amid their transmission is in fact reflected elsewhere in Jerome's corpus. For example, Jerome claims that Indian and Ethiopian Christians had traveled to Jerusalem or else settled in Palestine.[72] But despite his general tendency to distinguish Ethiopia and the Indian subcontinent, Jerome was describing Aksumite Ethiopians or Arabians as "Indians," just as he had done in his treatment of Pantaenus. By contrast, his reference to Ethiopians denoted either Meroitic Ethiopians, as distinct from Aksumite "Indians," or Aksumite Ethiopians, as distinct from Arabian "Indians." The presence of Aksumite Ethiopian or Arabian Christians in later Roman Palestine in fact receives independent corroboration (unlike those for subcontinental Indians), and whether Jerome had met them or simply had learned of them from other sources, it seems that these were commonly being called "Indians" by Christians of Palestine who encountered them. In turn, Jerome understood their identification as "Indian" to mean that they had originated from the subcontinent. Such tendencies probably informed the fourth-century statement of Epiphanius that merchants sailed from ports of the Sinai peninsula to "India." Even if he was distinguishing the

---

[68] Edward, *Hebrew Gospel* provides analysis, with discussion of Pantaenus (12), patristic witnesses (1–76), and the gospel's link to Matthew (243–52).
[69] Schneider, *L'Ethiopie et l'Inde*, 139–41.
[70] Von Gebhardt, *Hieronymus de viris inlustribus*, 7; Mayerson, "Confusion of Indias," 171–72; Johnson, "Real and Imagined Geography," 411 and *Literary Territories*, 133–37.
[71] This is the text of "ps.-Abdias": *Passion of the Holy Apostle Bartholomew* (ed. Bonnet) esp. 1.
[72] Jerome, *Ep.* (ed. Hilberg) 107.2.3 with 46.10. See Di Segni and Tsafrir, "Ethnic Composition of Jerusalem's Population," 453–54, who comment on Aksumite coin findings in Jerusalem/Palestine from this time.

subcontinent from east Africa or Arabia, the tendency for the sources of such information to call east Africa or Arabia "India" made him believe that "India" referred to the south Asian landmass.[73] The sixth-century CE testimony of the Procopius of Gaza that Indians frequented Jerusalem (or Hierapolis) raises the very same issues.[74]

The treatment of Frumentius' activity among ecclesiastical historians, as previously described, also reflects the instability and semantic drift that the terms "India" and "Indians" endured amid their late antique transmission. As noted previously, the ecclesiastical historians Rufinus, Socrates, Sozomen, and Theodoret all describe the Christian conversion of "farther India" or "inner India," and they depict it as occurring after the apostolic evangelization of Ethiopia by Matthew and "nearer India" or "India adjoining Ethiopia" by Bartholomew.[75] In such instances, Ethiopia and "nearer India" represent a conflation of the same basic place: Meroitic Ethiopia. By contrast, "farther/inner India" was Aksumite Ethiopia. The testimony of Athanasius (written in the late 350s) leaves no doubt. He describes Frumentius, one of his subordinate bishops, as overseeing Aksum, even if he conceives of these recent adherents to Christianity as Indians.[76]

In their description of how Christianity came to Aksum through Frumentius' activity, however, the ecclesiastical historians claim that "farther/inner India" was finally evangelized when a philosopher named Meropius traveled there in the accompaniment of two boys named Aedesius and Frumentius. Abducted by local inhabitants, the two boys worked for the administration of an unnamed king before returning to Tyre and Alexandria respectively. Athanasius of Alexandria then allegedly sent Frumentius back to "inner/farther India" in order to give Christianity a more stable footing. Nothing in these accounts is inconsistent with a Red Sea voyage to Adulis, an overland journey to Aksum, and then a return to Roman Egypt by a port on the Sinai peninsula.[77] On the return trip, Rufinus claims that while Aedesius "hastened" (*festinante*) to Tyre, Frumentius rushed (*pergit*) to Alexandria. Likewise, Sozomen maintains that Frumentius "delayed" or

---

[73] Epiphanius, *Pan.* (ed. Holl) 66.1.8–12. One can remark similarly for the *Itinerary of Antoninus Placentinus* (ed. Geyer) 40 and, later, Peter the Deacon, *Book of Holy Places* (ed. Weber) Y6.
[74] Proc. Gaz., *Pan.* (ed. Kempen) 18. See Jones, "Procopius of Gaza," 455–67 (esp. 456–59).
[75] Rufinus, *HE* (ed. Schwartz and Mommsen) 10.9–10; Socrates, *HE* (ed. Hansen) 1.19; Sozomen, *HE* (ed. Bidez and Hansen) 2.24; Theodoret, *HE* (ed. Parmentier and Hansen) 1.23–24. Also, Ps.-Gelasius, *HE* (ed. Hansen) 3.9; *Chronicle of Pseudo-Dionysius* (also known as *Zuqnin*) (ed. Chabot) 1.162–63.
[76] Athanasius, *Apologia ad Constantium imperatorem* (ed. Brennecke, Heil, and von Stockhausen) 29 and 31, with *Ep. ad Afros* (ed. Brennecke, Heil, and von Stockhausen) 1.2.2–3. Nedungatt, "Christian Origins," 421 interprets differently.
[77] Ramelli, "Cristianesimo," 104–10, and "Early Christian Missions," 228–30 interprets differently.

"deferred" (*anaballomenos*) an itinerary to Tyre and instead went to Alexandria.[78] Such testimony frames the two missionaries as having arrived at a port of the Sinai peninsula, like Clysma and Aila, which were the most active Roman ports on the Red Sea in late antiquity (as the next chapter discusses).

Nonetheless, all these late antique ecclesiastical historians apparently conceived of Frumentius' trip to Aksumite Ethiopia as emulating another figure's journey to an "India" that may have been conceived as the subcontinent. In their accounts, Meropius had brought Frumentius to "inner/farther India" in rivalry with the fourth-century Indian travels of a certain Metrodorus. In late antiquity, Metrodorus was famous for traveling to India, but during his return to the court of Constantine, the king of Persia had confiscated gifts that he had collected. This would suggest that Metrodorus traveled to the subcontinent, although it could mean that he had traveled to east Arabia or the Persian Gulf by crossing Mesopotamia.[79] But due to the fundamental instability of the term "India" during the fourth and fifth centuries, the ecclesiastical historians conceived of Metrodorus' journey to "India" (wherever he went) as being a trip to Aksumite Ethiopia. Accordingly, when they described how Meropius and Frumentius had traveled there, they construed the preachers as emulating Metrodorus' activity.

Conclusion

All told, all the sources analyzed in this chapter simply cannot be deemed reliable historical evidence for the movement of Christianity to India. Even if what they report is accurate, which is often debatable, it is clear that their referent is not the actual subcontinent of India. They were describing journeys and missions to places in east Africa and Arabia that they called "India." Eusebius misconstrues trips to Meroitic Ethiopia ("India") that his sources ascribed to Bartholomew and Pantaenus as treks to the subcontinent. Rufinus, Socrates, and Sozomen undoubtedly described the arrival of Christianity in Aksumite Ethiopia when they narrated the exploits of Frumentius (even if Rufinus conflated it with Arabia). Philostorgius was narrating how Christianity became embedded in south

---

[78] Rufinus, *HE* (ed. Schwartz and Mommsen) 10.9; Sozomen, *HE* (ed. Bidez and Hansen) 2.24.9.
[79] Ramelli, "Cristianesimo, 104–10," and "Early Christian Missions," 228–30. Ammianus (ed. Seyfarth) 25.4.23–24, seems to refer to how Metrodorus ran afoul of Persian authorities during his trek. An account of the trek appears in the Byzantine author Cedrenus; see Warmington, "Ammianus." For the Persian Gulf as "India," see pp. 143, n. 13, and 220.

Arabia and the island of Socotra. The testimony of the *Letter Regarding the Peoples of India and the Brahmins* conflates Arabia and India and Socotra and Sri Lanka, and even as they transpose the entire Red Sea region onto central and south Asia, the *Exposition of the Entire World* and the *Itinerary from Eden* place Christians in east African and Arabian "Indias," not the Indian subcontinent. In his works, Jerome construed his sources' references to Christian Ethiopians and Arabians as "Indians" to be descriptive labels for Indians of the subcontinent due to the semantic instability of the term. As the next chapter stresses, all the late antique sources just mentioned in fact cohere with reliable epigraphic, numismatic, and archaeological evidence for the formation of Christian communities in Aksumite Ethiopia, south Arabia, and Socotra, if not Meroitic Ethiopia as well, by the fourth century CE.[80] Their perspectives are also consistent with the contraction of the Roman Egyptian socio-commercial network after the third century. But they say nothing of value regarding India itself.

Late antique ecclesiastical historians describe how missionaries from the Roman empire, emulating the early apostles, had evangelized various regions of "Indians." But, however reliable their accounts may have been, all of them were in fact referring to phenomena that had putatively occurred in east Africa and Arabia. With these issues in mind, the next chapter illustrates how a Roman Egyptian socio-commercial network in fact transported Christianity to these regions, and explores how it never established Christianity in the Indian subcontinent.

---

[80] Bukharin, "Greeks on Socotra," 493–549; Bowersock, *Throne of Adulis*, 63–91, Power, *Red Sea*, 15–59; Haas, "Mountain Constantines," 111–13; and Phillipson, "Aksoum et le nord," 109–11 and *Foundations*, 91–106; Robin, "Arabia and Ethiopia," 273–81; Richter, "Beginnings of Christianity"; and Dijkstra, "Religious Transformation of Nubia." For evangelizing among the Nobatai during the reign of Justinian, see John of Ephesus, *HE* (ed. Brooks) 4.6.

CHAPTER 3

The Roman Egyptian Network, the Red Sea, and the Indian Ocean

In 70 CE, a Red Sea merchant lingering in the commercial and transport hub of Coptos in Egypt raised a dedicatory inscription in Greek for Isis and Hera.[1] The inscription, however brief, opens an illuminating window to the fascinating movements that facilitated the traffic of commodities, information, credit, and culture between the ancient Mediterranean and Indian Ocean worlds. As it states:

> For the sake of the emperor Caesar Vespasian Augustus and his house, to Isis and Hera, greatest goddesses. Hermeros, son of Athenion, Adenite (*Adaneitēs*), Red Sea merchant (*Erythraios emporos*), year 2, sixteenth day of the month Caesareus-Mesore.[2]

Although lacking in certain explicit points of detail, several features of the inscription demonstrate that it was raised by a Roman Egyptian merchant who resided at a durable residential community at Aden, a port city on the southwest coast of Arabia. Altogether, Hermeros' name and patronym, his use of Greek, his imprecation on behalf of the emperor, and his dating to the second year of the emperor's reign reflect the activity of a Roman imperial subject. As a resident of Aden, Hermeros was accordingly a Roman Egyptian who (or whose ancestors) had established a permanent residency at Aden but whose business activities prompted movement to Red Sea ports, the city of Coptos on the Nile River, and perhaps even Alexandria itself. His example therefore constitutes evidence for the presence of a residential community of Roman Egyptians at the port of Aden, even if it had suffered a brief period of first-century commercial decline.[3]

---

[1] Many parts of this chapter have been reproduced from Andrade, "Drops of Greek," published in *The Journal of Hellenic Studies*. They are reprinted with permission by The Society for the Promotion of Hellenic Studies.
[2] Bernand, *Portes du désert*, no. 65.   [3] *PME* (ed. Casson) 26, in which Casson, *Periplus*, 158–60.

94

The oft-frequented commercial lines extending from Red Sea Egypt to India, in which Hermeros the *Adaneitēs* participated, had the potential to move Christianity to the Indian subcontinent. Their existence ostensibly validates the late antique Christian sources that narrate the movement of Christianity from Red Sea Egypt to "India." For this reason, the activities and practices of merchants in the Red Sea merit scrutiny. Certainly, Roman Egyptian merchants could have transported Christianity to remote locations, but this does not mean that they actually did so. Roman Egyptian merchants in the Red Sea did not necessarily become Christians at an early date, and they therefore may not have begun to carry Christian culture to remote regions until late antiquity. Likewise, the movements and social relations of Roman Egyptian merchants were dynamic. They transformed and shifted over time, and they did not always maintain continual contact with the Indian subcontinent. It is therefore worth analyzing the dispositions of the Roman Egyptian socio-commercial network that extended into the Red Sea and Indian Ocean, and where it carried Christianity before 500 CE.

The Roman Egyptian trade network into the Red Sea and Indian Ocean does not receive the same illumination as the commercial players documented by the medieval Cairo Geniza. But it has nonetheless reaped the benefit of papyrus documents, archaeological work, and an accretion of recent scholarship. As such, this chapter does not aim to provide a comprehensive account of Indo-Mediterranean trade, and it therefore does not treat the nature and volume of the material goods that merchants and their interconnected networks transported between the Indian Ocean and the Mediterranean. It also does not probe the maritime and terrestrial technologies that facilitated it or the histories of all the ports, peoples, and empires that it brought into contact. It instead aims to address one significant issue: the social disposition of the commercial network of the Roman Egyptians that connected Alexandria, the Nilotic-Egyptian hinterland, the Red Sea, and the Indian Ocean. By doing so, this chapter will probe how and when this socio-commercial network transported Christianity from Alexandria and the Sinai peninsula to Nubian Ethiopia, Aksumite Ethiopia, and south Arabia. It also explains how this network did not transport Christianity to India or anchor it among its populations.

But before proceeding, we should clarify a couple points of terminology. A recent study has framed references to Indo-Mediterranean "trade" as problematic and has invoked the variety of forms that material exchange could assume in the Indian Ocean and subcontinent. It even maintains that at least certain peoples of India arguably engaged largely in forms of exchange not determined by price values, like gift-giving and barter, or material redistribution driven by social relations and hierarchies.[4] By this logic, the demand for external Mediterranean commodities could have been low. Scholars may or may not agree with these arguments, but the study reminds us of the immense diversity that characterized the kingdoms, economies, and identities of the various peoples that maintained contact with Roman traders. After all, in antiquity "India" and "Indian" were very broad Greek and Roman categories not indigenous to the subcontinent.[5] But even so, I retain the terms "trade" and "India" for present purposes. These after all reflect the activity and regional perceptions of the Roman Egyptian actors on which this chapter focuses. Finally, what "Roman Egyptian" means in the discussion to follow requires clarification. It must be stressed that "Roman Egyptian" does not constitute an ethnic or cultural category. It merely refers to the Egyptian regional origins of investors, merchants, and sailors that determined their network linkages with one another. What this chapter calls the "Roman Egyptian" network in fact included peoples of various ethnic, linguistic, and cultural persuasions, including the Jews and Palmyrenes of Roman Egypt. It was a diverse and multilingual network, even if Greek was commonly used within it.

Another issue is raised by this chapter's focus on the agency and vantage point of Roman Egyptian sailors, merchants, and travelers. One can perhaps criticize such a framing on many grounds.[6] The ancient Indian Ocean was an intricate web of connected social networks, each with its own regional and social anchorages. The Romans did not necessarily exercise primacy in motivating Indo-Mediterranean trade or even shaping the formation of Red Sea and Indian Ocean polities. The social networks of the Indian Ocean that intersected and interacted with the Roman Egyptian network were in many respects autonomous of it.[7] The material remains of Indian ports often treated as vectors of Indo-Mediterranean trade indicate that local and regional contacts were more intensive and vital. Only a sliver of the Indian Ocean's population had contact with Roman sailors and merchants or even their commodities that circulated. If this chapter focuses on the agency of a Roman Egyptian network, it is largely due to the nature of the textual sources, the specific expertise of the author, and above all the

---

[4] Gurukkal, *Rethinking Classical Indo-Roman Trade*. My thinking has also been shaped by personal conversations with Jeremy Simmons and others on these issues.
[5] Anuja, "British Museum," 259. I have benefited from discussing this with Jeremy Simmons.
[6] Darley, *Indo-Byzantine Exchange*; and Gurukkal, *Rethinking Classical Indo-Roman Trade* inform my considerations in the following paragraph.
[7] For example, see now Beaujard, *Mondes*; and the articles of Mathew, *Imperial Rome*; and Boussac, Salles, and Yon, *Ports*, with the works cited in the previous footnote.

fact that Christianity originated in the Roman Levant and Mediterranean. Barring the remote possibility that Indians or other Indian Ocean peoples adopted Christianity in Egypt or an intermediate location and then carried it to India before c. 500 CE (for which there is no credible evidence), the most obvious carriers of Christian culture from Roman Egypt or the Red Sea would be Roman Egyptians. For these reasons, this chapter will analyze where and with whom Roman Egyptians maintained direct contact and when they first became carriers of Christian culture in sufficient numbers to lay roots for it overseas. But it deems the Roman Egyptian network to be one of many vibrant and dynamic threads of a socially diverse, multi-lingual, and connected Indian Ocean in which local and regional cultures and structures were enduring.

Outline of the Roman Egyptian Network

At the peak of Indo-Mediterranean commerce (first to third centuries CE), Roman Egyptians usually used a trade route that extended from Alexandria.[8] One could sail up the Nile (which was navigable to the first cataract), transfer goods at Coptos or another transit point, and ship them overland to the Red Sea. From Berenike or Myos Hormos, merchants and sailors navigated the Red Sea and its ports. Moving east along south Arabia and the island of Socotra, they caught the monsoon winds during the late summer to north or south India, where they could navigate the Indian coast. They sailed west on the monsoon winds around January and made their return trip to the ports of Red Sea Egypt. From them commodities were transported to the Nile and shipped downriver to Alexandria. (Map 2)

A substantial portion of the cargo that the Roman Egyptian merchants acquired from Red Sea and Indian Ocean regions was eventually distributed to markets of the Mediterranean or the Egyptian hinterland. But most of it entered or passed through Alexandria, which constituted a vast market for consumption and a key hub of distribution for the goods that traveled elsewhere. In fact, since a round trip between Alexandria and India could occur within a year, while one between Italy and India could not, Alexandria was the central hub for merchants and investors whose commodities would eventually be transferred to Puteoli, Ostia, and Rome.[9] Such elements of long-distance trade should not prompt one to overlook the dense ties of local and regional connectivity that commerce prompted.

[8] The commercial route has been widely discussed in scholarship. See the references in n. 14-18 and 22.
[9] Cobb, "Exchange of Goods," esp. 107.

While the modalities of long-distance transit trade attract notice, the bulk of trade in Roman Egypt, as in most ancient societies, involved the trafficking and distribution of locally or regionally produced items for local, regional, or interregional markets.[10] Such was the tendency even among late antique Sogdians, the various commercial populations of the "Silk Road," and Jews of medieval North Africa.[11] Due to the primarily local and regional dimensions of trade, many Roman Egyptian merchants with aspirations of trading outside Egypt still oriented their activity on a primary commercial hub, like Alexandria, and the goods that could be produced or refined in the Egyptian hinterland. Their direct contacts outside the province extended to Rome, other sites of the Mediterranean, the Levant, or the Red Sea.[12]

Nonetheless, certain Roman Egyptian traders were more focused on acquiring, transporting, and distributing long-distance transit products originating from far eastern lands for Mediterranean markets. These merchants were embedded in a long-distance network that consisted in part of residential communities of Roman Egyptians (including Jews and expatriate Palmyrenes) living in the Red and Arabian Seas. Their intercrossed links and social relations facilitated the circulation of information, credit, cargo, bodies, and culture to and from the network's hub at Alexandria. They also generated trust among its members that their contacts would discharge reciprocal obligations despite the separation of distance. As anchor points, residential settlements enabled both people and culture to become established firmly in new localities, and as routing stations, they channeled the movement of information, commodities, credit, resources, and reciprocal obligations to and from the primary nodes.[13] But due in part to the activity of itinerant players who moved among the network's residential communities, the Roman Egyptian network was very much a "circulation society" that remained firmly connected

---

[10] Alston, "Trade and the City," 168–202, esp. 169–71, 182–86, and 192–98. Adams, *Land Transport in Roman Egypt*, 220–82; Gibbs, "Manufacture, Trade, and the Economy." For shifts in the tax structure, land tenure, and agricultural production from the Ptolemies to the Romans, see Monson, *From the Ptolemies to the Romans*.

[11] On the local and regional trade of Sogdians, which intersected with the transcontinental network that Sogdians formed for transit trade, see de la Vaissière, *Sogdian Traders*, esp. 165–67 and 186–90, with Hansen, *Silk Road*, 138–39, 196, and 235–42. On medieval Jews in a similar light, see Goldberg, *Trade and Institutions*," 211–46, esp. 214–15, with "Choosing and Enforcing Business."

[12] Noy, *Foreigners at Rome*, 245–51 and 298–300 (Rome); and Terpstra, *Trading Communities*, 120–123 (Egyptians and other foreigners at Ostia).

[13] Here I borrow the language of Aslanian, *From the Indian Ocean*, 15–16.

to its central hub (Alexandria).[14] For many centuries, it extended directly to India.

The empirical basis for reconstructing the Roman Egyptian socio-commercial network will be analyzed in this chapter, but for present purposes its basic dispositions can be outlined here. Environmental factors in Roman Egypt ensured that the bulk of transit commodities that arrived at Red Sea ports would be transported overland to the Nile, shipped along the river to Alexandria, and then undergo further distribution. Even if a canal meaningfully connected the Mediterranean to the Red Sea via Clysma, the unfavorable winds of the north Red Sea ensured that returning ships would dock farther south, at Berenike or Myos Hormos. The road to Coptos and the Nile would in turn be the primary conduits for the return trip.[15] Inscribed *ostraka* fragments demonstrate that a certain Nicanor maintained a thriving transport business for goods moving between Coptos and Myos Hormos and Berenike during the first century CE.[16] Commodities could also be shipped overland to the Nile farther south by roads; el-Kanais was a key transit point and watering station in that regard.[17] Similarly, export goods exited Egypt through these same ports, or they could be shipped from the Sinai peninsula harbors of Clysma or even Aila. But Alexandria was the primary place through which these goods traveled or through the activity of whose commercial investors such commodities were moved to the Red Sea. For this reason, merchants and investors there were the hub for the socio-commercial network involved in Red Sea and Indian Ocean transit trade, with Coptos on the Nile being a key transit point. While the diverse links of the Roman Egyptian network extended to various parts of the Mediterranean, Red Sea, and the Indian Ocean, they all converged at Alexandria.

But the Roman Egyptian network had mobile and expatriate elements too. Consisting of Roman Egyptian merchants (including Jews and Palmyrenes)

---

[14] Seland, "Networks and Social Cohesion," 375–81, and "Persian Gulf or Red Sea?" informs my analysis. See Aslanian, *From the Indian Ocean*, 15–16, for "circulation society."

[15] Sidebotham, *Berenike*, 179–82, and "Roman Ports" 132–39; Young, *Rome's Eastern Trade*, 75–78; and Aubert, "Trajan's Canal" discuss the canal. It could only be used during the Nile's inundation (September to December/January), which contrasted with the conventional July departure for India, even if Arabia and east Africa were accessible. For textual references, see Ptolemy, *Geog.* (Stückelberger and Graßhoff) 4.5; and Pliny, *NH* (ed. Jahn and Mayhoff) 6.33. Noticeably, Lucian, *Alex.* (ed. Macleod) 44 suggests that one could travel up the Nile to Clysma and then sail from there to India.

[16] The business of a certain Nicanor, son of Panis is best attested in this regard. Fuks, "Notes on the Archives of Nicanor," 207–16. The *ostraka* that provide documentation are O. Petr. 220–305. McLaughlin, *Roman Empire*, 80–81 discusses them.

[17] Sidebotham, *Berenike*, 126–76 and 212–20; and McLaughlin, *Roman Empire*, 79–86, treat such overland travel.

who traveled vast distances within the geographic span between the central hub of Alexandria, the Egyptian hinterland, the Red Sea basin, and even India, these also integrated residential communities that had formed within Red Sea and Arabian Sea ports in order to facilitate the movement of products, information, and people. Due to such long-distance networking and movement, merchants were able to arrange the seaborne transportation of goods from Indian Ocean sites to Red Sea harbors, their overland trek to Coptos, their river-ferried journey along the Nile, their arrival in Alexandria, and perhaps their distribution farther afield in the Mediterranean.[18] The anchor points that such merchants established in overseas ports also facilitated the movement of information, credit, bodies, commodities, and culture throughout a socio-commercial network (or circulation society) involving various dispersed overseas residential communities with links to one another. All such nodes were ultimately linked to the primary hub of Alexandria.[19]

Certainly, once Christianity had penetrated the Roman Egyptian circulation society that effectively connected the Mediterranean basin to the Red Sea and Indian Ocean worlds, it was quickly transported to Red Sea and Arabian Sea locations by the bodies of its traders. These bodies then transferred Christian culture to the bodies of contacts embedded in other socio-commercial networks, like those of Aksumite Ethiopians and south Arabians. But in order to evaluate when and how this process occurred, certain other factors require exploration. One is the issue of when exactly the itinerant merchants and residential communities of the Roman Egyptian network had become Christian in sufficient numbers to embed Christianity in new locations. Another is whether this network established actual residential communities in ports of the Indian subcontinent. Finally, a key problem is whether the network continuously extended to India directly or actually terminated at the threshold of the Red and Arabian Seas. At this chapter argues, Christianity had not yet penetrated this network during the period of its fullest extent to the Indian coast, between the first century BCE and the late third century CE. By the time that it did (during the mid-fourth century CE), it terminated in the ports and immediate hinterlands of Aksumite Ethiopia, south Arabia, and Socotra, where it transported and rooted Christianity in new bodies and socio-commercial networks. But the

---

[18] See Sidebotham, *Berenike*, 195–220, generally regarding ship sizes, transports costs, cargo costs, and funding.

[19] The Roman Egyptian network in this way shares many features with the early modern Julfa Armenian network. Aslanian, *From the Indian Ocean*, 14–16 and 86–165 (for empirical grounding among Julfa Armenian merchants).

Roman Egyptian circulation society no longer extended to India directly, and it therefore did not carry Christianity there.

Indo-Mediterranean Trade and Its Evidence

During the first through third centuries CE, Romans sailing from the Red Sea were certainly in direct contact with merchants and residents from various empires and realms of India. Along with the Kushans of north India, these included the territories of the Saka Kshatrapas located on the west coast of India roughly between the Indus River region and the Gulf of Barygaza; the Satavahana realm of the central Deccan plateau; the Chera, Chola, and Pandya realms of south India; and the Anuradhapura and other principalities of Sri Lanka.[20] Roman Egyptians also frequented ports in the south Arabian kingdoms of Saba, Himyar, and Hadramawt.[21] Due to archaeological illumination and scholarly attention, increased knowledge of the transit trade between the Mediterranean and these various Indian and Arabian kingdoms has emerged in recent years. A spate of excavations in Red Sea, Arabian Sea, and Indian ports has in fact yielded ample finds that illuminate the ebb and flow of trans-imperial commerce.[22] These materials in many respects cohere with the testimony of literary sources for the Roman imperial period, especially Strabo's *Geography*, the anonymous *Periplus of the Erythraean Sea*, and Pliny's *Natural History*, as well as the testimony of Dio of Prusa and Martial regarding Indians and Bactrians

---

[20] For discussion and analysis, see McLaughlin, *Rome and the Distant East*, 42–57, and *Roman Empire*, 113–206; Sidebotham, "Red Sea and Indian Ocean," 1056–59; Thapar, *Early India*, 217–34.

[21] Sidebotham, "Red Sea and Indian Ocean," 1046–48; McLaughlin, *Roman Empire*, 128–49.

[22] The bibliography and archaeological evidence for such movement of objects, especially coins, ceramic vessels, and botanical materials (particularly for the port of Berenike) is increasingly vast. Some examples are Tomber, "Rome and Mesopotamia," *Indo-Roman Trade*, "Beyond Western India," and "From the Roman Red Sea to Beyond"; Selvakumar, Shajan, and Tomber, "Archaeological Investigations," 29–41; Sidebotham, *Berenike*, esp. 175–94 and 203–58, "Red Sea and Indian Ocean," and "Roman Ports"; Peacock and Blue, *Myos Hormos–Quseir al-Quadim*; Sedov and Salles, "Place of Qâni'"; Salles and Sedov, *Qâni'*; Decker, "Settlement and Trade"; Suresh, *Symbols of Trade* and *Arikamedu*; Beaujard, *Mondes*, 1.354–91; Ray, "Inscribed Pots, Emerging Identities," 113–44; Schiettecatte, "L'Arabie du Sud," 237–73; Power, *Red Sea*, 12–59; Seland, *Ports and Political Power*; Cohen, *Hellenistic Settlements in Syria*, 306–344 (for Hellenistic Red Sea settlements); Seland, "Archaeology of Trade" and *Ports and Political Power*; Mairs, "Glassware from Roman Egypt"; Cobb, "Exchange of Goods" and "Balancing the Trade"; Bellina and Glover, "Archaeology of Early Contact" (from a southeast Asian perspective); de Romanis and Maiuro, *Across the Ocean*; Mathew, *Imperial Rome*; Boussac, Salles, and Yon, *Autour* and *Ports* (which contains numerous articles on the Godavaya shipwreck); Gurukkal, *Rethinking Classical Indo-Roman Trade*; Seland, "*Periplus of the Erythraean Sea*"; Darley, *Indo-Byzantine Exchange*; Tchernia, *Romans and Trade*, 39–50 and 229–47. The list is not comprehensive, and other works are cited as appropriate.

at Alexandria and Rome.[23] They also coincide with the famous "Muziris papyrus," a second-century document that sheds light on how the cargo of a ship was transported between the Red Sea and Alexandria.[24]

As inscriptions and papyri from Roman Egypt show, Romans traveled to India. A certain Gaius Numidius Eros even carved a Latin inscription at a grotto on the road between Berenike and Coptos in 2 BCE, and in it he claimed that he had returned from India. A document listing tax exemptions places a Roman Egyptian in India in 72/73 CE, and at some point in the late Ptolemaic or early Roman imperial period, a figure named Sophon claimed in an inscription between Berenike and Edfu that he was an *Indos*. In this instance, *Indos* could refer to his regional background, his occupational status as a driver of elephants, or his status as a Greek-speaking Roman Egyptian residing in India.[25] Whatever this inscription's significance may be, Pliny notably describes an imperial freedman of a certain Annius Plocamus who traveled to Sri Lanka, and this name corresponds with that of a figure whose slave left rock-cut graffiti in Greek and Latin on the road between Coptos and Berenike, precisely where the Gaius Numidius Eros, mentioned above, cut his graffito.[26] The link between these different attestations for a figure or figures named Annius Plocamus is yet unclear, but they certainly document direct contact with India.[27] In this vein, it is worth noting that studies focusing on the ancient ports of the Bay of Bengal sometimes report that a Greek inscription made by a sailor on a terracotta plaque was found near

---

[23] Strabo (ed. Radt) 2.3.4–5 and 2.5.12; Bukharin, "Greeks on Socotra," 510–11. Strabo claims that he witnessed 120 ships departing from Myos Hormos when Gallus was governor (29–26 BCE), and he indicates that a certain Eudoxus also tried to circumnavigate Africa to reach India; he did not succeed despite the success that Herodotus (4.4) reports regarding Phoenicians employed by the Persian monarchy. The *Periplus of the Erythraean Sea (PME)*, probably composed in the late first century CE (see pp. 117-18, n. 98), provides an itinerary for sailors of the Red Sea and Indian Ocean involved in trade between Roman Egypt and India. Pliny, *NH* (ed. Jahn and Mayhoff) 6 (esp. 104–106) treats Roman trade with India and Sri Lanka. Dio Chry. (ed. de Arnim) 32.40 and 32.43, with perhaps 72.3; and Martial (ed. Shackleton-Bailey) 7.30. McLaughlin, *Roman Empire*, 106–7, provides key discussion. For Ptolemaic contact with India, see Habicht, "Eudoxus of Cyzicus."

[24] P. Vindob G 40822=*SB* XVIII 13167. Thür, "Hypotheken-Urkunde," 229–45; Casson, "New Light," 195–206; Rathbone, "'Muziris' Papyrus," 39–50; Seland, "Ports, Ptolemy," 77–78; Sidebotham, *Berenike*, 217–19; Morelli, "Dal Mar Rosso"; and de Romanis, "Playing Sudoku" and "Comparative Perspectives," with bibliography, discuss the famous "Muziris papyrus," which documents the movement of objects from Muziris to Alexandria via a Red Sea port.

[25] Meredith, "Inscriptions," 281–87=Bernand, *Portes du Désert*, no. 64; *P. Lond.* 2.260, col. 3, line 42; Bernand, *Paneion*, no. 38. Sidebotham, *Roman Economic Policy*, 101; Strauch, "Socotra and the 'Indian Connection'," 371–72; Parker, *Making of Roman India*, 74 and 81–82.

[26] Pliny, *NH* (ed. Jahn and Mayhoff) 6.84; Meredith, "Two Inscriptions."

[27] De Romanis, "Romanukharaṭṭha and Taprobane," 167–71 (esp. 167–71 and 188); Tchernia, *Romans and Trade*, 43–44 and 46.

Tamluk. But its location is now unknown, and its reading has not been verified by epigraphers.[28]

The excavations at Arikamedu, located not far from the sacred site of Thomas' tomb at Mylapore, have revealed that the site was a key emporium during the first century CE, and Roman ceramic remains have surfaced there.[29] Roman coins certainly circulated in India and had a material and cultural impact on coins of the subcontinent.[30] Excavations at south Indian sites like Pattanam (probably ancient Muziris), among many others, have yielded Roman ceramic finds.[31] So far, inscribed pottery and graffiti found at Berenike have contained a dozen different languages; Ethiopic, south Arabian, Tamil, Sanskrit and the various languages normally written in Roman Egypt and the eastern Roman empire (Greek, Aramaic, Syriac, Hebrew, and Latin) are represented.[32] Similar forms of writing, including Prakrit and Tamil, have been found at Myos Hormos.[33] These inscriptions suggest a multiethnic presence at Egyptian Red Sea ports if one accepts that the vessels had been inscribed at the location where their fragments were found. A papyrus from Oxyrhynchus containing part of a burlesque of the Euripidean play *Iphigenia in Tauris* known as the "Charition mime" is set in India, and scholars have debated whether the Indian characters speak gibberish or actual Indian languages. If involving coherent spoken lines in a south Asian tongue, it is possible that the performance of the play included Indian actors or reflects authors or actors who were conversant in such languages.[34] Roman novels and poetry represent Indians (with

---

[28] Ghosh, "Museums and Exhibitions," 59–64; Chakrabarti, *Archaeological Geography*, 150–51, and "Relating History," 10–11; Tripati, Patnaik, and Pradhan, "Maritime Trade Contacts," 227. The inscription was reportedly found at the port site of Tildah, brought to the Asutosh museum of Calcutta, and translated by a Christian priest, who deemed it a religious dedication for the East Wind and the Dawn. I thank Roberta Tomber for providing helpful correspondence on this matter.

[29] Tomber, *Indo-Roman Trade*, 133–37; Begley et al., *Ancient Port of Arikamedu*; Gurukkal, *Rethinking Classical Indo-Roman Trade*, 32–33; Suresh, *Arikamedu*, 39–62.

[30] Turner, *Roman Coins*; de Romanis, "*Aurei*"; Falk, "Indian Gold," 106–113; Cobb, "Balancing the Trade," 187–93; Suresh, *Symbols of Trade*, 26–88; Gurukkal, *Rethinking Classical Indo-Roman Trade*, 47–52; Darley, *Indo-Byzantine Exchange*, including Appendix 6.

[31] For excavations, see n. 42 and 89 for Cherian's publications; Selvakumar, Shajan, and Tomber, "Archaeological Investigations." Suresh, *Symbols of Trade*, 89–122; and Tomber, *Indo-Roman Trade* account for the evidence available at the time of publication. Also see Gurukkal, *Rethinking Classical Indo-Roman Trade*, 29–32.

[32] Thomas, "Port Communities," 172; and Sidebotham, "Reflections of Ethnicity," 105–115, and "Roman Ports," 157–58, with n. 105. Many documents can be found in Bagnall, Helms, Verhoogt, et al., *Documents from Berenike*.

[33] Salomon, "Epigraphic Remains," with Sidebotham, "Roman Ports," 147, n. 73; and Tomber et al., "Pots with Writing." Mahadevan, *Early Tamil Epigraphy*, 49–50, includes most Tamil inscriptions from Roman Egypt and elsewhere in the Roman world.

[34] For in-depth discussion of the papyrus (*P. Oxy.* 413) and mime, see now Hall, *Adventures*, 111–35 (esp. 130–35).

uncertain reliability) as merchants living in Egypt or slaves throughout the Roman Mediterranean; Indian plays sometimes make references to or provide stage directions for Yavana ("Greek" or "foreigner") slave characters too.[35] Along with Tamil inscriptions on pottery fragments, material evidence for differences of consumption, diet, and technology suggest that various quarters of Myos Hormos and Berenike held foreign residential communities.[36] The presence of Indian tableware at Berenike, a ceramic arguably not intended for circulation, would seem to support that Indians resided at Red Sea ports.[37]

Much of the existing evidence can be ambiguous in its significance. Inscribed ceramic fragments and the presence of different material practices in circumscribed locations do not conclusively reflect ethnicity or illuminate different ethnic communities at ports. Similarly, objects produced for circulation, such as coins, transport pottery, and commodities, could have traveled well beyond the actual movements of their initial carriers. For this reason, it is significant that rock-carved graffiti demonstrate that Indians navigated common sacred space with Roman Egyptians, south Arabians, Aksumite Ethiopians, and Palmyrenes in a sacred grotto on the island of Socotra.[38] One of the visitors to the island may have been from the Kushan empire.[39] Clearly, travelers of diverse origins were in contact on the island. The activity of Indian traders from Barygaza, a well-known emporium for Roman sailors, is especially well attested on the island.[40] Palmyrene traders were certainly on the move in Roman Red Sea Egypt, south Arabia, the island of Socotra, north India, and the Persian

---

[35] For example, Horace, *Serm.* (ed. Shackleton-Bailey) 2.8.14 (slave named Hydaspes); Martial (ed. Shackleton-Bailey) 7.30; Tibullus (ed. Luck) 2.3.58; Juvenal (ed. Willis) 6.585, but the key word may be read "*inde*" not *Indus* (ed. Labriolle and Villeneuve); Philostratus, *VS* (ed. Kayser) 552–53; Kalidasa, *Vikramorvasiyam*, Act 5, and *Sakuntala*, Acts 2 and 6 in Vol. 1 of Devadhar, *Works*. McLaughlin, *Roman Empire*, 107–8 and 166, provides key discussion for Indians and other eastern or African peoples.

[36] Thomas, "Port Communities," discusses, with Sidebotham, "Reflections of Ethnicity," 105–115.

[37] Sidebotham, *Berenike*, 231, and "Roman Ports," 159–60. I thank Steven Sidebotham for also discussing this matter with me.

[38] These are now compiled in Strauch, *Foreign Sailors on Socotra*, with valuable commentary by scholars from diverse fields. See Strauch et al., "Catalogue."

[39] A short graffito containing a Bactrian personal name in both Greek and Brahmi script has been found on the island of Socotra (in the cave Hoq). Strauch et al., "Catalogue," 202–203 (16.8) is the Greek and Bactrian (Brahmi) inscription of Humiyaka, who bears a distinctly Iranian name. This is presumably the same figure who also made an inscription (14:13, 179–80 in a similar hand) in Middle Indic (Brahmi) and who is identified by the Sanskrit inscription (in a different hand) made by the "son of the captain Humiyaka" in the same cave (180–81, 14:15). See Strauch, "Indian Participants," 349.

[40] The cities of Barygaza (Bharukaccha) and Astakpra (Hastakavapra) are particularly well represented by Indian merchants on Socotra. Strauch, "Indian Participants," 344–45.

Gulf, although it is not clear how routine their direct travel between the Red Sea and Persian Gulf was.[41] It nonetheless remains uncertain whether or to what extent Roman settlers established residential communities in Indian ports, and the volume of movement between the Red Sea and south Asia is very difficult to calculate.[42] Many Roman Egyptian sailors may have had terminal points in south Arabia, a central location for frankincense and myrrh and a transit center for goods coming from India.[43] Some recent scholarship has asserted that market- or price-based "trade," as opposed to other forms of exchange structured by prevailing social relations, did not play a significant role in some Indian economies and that peoples of the subcontinent thus did not establish stable commercial networks that extended to Roman Egypt.[44] But Indian sailors certainly frequented Socotra, which Arabian, Ethiopian, and Roman Egyptians visited too.[45] We have already noted how they can arguably be placed at Berenike on the basis of ceramic tableware found there.[46] But altogether the connectivity of the Red Sea and Indian Ocean worlds is certain, and Roman sailors apparently sometimes even penetrated the Bay of Bengal and beyond.[47]

Unfortunately, many Indian sources, like the north Indian *Arthashastra* or the later copper and stone inscriptions of the south Indian Pallavas, make no specific mention of sailors from the Roman empire.[48] The guilds

---

[41] Gorea, "Palmyrene Tablette" and "Sea and Inland Trade."
[42] The Peutinger map places a temple of Augustus at Muziris, which can be identified with Pattanam, where excavations have produced Roman coins and ceramics. But the significance of the map is unclear. Gurukkal and Whittaker, "In Search of Muziris," 334–50; Young, *Rome's Eastern Trade*, 30–31; Fauconnier, "Graeco-Roman Merchants," 92–93. For Pattanam as Muziris, see Selvakumar, Shajan, and Tomber, "Archaeological Investigations," 29–41; Cherian, *Pattanam Excavations, Interim Report*, and *Unearthing Pattanam*; and Tomber, "Roman Pottery." Parker, *Making of Roman India*, 246, discusses the temple and map, and he also sees such a representation of India as part of the Romans' mental map of empire, even if the Roman empire did not enact political and military control and administration. Similarly, Talbert, *Rome's World*, 122 and 142–47. An objection to the premise that the Romans established a temple to Augustus at Muziris based on the Peutinger map was raised as early as Ray, *Winds of Change*, 66. Fauconnier, "Graeco-Roman Merchants," 90–92, discusses other interpretations that need not be treated here. Seland, "Ports, Ptolemy," 78, treats the map as inconclusive. For volume, Cobb, "Balancing the Trade," provides recent treatment.
[43] Peacock and Williams, "Introduction," 1–3; and Peacock, Williams, and James, "Basalt as Ships' Ballast," 28–70, esp. 28 and 59–63. Selvakumar, Shajan, and Tomber, "Archaeological Investigations," esp. 34–35. Shipwrecks discovered in the northern Red Sea unfortunately do not clarify ultimate destinations. Blue, Hill, and Thomas, "New Light," 91–100.
[44] Gurukkal, *Rethinking Classical Indo-Roman Trade*, 200–48 (esp. 248).
[45] Strauch, *Foreign Sailors on Socotra*.   [46] Sidebotham, *Berenike*, 231. See n. 37.
[47] Ptolemy's source, Marinos, was citing a certain figure named Alexander, who was presumably connected to Indian Ocean commerce. Ptolemy, *Geog.* (ed. Stückelberger and Graßhoff) 1.14 (Alexander), 7.1 (India, west of Ganges), 7.2 (India east of the Ganges), 7.3 (eastern lands). McLaughlin, *Rome and the Distant East*, 57–59: east of India.
[48] Mahalingam, *Inscriptions*; Francis, *Discours*; Sastri, *History of South India*, 101–13. For the *Arthashastra*, a guide to statesmanship that outlines modes of tariff collection that could have

of merchants and artisans and religious communities attested for later periods (the *anjuvannam, manigrammam, nanadesis*, and *ayyavole*) do not have strong documentation in the period under present discussion.[49] But possible exceptions are notable. Intriguingly, Tamil poems describe how Yavanas, a word for Greeks or foreigners in south Asian languages, frequented the ports of south India, especially Muziris, to which they brought wine and gold, and from which they transported pepper. Yavanas are also recorded as being residents of south India, where they worked as mercenaries or guards and sometimes manned ships with the swan-neck sterns that graced Mediterranean vessels.[50] It is unclear whether these Yavanas were always Roman Egyptians or simply "foreigners." According to the conventional dating, references to Yavanas who trade appear in the earlier poems, but the material depicting them as residential settlers and mercenaries tends to be later. It should however be noted that at least one scholar controversially dates the poems to the early medieval period of south India; this would undermine their value for early periods of Indo-Mediterranean trade.[51] The literary nature of the poems also raises issues for their reliability.[52]

been relevant to Roman sailors and merchants at Barbarikon and inland Minnagar, see McLaughlin, *Roman Empire*, 151–55.

[49] Sastri, *History of South India*, 164 and 200; Singh, *History*, 602; Wink, *Al-Hind*, 71 and 101; Malekandathil, *Maritime India*, 41; Narayanan, *Perumals of Kerala*, 277–84. For exchange and Indian economies before medieval times, see now Gurukkal, *Rethinking Classical Indo-Roman Trade*, esp. 200–91.

[50] See Zvelebil, "Yavanas," 401–9, who quotes significant passages and discusses the problems. Also, Seland, "Ports, Ptolemy," 71–72; Beaujard, *Mondes*, 1.370–71; Fauconnier, "Graeco-Roman Merchants," 95–97; Tomber, *Indo-Roman Trade*, 26–29, provides summary of the Tamil literature, including the *Sangam* poems, the post-*Sangam* Tamil epics, and bibliography; McLaughlin, *Rome and the Distant East*, 53–57, and *Roman Empire*, 98, 172–73, 182–83, and 200–1, cites many passages of Tamil literature that refer to Yavanas; Gurukkal, *Rethinking Classical Indo-Roman Trade*, 82–90, also discusses and comments on often overlooked weaknesses of the poems. Some frequently cited passages are: *Akananuru* 149.7–11 (Yavanas come to Muziris with gold, return with pepper), from de Romanis, "Rome and the *Notia*," 98 and 107–8; *Purananuru* 56.18–21 (wine of the Yavanas) and 343. 1–10 (pepper purchases), from Hart and Heifetz, *Four Hundred Songs*, 43 and 195–96; *Patirruppattu* 2.4–10 (attacks against Yavanas), from Zvelebil, "Yavanas," 404; *Perumpanarruppatai* 316–18 (Yavanas and swan-neck sterns), from Zvelebil, "Yavanas," 405; *Silappatikaram* 5.9–12 (abodes of Yavanas) and 14.66–67 (Yavanas as guards or mercenaries); *Mullaippattu* 59–62 (Yavanas as guards or mercenaries), from de Romanis, "Rome and the *Notia*," 104–5, 116–17, and 151. For additional references to Yavanas as artisans, see Zvelebil, "Yavanas," 406–407 and McLaughlin, *Roman Empire*, 182–83. The first four poems cited date probably to 150 CE or somewhat later. *Silappatikaram* most probably dates to the fifth century while integrating earlier material. *Mullaippattu* was composed c. 230 CE. Zvelebil, *Tamil Literature*, 78–115 (esp. 78–79, 107, and 110–15); and Hart, *Poems 7–12* represent standard dating.

[51] Tieken, *Kavya in South India* and "Old Tamil Cankam Literature." This view is criticized by Hart, "Review" and often dismissed (as in Selby, *Tamil Love Poetry*, 3-4). But see Darley, *Indo-Byzantine Exchange*, 352–59. Shulman, *Tamil*, 66–106 (esp. 82 and 105) stakes out a middle position.

[52] Darley, "Self, Other, and Use," 66–67, with n. 22.

Similarly, some Buddhists who made dedicatory inscriptions in Sanskrit or Prakrit (in Brahmi script) at monasteries in the western Ghats called themselves Yavanas or Yonakas during the first and second centuries CE (and perhaps earlier).[53] While sometimes believed to be traders from Roman Egypt, these could have been residents of areas near the Gulf of Barygaza who had links to the Greek Yavanas who had settled north India.[54] They in fact noticeably used forms of self-ascription similar to that (*Yona*) attested on the famous pillar that a certain Heliodoros, an ambassador from Taxila, raised at the court site of an Indian king near Besnagar in the late second century BCE.[55] In other words, such Buddhists were perhaps linked in some way to prior Greek residents of north India, but they or their ancestors had settled near the Gulf of Barygaza and the western Ghats, where they were living in the first and second centuries CE.

Certain factors support this interpretation. First, the overall absence of Greek or Roman cultural idioms in the inscriptions suggests that the Buddhists who made them belonged to populations that had participated in the cultural mainstream of north or west India for centuries. Elsewhere, Roman travelers, settlers, or soldiers maintained some connection to Greek, Latin, or other languages of the Roman empire, even if outside it.[56] The Yavanas living near the Gulf of Barygaza and the western Ghats, by contrast, bear hardly any traces of Mediterranean culture, and their assimilation into the cultural mainstreams of west India suggest that their ancestors had been in the subcontinent for numerous generations, if not centuries. Second, the Gulf of Barygaza was situated on arteries that were connected to the major thoroughfares that linked north and south India and especially facilitated the movement and networking of Buddhists from

---

[53] Lerner, "Greek Indians of Western India" for texts and analysis. For dating, see Shinde, "Early Historic Junnar"; Shinde et al., "Junnar"; and Ray, "King and Monastery."

[54] Lerner, "Greek Indians of Western India," posits links with Greek Yavanas of north India. McLaughlin, *Rome and the Distant East*, 46–59, and *Roman Empire*, 170–71; Fauconnier, "Graeco-Roman Merchants," 97–101; Thapar, "Early Mediterranean Contacts," esp. 34–35, and *Early India*, 241–43, and 260–67; Neelis, *Early Buddhist Transmission*, 106–7 and 205–17; Ghosh, "Understanding Transitions," 291; Gurukkal, *Rethinking Classical Indo-Roman Trade*, 39–42, provide varied viewpoints on the term or note its relative instability.

[55] Salomon, *Indian Epigraphy*, 265–66; *IGSK* 65.409; and Mairs, *Hellenistic Far East*, 117–33 (119 for text). The term "Yona" appears for Greeks in the Prakrit texts of Asoka's edicts. Schneider, *Grossen Felsen-Edikte Asokas*, 25, 39, 76–77, and 104–7, 118–19 (2A, 5J, 13Q-R).

[56] For Roman Greek inscriptions on Socotra and in south Arabia, see Bukharin, "Greek Inscriptions at Hoq" and "Greeks on Socotra," 531–37. For Latin inscriptions of south Arabia (esp. the Farasan Islands), see Phillips, Villeneuve, and Fahey, "A Latin Inscription from South Arabia"; Villeneuve, "Farasan Inscriptions"; Speidel, "Ausserhalb des Reiches?"; and Nappo, "Roman Policy," 65–68. Other Greek and Greek-Latin inscriptions of south Arabia are *IGSK* 65.435–438; and Marek, "Roman Period Inscription."

north India.⁵⁷ Yavanas living near the Gulf of Barygaza and the western Ghats thus could have called themselves by a name that Greek Yavanas of north India had previously put in circulation, even if they did not think of themselves as Greeks in a meaningful sense at all. It is even possible that Buddhist networks helped shape the movement of Yavana settlers from north India to places farther south. Indeed, in one inscription (at Nasik, Cave 17), a Buddhist describes his father as a Yonaka and a "northerner" from "Datamitiyaka." The location of "Datamitiyaka" is uncertain, but this figure clearly had roots in north India.⁵⁸

In other words, the Yavanas or Yonakas near the Gulf of Barygaza and the western Ghats during the first and second centuries CE, if anything, had inherited their name from Greek settlers of north India. For this reason, it should be borne in mind that in many instances Sanskrit/Prakrit inscriptions and Tamil poems could be making references to such Yavanas, not necessarily Roman Egyptian traders. Unfortunately, the poems are not always descriptive of the origins of Yavanas. One Tamil poem apparently refers to how a Chera king engaged in military exploits in the land of the Yavanas, which is described as both mountainous and fertile. Some have seen this as a reference to the Hindu Kush and Kushan kingdom.⁵⁹ These Yavanas are also described in the passage as being of barbarian speech, but for Tamil authors, this could refer to speakers of Sanskrit/Prakrit.

It is also worth noting that the Yavanas near the Gulf of Barygaza were not the only people in the area to bear an ethnic label previously used by settlers of north India. An inscription made by a Satavahana king in the western Ghats c. 100 CE or perhaps a bit later (in Cave 3 of Nasik) describes how a predecessor had wrested the region from the Saka Kshatrapas and therein credits him with crushing the "Sakas, Yavanas, and Pahlavas."⁶⁰ All of these were peoples who had had once ruled north India (modern scholars sometimes call Pahlavas "Indo-Parthians"),⁶¹ but in the first

---

⁵⁷ For discussion, see Neelis, *Early Buddhist Transmission*, 183–217.
⁵⁸ Lerner, "Greek Indians of Western India," 90–91, provides analysis. But see Cohen, *Hellenistic Settlements in the East*, 316, on problems with the association of Demetrias with Indian place names.
⁵⁹ As suggested by Zvelebil, "Yavanas," 406, who cites references from *Silappatikaram* 28.147 and 29.25. Also the commentary of Parthasarathy, *The Cilappatikaram of Ilanko Atikal*, 294.
⁶⁰ Neelis, *Early Buddhist Transmission*, 127; and Thapar, *Early India*, 227, with Senart, "Inscriptions," no. 2 and Mirashi, *History and Inscriptions*, 1.31–35 and 2.41–49 (no. 18) for the inscription. Ghosh, "Understanding Transitions," clarifies the ethnic basis of the references to Sakas and Pahlavas in the Indian literature. On cave 3 and other monasteries at Nasik (with images), see Ray, "King and Monastery," 45–59. For dating the Satavahanas and western Kshatrapas, see n. 61.
⁶¹ On the Greeks of Hellenistic Bactria and India, the Sakas, and the Indo-Parthians, see Burstein, "New Light," 181–92; Mairs, "Waiting for the Barbarians" and *Hellenistic Far East*; Coloru, *Alessandro a Menadro*. For Sakas and Indo-Parthians, see Puri, "Sakas and the Indo-Parthians";

century CE and perhaps subsequently, people bearing such identifying labels or being called by them were apparently living in the territories controlled by the Saka Kshatrapas in the vicinity of Barygaza. In the western Ghats, self-identifying Sakas have in fact left inscriptions.[62]

Significantly, both Yavanas and Sakas left traces in the cave Hoq on Socotra, where the Sanskrit and Prakrit inscriptions were written in a script that links their writers to the vicinity of the Gulf of Barygaza or sometimes even specify origins there.[63] Among them is a Brahmi Sanskrit inscription made by a man who identifies himself as "the Yavana Cadrabhūtimukha."[64] This figure bears none of the cultural characteristics of the Greek-speaking Roman Egyptians who also left inscriptions on the island; he was certainly from west India. As a Yavana, he was most probably among the Yavanas with links to north India who had settled farther south at the Gulf of Barygaza. He may have been a self-identifying Yavana, but he did not share the culture of Greeks or Greek-speakers from Roman Egypt.[65] It is for this reason that another figure from the region identified himself as a Saka in the inscription that he made on the island.[66] He too called himself by the name borne by people who had previously inhabited north India. It is worth adding that people apparently from the Gulf of Barygaza identified themselves as *kshatrapas* in texts written in the cave Hoq too.[67] Accordingly, the Buddhist inscriptions made by Yavanas and Yonakas in the western Ghats were most probably carved by Yavanas who had settled in areas near the Gulf of Barygaza but who owed their identifying label to the Greek Yavanas who had originally settled in north India. These also were perhaps Yavanas that appear in the later Tamil poems of south India as residential figures who served as guards or soldiers for local dynasts.

The socio-commercial networks that connected the Mediterranean and Indian Ocean worlds also facilitated relationships of international diplomacy that connected the far-flung regions of the Afro-Eurasian landmass. Indian embassies definitely visited Alexandria and other key

---

Bivar, "Gondophares"; Bopearachchi, "Indo-Parthians"; Thapar, *Early India*, 217–24; Neelis, *Early Buddhist Transmission*, 109–32. For chronologies (which are contested), Cribb, "New Evidence" and "Western Satraps and Satavahanas"; and Falk, "Ancient Indian Eras."

[62] Senart, "Inscriptions," nos. 14a, 15, 26, and 27; and Burgess and Indraji, *Inscriptions*, 45–46 (Burgess, *Report*, 96) for example.
[63] Strauch, "Brahmi Scripts," 341–42, and "Indian Participants," 344–45. Barygaza and Astakpra are specified.
[64] Strauch et al., "Catalogue," 183 (14:17).
[65] For different interpretation, Strauch et al., "Catalogue," 183, 14:17; and Strauch, "Indian Participants," 348.
[66] Strauch et al., "Catalogue," 96, 6:7 and Strauch, "Indian Participants," 348.
[67] Strauch et al., "Catalogue," 161 (12:2) and 194 (15:5); and Strauch, "Indian Participants," 350–51.

Mediterranean sites (including Rome, Athens, Antioch, Carthage, and Epirus) during the Hellenistic period.[68] Augustus received the embassies of Sakas from India too, and during one of them, a sage (perhaps a Buddhist) who appears in Greek sources as Zarmaros or Zarmanochegas from Barygaza burned himself alive at Athens. The sources differ regarding whether he did so because he had enjoyed his life and wanted to die before a reversal occurred or just simply wanted to amplify his reputation.[69] Zarmaros/Zarmanochegas was not the sage's actual name, but it referred to his status as a *sramana* or teacher of *sramanas*.[70] The arrival of additional Indian ambassadors to the Mediterranean littoral is documented for the Roman imperial period.[71] Certain inhabitants of Alexandria knew what Buddhists or ascetics called themselves in Sanskrit/Prakrit (sramanas/samanas) and the significance of a man called "Boutta" by the second century. This perhaps reflects contemporary contact with the subcontinent.[72] In turn, an Indian astronomer named Varahamira of the sixth-century CE consulted astrological works whose names suggest a Roman origin; these presumably arrived during the peak centuries (first-third CE) of Indo-Mediterranean trade.[73] Roman visitors to royal courts clearly landed in India, southeast Asia, and China by the sea-lanes of the India ocean and Pacific coast. The efforts of Han ambassadors to reach or record the Roman empire are likewise attested.[74]

As the durability of trade and diplomatic exchange between Egyptian Red Sea ports and India has received continued substantiation, so too has the premise that Christianity probably arrived and became established

---

[68] Schneider, *Die grossen Felsen-Edikte Asokas*, 76–77 and 118–19 (13Q-R), for the embassies sent by the Buddhist king Asoka to Hellenistic Greeks.

[69] Strabo, *Geog.* (ed. Radt) 15.1.73 (Nicolaus of Damascus: *FGrH* 90, F. 100); and Cass. Dio (ed. Boissevain) 54.9; Suet. *Aug* (ed. Ihm) 21.3; McLaughlin, *Roman Empire*, 157–59. Aug, *Res. Gest.* (ed. Scheid) 31 for Augustus' boast of having received Indian embassies. For Roman diplomacy with peoples of the Indian Ocean, see now Speidel, "War, Trade, and Treaties."

[70] Biffi, *Estremo oriente*, 244; McLaughlin, *Roman Empire* 158–59.

[71] Porphyry's *De Styge* in Stob. *Anth.* 1.3.56 (1.66.24–70.13), which is *Fragments* (ed. Smith) 376, with *de abstinentia* (ed. Nauck) 4.16–17 (together being *FGrH/BNJ* 719 F. 1–2). This, however, could be fictitious. Biffi, "Ciò che Bardesane venne a sapere sull'India?" See Chapter 4, pp. 141–42.

[72] Schneider, *Die grossen Felsen-Edikte Asokas*, 76–77 and 118–19 (13Q-R); Clement, *Strom.* (ed. Stählin and Früchtel) 1.15.71.3–6. Clement's information could have been derived from Megasthenes, however. *BNJ/FGrH* 715, T1 and F3a. Reed, "Beyond the Land of Nod," 66–67, n. 78 discusses sramanas/samanas.

[73] McLaughlin, *Roman Empire*, 171. The works cited are the *Romaka Siddhanta* and the *Paulisa Siddhanta*. For relevant passage in translation, see Sastry, *Pancasiddhantika*, 3–5.

[74] Leslie and Gardiner, *Roman Empire in Chinese Sources*, 42 (*Hou Hanshu* 86) and 61 (*Hou Han Chi*); see particularly *Hou Hanshu* 88 in Leslie and Gardiner, *Roman Empire in Chinese Sources*, 50–5; and Hill, *Through the Jade Gate*, 27. Romans coins found in China are later and are concentrated on overland routes. Li, "Roman Coins." McLaughlin, *Rome and the Distant East*, 111–41, treats diplomatic contacts.

on the shores of India at an early date. The stability of the transit trade and a spate of sources regarding the travel of Christian apostles or early Christian churchmen to India could suggest that by the fourth century, Roman imperial residents had transported Christianity to India and that Indians had adopted it. Indeed, due to such evidence for "global" connectivity, scholars have deemed the early movement of Christianity to India to be quite plausible, even if empirically obscure. Increased credence has accordingly been given to the Indian *Acts of Thomas* and other south Asian traditions pertaining to the apostle's travels. Some scholars accept that Thomas did in fact travel throughout India based on these narratives, whether this meant he arrived there via the Persian Gulf or via the Red Sea.[75] Otherwise, they sometimes posit the validity of late Roman narratives regarding the arrival of Christianity to a place labeled "India" through Egypt and its Red Sea connections to the Indian Ocean. Since these texts ostensibly document how Christianity arrived in India, they offer putative support to the premise of the Thomas narrative or at least the likelihood for its early travel and permanence in the subcontinent, either via the Red Sea or the Persian Gulf.[76] After all, recent scholarship has demonstrated how religious ideas and culture traveled among the various societies of the Afro-Eurasian world system and that the commercial and diplomatic webs that certainly existed were especially exploited by the Manichaeans.[77] The far-flung movement of culture, ideas, and the people that carried them could likewise explain similarities among literary tropes in Mediterranean (including Christian) and Indians texts, as well as iconographic parallels in visual representations. One thinks, for example, of consistencies in narratives told about Jesus of Nazareth and Krishna.[78] In theory, such "global" connections could have facilitated the movements of the apostle Thomas or other early Christians and perhaps even constitute supporting evidence for them.

---

[75] McGrath, "History and Fiction," esp. 307–10; Kurikilamkatt, *First Voyage*; Baumer, *Church of the East*, 15–19 and 235–36; Jullien and Jullien, *Apôtres des confins*, 11–21 (on Bartholomew, Thomas, and Addai/Thaddaeus); Nedungatt, *Quest for the Historical Thomas*, 81–96, and "Apocryphal *Acts of Thomas*"; Hage, *Orientalische Christentum*, 315–17; Frykenberg, *Christianity in India*, 92–110; McDowell, *Fate of the Apostles*, 157–74.

[76] Ramelli, "Tradizione su Tommaso," 59–82, esp. 65; Seland, "Trade and Christianity," 78–79, and "Networks and Social Cohesion," 385–86; Tubach, "Historische Elemente," 49–116; Ellerbrock and Winkelmann, *Die Parther*, 273–75; Debié, Perrin, and Mahé, "L'Orient," 614–16.

[77] Gardner, "Comments on Mani"; Klein, "Epic Buddhasarita"; Dilley, "Religious Intercrossing," 58–70, "Mani's Wisdom," "Also Schrieb Zarathustra?" and "'Hell Exists'"; BeDuhn, "Iranian Epic" and "Mani and Crystallization"; Jones, "Things Mani Learned."

[78] On Christian and Indian narratives (and similarities between stories about Jesus and Krishna), see Dognini, "Nascita" and "Primi contatti," but note reservations of Sidebotham, *Berenike*, 257.

But the movement of culture and ideas and their impact on any artistic or literary forms across vast geographies do not necessarily constitute evidence for direct contact. Intermediaries could be responsible, and literary or artistic forms can be transmitted by various connected actors and then shared by people living in various regions over time. As the previous chapter has emphasized, the late antique ecclesiastical historians that described the evangelization of "India" were actually referring to regions in east Africa and Arabia. Otherwise, the evidence for the early arrival of Christianity in the Indian subcontinent is weak, and the Roman Egyptian network that extended into the Red Sea and Indian Ocean betrays no indication that it carried Christianity in a meaningful capacity before the fourth century CE. For this reason, the remainder of this chapter pinpoints the key dispositions of this network (or circulation society) and its placement of residential communities (anchor points or routing stations) at various overseas ports. It also examines the chronological vicissitudes of this network and how it eventually transported Christianity to Aksumite Ethiopia and south Arabia, but not ultimately to the Indian subcontinent itself.

The Roman Egypt Network (First Century BCE to Third Century CE)

As the previous discussion has emphasized, traders from Roman Egypt were certainly in direct contact with the Indian subcontinent between the first century BCE and the third century CE. But certain features of such trade are difficult to establish. The volume of shipping and direct trips that Roman Egyptians undertook cannot be measured precisely, and it is yet unclear whether Roman Egyptians established actual residential communities in India (which is probable). Nonetheless, textual sources and archaeological material show that Alexandria was the central node of a network that connected numerous residential communities of Roman Egyptians between the Red Sea and the Indian subcontinent. It facilitated the flow of goods, information, credit, trust, culture, and people.

As previously noted, the presence of inscribed pottery fragments, of material remains that indicate differences in social practice, and of foreign objects intended for circulation at specific ports may indicate the general existence of various ethnic or linguistic groups involved in Red Sea and Indian Ocean trade. But whether these are reliable for establishing self-ascribed identities, the specific characteristics of communities in a given place, or the existence of foreign residential communities in Red Sea and

Indian Ocean ports is yet unclear.[79] These arguably do not provide reliable evidence for the presence of residential communities of a specific social or ethnic background, and any effort to determine where the Roman Egyptian socio-commercial network established them requires alternate forms of support. For this reason, epigraphic remains of a more monumental or noncirculatory nature are of immense value: these include honorific inscriptions that accompanied statues, religious dedications associated with specific sacred sites, building inscriptions, or graffiti carved into immobile geologic formations. Such epigraphic forms were typically created in an identifiable location by expatriates who resided there or by itinerant merchants who tarried in a place in which compatriots resided. Along with such epigraphic materials, various textual sources, especially the "Muziris papyrus" and the *Periplus of the Erythraean Sea*, help create a fuller picture of the Roman Egyptian network. All told, the dispositions of the Roman Egyptian network can be described as follows.

First, it seems that many investors and merchants who were involved in Red Sea and Indian Ocean trade resided in Alexandria or maintained a permanent proxy presence there. But these acquired transit goods through subordinate employees, business associates, or even merchants who had accepted loans from them for the acquisition of goods. Such figures were typically located at Red Sea locations, although they were often quite mobile. The second-century "Muziris papyrus," a document previously mentioned, illuminates the basic contours of one variation on such forms of social relations. Even if certain features remain debatable, the papyrus (which is not entirely intact) most probably permitted an investor and his agents to confiscate a cargo of transit commodities if an indebted merchant did not repay a prior loan or loans within a certain time after the cargo arrived at a Red Sea port.[80] The document does not indicate that the parties involved had contracted a bottomry loan, by which a merchant or ship's captain would have borrowed money against a ship as collateral.[81] Instead, it apparently indicates that a similar type of loan had been made for the acquisition of cargo, or perhaps just to cover the expensive cost

---

[79] Thomas, "Port Communities," focuses on these approaches.
[80] P. Vindob G 40822=*SB* XVIII 13167. The interpretation posited here and many to follow are informed by Casson, "New Light," 202–6; and Rathbone, "'Muziris' Papyrus," with recent new readings (especially of the verso) by Morelli, "Dal Mar Rosso," esp. 207–10, and analysis by de Romanis, "Playing Sudoku" and "Comparative Perspectives," 135–39. Ruffing, "Trade with India," 204–210, informs my views on the papyrus and social networking. See also Thür, Hypotheken-Urkunde"; Seland, "Ports, Ptolemy," 77–78; Sidebotham, *Berenike*, 217–19; and McLaughlin, *Roman Empire*, 89–93.
[81] Sidebotham, *Berenike*, 219, discusses bottomry loans.

of transport to Coptos and down the Nile to Alexandria.[82] In fact, the document may refer to two separate loans to be repaid: one that covered the costs of transport from the Red Sea to Alexandria and a prior one that funded a maritime trip into the Indian Ocean.[83] The commodities purchased constituted the collateral, which the investor could confiscate if repayment did not happen according to schedule (although if the value of the cargo exceeded the loan amount, the creditor was obligated to pay the merchant a proper portion). Given the amount of Italian or Laodikean wine documented by *ostraka* as being loaded onto ships at Berenike, it is possible that wine was part of an export cargo that the merchant had bought with money loaned by the investor.[84] In turn, the money derived from the cargo's overseas sale was to purchase the import goods that were transported to Egypt (like nard, ivory, pepper, and others).[85] As part of the agreement, the document, apparently contracted at a Red Sea location, outlines how the indebted merchant was supposed to transfer the cargo of a ship called the *Hermapollon* from an unnamed Red Sea port to Coptos, where it would be shipped down the Nile to Alexandria.[86] The merchant was also to pay certain fees at Coptos, have the 25 percent custom tax (*tetartē*) assessed at Alexandria, sell the cargo, and repay the loan from the proceeds.[87] But beyond that, it seems that the investor was the one absorbing the financial risk for the loss or destruction of cargo; the risk that the merchant endured was perhaps death or captivity on the sea.[88]

Although the precise ports visited by the *Hermapollon* are not named, the document indicates that many of the goods on the ship originated from the south Indian port of Muziris, now increasingly identified with

---

[82] Rathbone, "'Muziris' Papyrus," 41–42; McLaughlin, *Roman Empire*, 90–91.
[83] For example, Morelli, "Dal Mar Rosso," 205–6; and Ruffing, "Trade with India," 202, n. 14.
[84] Bagnall, Helms, and Verhoogt, *Documents from Berenike*, Vol. 1, esp. 8–14 (for key discussion) and 37–73 (for inscribed *ostraka*). For references regarding *ostraka* and other documents of Berenike, see Sidebotham, "Ports," 158, n. 105. For export wine, see now Cobb, "Balancing the Trade," 193–96, with Seland, "*Periplus of the Erythraean Sea*," 202.
[85] For cargo, Morelli, "Dal Mar Rossi," 216–31; and de Romanis, "Playing Sudoku," "Comparative Perspectives," 135–39, and "Muziris Export."
[86] For details regarding the labor, economic relations, social mechanisms, and infrastructure that facilitated the transport of transit goods from Red Sea ports to Alexandria by means of the Nile, see Sidebotham, *Berenike*, 126–76 and 212–20; Young, *Rome's Eastern Trade*, 38–78; and Wilson, "Red Sea Trade." For probable Red Sea location of composition, see Casson, "New Light," 203; and Morelli, "Dal Mar Rosso," 205.
[87] *SB* XVIII 13167, recto, col. 2 generally. Along with the contents of the papyrus, see *OGIS* 674; and Young, *Rome's Eastern Trade*, 47–54.
[88] Rathbone, "'Muziris' Papyrus," 42–43.

Pattanam.⁸⁹ It even refers directly to previous loan contracts, probably for the purchase of cargo, that scholars have variously construed as "loan contracts (drawn up at) Muziris" or "loan contracts (for the trip to) Muziris" (ταῖς κατὰ Μουζεῖριν τοῦ δα[νείου σ]υνγραφαῖς).⁹⁰ Due to such ambiguity, the reference could mean that an investor in Alexandria had managed to front credit to a merchant who primarily resided on the Red Sea coast of Egypt but who was also quite mobile. Perhaps the merchant had been in Muziris and made the contract with subordinates or the proxies of the investor. Investors and merchants in Egypt could have arranged loans and purchases that personal proxies or contacts contracted at foreign ports, just as Jewish businessmen in medieval Egypt are famous for doing.⁹¹ But according to another line of interpretation, the document was describing loan contracts for a trip to Muziris, and these documents were created at a Alexandria or a Red Sea site.⁹² In this way, the investor had given the merchant a sum of money at Alexandria or enabled credit to be fronted to him at a Red Sea port. From there, the merchant set about the business of buying and transporting cargos in overseas places.

Wherever the loan contracts cited in the Muziris papyrus may have been created, the papyrus and its contents reflect how premodern sociocommercial networks facilitated the movement of credit, commodities, people, and trust over vast distances. An investor at Alexandria or his subordinates fronted a substantial amount of money to a merchant operating primarily along the Red Sea. In turn, the merchant, whether he did it by himself or through proxies, purchased an outgoing cargo, transferred it to the *Hermapollon*, and arranged its overseas sale. He then acquired an incoming cargo from Muziris, oversaw its movement to the Red Sea on the *Hermapollon*, and then arranged its transport to Coptos and down the Nile. In order to accomplish this feat, the investor and merchant relied on a web of transport providers, sailors, customs officials, and residential contacts in ports of the Red Sea and Indian Ocean. We have already witnessed how transport businesses operated between Coptos and Red Sea ports, and one of these presumably moved the cargo to Alexandria.⁹³ But merchants needed the aid of sailors too.

---

[89] Selvakumar, Shajan, and Tomber, "Archaeological Investigations"; Cherian, *Pattanam Excavations, Interim Report*, and *Unearthing Pattanam*; and Tomber, "Roman Pottery."
[90] *SB* XVIII 13167, Recto, col. 2, line 12. As interpreted by Casson, "New Light," 196, 200, and 206; and Rathbone, "'Muziris' Papyrus,"41.
[91] Goitein and Friedman, *India Traders*, 22–24, 59–66, and 137–40. For investors and agents, see Ruffing, "Trade with India," 204–10.
[92] Rathbone, "'Muziris' Papyrus,"41; with Morelli, "Dal Mar Rosso," 216.
[93] Fuks, "Notes on the Archives of Nicanor," 207–16. The *ostraka* that provide documentation are *O. Petr.* 220–305.

The Muziris papyrus provides no details regarding the sailors who actually traveled to India in the *Hermapollon*, but parallel inscriptions suggest that sailors and technicians lived at Red Sea ports, belonged to naval associations, and maintained (ideally) symbiotic relationships with merchants. At some point in the late second or early third century, Palmyrene merchants accordingly made an honorific inscription and statue at Coptos for a member of an association of Palmyrene sailors, ship outfitters, or ship owners of the Red Sea (*Palmyrenoi naukleroi Erythraikoi*).[94] It is possible that the owner or captain of the *Hermapollon* was fulfilling a contract or agreement with the merchant who borrowed from the investor in Alexandria. The captain and his crew would have been paid after their voyage from the sale of cargo or by a fixed rate, whether the merchant had traveled with them or remained on the Red Sea. Certainly, the goods on the *Hermapollon* would have made a huge profit at market, even after Roman custom officials claimed a quarter of it. Intriguingly, the papyrus lists a cargo containing nard and ivory, and presumably pepper and other commodities, that was worth nearly seven million drachmas, but this was apparently about three-fourths of one consignment that may have only filled a part of the *Hermapollon*.[95] In other words, the ship captain, or at least the ship owner, was probably selling cargo space or accepting fees from numerous merchants.[96]

Whichever the scenario may have been, the key point here is that the acquisition of high-risk, high-profit transit goods frequently involved the intervention and interrelation of numerous interconnected figures who were separated by vast geographical distances. These figures had established sufficient trust that their associates would fulfill the mutual obligations necessary to ensure the movement of credit, money, and commodities. In this instance, on the basis of the Muziris papyrus and supporting documents one can reconstruct the reciprocal agreements of an investor in Alexandria, a merchant at a Red Sea port, the owner or captain of a ship sailing between the Red Sea and Egypt, and members of overland or Nilotic transport businesses linking Coptos to the Red Sea and to Alexandria. These were all in some way involved with the acquisition

---

[94] Bernand, *Portes du Désert*, no. 103.
[95] *SB* XVIII 13167, verso, col. 2 generally; with the recent reading and analysis of Morelli, "Dal Mar Rosso," esp. 207–10; and de Romanis "Playing Sudoku," "Comparative Perspectives," and "Muziris Export," 135–39. Sidebotham, *Berenike* 217 notes the single consignment. For the *Hermapollon*'s size and cargo capacity, see Morelli, "Dal Mar Rosso" 216–31; and de Romanis, "Playing Sudoku," "Comparative Perspectives," 135–39, and "Muziris Export."
[96] Sidebotham, *Berenike*, 217.

and transport of the cargo in a specific consignment of the *Hermapollon*. The Muziris papyrus accordingly reflects how members of a self-regulating network transmitted information, moved goods, and established trust over vast geographic spaces extending from Alexandria, along the Nile, to Coptos and the Red Sea, and even to India.

Of course, the social relationships represented by the Muziris papyrus constituted a specific variation of a broader array of possibilities responsible for moving commodities, people, and trust. Some wealthy merchants with ties to Alexandria did not necessarily lend money to Red Sea merchants or have them move cargo through the ships of another. They simply owned their own ships and purchased their own cargos, thereby leaving the tasks of trafficking to paid employees or subordinates. A religious dedication raised at Medamud, a Nilotic site located somewhat south of Coptos, shows how this was so. In this inscription two women named Aelia Isidora and Aelia Olympias (apparently relatives) described themselves as "Red Sea ship-owners and merchants" (*naukleroi ka[i empo]roi Erythraikai*) and, in a lacunose part of the inscription, they seem to provide the name of the captain of their fleet (Apolinarios).[97] Since they were Roman citizens, it appears that the women were foremost inhabitants and citizens of Alexandria who owned property in the hinterland and managed a fleet of merchant ships on the Red Sea from afar. Otherwise, they could have resided in the Egyptian hinterland but maintained permanent proxies at Alexandria to ensure the distribution of their transit goods to Mediterranean markets. The captain that they employed, whatever his origins, operated at a Red Sea port. As it appears that all parties were involved in the dedication of the inscription, it is possible that they had convened at an intermediary point in order to transfer commodities moving (in either direction) between Alexandria and the Red Sea. In such a scenario, Aelia Isidora and Aelia Olympias would have traveled from Alexandria, and Apolinarios would have come from his Red Sea location.

Although the Muziris papyrus casts light on the social relationships through which various figures of the Roman Egyptian network connected Alexandria to Indian ports like Muziris, our knowledge regarding where the network maintained residential communities must come from other sources. The Red Sea extension of the Roman Egyptian socio-commercial network receives significant, if incomplete, elucidation from varied documents. One is the aforementioned *Periplus of the Erythraean Sea*,

---

[97] *SB* V 7539=Jouguet, Dédicace, 1–29. See Sidebotham, *Roman Economic Policy*, 86–87; and Ruffing, "Trade with India," 209.

a description of ports and markets of the Red Sea and Indian Ocean apparently written by a Roman Egyptian during roughly the mid-first century CE, if not produced later through an accretive process.[98] Starting with west coast of the Red Sea, it proceeds along east Africa, the east coast of the Red Sea, south Arabia, and then the coast of India. As it does so, it describes key ports, commodities that are available or in demand, and expected sailing times.

A vital feature of the *Periplus* is that it sheds light on where exactly "Greeks," by which it appears to describe Roman Egyptians, had established residential communities. Such a permanent community of expatriate settlers had formed, for instance, on the island of Socotra, from which Roman Egyptian expatriates could more easily make the round trip to India, especially Muziris.[99] Its claim that a dynast named Zoskales, located in Ethiopia or the Horn of Africa, was literate in Greek suggests a Roman Egyptian residential presence. If the Roman Egyptian network had established residential communities on the Horn of Africa and on Socotra, it probably established one at Adulis too. Finally, in an intriguing passage regarding Muziris and nearby ports in India, it notes that these constituted limited markets for grain on account of the fact that those involved in shipping or navigation alone consumed it and *emporoi* did not. The text here seems to differentiate between grain-consuming sailors from Roman Egypt who resided at the port and local merchants who ate rice.[100] Such a line of interpretation is corroborated by a census list from Egyptian Arsinoe (72/73 CE), which declares exemptions for a certain figure named "Gaion, who is also Diodorus" on the grounds that he was in India.[101]

The evidence provided by the explicit statements of the *Periplus* can be amplified greatly by what the text implicitly conveys regarding the formation of residential communities of "Greeks" (by which it seems to mean Roman Egyptians) throughout the Indian Ocean. This claim is justified by two reasons. First, the reason why the text explicitly locates a residential

---

[98] For conventional author/date, see Casson, *Periplus*, 6–8; Belfiore, *Periplo*, 77–84, with Cribb, "Numismatic Evidence"; Robin, "Date"; Boussac, "Revisiting," 179–81, with notes. Arnaud, "*Periplus*," however, suggests a second-century author enmeshed in a context of Latin and Greek learning.

[99] *PME* (ed. Casson) 30 and 54, with 4-5. In its discussion of the island of Socotra, the *Periplus* states explicitly that Arabians, Indians, and "Greeks" established residential communities there.

[100] *PME* (ed. Casson) 56. Casson, *Periplus*, 24 and 264; Fauconnier, "Graeco-Roman Merchants," 92–93.

[101] See *P. Lond.* 2.260, col. 3, line 42; Casson, "P. Vindob G 40822"; Fauconnier, "Graeco-Roman Merchants," 93.

community of "Greeks" on the island of Socotra is due to its uniqueness as a place whose only inhabitants were foreign settlers. The text frequently conveys to readers what the local inhabitants of various ports and hinterlands were like and occasionally comments on the sort of foreigners that frequented them. It typically is silent on where Roman Egyptians themselves were located, and it could be argued that the text assumes that readers would expect Roman Egyptians (which it calls "Greeks") to be residing in most of the ports whose markets or *emporia* it describes, even if it does not provide explicit commentary. Accordingly, it is perhaps due to Socotra's unique stature as an island with no "indigenous" population that the *Periplus* describes its inhabitants as foreigner settlers, including some "Greeks." Elsewhere, the text explicitly discusses local indigenous populations and implies the residential presence of Roman Egyptians.

Second, in the ancient and premodern world the forms of local knowledge that traveled throughout socio-commercial networks typically were transmitted by mobile traders. But such knowledge was initially produced or acquired by residential communities whose anchorage in local settings enabled them to form the most intensive social bonds and lines of communication with the indigenous inhabitants and foreign resident traders.[102] As the anchor points, residential communities of the Roman Egyptian network also meaningfully constituted the core fixed nodes of their broader circulation society. They foremost produced information regarding local areas and then conveyed it along the physical and social pathways that the Roman Egyptian socio-commercial network maintained. For such reasons, the *Periplus* does not merely reflect the experience of its historical author, who presents himself as a member of the Roman Egyptian network. It also encapsulates the knowledge (albeit of varying accuracy and at times flawed) that traveled throughout the Roman Egyptian network and that was therefore accessible to its members, including the author.[103] It in fact conveys how the author experienced the forms of knowledge that expatriate residential communities generated and that the network in its totality circulated.[104] Since residential communities of Roman Egyptians constituted the founts of information that the *Periplus* documents, these should therefore be deemed

---

[102] Aslanian, *From the Indian Ocean*, 14–16; and Markovits, *Global World of Indian Merchants*, 181–84, inform my perspectives.

[103] See significantly Bukharin, "Coastal Arabia," who surmises that the author, who had some personal experiences of the regions in his account, still exhibits omissions and erroneous perspectives on Arabia that suggest a reliance on popular knowledge.

[104] For network analysis approaches to the author's knowledge of ports and products, see Seland, "*Periplus of the Erythraean Sea*."

the origin points for the information that the *Periplus* conveys for the various ports of the Red Sea and Indian Ocean worlds.

According to such a reading of the *Periplus*, the ports or localities at which the text implies the presence of Roman Egyptian residential communities include Adulis (Ethiopia); Muza, Aden, Qane, and Moscha Limen (Arabia); and Barbarikon, Barygaza, and Muziris (India), just to name a few. By contrast, the interior of the Persian Gulf, Sri Lanka, and the east coast of India, on which the text is mostly silent, did not house them by the time of its probable composition in the mid-first century CE. Nonetheless, east India and Sri Lanka may have harbored residential communities of the Roman Egyptian network by the time that Pliny (mid- to-late first century CE) and Claudius Ptolemy (mid-second century CE) were writing. In fact, the detailed treatment that Claudius Ptolemy gives to both coastal and interior India in his *Geography* indicates that the Roman Egyptian residential presence in India must have been quite ample.[105]

Such an interpretation of the *Periplus*' testimony is supported by epigraphic evidence, which also amplifies our knowledge of where Roman Egyptian networks established residential communities. We have already noted the Roman Egyptian who resided at Aden but traveled on business to Coptos, where he left an epigraphic trace. Likewise, a Latin inscription found on the Farasan Islands of the south Red Sea indicates that a detachment of a Roman legion was stationed there during the 140s CE. The inscription also seems to indicate that its commanding officer was overseeing the *Ferresani portus* (even if most letters of *portus* are now barely visible). This apparently refers to a port or customs post and implies, by extension, a residential community.[106] The fact that Roman soldiers were deployed on the Farasan Islands to manage the affairs of a port and presumably a residential presence of Roman Egyptians in the mid-second century is significant for another reason. Being stationed far from the Egyptian and Arabian provinces, these were most certainly protecting merchants and expatriate settlers from the Roman empire who were conducting commerce in the south Red Sea and Arabian Sea, including those at nearby Adulis (on the African side) and Muza (on the Arabian side). The inscription, one of several Latin or Greek texts linked to Roman military figures in south Arabia, may reflect an effort to integrate the region

---

[105] Ptolemy, *Geog.* (ed. Stückelberger and Graßhoff) 7.1–3; Pliny, *NH* (ed. Jahn and Mayhoff) 6 (esp. 104–6). McLaughlin, *Rome and the Distant East*, 57–59; Nappo, "Roman Policy," 70–71.

[106] Phillips, Villeneuve, and Fahey, "A Latin Inscription from South Arabia," esp. 246–47; Villeneuve, "Farasan Inscriptions"; and Speidel, "Ausserhalb des Reiches?" esp. 637–39, and "War, Trade, and Treaties," 89–84; Nappo, "Roman Policy," 65–68, all inform my discussion.

into the Roman imperial system during the first half of the second century CE.[107] Adulis and Muza are described as being prominent harbors by the author of the *Periplus*, and the Latin inscription suggests that Roman Egyptians resided there permanently.[108]

Most significant of all for establishing the reach of the Roman Egyptian network are the recent epigraphic finds from the island of Socotra. These provide every indication that the island was a contact point for merchants and sailors from south Arabia, Aksumite Ethiopia, the Indian subcontinent, and Roman Egypt. As noted above, the *Periplus* states explicitly that Arabians, Indians, and "Greeks," (presumably Roman Egyptians) established residential communities there,[109] but the inscribed texts from the cave Hoq contribute additional layers of significance for two reasons. First, they indicate that the island of Socotra was a vital point of face-to-face contact for sailors and merchants who arrived from various parts of the Indian Ocean littoral. A preponderance of texts from the second to the late-fourth centuries CE was created by Indian travelers in Sanskrit, and many specify that the Indians in question were from Barygaza and Astakpra or bear script styles that indicate origins near the Gulf of Barygaza.[110] One of them suggests a trickle of movement from Kushan north India to Socotra, presumably via Barbarikon.[111] These texts, along with those inscribed in south Arabian or Ethiopic during the second and third centuries, confirm the statement of the *Periplus* that the island was frequented by Indian and Arabian sailors.[112]

Second, the inscriptions at the cave Hoq on Socotra substantiate the premise that Roman Egyptians established residential communities on the island or at least lingered there as a key stopover point. In the early third century CE, a Roman Egyptian inscribed a graffito in Greek;[113] this corroborates the claim of the *Periplus* that Arabians, Indians, and "Greeks" (that is, Roman Egyptians) established residential communities there.[114] Similarly, in 258 CE, a Palmyrene traveler dedicated a wooden tablet in the grotto.[115] Even if he was probably traveling foremost as an emissary, he likely participated in a Palmyrene subset of the Roman Egyptian network whose traces can be detected at Coptos and Berenike. Perhaps initiated by the deployment of

---

[107] Other Greek and Greek-Latin inscriptions of south Arabia are *IGSK* 65.435–438; and Marek, "Roman Period Inscription."
[108] *PME* (ed. Casson) 7, 16–17, and 20–29. [109] *PME* (ed. Casson) 30.
[110] Strauch, "Brahmi Scripts," 342, and "Indian Participants," 344–45.
[111] For details and references, see n. 39.
[112] South Arabian and Aksumite texts are treated by Robin, "Sudarabiques et Aksūmites," 438–42, and "Suquṭra dans les inscriptions," 443.
[113] Bukharin, "Greek Inscriptions at Hoq"; Strauch et al., "Catalogue," 11:26.
[114] *PME* (ed. Casson) 30. [115] Gorea, "Palmyrene Tablette."

Palmyrene auxiliaries at Coptos and Berenike in the second century CE, it soon attracted merchants or ship maintainers too.[116] The Greek and Palmyrene inscriptions represent only a small fraction of the inscriptions from the grotto, and this suggests that the residential presence of Indians was denser than that of Roman Egyptians. Still, it is clear that Roman Egyptians and Palmyrenes with links to Egypt were residing on or frequenting Socotra, if in smaller numbers. They were probably at this time also residing at Qane, which was located northwest across the Arabian sea on the mainland; the *Periplus* emphasizes its importance, and, as we will see, inscriptions place Roman Egyptians there in late antiquity.[117]

Finally, as noted previously, the *Periplus* implicitly locates a residential community of Roman Egyptians at the Indian port of Muziris. It indicates that shippers ate grain and merchants at the port did not eat it, and it thereby suggests that grain-eating Roman Egyptians resided at the port, whereas local merchants ate rice. The *Periplus'* apparent depiction of a Roman Egyptian residential community at Muziris, as well as its implicit location of such expatriate settlements at Barbarikon and Barygaza,[118] is worth further emphasis in light of the ambiguities of other evidence. The material remains of Roman transport vessels and coins at Pattanam, Arikamedu, and other Indian coastal sites are not necessarily conclusive support for residential communities, even if they are suggestive.[119] In fact, recent excavators of Arikamedu have noted that the architecture at the site does not follow Mediterranean patterns, and the amount of pottery from the Mediterranean world constitutes only a sliver of the total finds there (as at Pattanam).[120] This renders extremely suspect any claim that the first-century CE date and Roman origins of the apostle Thomas' putative tomb at Mylapore can be established through comparisons to the brick buildings of Arikamedu, including an allegedly "Roman warehouse."[121] Similarly, the evidence for a Jewish presence during the first half of the first millennium BCE is very tenuous, as is any claim of sustained direct contact

---

[116] Bernand, *Portes du Désert*, nos. 39 (=*PAT* 0256: Tentyris), 85 (Coptos) and 103 (Coptos); Dijkstra and Verhoogt, "Greek-Palmyrene inscription," 208–10, represent certain attestations. For others (including the uncertain), see Dijkstra and Verhoogt, "Greek-Palmyrene inscription," 213–18.

[117] *PME* (ed. Casson) 27–28. For Qane, Sedov and Salles, *Qâni'*. [118] *PME* (ed. Casson) 38–41.

[119] For references, see n. 22, 29, 31, 42, and 89.

[120] Begley, "Changing Perceptions of Arikamedu," 23; Suresh, *Arikamedu*, 51. Similarly for Pattanam, Cherian, *Pattanam Excavations, Interim Report*, and *Unearthing Pattanam*. On sites near Arikamedu, Suresh, *Arikamedu*, 63–76. In my view, Gurukkal, *Rethinking Classical Indo-Roman Trade*, 182–94, often conflates the presence of Mediterranean circulatory materials and the presence of Mediterranean/Roman traders at Arikamedu and Pattanam in a problematic way, even if the stable presence of some Roman Egyptians or otherwise Roman settlers was probable.

[121] Schurhammer, "New Light," 99–101; Nedungatt, *Quest for the Historical Thomas*, 308–12.

between Mediterranean peoples and India during that period.[122] But Jewish traders from Roman Egypt or Mesene may very well have gone to India or settled there during the Roman, Parthian, and Sasanian periods, as they certainly settled in south Arabia.[123]

The Peutinger map famously depicts a temple of Augustus at Muziris. The Romans' ideological pretensions of having conquered India may have informed this representation. It probably has nothing to do with actual Roman settlement.[124] But other signs of Roman residential settlement can be noted. As we have seen, the Muziris papyrus may refer to loan contracts made by an Alexandrian investor and a Red Sea merchant at Muziris through various proxies. If loans could be contracted exclusively among Roman Egyptians at Muziris (and this is far from certain), it follows that some of Roman Egyptians were living there. Likewise, even if the Yavanas that Tamil poems claimed to have established residential communities in south India are not easy to identify concretely, they nonetheless lend further credence to the possibility that the Roman Egyptian network had established residential communities there.[125] As noted previously, a census list from Egyptian Arsinoe (72/73 CE) declares an exemption for a certain figure who is "in India." The cumulative weight of such documents indicates that some Roman Egyptians resided in Indian ports.

An additional body of texts that support the premise for Roman Egyptian residential communities in India comes from an unlikely source. This is the Chinese *Hou Hanshu*, whose material pertains to the third century CE even if its compilation was in the fifth century or so. According to the text, an embassy from Da Qin (the Roman empire) arrived at the Han court after having traveled via southeast Asia. This source thereby indicates that the embassy from Roman arrived by sailing through the India Ocean, and it also names the contemporary Roman emperor as "Antun," who could be Antoninus Pius or Marcus Aurelius Antoninus.[126] Roman coins found in Vietnam and Thailand strengthen the premise that

---

[122] Puthiakunnel, "Jewish Colonies," is based on a fanciful collation of Hebrew Bible toponyms with Indian ports, the presence of Indian products in the Mediterranean that could have been acquired through intermediaries, and evidence from the second millennium CE. Nothing suggests that the references to Ophir and Tarshish in 1 Kings denote sites of India. Cogan, *1 Kings*, 306 and 319. The attestation of loan words for commodities and animals from India in the Hebrew Bible is also not evidence of direct contact. Gurukkal, *Rethinking Classical Indo-Roman Trade*, 108.
[123] For details and references, see this chapter, pp. 131–32, n. 151–55 and Chapters 5–6, pp. 197–98 and 214.
[124] For details and references, see p. 105, n. 42.   [125] For details and references, see p. 106, n. 50.
[126] *Hou Hanshu* 88, in Hill, *Through the Jade Gate*, 27; and Leslie and Gardiner, *Roman Empire in Chinese Sources*, 50–51.

Romans could have traveled to China from there,[127] and it is improbable that such an embassy would have happened without the well-laid social and physical pathways generated by the Roman Egyptian network in the Indian Ocean and without a meaningful residential presence of Roman Egyptians in Indian Ocean ports. As these Roman Egyptians would have formed the most intensive social bonds with Indian locals and eastern traders who arrived in south Indian ports, they were primarily responsible for generating the knowledge that facilitated further navigation and travel eastward. In this sense, the Chinese sources offer corroboration to the testimony of Tamil poems that place residential communities of Yavanas in south India. These could very well have been Roman Egyptians, even if these also could have been members of an enduring population along the Gulf of Barygaza and the western Ghats who had expatriated to south Indian ports.

All told, the Roman Egyptian network, which included the Palmyrene expatriates of Red Sea Egypt and maintained a key hub at Alexandria, had established residential communities at various sites of east Africa, south Arabia, Socotra, and even India during the first through third centuries CE. These communities facilitated the movement of itinerant merchants, sailors, objects, and information between Alexandria, Red Sea Egypt, and the Indian Ocean. They also enabled economic transactions and reciprocal exchanges among commercial players who worked in various places and fulfilled various roles over a vast geographic expanse The merchants of this network certainly maintained direct contact with India and traveled there. They may have even established residential communities on the subcontinent itself. The abundant details that the Roman Egyptian geographer Claudius Ptolemy provides regarding the cities along the coast and within the hinterland of India, as well as in southeast Asia, testify to this reach.[128]

Christianity and the Roman Egyptian Network (Third to Sixth Centuries CE)

It is difficult to establish why no reliable contemporary evidence has surfaced for Christianity in the Indian subcontinent before or during the fourth century CE, especially in light of the fact that Roman Egyptians

---

[127] Young, *Rome's Eastern Trade*, 29; McLaughlin, *Roman Empire*, 206; Bellina and Glover, "Archaeology of Early Contact," 71–72.
[128] Ptolemy, *Geog.* (Stückelberger and Graßhoff) 7.1–3; McLaughlin, *Rome and the Distant East*, 57–59 and *Roman Empire*, 203–6; Nappo, "Roman Policy," 70–71.

had direct commercial links there. Perhaps the formation of Christian communities has simply left no empirical traces. Maybe Romans never established commercial communities in ways that enabled Christianity to take root among local communities. But the most plausible reason for this deficit of evidence pertains to fundamental transitions that the Roman Egyptian network into the Red Sea experienced during the very late third and early fourth centuries CE. During this time, the network lost direct contact with the Indian subcontinent, and it was only after losing such contact that it began to integrate a critical concentration of Christians. In other words, the network's members had maintained direct contact with India during the first and second centuries CE and throughout much of the third century, but this phenomenon had occurred before they had become Christians in sufficient numbers for Christianity to take root in far-flung regions through their trans-imperial movement. By the time that this network included a concentration of Christians, its points of direct contact and placement of residential communities were limited to Aksumite Ethiopia, Meroitic Ethiopia, south Arabia, and Socotra. These regions therefore yielded Christian communities or converts.[129] But the network no longer extended its direct contact to India, and it therefore did not facilitate the movement and anchorage of Christian culture in India.

It is generally accepted that the Roman Egyptian trade network suffered disruption in its direct links to India during the late third and early fourth centuries due to internal instability in Roman Egypt and the broader empire, increased hostilities with Sasanian Persia, and various forms of strife in or between Aksumite Ethiopia and Himyarite south Arabia.[130] Certainly, a hiatus in the material traces for both botanical and inorganic matter from India at Berenike and the complete abandonment of Myos Hormos have encouraged this interpretation. As the Roman Egyptian socio-commercial network contracted, the disruption to the movement of transit commodities made Myos Hormos less valuable as a port and reduced the amount of matter that reached Berenike. The inscriptions from Socotra indicate that Indians continued to sail to the

---

[129] Bukharin, "Greeks on Socotra," 493–549; Bowersock, *Throne of Adulis*, 63–91; Power, *Red Sea*, 15–59; and Haas, "Mountain Constantines"; Phillipson, "Aksoum et le nord," 109–11 and *Foundations*, 91–106; Robin, "Arabia and Ethiopia," 273–81; Richter, "Beginnings of Christianity"; and Dijkstra, "Religious Transformation of Nubia."

[130] For the discussion that follows, see for instance Sidebotham, *Berenike*, 221 and 259–62, "Red Sea and Indian Ocean," 1044–45, and "Roman Ports," 148–49; and Tomber, *Indo-Roman Trade*, 154–70; Decker, "Settlement and Trade"; Schiettecatte, "L'Arabie du Sud," 250–54; Power, *Red Sea*, 51–52; Nappo, "Impact."

island at this time, but Roman Egyptians apparently stopped sailing there in the late third century CE and only resumed doing so in the mid-fourth.[131]

The hiatus in Roman Egyptian commercial activity nonetheless was short. For various reasons, it seems that the Roman Egyptian network had reasserted its position within the Red Sea after just a few decades of interruption, and some have detected signs of direct contact between Roman Egypt and India in their respective material cultures.[132] Despite Berenike's continued importance, the network was increasingly reoriented farther north at ports like Clysma and Aila, which were perhaps made more accessible to northbound vessels through new sailing techniques.[133] But altogether the material evidence from Berenike and other Red Sea ports indicates that the movement of long-distance transit goods and even domestic wares from the Indian Ocean world had resumed by the mid-fourth century CE. Beads with production sites in India, Sri Lanka, or southeast Asia, along with cooking ware from India and belts apparently reflecting an Indian style of fabrication, are likewise among the finds at Berenike.[134] A form of ceramic vessel produced at Aila has been found in many Red Sea or Arabian locations too.[135] Diplomatic activity also became more frequent. As we have seen, an edict of Constantius II from the Theodosian Code even apparently regulates how long ambassadors to Aksum and Himyar could linger at Alexandria.[136] Coins of Constantine and subsequent emperors, mostly of copper, have been found in India, and some later Roman ceramics have been too.[137] Intriguingly, people in India may have been seeking Roman coins for uses that were not strictly economic, including ritualistic purposes.[138]

---

[131] Of relevance are Strauch, "Brahmi Scripts" and "Indian Participants"; Bukharin, "Greeks on Socotra." For inscriptions, Bukharin, "Greek Inscriptions"; and Strauch et al., "Catalogue," 142–44 (11:26 and 11:28).

[132] Sidebotham, *Berenike*, 221, 231, and 259–62, "Ethnicity," 112, and "Red Sea and Indian Ocean," 1044–45; Tomber, *Indo-Roman Trade*, 154–70; Decker, "Settlement and Trade"; Schiettecatte, "L'Arabie du Sud," 254–58; Power, *Red Sea*, 52–53, are some key discussions.

[133] Decker, "Settlement and Trade," 217; Nappo, "Impact," 243; Sidebotham, *Berenike*, 177–79 and "Roman Ports," 129–33. Epiphanius, *Pan.* (ed. Holl) 56.1.8-12 argues that these ports received substantial trade from "India" and that merchants were traveling there during the fourth century CE, but it is unclear which "India" he means.

[134] Power, *Red Sea*, 39–41; Sidebotham, *Berenike*, 75, 238 and 261–62. I thank Steven Sidebotham for discussing the cooking ware with me.

[135] Power, *Red Sea*, 29–30, with n. 32 containing references for finds; Tomber, *Indo-Roman Trade*, 162–63 and 166; Sidebotham, *Berenike*, 259–62.

[136] *CT* (ed. Mommsen) 12.12.2; Munro-Hay, *Aksum*, 80.

[137] Suresh, *Symbols of Trade*, 38–40; Tomber, *Indo-Roman Trade*, 165–67; Gurukkal, *Rethinking Classical Indo-Roman Trade*, 47–48; Darley, *Indo-Byzantine Exchange*, including Appendix 6; Krishnamurthy, *Late Roman Copper Coins*; Walburg, *Coins and Tokens*, 51–57, 81–84, 231–36, 267–78, and 319–44.

[138] Darley, *Indo-Byzantine Exchange* (throughout) and "Self, Other, and Use"; similarly for earlier periods de Romanis, "*Aurei*," 69–81.

In terms of its activity and movement of objects and wealth, the Roman Egyptian network may have been robust and active. But it did not necessarily extend as far as it had in preceding periods. The resurgent movement of commercial objects, coins, and circulation vessels, and the presence of Indian cooking wares at Berenike, does not clarify how far the Roman Egyptian network extended in this period. Roman Egyptian merchants could have been exchanging objects or commodities without traveling to India. Indian cooking wares may suggest that Indians or other foreign traders frequented Berenike, but they do not highlight where Egyptians were traveling. Most plausibly, members of the Egyptian network were overwhelmingly acquiring or distributing products and coins through intermediaries in south Arabia.[139] It is even possible that Indians increased their activity in the Red Sea as the Egyptian network regressed.[140] In fact, various factors suggest that the network, while vibrant and active, did not reassert routine, direct contact with India (especially before the sixth century CE). It accordingly was able to transport Christian culture to Aksumite Ethiopia, south Arabia, Socotra, and Nubian Ethiopia but not to the Indian subcontinent.

Certain archaeological materials support this premise. As noted previously, finds of coins, circulation pottery, commodities (like pepper or wine), and even domestic vessels, being earmarked for exchange, can travel beyond the movements of their initial set of carriers. But the travel of materials specifically loaded onto ships for segments of a trip and then discarded can suggest specific legs between the Red Sea and India that sailors and merchants traveled. Finds of basalt rocks from the ports of Berenike and Myos Hormos are typically traceable to Yemen but not to India, and this suggests that many Romans only traveled as far as ports in south Arabia, where they loaded their ships with ballast, which was discarded upon arrival in Egyptian Red Sea ports.[141] Certainly, even at the height of Indo-Mediterranean contact certain Roman Egyptian merchants awaited the arrival of eastern goods from Arabian harbors, from which they could acquire local frankincense. The deposition of some ballast stones can be dated explicitly to this period, and since Myos Hormos was abandoned in the late third century CE, the basalt finds there were probably deposited

---

[139] Walburg, *Coins and Tokens*, 319–44 (esp. 327–29), informs my thinking, though I differ in some interpretations. Also, an implication of Darley, *Indo-Byzantine Exchange*, 382, and "Self, Other, and Use," 73–75; and Decker, "Settlement and Trade," 213.
[140] Sidebotham, *Berenike*, 261–62.
[141] Peacock and Williams, "Introduction"; and Peacock, Williams, and James, "Basalt as Ships' Ballast," 28–70, at 28 and 59–63.

earlier.[142] Unfortunately, many ballast stones lack firm dates of deposition at Berenike. Some such ballast stones probably were deposited there in late antiquity. They would in such an instance reflect the geographic retraction of the Roman Egyptian network during the fourth and fifth centuries and the tendency for merchants and sailors of the period to terminate their journeys in Arabian ports, which represented the southern and eastern loci of Roman residential communities.

As discussed in Chapter 2, textual sources corroborate the premise that the Roman Egyptian network, while maintaining a robust presence in the Red Sea and south Arabia, had retracted geographically. Indeed, they suggest the loss of direct contact with the subcontinent. Such sources no longer describe direct commercial contact in the same manner that the *Periplus of the Erythraean Sea*, Strabo, Pliny, and Claudius Ptolemy had for previous centuries. Similarly, the tendency for late antique sources to describe Arabia and Ethiopia as regions inhabited by "Indians" reflects the shrinking horizons of the period. In certain instances, it indicates geographic confusion (*Letter Regarding the Peoples of India and the Brahmins; Exposition of the Entire World; Itinerary from Eden*) or the belief that east Africans and Arabians were specific types of Indians (Rufinus, Socrates, Sozomen, Philostorgius; Theodoret; ps.-Gelasius). In others, it reveals how authors could believe that sources citing east Africans and Arabians as "Indians" were referring to actual inhabitants of the subcontinent (Eusebius, Jerome, and Epiphanius).

Such tendencies in the sources reflect the substantive shifts that the Roman Egypt network was experiencing at the time. Because the network no longer extended to India directly, fourth- and fifth-century CE Romans would have encountered Indians of the subcontinent in intermediary locations, or possibly at their Red Sea ports. Their commerce with Indian Ocean peoples thus assumed a new dynamic. To a certain degree, they relied on Aksumite Ethiopian and Arabians contacts to purchase their commodities in the same way that inhabitants of the subcontinent previously had. They also shipped commodities to the ports of Aksumite Ethiopia or Arabia so that their intermediaries could complete the seaborne trek to India itself. Finally, as we have seen, Indians may have continued to frequent or even reside at ports of the Red Sea.[143] As such modes of exchange became dominant, Roman Egyptians increasingly conflated the various peoples

---

[142] Peacock, Williams, and James, "Basalt as Ships' Ballast," 59–60.
[143] Sidebotham, *Berenike*, 261–62. By contrast, Gurukkal, *Rethinking Classical Indo-Roman Trade*, 200–48 (esp. 248) doubts the westward extension of Indians' networks due to a disassociation from price-based networks.

who acted as contacts for overseas trade between the Red Sea and India and labeled them "Indian." But despite their contact with Red Sea ports and the subcontinent, no reliable evidence indicates that Indians, Arabians, or Ethiopians were responsible for bringing and anchoring Christianity in India in a significant way. As we will see in a moment, the textual and epigraphic sources for Christianity's movement into the Arabian Sea link the phenomenon to travelers from the Roman empire, but these were not moving beyond south Arabia.

Accordingly, even if some of the sources that describe "Indian" Christians express cognizance of the existence of the Indian subcontinent, they were still treating east Africa and Arabia as containing Christian "Indians" and "Indias." Their treatment was shaped by the fact that Arabians and Ethiopians were now oftentimes the "Indian" contacts with whom the Roman Egyptian network maintained the bulk of its direct contact and through whom it managed trade with India. This is why, as noted in the previous chapter, the *Itinerary from Eden* locates Christian communities among the "Indians" of Ethiopia, Arabia, and Socotra during this period but has little to say about the actual Indian subcontinent. It explains why the *Letter Regarding the Peoples of India and the Brahmins* similarly appears to assume that India was not far from the horn of Africa and was embedded in the Roman empire's framework of international diplomacy; the text had in fact conflated Arabia and Socotra with the Indian subcontinent and Sri Lanka. In their own ways, Eusebius, Rufinus, Jerome, Epiphanius, Philostorgius, Sozomen, Socrates, and Theodoret all described places in Africa or Arabia as "India."[144] Moreover, no reliable epigraphic or material evidence for Roman Egyptian Christians or their impact in India has surfaced. This is probably because the Roman Egyptian network no longer maintained a well-laid social pathway to India or had residential communities (anchor points) there by the time that it had integrated Christian culture.

When the revitalized Roman Egyptian network had begun to carry Christianity throughout the Red and Arabian sea during the fourth century, it could no longer carry it to India. Christianity had in fact lingered at Alexandria for centuries before penetrating the Roman Egyptian socio-commercial network and traveling to Red Sea harbors. Being firmly established in Alexandria and its environs by the end of the first century CE, the activity of Clement of Alexandria demonstrates that it had become deeply rooted there during the second. But it was only during

---

[144] These issues are examined in Chapter 2.

the second and third centuries CE that it (along with its Gnostic strands) slowly penetrated the Egyptian hinterland. By the fourth century CE, it had been anchored in most Egyptian urban centers and their immediate rural hinterlands; the majority of Egyptians, as some believe, were Christian by the time of Constantine's death.[145] But amid its slow circulation throughout Egypt, Christian culture did not travel and become established at Red Sea Egypt in any substantive way until roughly the time of the tetrarchy.[146] What some have identified as a Christian church at Aila, the earliest of its kind along the Red Sea, dates to c. 300 CE,[147] and no Christian remains are yet attested at Berenike until the fifth century.[148] Myos Hormos, abandoned during the late third century, was apparently evacuated before Christian communities had taken hold there, and the Roman fort at Abu Sha'ar, established in the early fourth century, only housed Christian practitioners decades later.[149] Despite the early arrival and establishment of Christianity at Alexandria, the Roman Egyptian network whose hub was at Alexandria apparently did not adopt Christianity or its culture in any substantive capacity before its third-century regression. But when the network was revived during the fourth century, its members had become carriers of Christianity in sufficiently concentrated numbers to bear Christianity to the residential communities that it had placed in the Red Sea and the Arabian Sea.

As the Roman Egyptian socio-commercial network carried Christianity into the Red Sea and south Arabia, it had the support of churchmen in Alexandria. After all, the Christian culture that it transmitted overseas often had links to Alexandria and the Christian communities there. Yet such ecclesiastical activity was not the primary motor for Christianity's movement. Certainly, as bishops such as Athanasius amplified the strength of their episcopal institutions over the course of the fourth century CE, they endeavored to yoke for their purposes the movement and anchorage of Christianity that the Roman Egyptian network had facilitated beyond the

---

[145] Pearson, "Earliest Christianity," 97–112, and *Gnosticism and Christianity*, 32–37 and 223; Clarke, "Third-Century Christianity," 605–8 and 638.
[146] It was noticeably in and after the fourth century CE that Christian ecclesiastical involvement in Red Sea trade and importation of south Asian products can be detected. Seland, "*Liber Pontificalis* and Red Sea Trade."
[147] Power, *Red Sea*, 28–29; Parker, "Roman 'Aqaba Project" (the 1997–1998, 2000, and 2002 Campaigns).
[148] Sidebotham, "Roman Ports," 161, with Fig. 6.21–22.
[149] Sidebotham, *Berenike*, 182–83, and "Roman Ports," 139–42 and 148–49; Nappo, "Impact," 238. The site of Abu Sha'ar does not appear to have played a heavy role in trade, but it was still connected to other Red Sea ports.

immediate confines of Egypt.[150] But the reestablishment of the network was the key factor. As it regained its former extent, it transmitted the strains of Christian culture flourishing at Alexandria and Egypt to the various parts of the Red Sea and south Arabia. It anchored them at sites where the network's members had established residential settlements. This premise is supported by several observations regarding the activity of Christians at Aksum and south Arabia, which in fact constitute the "Indias" whose evangelization the late antique ecclesiastical historians narrated (as described in the previous chapter).

Significantly, epigraphic evidence indicates that the Roman Egyptian network maintained residential communities in south Arabia and Socotra during late antiquity. At Qane in south Arabia, certain of its Jews founded a synagogue building, and either a resident Jew or Christian was responsible for a Greek inscription discovered in the building's earlier phases.[151] Likewise, a Roman Egyptian Christian inscribed a text at Socotra, most probably in the late fourth century CE.[152] Such articles of evidence are consistent with the text of Philostorgius discussed in the previous chapter. According to him, Theophilus, a native of Socotra, engaged in evangelizing efforts in south Arabia and Socotra during the mid-fourth century in ways that cohered with embassies that the Roman emperor Constantius had dispatched.[153] But the missionary activities of fourth-century CE evangelizers in south Arabia, just like the embassies sent by Constantius, were following the social pathways generated by the Roman Egyptian network. When Theophilus arrived in south Arabia, as Philostorgius asserts, he found that communities of Jews and Christians were already there.[154] Many of these Jews and Christians were connected to Roman Egypt and represented the residential communities it had established there. Of course, the Jews of Yemen also maintained ties to Palestine and cultivated Hebrew, Aramaic, and Sabaic over late antiquity, and their presence in south Arabia could have been informed in part by overland commercial networks that traversed Arabia.[155] But some such Jews were certainly

---

[150] For Athanasius, the episcopal institutions of Alexandria, and pro-Nicene/anti-Nicene factions, see Haas, *Alexandria in Late Antiquity*, esp. 173–277.

[151] Sedov, "Fouilles du secteur 3: la synagogue," 87–122; and Bukharin, "Greeks on Socotra," 531–37. Also, *IGSK* 65.437.

[152] Bukharin, "Greek Inscriptions at Hoq," 497–98; and Strauch et al., "Catalogue," 144, 11:28.

[153] Philostorgius, *HE* (ed. Bidez and Winkelmann) 3.4–6. See Chapter 3, pp. 74–77, n. 7–20.

[154] Philostorgius, *HE* (ed. Bidez and Winkelmann) 3.4–6; Bukharin, "Greeks on Socotra," 493–549.

[155] Tobi, "Jews of Yemen," provides treatment. For inscriptions of Himyarite Jews in Palestine, see Schwabe and Lifschitz, *Beth She'arim*, no. 111; and Nebe and Sima, "Grabinschrift." For south Arabians in the Levant, see Schiettecatte and Arbach, "Political Map."

connected to Egypt and Alexandria, and the Christians who settled in south Arabia in the fourth century CE were too. The residential communities of the Roman Egyptian network had anchored Christianity in south Arabia. Evangelizers like Theophilus were contributing to and amplifying its cultural impact in the region.

Likewise, material evidence, especially coins and inscriptions, leaves no doubt that the Aksumite monarchy had become Christian during the first half of the fourth century; Athanasius had established a subordinate bishop named Frumentius at Aksum at this time.[156] While romantic in their narrative style, the ecclesiastical sources specify that "farther/inner India" (Aksumite Ethiopia) had been evangelized by figures (including Frumentius) who had traveled from Roman Egypt along the physical and social pathways generated by the trade network in the Red Sea. The presence of Frumentius at Aksum was facilitated by the existence of a Roman Egyptian residential community at Adulis. Such a community surely channeled the movements of Roman Egyptians who carried Christian culture and enabled them to form social connections with Ethiopians at Aksum. Rufinus' treatment even indicates that Frumentius sought out Roman traders (*negotiatores Romani*) who were in the kingdom to inquire about whether any Christians were among them and found such a presence.[157] "Cosmas Indicopleustes" (or a passage attributed to him) verifies that such a community of Roman Egyptians was present at Adulis c. 515–525 CE.[158] Frumentius' activity indicates that it was already at Adulis centuries earlier. From there residential or itinerant Egyptian preachers carried out their evangelizing efforts in the interior. It was only after the Roman Egyptian network had anchored Christianity at Aksum that Athanasius, the bishop of Alexandria, amplified the process and expanded his own reach by making Frumentius (whatever his previous role had been) his subordinate bishop at Aksum.

Moreover, along with the material remains at Aksum that reflect an engagement with Alexandrian Christian culture, a Ge'ez inscription on a fragment of pottery found near Roman Egyptian Berenike is of some value. Its reading and reconstruction are somewhat controversial, but it

---

[156] Munro-Hay, *Aksum*, 77–78 and 202–5; and Munro-Hay and Juel-Jensen, *Aksumite Coinage*, 134–38; Bowersock, *Throne of Adulis*, 63–77; Power, *Red Sea*, 15–59; Robin, "Arabia and Ethiopia," 273–76; and Haas, "Mountain Constantines," esp. 111–13.
[157] Rufinus, *HE* (ed. Mommsen) 10.9.
[158] Cosmas Indicopleustes (ed. Wolska-Conus) 11.13–19. On authorship, see de Romanis, "Romanukharaṭṭha and Taprobane," 196, n. 133; and Darley, *Indo-Byzantine Exchange*, 108–24. For dating his activity at Adulis (perhaps 518–520), see Robin, "Nagrān," 77–79; and Speidel, "Wars, Trade, and Treaties," 83.

indicates the presence of an Aksumite merchant or traveler, or at least a contact of his, at Berenike during the fourth century CE. Like the Aksumite king Aezanas, he calls the Christian god Ariam, and his activity suggests that Aksumite traders at Adulis had adopted the Christian culture of the Roman Egyptian network (either at Adulis or a Red Sea Egyptian port), reconstituted it, and carried it elsewhere.[159] Accordingly, the fact that Aezanas, the first Christian Aksumite king, began to display Christian imagery c. 330 CE, raised inscriptions in Greek and Geʿez (in both Ethiopic and south Arabian scripts), and minted coins with Greek legends illustrates the social connectivity that Aksum and Alexandria enjoyed.[160] The residential settlement of Roman Egyptians at Adulis was a key node for this contact, even if Aksumites who forged their own network to Red Sea Egypt certainly contributed too.

If the Roman Egyptian network had anchored Christianity in the ports and interior cities of Aksumite Ethiopia and south Arabia during the fourth century CE, it no longer had the capacity to bring it to India. It was only during the late fifth and sixth centuries that Romans reestablished a certain measure of direct trade and contact with India, even if Aksumite, Arabian, and Indian contacts, as "Indians," still played centrals roles. For this period, the work transmitted under the name "Cosmas Indicopleustes" specifies that Roman Egyptians were dwelling in the port of Adulis and, with the help of Aksumite sailors, were voyaging to Sri Lanka. It also states that Persian Christians had established settlements of their own in south India and Sri Lanka, even if it does note the presence of Greek-speaking Christians on Socotra itself.[161] Such testimony significantly indicates that by the time Roman Egyptians had re-established direct contact with the Indian subcontinent, Persian Christians had already been evangelizing the populations of certain port cities and coastal regions. By contrast, the Roman Egyptian network had only moved Christianity as far as Socotra, where, as we have seen, a Roman Egyptian Christian did in fact inscribe a graffito in Greek. As Procopius indicates, Persians were also much more successful at establishing direct socio-commercial networks with India and at forging commercial bonds with Indians, even if "Cosmas" (or

---

[159] Littmann and Meredith, "An Old Ethiopic Inscription"; Ullendorf, "Ethiopic Inscription"; Haas, "Mountain Constantines," 112–13; Power, *Red Sea*, 40; Robin, "Arabia and Ethiopia," 273–81.
[160] Munro-Hay, *Aksum*, 77–78 and 202–5; and Munro-Hay and Juel-Jensen, *Aksumite Coinage*, 134–38; Bowersock, *Throne of Adulis*, 61–77; Haas, "Mountain Constantines," esp. 111–13; Phillipson, "Aksoum et le nord," 109–11 and *Foundation*, 91–106; Robin, "Arabia and Ethiopia," 273–81. Aksum's conversion to Christianity was not seamless. See Rubin, "Greek and Geʿez."
[161] Cosmas Indicopleustes (ed. Wolska-Conus) 2.54 and 3.65, with 11.17.

a passage attributed to him) depicts a king of Sri Lanka as being especially impressed with Roman coinage.[162]

If such premises are correct, the disruption that the Roman Egyptian commercial network extending directly to India suffered over the late third and early fourth centuries CE best explains how Christianity did not become anchored in Indian ports due to the activity of Roman Egyptians. When the network did extend to India (during the first-third centuries), its merchants and sailors were not yet carrying and transmitting Christian culture. After the network had begun to carry Christian culture (during the fourth-sixth centuries CE), it no longer maintained a residential presence in India itself, but it did extend to various ports of the Red Sea and Arabian Sea. It is for such reasons that epigraphic and archeological indications for late antique Christianity in Aksumite Ethiopia, Nubia, and south Arabia have been detected,[163] and this evidence coheres with the testimony of ecclesiastical histories, even if these are anecdotal and dubious on points of detail. Accordingly, Roman traders who traveled to India in the first through mid-third centuries CE were not carriers of Christian culture, and Roman traders who carried Christian culture to various parts of the Red and Arabian Seas during the fourth and fifth centuries CE were no longer traveling to India. This attenuation of the Roman Egyptian trade network therefore spelled a delay for Christianity's anchorage in the Indian subcontinent. In other words, Christian communities took shape in Aksumite Ethiopia, south Arabia, and Socotra during the fourth century CE because it was precisely by that time that Christianity had penetrated a resurging Roman Egyptian network. Late antique ecclesiastical historians were referring to such phenomena when they described the arrival of Christianity in "India." But the network could not anchor Christian culture in the Indian subcontinent itself.

In light of such issues, the testimony of "Cosmas Indicopleustes" regarding the formation of Christian communities in the Indian Ocean is significant. Of all our classical or late antique authors that depict Ethiopia, Arabia, and India, "Cosmas" is the one who provides authentic indication that he visited most of these places firsthand, understood their

---

[162] Cosmas Indicopleustes (ed. Wolska-Conus) 11.13–19 (on authorship, de Romanis, "Romanukharaṭṭha and Taprobane," 196, n. 133; and Darley, *Indo-Byzantine Exchange*, 108–24); Procopius, *Bell. Pers.* (ed. Haury) 1.20.

[163] Bukharin, "Greeks on Socotra," 493–549; Bowersock, *Throne of Adulis*, 63–91; Power, *Red Sea*, 15–59; and Haas, "Mountain Constantines," esp. 111–13; Phillipson, "Aksoum et le nord," 109–11, and *Foundations*, 91–106; Robin, "Arabia and Ethiopia," 273–81; Richter, "Beginnings of Christianity"; and Dijkstra, "Religious Transformation of Nubia."

geography, and could differentiate among their different societies, even if he nonetheless conceived of east Africa, Arabia, and the subcontinent as populated by various types of "Indians." Having traveled in the Red Sea and Indian Ocean c. 515–525 CE and having composed his narrative c. 550 CE, "Cosmas" locates Christian communities overseen by the Persian Church of the East at Sri Lanka, Kalliena (likely near Mumbai or Quilon), pepper-producing Male (most reasonably Malabar/Kerala), and Socotra.[164] How these Christian communities became established in south India is the topic of Chapter 6, but for now, it is worth emphasizing that "Cosmas" does not accredit Roman Egyptians with bringing Christianity to south Asia. Intriguingly, he notes that the Christians of Socotra spoke Greek despite having Persian bishops, and this coheres with the textual and material evidence for Greeks-speaking Christians on Socotra by the late fourth century. But that is as far into the Indian Ocean that the Roman Egyptian network had carried Christianity; otherwise the Persians had evangelized south India and its environs.

Conclusion

In antiquity, commercial networks meaningfully connected the various societies of the Mediterranean and Indian Ocean worlds. Commodities, people, and ideas traveled among these societies through the social pathways that these networks laid. Due to such connectivity, the various late antique testimonies regarding Christianity's arrival in "India" have ostensible value as sources for the arrival of Christianity in the Indian subcontinent. But as we have seen, late antique treatments of Christianity in "India" were referring to places and peoples in east Africa and Arabia.

Roman Egyptian traders and preachers did not bring and anchor Christian culture in the Indian subcontinent. For much of the Roman imperial period, the Roman Egyptian socio-commercial network and its circulation society moved people and culture to and from India. But they did not carry Christianity there. When the network was at its peak, its members had not yet begun to carry the culture of Christianity in any substantive capacity. When they had begun to do so, the network no longer extended to India. It instead carried Christianity to various ports

---

[164] Cosmas Indicopleustes (ed. Wolska-Conus) 3.65, with 11.13–19 (on the authorship of Book 11, see De Romanis, "Romanukharaṭṭha and Taprobane," 196, n. 133 and Darley, *Indo-Byzantine Exchange*, 108–24). For "Cosmas'" claims of personal autopsy, see p. 83, n. 44. His toponyms are treated by Banaji, "'Regions that Look Seaward'," 114–19.

in the Red Sea and south Arabia; these were the "Indias" to which the late antique ecclesiastical historians were referring. By the time that the network refashioned direct links with the Indian subcontinent, a strand of Christianity carried there by Persians had already arrived and been established.

PART III

Christianity, Networks, and the Middle East

CHAPTER 4

The Movement of Christianity into Sasanian Persia: Perspectives and Sources

According to the Parthian *Acts of Thomas*, which does not survive but can be reconstructed in general outline (see Chapter 1), Judas Thomas evangelized peoples of Iran, central Asia, and even parts of north India. In this relatively early version of the Thomas narrative, the transaction between Jesus and Habban would have occurred at a Persian Gulf site. Habban and Judas Thomas would have sailed downriver and into the open sea to north India, where the realm of the Indo-Parthian king Gudnaphar was located. When composing the surviving third-century Indian *Acts*, the author drew upon, engaged with, and manipulated this basic tradition. In such ways, the Parthian *Acts*, composed in the later second century or so, attributed the rapid evangelization of the Parthian empire and adjacent territories of central Asia and north India to the itinerant apostle Judas Thomas.

The actual trek of Christianity to the Iranian plateau and central Asia, however, happened much later and slower than the itinerary that Thomas' Parthian *Acts* or any other late antique text conveyed. As we have seen, late antique Christians who encountered the narrative tradition of the Parthian *Acts* believed that Christians inhabited these places due to a first-century Christian mission. The Syriac *Book of the Laws of the Countries* and, by extension, the *Clementine Recognitions* and Eusebius therefore conceived of Christianity as being practiced by Parthians, Medians, Persians, and Kushans/Bactrians.[1] Such premises of Christianity's early and rapid movement have similarly been replicated by modern scholarship due to a variety of sources that presumably document the process.[2] Yet, a substantial gap exists between the actual movement of Christianity into the Iranian plateau

---

[1] Andrade, "Syriac *Book*."
[2] Koshelenko, Bader, and Gaibov, "Beginnings of Christianity in Merv," 55–70; Ramelli, "Tradizione su Tommaso," esp. 65; Harrak, "Trade Routes," 57; but see "Edessa or Adiabene?" 172–77; Tomber, "Bishops and Traders," 225; Jullien and Jullien, *Apôtres des confins*, 201–6 and 215–22; Jullien, "Minorité chrétienne 'grecque'," 107–9; Debié, Perrin, and Mahé, "L'Orient," 616.

and central Asia and the historical experiences that Upper Mesopotamian and Mediterranean Christians cultivated. This chapter probes it.

Socio-commercial networks played a vital role in shaping the movement of Christianity from the Roman Levant to regions farther east. Chapter 5 in this vein analyzes the socio-commercial networks that connected the Roman Levant to central Asia and India, and as we will see, their dispositions shaped where Christianity traveled before the fifth century CE. But before such analysis can be implemented, it is important to examine the existing sources for the presence of Christianity in Parthian and Sasanian territories and to assess where one can reasonably posit its anchorage during that time. This chapter therefore provides such an assessment of the evidence for where Christianity had traveled, and by doing so, it enables the chapter to follow to posit how socio-commercial networks carried Christianity to new places and transferred it to the bodies of new networks.

Early Christianity in India: Complexities and Problems

Due to the complicated nature of the traditions pertaining to the apostle Judas Thomas, certain issues must first be clarified before one can proceed to analyze the secure evidence for Christianity's eastward trek and arrival. Late antique apostolic apocrypha, hagiographies, and chronicles ostensibly suggest direct contact between the Roman Levant and India and, thereby, the early transmission of Christian culture to India. As a result, they have often influenced scholarly perspectives. But Roman Syrians and Upper Mesopotamians did not carry Christianity directly to India, and Indians rarely if ever traveled to Roman Syria and Upper Mesopotamia. Direct contact between the populations of these regions was in fact quite limited, and if it did occur, it happened at sites on the north Persian Gulf littoral.

Certainly, strands of Christianity with intimate ties to the Syriac language took root in Sasanian Persia and eventually central Asia and parts of coastal India. As stated previously, "Cosmas Indicopleustes" is the earliest source that unambiguously places the Persian Christians in the Indian Ocean. Aside from his testimony, various literary sources indicate or hint that Christianity had been anchored in parts of coastal India at some point in the fifth century (see Chapter 6). They also suggest that a vital transit point for such strands of Christianity was Upper Mesopotamia. This was the home of the Syriac dialect of Aramaic that eventually became a liturgical language of Thomas Christians, even if the terms of its transmission to India are poorly documented.

Nonetheless, the evidence for the movement of Christianity from Upper Mesopotamia to India before c. 400 CE poses certain difficulties. It is often posited that direct commercial or diplomatic movement between Upper Mesopotamia and India was fairly routine in antiquity. If so, Christianity could have traveled to India at an early date.[3] Certainly, various imperial and royal centers in the geographic span between the eastern Mediterranean and India or China were connected by a web of diplomatic exchange. Such connectivity facilitated the dissemination of the Manichaean religion and the movement and exchange of religious ideas throughout a broader Afro-Eurasian world system.[4] But as noted in the Introduction, the belief that inhabitants of the Roman Levant and Upper Mesopotamia were in direct contact with India is based primarily on the testimony of the Indian *Acts*. Since the surviving text is the product of a specific mid-to-late third-century agenda whose primary aim was to remove Judas Thomas from Parthia, it is not reliable.[5]

As we have seen, Indians who traveled to the Roman Mediterranean typically followed the Red Sea passage. It would seem that Indian ambassadors sometimes traveled there by moving overland across Mesopotamia and the Roman Levant. According to Porphyry, who wrote in the late third century, the Edessene philosopher Bardaisan had written about Indians' customs and even discussed the distinction between Brahmins and "Samanaeans." Having consulted Indian ambassadors who were on a diplomatic mission during the reign of an Antoninus from Emesa (that is, Elagabalus, 218–222 CE), he learned from them how Brahmins conducted trials by ordeal but refused to put anyone to death.[6] His discussion is consistent with that of *The Book of the Laws of the Countries*, which was composed by one of Bardaisan's students c. 200–225 CE but may be an iteration or expansion of a late second-century CE text of Bardaisan cited

---

[3] Ramelli, "Tradizione su Tommaso," esp. 65, and "Early Christian Missions," 223–25; Harrak, "Trade Routes," 57, but see "Edessa or Adiabene?" 172–77; Tomber, "Bishops and Traders," 225, for instance.
[4] Some examples are Dilley, "Religious Intercrossing," "Also Schrieb Zarathustra," and "'Hell Exists'"; BeDuhn, "Iranian Epic" and "Mani and Crystallization"; Gardner, "Comments on Mani"; Klein, "Epic Buddhasarita"; Dognini, "Nascita" and "Primi contatti"; Lieu, "Diffusion, Persecution, and Transformation of Manichaeism."
[5] For a different interpretation, see Reger, "On the Road to India," 252.
[6] Porphyry's *De Styge* in Stob. *Anth*. 1.3.56 (1.66.24–70.13), which is *Fragments* (ed. Smith) 376, with *de abstinentia* (ed. Nauck) 4.16–17 (together being *FGrH/BNJ* 719, F. 1–2). The correct Greek text of the reference to Antoninus from Stobaeus is a matter of dispute, but I favor a reconstruction that identifies Antoninus as being from Emesa in Syria, not as coming from Emesa into Syria. For some key discussion, see Reed, "Beyond the Land of Nod," 66–68, who regards some of Bardaisan's knowledge (esp. on the "Samanaeans") to be new and not based on Greek source tradition.

by Eusebius and entitled *On Fate* by him.[7] According to this text, the Brahmins followed a law that prohibited killing.

But as recently argued, such testimony regarding Indians may have been in fact derived from Greek and Roman sources produced after the conquests of Alexander the Great, thereby suggesting that neither Bardaisan nor his students had consulted Indian informants.[8] In fact, one of the principal informants mentioned is called Dadamamis or Damadamis in the various manuscripts. He is therefore often deemed to be named after a prototypical Indian sage of Greek literature (Dandamis) and, if so, is probably invented.[9] Moreover, if a member of Bardaisan's intellectual circle had in fact encountered an actual Indian embassy to "Elagabalus," the meeting did not occur in Mesopotamia or Syria. It would have occurred in the city of Rome. By this interpretation, "Dadamamis" or "Damadamis" (or Dandamis), if not a complete invention of the writer, would be an Indian named Dahardah who attended the investiture of a king in Yemen late 218 or 219 CE.[10] If "Dadamamis" or "Damadamis" was this Dahardah, and if Dahardah had continued to Rome to meet Elagabalus in c. 219–220 CE, he was traveling by the Red Sea, not Upper Mesopotamia.

Ostensibly, the *Nisibene Hymns* of Ephrem provide support for the activity of Judas Thomas, the early movement of Christianity to India, and direct contact between Edessa and the Indian subcontinent. One of his hymns famously echoes an Edessene claim that a merchant had brought Thomas' relics from India to Edessa.[11] In the poem, the Devil laments their arrival. Certainly, Ephrem's testimony attests to the formation of a relic cult for Thomas at Edessa by the mid-fourth century. But it also reflects the influence that the *Acts of Thomas* had exerted on Edessene historical memories by that time. Due to its influence, Ephrem and his contemporaries treasured a narrative that linked Thomas' relics to India, and it is noticeable

---

[7] *The Book of the Laws of the Countries* (ed. Drijvers) 42 and (ed. Ramelli) 179. Ramelli, *Bardesane di Edessa*, 18–32 and *Bardaisan of Edessa*, 54–60 and 115–22, treats date and relationship to the text cited by Eusebius. For Eusebius' citation of *On Fate*, see *HE* (ed. Schwartz and Mommsen) 4.30. For his version of passages of the Syriac *Book of the Laws of the Countries*, see *Preparation for the Gospel (Praeparatio Evangelica)* (ed. Mras and des Places) 6.9.32–6.10, with *FGrH/BNJ* 719, F. 3. Eusebius' iteration coheres with the Syriac *Book*, but Ramelli surmises that it could be based on Bardaisan's text.

[8] Biffi, "Ciò che Bardesane venne a sapere sull'India?" and *FGrH/BNJ* 719, F. 2 discuss.

[9] See previous note. For the Greek tradition on Dandamis, see Martin, "Un recueil de diatribes cyniques"; and Photiadès, "Diatribes cyniques."

[10] Since Dahardah's embassy can be traced to south Arabia, from which it could reach Rome by the Red Sea and Egypt, it is most probable that Bardaisan (or a disciple) encountered Indian diplomats in Rome while on embassy there. See Robin, "Palmyréniens en Arabie du Sud," 490–92.

[11] Ephrem, *CN* (ed. Beck) 42.1–3.

that like the *Acts*, Ephrem does not mention a specific site in India where Thomas had died and been interred. In the same way that the Indian *Acts* reflects an Edessene tendency to associate the preaching of Judas Thomas vaguely with India, Ephrem's narrative in fact exhibits a similar lack of knowledge of India or the nature of trade between it and Upper Mesopotamia. If he was ascribing the arrival of Thomas' relics at Edessa to commercial activity between India and Upper Mesopotamia, he was emulating the contrived narrative of the surviving *Acts* and similar local traditions of the Edessenes, which portrayed the arrival of Judas Thomas in India through a similar device. But like the Indian *Acts*, his testimony was not based on any referential knowledge of India or how to travel there. It simply perpetuated the Edessene inventions responsible for the Indian *Acts* and the relic cult for Thomas at Edessa, from which it was ultimately derived.

The *Chronicle of Se'ert* in several instances describes Christian movement between Sasanian territory and India, but its compilation was late, and its reliability for the period before the fifth century is an issue. For instance, in two nearly identical passages it states that a bishop of Basra named David (Dodi), who may correspond to a third-century bishop of Phorat-Maišan, had traveled to India (*al-Hind*) to evangelize the region; it first dates this episode to c. 295–300 CE and the second time to c. 360 CE.[12] Complicating the matter, however, is the fact that Islamic-era texts like the *Chronicle* often referred to the Persian gulf littoral as *al-Hind* or *bēṯ hendwāyē*.[13] Even if the passage reflects authentic activity, it is not certain that David (Dodi) traveled to the subcontinent to preach; he may have been evangelizing people of the Persian Gulf or parts thereof. The chronicle's treatment of the arrival of asceticism in the Persian Gulf during the fourth century poses similar difficulties.[14]

Nonetheless, *the Chronicle of Se'ert* and other Islamic-era sources provide plausible testimony for the fourth- or fifth-century arrival of Christianity in India. According to the *Chronicle*, a bishop of Rev-Ardashir at coastal Persis (Fars), about whose identity the text is somewhat confused, sent materials for use among Christians in India c. 470 CE.[15] In the ninth century CE, Ishoʻdad

---

[12] *Chronicle of Se'ert* (ed. and trans. Scher) in 4.236–37 and 292–93. The *Ecclesiastical Chronicle* of Barhebraeus (thirteenth century) describes a David of Phorat-Maišan who lived in the mid-third century and laid hands on Papa, thus ordaining the controversial bishop of Seleucia-Ctesiphon. Barhebraeus, *Ecclesiastical Chronicle* (ed. Abbeloos and Lamy) 3.27–28.

[13] Brock, "Syriac Life," 166 and 187. Perhaps used in this way by the putative author of *The History of Mar Yaunan*, in Bedjan, *AMSS* 1.466 and in the *Life of Mar Giwargis* (ed. Bedjan) 561.

[14] *Chronicle of Se'ert* (ed. and trans. Scher) 5.310–12 for fourth-century ascetics in the Persian Gulf.

[15] According to the *Chronicle of Se'ert* (ed. and trans. Scher) 7.116–17, Maʻna, bishop of Rev-Ardashir and metropolitan of Fars, sent Syriac translations of some Greek works of Diodore of Tarsus and Theodore of Mopsuestia and other texts that he wrote in Persian to Persian Gulf locations and India. It should be

of Merv described how what he called the "Letter to Romans" (most likely Theodore of Mopsuestia's commentary on the Pauline Letter to Romans, not the actual epistle) was translated from Greek to Syriac by Mar Koumi for Mari the priest, with the help of Daniel the priest, an Indian.[16] As such, the translation would have occurred in the mid-fifth century or so; at that time Mari may have been the bishop (or future bishop) of Rev-Ardashir, and Daniel would have been an "Indian" Christian with links to Fars. Two letters of Isho'yabh III, bishop of Seleucia-Ctesiphon, verify that the metropolitan of Fars administered Indian sees and even a Christian congregation at "Qalah" (that is, Qalang) in the Malay peninsula by the mid-seventh century.[17] The *History of Mar Yaunan*, clearly late Sasanian or early Islamic, places Christian monasteries deep in the Persian Gulf area.[18] One can also refer to Persian merchants and monks in *bēt hendwāyē* according to Isho'denah of Basra (eighth century).[19]

All such testimony from these later sources is difficult to verify and is in itself insufficient as testimony for the movement of Christianity to India in substantially earlier periods. But it coincides with the sixth-century testimony of "Cosmas Indicopleustes," who maintains that Christian communities had formed stable roots in coastal India by c. 515–525 CE. Also, by c. 500 CE the tradition had begun to circulate in Greek, Latin, and Syriac sources that Thomas had died in Kalamene/Calamina of India. The name of the site for Thomas' martyrdom may constitute a Greek and Latin rendering and shortening of *Cholamandalam*. It at least reflects the establishment of a tomb ascribed to Thomas on the Coromandel coast or elsewhere in south India.[20] The tradition regarding Kalamene/Calamina is therefore quite

---

noted that the *Chronicle of Se'ert* also conflates Ma'na, a shadowy bishop of Rev-Ardashir whom the *Chronicle* claims to have become metropolitan of Seleucia-Ctesiphon in 420, and Ma'na, metropolitan of Fars c. 470 CE. For the first Ma'na, see *Chronicle of Se'ert* (ed. and trans. Scher) 5.328–30.

[16] Isho'dad, *Commentaries* (ed. Gibson), Vol. 5, ܐ, with xiii–xiv. It is often assumed that this translation occurred c. 425 CE, which coincides with the death of Theodore of Mopsuestia. But it could have been accomplished in the decades that followed. Baum and Winkler, *Church of the East*, 53.

[17] Isho'yabh III, *Liber epistularum* (ed. Duval) 247–55 (esp. 252) and 255–60. Whitehouse and Williamson, "Sasanian Maritime Trade," 45–49; and Colless, "Persian Merchants."

[18] Payne, "Monks, Dinars, and Date Palms," 99–101. The author associates himself with a monastery in India, in Bedjan, *AMSS* 1.466, but this could refer to the Persian gulf generally. Similarly, *Life of Mar Giwargis* (ed. Bedjan) 561. See n. 13.

[19] Isho'dnah of Basra, *Book of Chastity* (ed. Bedjan) 487; see also Mingana, "Spread of Early Christianity," 455–56, who cites other passages from the Syriac tradition. For text and manuscripts, see Fiey, "Icho'dnah," 435–38.

[20] Nedungatt, "Calamina, Kalamides, Cholamandalam," with Tubach, "Historische Elemente," 106–7, argues for the link to *Cholamandalam*. As Nedungatt indicates, this is perhaps a Sanskritized Tamil word. See Monier-Williams, *A Sanskrit Dictionary*, 775 (*maṇḍalam*=territory) and Burrow and Emeneau, *A Dravidian Etymological Dictionary*, 413 (*maṉ*=land). For more detailed discussion, see pp. 222–25, n. 57–66.

significant for establishing a date by which Christianity had become anchored in south India and a tomb ascribed to Thomas's burial had emerged there. Its implications are developed more thoroughly in Chapter 6.

Additional evidence for the movement of Christianity from Sasanian Persia to India by the fifth century is provided by the *Ecclesiastical History* that has traditionally been attributed to Gelasius of Cyzicus.[21] According to this history, one of the signatory bishops that attended the council of Nicaea was a certain John, who represented the churches of all Persia and "greater India," by which, as noted previously, the author is clearly referring to the Indian subcontinent.[22] This statement, however, is based on an anachronism. Eusebius' *Life of Constantine* claims that a Persian was present at the council, and some recensions of the *Names of the Fathers at Nicaea* list a certain John the Persian. But these texts make no mention of India.[23] Moreover, the identity of this figure is obscure; he presumably was a bishop along one of the frontier provinces of Persia, not a resident or native of Fars/Persis.[24] Since Eusebius and the *Names of the Fathers at Nicaea* make no mention of India at all, their testimony suggests that the Persian Church of the East did not yet have jurisdiction over Christians there. But the testimony of the ecclesiastical history, in its anachronism, is significant. It suggests that by the late fifth century, when it was composed, the churches of coastal India were being administered by the Church of the East of the Sasanian empire and that the episcopal sees of Persia and India could therefore in theory be represented by a single signatory bishop at an ecumenical conference. The author of the anonymous church history had accordingly assumed that this was the function of the "John the Persian" known to have attended the council of Nicaea in the early fourth century.

Early Christianity in Iran and Central Asia: Complexities and Problems

As remarkable as the traditions of Thomas' travels are, they are easily rivaled by the putative exploits of a figure named Bar Shabba or Mar Shabbay. According to later texts that circulated in Syriac, Arabic, and

---

[21] Jullien and Jullien, *Apôtres des confins*, 110 inform much of what follows.
[22] Ps.-Gelasius, *HE* (ed. Hansen) 2.28.4 and 2.38.1: Ἰωάννης Πέρσης ταῖς ἐν Περσίδι πάσῃ καὶ τῇ μεγάλῃ Ἰνδίᾳ.
[23] Eusebius, *VC* (ed. Winkelmann) 3.7; *Names of the Fathers at Nicaea* (ed. Gelzer, Hilgenfeld, and Cuntz) 23, 64, 87, 103, 127, 149, and 197. Jullien and Jullien, *Apôtres des confins*, 110 provide insight.
[24] Jullien and Jullien, *Apôtres des confins*, 110, discuss various theories regarding this figure and provide bibliography. The identity of this bishop, however, is too obscure to reconstruct despite efforts. Ramelli, "Cristianesimo," 110–14; and Kollaparambil, "Identity of Mar John."

Sogdian (at the least) and that might have a basis in sources as early as the seventh century, the holy man's parents were from Roman Syria, but they were abducted by the Persians when the forces of Shapur I overran the region. Raised as a Christian and a subject of Shapur II at Ctesiphon, the saint exorcized and baptized a woman from the royal court. Forced by the king to relocate to Merv and to marry the magistrate there, the woman eventually summoned her holy patron, and they were responsible for evangelizing the city and its hinterland.[25] Due to their lateness and their romantic nature, tales about figures like Bar Shabba or Mar Shabbay strain plausibility. Yet, in this specific instance, the narrative may have a meaningful historical kernel. The existence of a bishop of Merv named Bar Shabba, active in the early fifth century, is secure, and additional sources show that Christianity had become anchored at Merv by the end of the fourth century.[26]

Like the narratives regarding Bar Shabba/Mar Shabbay, the testimony for the movement of early Christianity into the Iranian plateau, central Asia, and even the Parthian/Sasanian lowlands is generally laden with difficulties. Aside from the Manichaean example, the sources for whether Christian communities had been established in the Iranian plateau by the third century are quite vexing.[27] In particular, it is unclear when the strand of Syriac Christianity that would constitute the basis for the ecclesiastical hierarchy of the late antique Church of the East effectively arrived in the Iranian highlands. While the Syriac *Book of the Laws of the Countries* places Christianity at Edessa and Hatra with considerable reliability,[28] we have already witnessed (in Chapter 1) how its claim that Christians dwelled among the Kushans, Parthians, Persian, and Medians was probably based on the apocryphal and invented tradition of the Parthian *Acts of Thomas*.[29] The text's reference to promiscuity among Kushans, while perhaps

---

[25] Various late sources accredit a certain Bar Shabba or Mar Shabbay with becoming the first bishop of Merv c. 360 CE, but these are late and cannot be traced to a period before the seventh century CE. Brock, "Bar Shabba/Mar Shabbay." Bar Shabba's conversion of Merv is in *Chronicle of Se'ert* (ed. and trans. Scher) 5.253–58. Excavations have not established the presence of a Christian community at Merv before the fourth century CE. Comneno, "Nestorianism in Central Asia," 28–34.

[26] The first signatory bishop of Merv, who bears the name Bar Shabba, was active in 424 CE; it is unclear how long he had been bishop previously. See *Synodicon orientale* (ed. Chabot) 43.

[27] In a very useful overview to the Church of the East, Walker, "From Nisibis to Xi'an," 997–1000, describes the evidence for early Christian communities in Parthian/Sasanian territory without relying on dubious sources.

[28] Kaizer, "Capital Punishment," demonstrates that Bardaisan's understanding of Hatra is generally accurate.

[29] For a different understanding, see Jullien and Jullien, *Apôtres des confins*, 130–32; Debié, Perrin, and Mahé, "L'Orient," 616.

referring to the practice of polyandry that is attested in Bactrian documents, also conforms to statements made by previous Greek sources, which could ultimately be the origins for it. It is therefore not certain that the *Book*'s statement reflects first-hand knowledge of Bactria's actual residents or direct contact between Christians of Upper Mesopotamia and central Asia.[30] The rock-cut inscriptions of Kirdir located at various sites in Fars show that Christians inhabited Sasanian territory by the late third century, but they unfortunately do not state where exactly the Christians were located.[31] Otherwise, the movement of Christianity to India through Sasanian territory is attested by Islamic-era material that may have had decent seventh-century sources. An example is the *Chronicle of Se'ert*.[32]

A few chronicles situate Christians firmly in the Iranian plateau and, of course, lowland Iraq by the fourth century, but they were written much later or, in one instance, are suspected of being modern forgeries. The authenticity of the *Chronicle of Arbela*, for instance, is not certain.[33] But we have already learned how the testimony of the *Chronicle of Se'ert*, probably compiled in the tenth or eleventh century, may be of some value. It describes how a figure named Bar Shabba or Mar Shabbay evangelized the residents of Merv c. 350 CE. While romantic in nature, this testimony may be based on sources from the seventh century or so CE.[34] It may be virtually impossible to establish the veracity of the tradition. But even so, as we will see later in this chapter, other sources significantly indicate that Christianity had arrived and had begun to find anchorage in the Persian Gulf, Iran, and even Merv in the later fourth century.[35]

Certain late antique hagiographies associate Christianity's movement through lowland Parthian/Sasanian territory and Iran with solitary itinerant apostles or disciples working in the first century CE. These also link the successes of such missionary apostles or disciples with mobile merchants,

---

[30] Crone, *Nativist Prophets*, 400–8 discusses polyandry in Iran. For document, see Sims-Williams, *Bactrian Documents*, 32–35. See also Andrade, "Syriac Book."
[31] The edition/translation of Gignoux, *Quatre inscriptions du mage Kirdīr*, 60 and 69–70.
[32] Walker, "From Nisibis to Xi'an," 1028, n. 28; Brock, "Syriac Sources," 25–26. The source seems to have incorporated material from ecclesiastical histories written by the seventh-century author Daniel bar Mariam and the ninth-century writer Isho'dnah. For recent discussion of sources, see Wood, "*Chronicle of Seert*," 43–60 (44 for citations of Eusebius, Socrates, and Theodoret) and *Chronicle of Seert*, 3–14.
[33] The modern reception of the *Chronicle of Arbela* (ed. Kawerau) has indeed been tortuous, and the text will not be a factor of this account. See namely the discussion of Brock, "Syriac Historical Writing," 23–25; and Walker, *Legend of Mar Qardagh*, 287–90, for its doubtful utility. Some nonetheless use the text to reconstruct the history of this period and argue for its authenticity. Jullien and Jullien, "*Chronique d'Arbèles*," 41–83, and *Apôtres des confins*, 133–36; Ramelli, *Chronicon di Arbela*.
[34] See n. 25.   [35] *Synodicon orientale* (ed. Chabot) 43.

and they thereby indicate that trade connections played a key role in Christianity's putatively rapid movement.[36] In *The Teaching of Addai*, the apostle Judas Thomas sends Addai to evangelize the kingdom of Osrhoene after its king had engaged in epistolary correspondence with Jesus.[37] Amid Addai's successes, easterners disguised as merchants come to Edessa from "Assyria" to hear Addai preach. In the *Acts of Mar Mari*, the preacher Mari, putatively a disciple of Addai in the first century, travels from Edessa to evangelize Iraq and Iran, and he discovers that Khuzistan and Fars had already been evangelized by merchants who had visited Edessa.[38] But the reliability of these accounts is dubious. These hagiographies represent episodes produced by Christians to give apostolic origins to Christian communities, often centuries after the missions that they record. The extant Syriac text of the *Teaching of Addai*, which recounts the movement of Christianity to Upper Mesopotamia, dates to the early fifth century. Its earliest instantiations can be traced to the late third century through the work of Eusebius.[39] Similarly, the *Acts of Mar Mari* was composed in the sixth or seventh century, and it creates a historical narrative for the origins of Christianity communities in the Parthian/Sasanian lowlands that meaningfully coheres with the *Teaching of Addai* (Mari is Addai's disciple).[40]

Like the Parthian and Indian *Acts of Thomas*, the hagiographies just described bear the hallmarks of contrived literary elements that circulated widely during late antiquity. As emphasized in the Introduction, their treatment of the world's peoples as apportioned to distinct apostles or preachers for evangelization emulated the narrative of the Acts of the Apostles, the tropes of the ancient novel, and literary representations of Mani and his disciples.[41] No sources from the first century or the early second century attribute the evangelization of Asian regions to the

---

[36] Jullien and Jullien, *Apôtres des confins*, 201–6 and 215–17; Jullien, "Minorité chrétienne 'grecque'," 107–9; Harrak, "Trade Routes," 49–50, with "Edessa or Adiabene?" 172–77; Baumer, *Church of the East*, 19; Debié, Perrin, and Mahé, "L'Orient," 616.
[37] *The Teaching of Addai* (ed. Phillips). Also, Eusebius *HE* (ed. Schwartz and Mommsen) 1.13.
[38] *Acts of Mār Mārī* (ed. Jullien and Jullien; ed. Harrak) generally, with 31 representing the reference to merchants. See p. 195, n. 87–88.
[39] Griffith, "*Doctrina Addai*"; Wood, "*We Have No King but Christ*," 101–10; Ramelli, "Addai-Abgar Narrative."
[40] Jullien and Jullien, *Origines*, 41–60 and 111–13, for date and relation to the Addai tradition. Also Jullien, "Figures fondatrices."
[41] In Acts of the Apostles (ed. Nestle-Aland) 1:8, the Holy Spirit bids the apostles to be witnesses of their faith throughout the earth and to its uttermost ends. The apocryphal *Acts*, being informed by many conventions of the ancient novel, depict apostles doing just that. Spittler, "Christianity at the Edges," 353–75; and Klauck, *Apocryphal Acts*, 1–14. Drijvers, "Addai und Mani," 171–85; Jullien and Jullien, *Origines*, 73–80; BeDuhn and Mirecki, "Placing the *Acts of Archelaus*," 2.

figures of Judas Thomas, Addai, Aggai, or Mari. The Christians who read and heard such works, of course, treated the invented traditions of the literature as representing historical phenomena, and it shaped their experiences of Christianity's historical movement and geography (as discussed in Chapter 1). But this does not mean that the late antique hagiographies reliably depicted how Christianity traveled.

As a result, most textual sources that document the movement of Syriac-speaking Christianity into Parthian and Sasanian territory impart little reliable evidence. Archaeological endeavors do not provide much either. In general, little material evidence sheds light on Christian activity in Parthian or Sasanian territory before the fifth century CE.[42] What has surfaced or been excavated has often generated substantial confusion. For instance, the Christian tombs and monastic complex on the island of Kharg in the Persian Gulf, originally deemed to have been built as early as the third century, were in fact created between the fifth and seventh centuries.[43]

In the discussion above, we have explored how the late antique texts that depict direct movement between the Roman Levant and India or the arrival of Christianity in various regions of Asia are not reliable sources for such historical phenomena. In Chapter 5, we will in fact establish the forms of commercial movement and relationships that provided the social pathways along which the culture of Christianity traveled. But first, the following sections will analyze the sources that illuminate the timeline for Christianity's arrival and anchorage in Parthian/Sasanian imperial space. The pace by which Christianity traveled eastward through lowland Sasanian territory and into the Iranian plateau was much slower than late antique apocrypha and hagiographies would suggest. The remainder of the chapter examines how this is so.

Christianity in Upper Mesopotamia and Parthian Lowlands

As noted in the previous section, Roman Syrians and Upper Mesopotamians did not carry Christianity directly to India, and they did not maintain direct contact with the Indian subcontinent. The sources that suggest the rapid and

---

[42] Cassis, "Kokhe, Cradle of the Church of the East," 62–78; Hauser, "Christliche Archäologie im Sasanidenreich," 93–136, and "Christen," 29–57. For Sasanian archaeology in general, Payne, "Archaeology," which introduces a journal volume devoted to the topic.
[43] Calvet, "Monuments paléo-chrétiens à Koweit," 678–80; Steve, *Ile de Khārg*; Carter, "Christianity during the First Centuries," 71–108, and "Christianity after the Coming of Islam," 311–30; Briquel-Chatonnet, "Expansion," 178–81.

uninterrupted movement of Christianity to India from the Roman Levant are also problematic on various grounds. But it is possible to establish where Christianity had traveled and found anchorage through an assessment of relatively reliable contemporary sources, and this section accordingly analyzes the timeline for Christianity's movement into lowland Parthian and Sasanian territories.

Syriac-speaking Christians in Upper Mesopotamia clearly had a strong impact on the formation of Christianity in the Parthian and Sasanian empires. It would be otherwise difficult to explain how Syriac came to be a preeminent language used by members of the Sasanian Church of the East in religious texts, formal documents, or quotidian matters.[44] Several contemporary sources verify that Christianity had been well established among Upper Mesopotamians, including inhabitants of Edessa and Nisibis, by the third century CE.[45] *The Chronicle of Edessa* indicates that in 313 CE, a bishop named Qone "placed the foundations for the church of 'Urhāy; he built and completed its building."[46] If the *Chronicle*'s report is regarded as accurate, it shows that by the early fourth century, Edessa possessed a municipal church building and the sort of ecclesiastical and episcopal primacy that had the means and organizational power to build it. Nisibis likewise featured a (now partially preserved) church patronized by the notable bishop Jacob and his eventual successor Vologases by the mid-fourth century.[47] But in a particularly intriguing part of the *Chronicle*, an account of a massive flood that occurred in 201 CE indicates that "the temple (ܗܝܟܠܐ) of the church of the Christians" (presumably a house church) was among the destroyed buildings of Edessa. This portion of the chronicle purports to have been derived from material archived at Edessa and may be contemporary to c. 200 CE, and it indicates that a house church modeled on a similar scale to the third-century one excavated at Dura-Europos existed at the time.[48]

Independently of the *Chronicle of Edessa*, texts of more certain contemporaneous origins indicate that Christianity had moved into Upper Mesopotamia and had taken root there by the late second century, even if church communities in cities like Edessa were not fully hierarchized. These sources also suggest that Christian practice was informed to some

---

[44] Healey, "Variety in Early Syriac," 221–30, and "Edessan Milieu and the Birth of Syriac."
[45] Ramelli, "Edessa e i Romani fra Augusto e i Severi," 137–43, with "Epitafio di Abercio" and "Iscrizione cristiana," cogently presents the existence of an organized church at Edessa by c. 200 CE.
[46] *Chronicle of Edessa* (ed. Guidi) 4.
[47] Sarre and Herzfeld, *Archäologische Reise*, 2.336–48, with the inscription also in *IGSK* 65.62.
[48] *Chronicle of Edessa* (ed. Guidi) 2. For the house church of Dura-Europos, see n. 59.

extent by the Greek-speaking Christian movement in Antioch and Roman north Syria. The funerary inscription of the Phrygian churchman Abercius (apparently 216 CE) records his prior travels through Syria and Mesopotamia as far east as Nisibis. His movements seem to have been mediated by the ecclesiastical network of north Syria, in which Antioch claimed a certain preeminence.[49] The notable influence that Greek philosophical concepts had on the works of Bardaisan, along with the impact that he had on Greek-speaking churchmen, likewise spells the transmission of intellectual culture by or through Antioch and north Syrian Greek polities. The *Book of the Laws of the Countries*, transmitted in Syriac by Bardaisan's disciples in the early third century, securely locates Christianity at Edessa and in north Parthian Mesopotamia.[50] Bardaisan himself was active in the late second century. When Eusebius composed his *Preparation for the Gospel* in the early fourth century, he included within in it excerpts from the Syriac *Book*, even if his *Ecclesiastical History* also perhaps cites a previous version written by Bardaisan himself (under the title *On Fate*).[51] Eusebius also integrated a famous epistolary correspondence that putatively occurred between Jesus and a member of the Abgarid dynasty at Osrhoene and a narrative tradition by which an apostle named Thaddaeus, usually called Addai in Syriac accounts, evangelized Upper Mesopotamia. The extant narrative of Addai's exploits and Jesus' correspondence with "Abgar the Black" (Abgar Ukkama) was composed in Syriac in the early fifth century CE. But Eusebius clearly had access to versions in circulation since at least the late third century CE and claimed to have obtained such documents, written in Syriac, from Edessa's archives.[52] All told, Christian communities can be securely located in the cities and client principalities of Roman and

---

[49] The epitaph with analysis is accessible in Ramelli, "Epitafio di Aberico," who presents the text of Wischmeyer, "Aberkiosinschrift, 24–26 (193–94). For date, Ramelli, "Epitafio di Abercio," 191–92.

[50] Notably Drijvers, for instance, in *East of Antioch*, 1–27, and "Bardaisan von Edessa," 109–22. Schwemer, "Ersten Christen in Syrien," treats the movement of Christianity and the formation of communities throughout Syria and eventually Upper Mesopotamia. Ramelli, *Bardaisan of Edessa*, 1–29 and 51–91, and *Bardesane di Edessa*, 12–18, discusses Greek influences on Bardaisan and his favorable reception among Greek-speaking churchmen of the third century CE, namely Origen.

[51] Ramelli, *Bardaisan of Edessa*, 18–32, and *Bardesane di Edessa*, 54–60 and 115–22. For Eusebius' citations, *Preparation for the Gospel* (*Praeparatio Evangelica*) (ed. Mras and des Places) 6.9.32–6.10, with *FGrH/BNJ* 719, F. 3; *HE* (ed. Schwartz and Mommsen) 4.30.

[52] Drijvers, "Addai and Mani"; Griffith, "*Doctrina Addai*"; and Wood, "*We Have No King but Christ*," 101–10; Brock, "Eusebius"; Ramelli, "Addai-Abgar Narrative." For the *Teaching of Addai* and its citation of early Roman material, Ramelli, *Possible Historical Traces*. Most of the extant version of Eusebius' *Ecclesiastical History* was completed by c. 315 CE (with the tenth book being produced in an update of c. 325), but the first seven books were perhaps composed before the tetrarchic persecutions of 303–311 CE. See Barnes, "Editions" and *Constantine and Eusebius*, 126–63; Louth, "Date"; and Burgess, "Dates and Editions."

Parthian Upper Mesopotamia, especially in urban centers like Edessa and Nisibis, from the mid-second century onward.

Strands of early Syriac Christianity in Upper Mesopotamia were in many ways mediated by Greek-speaking north Syrians, but they also integrated the practices of Palestinian Jews and, as such, were not isolated or completely distinct from Judaism.[53] In the second century, books of the Hebrew Bible were being translated into Syriac in what would become the Old Testament Peshitta. The fact that these books were being translated directly from Hebrew suggests the work of Jewish converts to Christianity, Jews who venerated Christ, or otherwise non-Jews who had mastered Hebrew through close contacts with local Jewish communities.[54] The prominence of Jewish communities in Upper Mesopotamia, especially along well-traveled commercial networks that facilitated movement between the Jews of Palestine and Babylonia, explain such a visible Jewish influence. But it should also be noted that early Christians of Mesopotamia, which included ethnic Jews, were forging direct links to Palestine; the frequent reference to Jesus as "king Christ" or "king Messiah" (*malkā mešīḥā*) is derived from phrases in Palestinian Targumim that often referred to "king, the anointed one."[55] As Josephus clarifies that an Aramaic version of his *Jewish Wars* circulated throughout Mesopotamia and describes how a Jewish merchant at Charax Spasinou converted members of the royal dynasty of Adiabene/Assyria to Judaism, it is certainly a realistic premise that Jews and Christians in Upper Mesopotamia and Assyrian territories to the east had direct links with Jews of Palestine.[56] Likewise, the *Letter of Mara bar Serapion* may have been written by a Jew well versed in Greek philosophy. The author was apparently fleeing north Syria for Osrhoene at a time of increased military activity. If the *Letter* did in fact have a first- or second-century Jewish author (which is far from certain), it could also be evidence for both Jewish ethnic communities and the influence of Greek philosophical trends on Jewish thought in north Syria and Upper

---

[53] Boyarin, *Border Lines*, discusses how strands of Christianity and Judaism intersected or diverged in antiquity. Likewise, Becker and Reed, *Ways That Never Parted* and, for north Syria and Upper Mesopotamia, Reed and Voung, "Christianity in Antioch." Jullien and Jullien, *Apôtres des confins*, 189–225, hypothesize how the "Judaeo-Christianity" of Parthian/Sasanian space was influenced by the practices of various Jews in the Levant, Upper Mesopotamia, and Lower Mesopotamia.

[54] Haar Romeny, "Syriac Versions of the Old Testament," esp. 74–75. Weitzman, *The Syriac Version of the Old Testament*. Jullien and Jullien, *Apôtres des confins*, 189–95; and Shepardson, "Syria," 458–59, treat connections to Judaism.

[55] Schwemer, "Ersten Christen in Syrien," esp. 189–93. Brock, "Syria and Mesopotamia," 171–82. Along similar lines, Amar, "Shared Voice," 15.

[56] Josephus, *AJ* (ed. Niese) 20.34–37; *BJ* (ed. Niese) Preface 3 and 6.

Mesopotamia at this time.[57] Altogether, the anchorage of Christianity in Upper Mesopotamia during the second century, along with the Jewish presences that helped facilitate it, is reasonably well attested.

Ample evidence demonstrates that Christian communities resided in lowland Roman territory along the middle Euphrates by the third century CE. Dura-Europos was a common stopover along the trade routes between the Levant and Seleucia-Ctesiphon, and it was under Parthian control until the 160s CE. It was then captured by the Romans, in whose hands it remained until the Sasanian Persians conquered it in 256 CE.[58] The site is also famous for the discovery of a third-century Christian house church, among the earliest of its kind.[59] The inscriptions and civil documents found at the site, including the fragment of what is either the *Diatessaron* commonly attributed to Tatian or a gospel harmony, are overwhelmingly in Greek.[60] Such texts indicate that the Christian culture of the site was shaped by a strand of Christianity with links to Antioch and north Syria. In fact, as the next chapter shows, north Syrian merchants frequently traveled through Dura-Europos on their way to lowland Parthian and Sasanian destinations. Nonetheless, the site also housed a famous Jewish synagogue in which Hebrew inscriptions have been unearthed,[61] and this shows that the Jewish community too inhabited Dura-Europos and even constituted a vector for interaction between Palestinian and Babylonian Jews. Accordingly, a Greek-speaking strand of Christianity from the north Levant had taken root in Dura-Europos by the third century CE. Like the

---

[57] The articles of Merz and Tieleman, *Letter of Mara bar Sarapion*, constitute the most recent organized effort among scholars to place the *Letter* in its historical, literary, and philosophical context. For discussion regarding date, among other issues pertaining to the letter, see Ramelli, "Lettera di Mara bar Serapion," "Gesù tra i sapienti greci perseguitati," and *Stoici Romani minori*, 2561–66; Chin, "Rhetorical Practice"; Merz and Tieleman, "*Letter of Mara bar Sarapion*"; Rensberger, "Reconsidering the Letter"; McVey, "*Letter of Mara bar Sarapion*."

[58] Recent work is Brody and Hoffman, *Dura-Europos: Crossroads of Antiquity*; Chi and Heath, *Edge of Empires*; Leriche, Coqueugniot, and de Pontbriand, *Europos-Doura*. For ethno-cultural politics among the city's constituents (non-Jewish and non-Christian), see now Andrade, *Syrian Identity*, 211–41.

[59] Kraeling, *Excavations at Dura-Europos: The Christian Building* (esp. 34–39, which discusses date). Peppard, "Illuminating the Dura-Europos Baptistery" and *World's Oldest Church* are recent studies. See also articles in Brody and Hoffman, *Dura-Europos: Crossroads of Antiquity*.

[60] *P. Dura* 10. Parker, Taylor, and Goodacre, "Dura-Europos Gospel Harmony"; Joosten, "Dura Parchment and the *Diatessaron*." Koltun-Fromm, "Re-Imagining Tatian," 18–30, challenges the view that Tatian authored the *Diatessaron*. Greek inscriptions can be found in the various volumes of *TEAD*. For the inscriptions in Palmyrene, Syriac, Hatrean, Hebrew, and other Semitic language dialects, see Bertolino, *Corpus*. Most (but not all) Greek inscriptions of Dura-Europos can be found in the volumes of *TEAD* and Cumont, *Fouilles de Doura-Europos*.

[61] Kraeling, *Excavations at Dura-Europos: The Synagogue*. A recent analysis is Stern, "Mapping Devotion in Roman Dura-Europos." Also see the articles of Brody and Hoffman, *Dura-Europos: Crossroads of Antiquity*.

elements of Jewish culture that found anchorage there, its presence can be explained by the close commercial contacts between the Roman Levant and lowland Parthian/Sasanian territory.

Such commercial contacts also brought Christianity to the Parthian lowlands fairly rapidly. Despite the scarce documentation, Christianity was clearly embedded in lowland urban areas of the Parthian and Sasanian empires by the third century CE. Because Dura-Europos was a key commercial stopover for merchants traveling from the Roman Levant to lower Mesopotamia, its Christian material remains represent the local anchorage of a Christian strand that merchants, travelers, or preachers were carrying into Parthian and Sasanian territory. According to the *Cologne Mani Codex*, Mani and his father were members of one of many "Judaeo-Christian" (or "baptist") sects that had taken root in lower Mesopotamia and Mesene by c. 200 CE.[62] Even if their origins are obscure, they were probably facilitated or amplified by the movement of Christian strands along the trade segments connecting north Syria and Upper Mesopotamia to lower Mesopotamia.[63] Finally, in the mid-third century, amid several successful military campaigns, the Sasanian Persians deported Roman Syrian captives, including some who were presumably Greek-speaking Christians, into their interior.[64] A segment of the captives was settled in cities of lowland, southwest Iran and Assyria. This phase of deportation may have amplified the Christian presence in lowland Sasanian territory, but when it occurred, Christian communities were probably already there. A number of deportees were also apparently settled in the interior of Parthia and Fars, including perhaps the new palace site of Bishapur. But according to some recent reckonings, the cultural and religious impact of this phase of deportation, attested largely by later sources, was minimal.[65]

---

[62] Jullien and Jullien, *Apôtres des confins*, 137–50.

[63] The testimony of *Refutation of All Heresies* (ed. Marcovich/ed. Litwa) 9.13.1 and 4, with 19.16.4, well represents such connectivity between Christians of north Syria and Judaeo-Christians sects (including "baptist" ones) in Parthia from the early second through the early third century. For more (with differing interpretations), see Jullien and Jullien, *Apôtres des confins*, 141–45; and Luttikhuizen, "Elchasaites."

[64] *Res Gestae of Shapur* (ed. Huyse) esp. 30 (deportation of Romans); *Chronicle of Se'ert* (ed. and trans. Scher) 1.220–21 (deportation of Christians). Jullien and Jullien, *Apôtres des confins*, 153–88, provide full discussion of evidence, and they suggest that episcopal divisions detectable in the fourth and fifth centuries could be attributable to the presence of Greek-speaking deportees of Roman Syria who did not mesh with the Syriac-speaking Christian presence. Otherwise, bids for ecclesiastical authority could just as easily have been the divisive issue. Also see Jullien, "Minorité chrétienne 'grecque,'" 110–13 and 120–36; and Debié, Perrin, and Mahé, "L'Orient," 619, for Greek-speaking Christians in Persian territory.

[65] Mosig-Walburg, "Deportationen"; Morony, "Population Transfers," 165–70; Smith, *Constantine and the Captive Christians*, 131.

It is not altogether clear whether enduring Christian communities were firmly implanted in these areas through the deportations of Shapur I. Various sources also narrate how Shapur II initiated another wave of deportations in the mid-fourth century.[66] The *Martyr Act of Pusai* indicates that deportees were then settled, for example, at Bishapur in Fars and in Khuzistan.[67] The impact of these deportations, primarily attested by texts after the fourth century CE, is also ambiguous. But as we will see, such settlement may have coincided with the anchorage of Christianity in the Iranian highlands during the latter half of the fourth century.

In many respects, the activity of Mani and his disciples represents a watershed moment in the history of the movement of religion across the Afro-Eurasian landmasses. Initiating a religion that was to be truly cosmopolitan and integrative (if hierarchal), Mani traveled from south Mesopotamia to north India, Iran, and central Asia, and as Chapter 5 stresses, his movement followed the well-laid social pathways created by a lowland Sasanian socio-commercial network. Within a generation of Mani's death, his disciples and converts carried his religion, which interwove Christian, Zoroastrian, Buddhist, and Jain practices and had a substantial impact on the future formation of Christian activity, into the Roman empire and east Asia. Mani and his successors actively moved their religious culture primarily by frequenting the courts of kings and local dynasts. They clearly intended to evangelize at an unprecedented scale and speed.[68] But as emphasized in the Introduction, the trans-imperial and intercontinental example of Mani and the proponents of his religion can be deceptive for many reasons. It runs the risk of being treated as exemplary despite its uniqueness. Having earned the ear of various emperors, governors, and client kings, Mani and his disciples rigorously and rapidly disseminated their religion throughout the geographical span between the Roman Mediterranean and west China. Their endeavors exposed Roman Egyptians to Indian religions in new ways.[69] But not all religions

---

[66] Smith, *Constantine and the Captive Christians* treats the sources for this.
[67] The *Martyr Act of Pusai* and *The Martyr Act of the Captives*, ed. Bedjan in *AMSS* 2.208–32 (208–209 for deportations) and 316–24 (316–19 for deportations), dating to the fifth–sixth century CE, treat this episode of history. See Payne, *State of Mixture*, 64–66.
[68] Dilley, "Religious Intercrossing," 58–70, and "Mani's Wisdom"; BeDuhn, "Parallels"; Gardner, "Mani's Last Days"; Lieu, *Manichaeism*, 86–120, *Manichaeism in Mesopotamia*, 26–38, *Manichaeism in Central Asia*, and "Diffusion, Persecution, and Transformation of Manichaeism."
[69] Gardner, "Comments on Mani"; Klein, "Epic Buddhasarita"; Deeg and Gardner, "Indian Influence"; Jones, "Things Mani Learned"; Dilley, "Religious Intercrossing," 58–70, "Mani's Wisdom," "Also Schrieb Zarathustra?" and "'Hell Exists'"; BeDuhn, "Iranian Epic" and "Mani and Crystallization"; De Jong, "*Cologne Mani Codex*."

were characterized by the inclusiveness and outreach that typified the Manichaeans. Most strands of Christianity acted more exclusively and traveled more slowly.

In fact, contemporary sources illustrate that the movement of Christianity was much more modest. They indicate that various and diverse Christian communities populated lowland Parthian/Sasanian territories by c. 200 CE, and probably even earlier. These communities cultivated strands of Christianity that had arrived from the Roman Levant, and they had also adapted and reconstituted these strands in ways that cohered with lower Mesopotamian cultural contexts. But the diverse strands of Christianity that these communities practiced had not yet traveled into the Iranian highlands by the third century. The movement of Manichaeism was much different. Of all the diverse religious communities that inhabited lowland Parthian and Sasanian territory, the innovative strands of Manichaean religious culture traveled most rapidly. Manichaeism did not merely find anchorage in lowland regions during the third century, but it soon accumulated followers throughout the Roman east, the Iranian plateau, and central Asia, apparently even while Mani was still alive. Chapter 5 analyzes how a Levantine socio-commercial network was responsible for anchoring Christian culture in lowland Parthian/Sasanian regions, and it examines how a lowland Sasanian network adopted and carried Manichaeism eastward at a much quicker pace than other Christian strands. But first, the timeline for the arrival of Christianity in Sasanian Iran and central Asia must be established.

Christianity in Sasanian Persia in the Third and Fourth Centuries CE

During the third century CE, Christians inhabited the Sasanian empire. The rock-cut inscriptions of Kirdīr that celebrate his aggression against them (if with complicated terminology) leave no doubt.[70] But while located in Fars, Kirdīr's texts do not specify where the Christians were resident, and Christianity did not have the regional dimensions that the Church of the East had obtained by the seventh century.[71] It also had not attained to the same trans-continental scope as Manichaeism. Contemporary homilies and conciliar records in fact clarify that the strand(s) of Christianity cultivated by the Persian Church of the East was firmly anchored in lowland Sasanian

---

[70] The edition/translation of Gignoux, *Quatre inscriptions du mage Kirdīr*, 60 and 69–70. For terms, see now Smith, *Constantine and the Captive Christians*, 130–35.
[71] Walker, *Legend of Mar Qardagh*, 87–104, discusses the church in its early seventh-century manifestation.

areas by the fourth century CE. They likewise suggest that it had only begun to move farther eastward after c. 350 CE.

By the 340s CE, urban Christian communities administered by the Church of the East had been established in Mesopotamia and north Iraq. It is often surmised, but perhaps quite problematically, that certain homilies of Aphrahat circulated in 337 or 344 CE (during the "Great Slaughter" of Shapur II) and were fashioned in part for a Christian community at Seleucia-Ctesiphon.[72] Aphrahat's homilies also suggest that social and religious divisions between Jews and Christians had not yet been entirely consolidated and that their beliefs, practices, and communities intersected in many ways.[73] The community at Seleucia-Ctesiphon may have been quite large; those elsewhere were probably more modest and on the scale represented by the house-church of Dura-Europos. In 410 CE, a church council at Seleucia-Ctesiphon organized the Christian communities in the Persian empire's lowland areas, including those in lower Mesopotamia, classical Assyria, the Zab River region, Elymais (Khuzistan), and Mesene, into six metropolitan regional districts. This same council indicates that Christian communities were located along or in the Persian Gulf and in the Iranian highlands, but they were apparently in too incipient a stage to be organized into the type of metropolitan districts that the lowlands had.[74] A manuscript of 411 CE, composed at Edessa, compiles the names of fourth-century Persian martyrs; it presumably reflects information brought to Roman Upper Mesopotamia by Marutha, a bishop of Martyropolis who attended the council at Seleucia-Ctesiphon in 410 CE.[75] All of the named martyrs are from the six lowland metropolitan districts. The abbreviated

---

[72] Walker, "From Nisibis to Xi'an," 1000–1001, provides summary and discusses that date in which Shapur II initiated the "Great Slaughter." Aphrahat, *Demonstrations* (ed. Parisot) 16 and 19–20 (759–84, and 845–930) are often deemed references to contemporary events (such as the conflict between Rome and Persia in 337), to relationships with Jews and Judaism, or to the "Great Slaughter." *Demonstrations* 14.1 (573, of 573–726), as some surmise, places Aphrahat in Seleucia-Ctesiphon during the persecution of 344; 5.1 (184, of 184–238) refers to the wars of 337; 21 treats persecutions (931–990). But see now the critiques of the conventional views by Smith, *Constantine and the Captive Christians*, 103–9. Two notable accounts of a famous bishop of Seleucia-Ctesiphon named Simeon bar Sabba'e (*Martyr Act* and *Narration*, ed. Kmosko), which probably date to the fifth century CE, are now translated in Smith, *Martyrdom* and treated in Smith, *Constantine and the Captive Christians*, 102–3 and 109–24. AMSS 2 and 4 contain many other martyr acts, with Brock, *History of Mar Ma'in*, 77–125, cataloging a comprehensive list.

[73] Becker, "Anti-Judaism and Care for the Poor," 305–27; and Lizorkin, *Aphrahat's Demonstrations*.

[74] *Synodicon orientale* (ed. Chabot) 33–36 (esp. 34 for Persian Gulf/Iranian highlands). For Persian Gulf/Arabia, see Briquel-Chatonnet, "Expansion," 179; and Brock, "Syriac Writers," 85.

[75] Brock, "Saints in Syriac," 185–86. Nau, "Martyrologes et ménologes," 23–26, presents the manuscript. The list of names is easily accessible in Brock, *History of the Holy Mar Ma'in*, 123–25, who includes names from a fragment at Deir al-Surian of Egypt (on which, see Brock and Van Rompay, *Catalogue*, 389–92, Fr. 27).

accounts of Sozomen, based on Syriac testimony that existed by the 440s–450s CE, mentions no highland martyrs either.[76]

With such contemporary evidence, many *Persian Martyr Acts* narrating the mid-fourth century CE violence that occurred during the reign of Shapur II date variously in composition to the late fourth through seventh centuries CE.[77] These narratives frame Shapur's aggression as a uniform persecution, but recent scholarship argues that Christians, primarily clerics, were suffering execution simply for breaking specific laws.[78] Moreover, since the martyr accounts constitute historical memories circulating long after the putative persecutions, it is often uncertain to what extent they capture the mid-fourth century CE context.[79] Work on these texts in the last decade has been illuminating. But much still remains to be done in terms of collating manuscripts and producing critical editions, and it should be stressed that these texts are widely recognized to be of variable and oftentimes dubious historical reliability.

Despite such issues, it is probably significant that the Persian martyr accounts, especially those set in the third or fourth centuries CE, almost always portray Christian dissidence and martyrdom as occurring in lowland areas.[80] The few exceptions depict lowland bishops who die while converting highland "pagans," represent lowland Christians transported to the highlands and martyred there by Sasanian authorities, or constitute late outliers that reflect opposition to the supremacy of the bishop of Seleucia-Ctesiphon amid his lowland primacy. One source, which likely dates to the late Sasanian period, describes the execution of Christians in Media, but it also indicates that the Christians who suffered martyrdom had been transported from Adiabene in pursuit of the king's court.[81] Christian

---

[76] Sozomen, *HE* (ed. Bidez and Hansen) 2.9–14. Sozomen was using the Syriac versions. Devos, "Sozomène et les actes syriaques," 443–56.

[77] Brock, *History of the Holy Mar Ma'in*, 77–125, documents these. Jullien, "Contribution des Actes des martyrs perses," 140–67, and "Contribution des Actes des martyrs perses (II)," 81–102; and Wood, *Chronicle of Seert*, 32–65, provide useful discussion. Note that Jullien treats the *Chronicle of Arbela* as authentic, and her lists of place names includes more than references to sites of persecution and martyrdom.

[78] Payne, *State of Mixture*, 23–58.

[79] Smith, *Constantine and the Captive Christians*, is thoughtful on this issue.

[80] Jullien, "Actes des martyrs perses," 129. Since they are set in the reign of Yazdgird I and tend to be from later manuscripts, the accounts edited and translated by Herman, "Passion of Shabur" and *Persian Martyr Acts* do not play a significant role in my discussion. In my view, the references to Persia in the *Martyr Act of Candida* (ed. Brock) 1, probably composed in the fifth century CE but set in the late third, refers generally to the Sasanian Persian empire, not Fars.

[81] *Martyr Act of 'Aqebshma*, ed. Bedjan, in *AMSS* 2.371–74. The *Martyr Act of 'Aqebshma* is attested by manuscripts dating as early as the sixth century CE. Vat. Syr. 160–61 are now online. The martyrdom of this bishop is reported by Sozomen, *HE* (ed. Bidez and Hansen) 2.13. But in the surviving

captives from a Roman army camp are likewise transferred to Iran in the *Martyr Act of the Captives* (probably a fifth- or sixth-century CE text), where they die late in Shapur II's reign.[82] Similar issues are raised by a martyr act involving a Persian governor of Media who, as a Christian, affiliated with Christians there and converted children of Shapur II in ways that led to their deaths. It depicts no actual executions in Media (these happen at one of the king's lowland courts), and its description of Christians in Media appears tendentious. The source is generally considered suspect and probably does not date before the sixth century CE.[83]

The martyr act regarding Miles, bishop of Susa, constitutes a notable exception.[84] According to this account, Miles was born in the Median highlands, in *bēṯ Raziqāyē*, but he only received baptism after migrating to the king's court at Karka d-Ledan in Khuzistan. Having become bishop of Šušan (Susa), where he apparently failed to curb paganism, he traveled to Jerusalem, Alexandria, the deserts of Egypt, Nisibis, Seleucia-Ctesiphon (where he confronted its power-hungry bishop Papa), and then Maišan, where he interacted with various Christians and made additional converts. Upon returning to the Zagros mountains with two disciples, he was martyred while trying to convert a largely "pagan" landscape in the region.[85] The names of Miles (Milos) and his two martyred companions in fact appear in the Persian martyr list contained in the Edessene manuscript composed in 411 CE.[86] But significantly the martyr act of Miles does not depict the general imprisonment or execution of Christians in the region, and it indeed indicates that Media (*bēṯ Raziqāyē*) consisted largely of non-Christians whom Miles endeavored to evangelize.

---

account, 'Aqebshma is treated as the bishop of a see that is not reliably attested before the fifth century; see Jullien, "Contribution des Actes des martyrs perses," 155. Brock, *History of the Holy Mar Ma'in*, 87–91, for manuscripts.

[82] *Martyr Act of the Captives*, ed. Bedjan in *AMSS* 2.316–19 (deportation) and 320–24 (executions). See Smith, *Constantine and the Captive Christians*, 135–38 and 184–90 (185–86 for date; translation on 186–90).

[83] *Martyr Act of Gubralaha and Qazo*, ed. Bedjan in *AMSS* 4.141–63. The earliest manuscripts are tenth-century, and this figure is not attested among the names of the manuscript of 411 or in the narrative of Sozomen, *HE* (ed. Bidez and Hansen) 2.9–14. Nau, "Martyrologes et ménologes," 23–26, with Brock and Van Rompay, *Catalogue*, 389–92, Fr. 27. The list of names is easily accessible in Brock, *History of the Holy Mar Ma'in*, 123–25. Fiey, *Saints syriaques*, 87 discusses this text.

[84] *Martyr Act of Miles*, ed. Bedjan in *AMSS* 2.260–75 survives in manuscripts that date as early as the fifth century CE (and which closely correspond to Bedjan's text). Vat. Syr. 160–61 are now online. An abbreviated account of his martyrdom is contained in Sozomen, *HE* (ed. Bidez and Hansen) 2.14. See Brock, *History of the Holy Mar Ma'in*, 87–91, and "Saints in Syriac," 185–86 for manuscripts.

[85] *Martyr Act of Miles*, ed. Bedjan in *AMSS* 2.263–74 (with the reference to paganism on 270).

[86] Nau, "Martyrologes et ménologes," 23, with Brock, *History of the Holy Mar Ma'in*, 123–25; Sozomen, *HE* (ed. Bidez and Hansen) 2.14. The companions were Abursam and Sinai, named in the *Martyr Act of Miles*, ed. Bedjan in *AMSS* 2.272–74.

The tradition regarding the martyrdom of Miles and the bishop's highland origins apparently stimulated subsequent efforts to narrate highland martyrs, although in an anachronistic way. Several martyr acts are contained in the same surviving manuscripts as that of Miles and in fact are dated according to his martyrdom. The composition and compilation of these acts seem to reflect a single vein that celebrated Miles and other highland saints.[87] One of them describes the execution of monks, including a figure named Barshebya, in Ishtakhar of Persis/Fars in the year that Miles died. But its depiction of monks in communal monasteries as being targeted by Sasanian authorities is arguably anachronistic. Coenobitic monasteries (which took form later in Sasanian Persia) are not known to have suffered the violence of fourth-century CE Sasanian authorities, and no coenobitic monks are listed as martyrs in the Edessene manuscript of 411 CE (even if the text breaks off abruptly). The aggressor is also described as the "*mawpāṭā*" (mobad) of Ishtakhar, a sort of regional priestly title that suggests a date later than the fourth century CE.[88] Another such martyr act very briefly recounts the death of two other residents of *bēṯ Raziqāyē* two years after the death of Miles. It too describes the violence as being initiated by the regional *mawpāṭā*, again a reference to a relatively late provincial hierarchy of priests and a title not cited in the account of Miles' martyrdom.[89] These texts, modest in scope, seem to expand the example of Miles so as to indicate that Christians of Media and Fars had suffered violence under Shapur II. But they lack plausibility in comparison to Miles' account and were likely written substantially later. Also, unlike Miles and his two companions, their names do not appear in the martyr list of 411 CE or in Sozomen's narrative.

---

[87] Devos, "Martyrs persans," 223–24.
[88] *Martyr Act of Barshebya*, ed. Bedjan in *AMSS* 2.281–84. The work is attested in manuscripts as early as the sixth century CE (Vat. Syr. 160–61 are now online), and it probably dates to the period. See the important observations of Smith, *Constantine and the Captive Christians*, 192 (translation of text at 194–96), on this issue, including regarding coenobitic monasticism. Noticeably, this figure is not listed among the martyrs of the manuscript of 411 or the account of Sozomen, *HE* (ed. Bidez and Hansen) 2.9–14. Vööbus, *History of Asceticism*, 1.229–34, treats early asceticism, and Jullien, *Monachisme en Perse*, covers coenobitic monastic reform and the links to Egyptian models (with bibliography for previous treatment). Gignoux, "Titres et fonctions," 196–98, discusses priestly titles and provincial hierarchies. See Ciancaglini, *Iranian Loanwords in Syriac*, 202–3, on the terms in Syriac. Jullien, "Martyrs en Perse," 279–90, also provides discussion. Brock, *History of the Holy Mar Ma'in*, 87–91, lists manuscripts.
[89] *Martyr Act of Daniel and Warda*, ed. Bedjan in *AMSS* 2.290, with *Martyr Act of Miles*, ed. Bedjan in *AMSS* 2.271. The work is attested in manuscripts as early as the sixth century. Vat. Syr. 160–61 are now online. But this figure is not listed among the martyrs of the manuscript of 411 or the account of Sozomen, *HE* (ed. Bidez and Hansen) 2.9–14. For title, see Gignoux, "Titres et fonctions," 196–98, with Ciancaglini, *Iranian Loanwords in Syriac*, 202–3.

All told, the *Persian Martyr Acts*, regardless of their historical accuracy or inventive embellishments, overwhelmingly situate the dissidence and executions of Christians in lowland areas during the reign of Shapur II. Those that place such activity in the Iranian highlands bear signs of anachronism. This further suggests that well-embedded Christian communities did not yet exist within the Iranian plateau by the 340s and 350s CE. Even if Shapur II may have begun to settle Christians there amid his wars against the Roman empire, these communities only started to take shape in the second half of the fourth century. The presence of signatory bishops from these regions at a council that convened in 424 CE, and references to bishops from Fars who had previously been reprimanded by metropolitans from Seleucia-Ctesiphon, in part reflect an increasingly centralized, ecclesiastical initiative to expand the authority of the bishop of Seleucia-Ctesiphon by consolidating and amplifying relatively new, inchoate communities.[90] They suggest that the formation of enduring Christian communities in Fars and Media was relatively recent. Otherwise, the presence of urban Christian communities by the 350s CE is attested reliably only for lowland Sasanian areas, namely the regions that were integrated into one of six discrete dioceses by the council of 410: lower Mesopotamia, classical Assyria, the Zab river region and *bēṯ Garmai*, Nisibis and its environs, and Maišan.[91] Only in 410, 420, and 424 CE do church councils provide secure documentation of Christian communities governed by bishops in the Iranian plateau or at Merv, but it is not evident that these belonged to discrete dioceses by then or had existed for very long.[92] It is of course possible that bishops in the Iranian highlands, notable for opposing the supremacy of the bishop of Seleucia-Ctesiphon, simply were not attending lowland councils.[93] But the lack of relatively early witnesses to the execution of Christians in the Iranian highlands during the reign of Shapur II would suggest that Christianity was absent before the second half of the fourth century CE altogether. The councils suggest that the formation of Christian communities and the appointment of episcopal overseers in these regions constituted a recent phenomenon, one whose gestation was between 350 and 400 CE.

Regardless of the debatable accuracy and oftentimes late dating of Persian martyr acts, the fact that Sasanian lowlanders almost exclusively narrated

---

[90] *Synodicon orientale* (ed. Chabot) 43–44. The record for this synod, however, does suffer from later interpolations. See Smith, *Constantine and the Captive Christians*, 192, n. 4.
[91] *Synodicon orientale* (ed. Chabot) 33–36.
[92] *Synodicon orientale* (ed. Chabot) 33–36 (esp. 34), 37, and 43–44.
[93] Payne, *State of Mixture*, 64–65 raises this possibility.

experiences of such putative mid-fourth-century CE episodes and set them in a distinctly lowland topography of violence is of value. It indicates that the form of Christianity represented by the Church of the East was only firmly anchored in the Iranian highlands in the mid-to-late fourth century CE. This date coincides with the presence of actual signatory bishops from Christian communities in the Iranian highlands and at Merv at the church council of 424. It also aligns with the *Martyr Act of Pethion*, a fifth- or sixth-century CE text that may reliably place Christians in Media during the reign of Yazdgird II (438–57 CE).[94] Excluding Manichaeism, whose communities certainly populated the Iranian plateau by the end of the third century CE, one can therefore separate the movement of Christianity into two phases. Over the second and third centuries CE (and by the early fourth), numerous strands of Christianity found anchorage in lower Mesopotamia, classical Assyria, the Zab river region, lowland southwest Iran, and the north Persian gulf littoral. Some of the prominent strands constituted the basis for the Persian Church of the East and its institutional formation. Nonetheless, as the next chapter (5) argues, these strands of Christianity had followed the physical and social pathways forged by a Levantine Roman socio-commercial network that had established residential communities in lowland Parthian/Sasanian regions. Only subsequently, starting in the mid-late fourth century CE, did the Christianity of the Church of the East begin to become established in the Iranian highlands, central Asia, east Arabia, and eventually India. As it did so, it exploited the pathways and anchor points created by a lowland Sasanian commercial network that extended into these regions.

Conclusion

No reliable contemporary evidence situates Christian communities in the Iranian plateau or central Asia before 350 CE. The later sources that do so are typically of dubious validity. Archaeology has yet to provide any clarification or support on this score. The *Book of the Laws of the Countries* (c. 225 CE) claims that Christians lived in the Iranian plateau and central Asia, but this observation was probably based on the lost Parthian *Acts of Thomas*. All told, the sparse reliable contemporary evidence that exists situates Christianity (non-Manichaean) in the Iranian plateau and central Asia only in periods subsequent to 350 CE. Even the Syriac *Persian Martyr Acts* typically do not narrate any fourth-century executions that afflicted the highlands, and when they do, their

---

[94] *Martyr Act of Pethion*, in *AMSS* 2.559–641. See Payne, *State of Mixture*, 59–92.

anachronisms are obvious. Nonetheless, as noted in previous chapters, Christians in the Mediterranean and proximate regions of the Near East often believed that Christians dwelled in the Iranian plateau and central Asia by the fourth century CE. This was due to the lost Parthian *Acts of Thomas*.

In the lost Parthian *Acts*, composed in the late second century CE or so, the apostle Judas Thomas apparently evangelized the Iranian highlands and parts of central Asia and north India controlled by the Kushan empire at the time of the text's production. This narrative generated among subsequent Christians the historical experience that their Christian brethren inhabited remote parts of Asia. But these experiences were independent of the actual movement of Christianity to Iran, central Asia, and north India (or lack thereof) during late antiquity. The culture of Christianity in fact was carried to these regions during the late fourth century CE by a socio-commercial network that effectively connected lowland Sasanian territories to these regions. The next chapter examines how.

CHAPTER 5

Social Connectivity between the Roman Levant, Persian Gulf, and Central Asia

According to the *Acts of Mar Mari*, Mari was an Edessene saint who had converted to Christianity under the guidance of Addai, the famous evangelizer of Edessa (a figure discussed in Chapter 1).[1] As the narrative claims, Mari had already evangelized communities throughout Mesopotamia, the Zab River region, classical Assyria, and Mesene when he decided to confront the populations of Iran.[2] But when he arrived in Khuzistan and the highlands of Fars, he discovered that people there had already become Christians. Upon asking how they had become so, he learned that merchants from Khuzistan (*bēṯ Hūzāyē*) and Fars (*bēṯ Parsāyē*) had been at Edessa when Addai had evangelized it, and they had transported the religious culture of its population to their home regions. There it had taken root. After reaching Fars and proceeding farther, Mari also reportedly smelled the sweet scent of the apostle Thomas.[3]

As this chapter argues, the range of movement with which the *Acts of Mar Mari* endows these merchants is generally consistent with commercial movement between the Roman Levant/Upper Mesopotamia and Sasanian territory. While direct movement between the Levant and the Iranian plateau was for various reasons very rare, merchants from Roman territory traveled to lowland Parthian and Sasanian territory, including Khuzistan. Likewise, traders from lowland Parthian/Sasanian regions frequented the Roman Levant. In this regard, the invented movements of such putatively first-century CE merchants serve as a point of ostensible contrast with the activity of a certain Maes Titianos.

According to the second-century CE geographer Ptolemy, a merchant named Maes Titianos is most famous for obtaining measurements for the distance between the Euphrates River and the "land of the Seres." Due to

---

[1] Many parts of this chapter have been reproduced from Andrade, "Voyage of Maes Titianos," with permission from *Mediterraneo Antico*.
[2] *Acts of Mar Mari* (ed. Jullien and Jullien; ed. Harrak) 1–30.
[3] *Acts of Mar Mari* (ed. Jullien and Jullien; ed. Harrak) 31–32.

Ptolemy's testimony, it is often surmised that Maes Titianos traveled from the Roman Levant to central Asia and dispatched associates farther east to west China. Some have in fact deemed his example as relatively typical for the times; others have reckoned it exceptional. In either instance, it is impossible to deny that the intersection of socio-commercial networks transported commodities across the Asian landmass, both to and from the Roman Levant. This issue has much bearing on the movement of early Christianity from the Roman Levant to regions farther east. If inhabitants of the Roman Levant and Upper Mesopotamia had forged direct contact with those in the Iranian plateau and central Asia, one could expect Christianity to have traveled to these regions at a rapid and uninterrupted pace.

The existence of trade routes and a flow of commodities, however, can be misleading indicators of Christianity's movement. Like the *Acts of Mar Mari*, late antique narratives sometimes invoked merchants as agents for Christianity's movement, and such trade routes and commercial activity provide ostensible support for the premise that Christianity moved in a diffuse and rapid fashion.[4] But the social relations and pathways generated by socio-commercial networks and their placement of residential communities were mainly responsible for shaping how and when Christianity traveled, and it is therefore important to discern where the members of such networks actually traveled and established expatriate residential settlements. Ancient and late antique sources in fact only verify the routine movement of merchants from the Roman Levant into lowland Parthian and Sasanian territory, and the documentary basis for direct travel and contact between the Roman Levant and the Iranian plateau or central Asia is quite weak. Although the example of Maes Titianos ostensibly supports the premise of direct contact between merchants of the Roman Levant and those of central Asia or west China, he in fact most probably never traveled east of Mesopotamia or Assyria. Since Roman merchants maintained commercial contacts and residential communities primarily in lowland Parthian and Sasanian territory, Christianity traveled rapidly from the Roman Levant to various parts of Iraq and Khuzistan. But Roman Levantine merchants did not routinely travel to the Iranian plateau or central Asia directly, and they had to transfer the culture of Christianity to Parthian/Sasanian merchants before it could be carried to those regions

---

[4] Ramelli, "Tradizione su Tommaso," esp. 65; Harrak, "Trade Routes," 57; Tomber, "Bishops and Traders," 225; Jullien and Jullien, *Apôtres des confins*, 201–6 and 215–22; Jullien, "Minorité chrétienne 'grecque'," 107–9; Koshelenko, Bader, and Gaibov, "Beginnings of Christianity in Merv," 55–70; Debié, Perrin, and Mahé, "L'Orient," 616.

and embedded there. Christianity therefore traveled to Iran and central Asia at a relatively slow pace.

As Chapter 4 has discussed, many of the literary texts that record the evangelization of Mesopotamia, Iran, and central Asia are problematic as historical sources. More reliable textual material indicates that Christian communities did not inhabit the Iranian plateau, the Persian Gulf, or central Asia until the late fourth century. What is known about socio-commercial networks (or circulation societies) in the Roman Near East and Parthian/Sasanian Mesopotamia supports this perspective. Such interconnected social networks may have enabled an ancient Afro-Eurasian world system to cohere, but these networks still had their distinct regional orientations and geographic segmentations. Because the Levantine Roman socio-commercial network only extended as far as lowland Parthian/Sasanian territory, it relied on contacts from a lowland network anchored there for transit commodities and information pertaining to them. This lowland network itself extended into the Iranian plateau, central Asia, and India (via the Persian Gulf), and it generated the social pathways by which the charismatic preacher Mani traveled and transmitted his religious culture to converts. Because it terminated in lowland Parthian and Sasanian territory, the Levantine Roman network carried and anchored Christian culture (or cultures) there at an early date, by or during the second century CE. But there Christian culture took root and transformed as various Christian communities took shape. It was only when members of the lowland Sasanian network had adopted Christianity and its culture in sufficient numbers that it carried it into highland Iran, central Asia, and the Persian Gulf.

The Levantine and Lowland Parthian/Sasanian Socio-Commercial Networks

The major trade arteries that connected the Levant to central Asia have long been known. This chapter will mention them frequently. Merchants and travelers from north Syria could travel eastward among the urban centers of Upper Mesopotamia and classical Assyria. Or they could follow the Euphrates southward to Seleucia-Ctesiphon. Farther south, they could cross the dry Syrian steppe toward the Euphrates. As we have seen, Palmyra was a key stopover and, during the Roman period, a site for major caravan endeavors. From it, merchants followed caravan tracks to the Euphrates and the Persian Gulf. From Mesopotamia, merchants moved east into the Iranian plateau and central Asia. Or they sailed south through the Persian Gulf to north India or south Arabia. (Map 3)

As this chapter describes, a Levantine socio-commercial network was primarily responsible for transporting and anchoring Christianity in lowland Parthian and Sasanian territories. This network included Greek- and Aramaic-speaking Syrians, Syriac-speaking Upper Mesopotamians, Palmyrenes, Nabataeans, and Jews inhabiting various Syrian localities, including Palestine. But its general disposition was vastly different from the Roman Egyptian network that extended into the Red Sea and Indian Ocean, and certain elements of the network should be noted. The various sections of this chapter analyze the empirical evidence for these elements. But its generic features were as follows.

In contrast to the Roman Egyptian network, which was centered on Alexandria, the Levantine network was divided into various discrete segments that maintained their own hubs and nodes. The structuring force of Roman imperialism, however, ensured that these maintained sufficient contact, coordination, cooperation, and competition for them to be conceived of as a network of Levantines. Even if Antioch, located on a river that let into the Mediterranean, was perhaps the location of its most central hub, it did not occupy the hegemonic position of its Alexandrian counterpart. A cadre of investors and merchants at Antioch acquired both regional and eastward products and distributed them throughout the Mediterranean, but Antioch did not attract all the flows of information and products or serve as the main organizational point for all Levantine commercial activity. The geography of the Near East in fact enabled investors and merchants to establish hubs elsewhere, and these maintained links to one another. For example, during its economic and political peak, investors and merchants at the city of Palmyra, whose inhabitants established direct contact with India, also played a central role and transmitted commodities and information to contact points at Antioch, Emesa, and Damascus.[5] While a first-century CE Nabataean segment that extended deep into Arabia established its hub at Petra, it also dispatched merchants eastward across the Omani desert and to the Persian Gulf.[6] Over the second and third centuries CE, Syriac-speaking Edessenes were part of the network too, with Edessa probably being a key site of contact and distribution. As we will see, commercial figures located in Palestine, Phoenicia, or the Syrian interior, including Jews, could follow

---

[5] Seland, "Persian Gulf or the Red Sea?," "Organisation," "Palmyrene Long-Distance Trade," and *Ships of the Desert*; Gorea, "Sea and Inland Trade," 463–65; Terpstra, *Trading Communities*, 152–60 and "Palmyrene Temple"; Smith, *Roman Palmyra*, 68–80; Young, *Rome's Eastern Trade*, 123–68 for details.

[6] Young, *Rome's Eastern Trade*, 90–135; McLaughlin, *Rome and the Distant East*, 61–82; Sidebotham, *Berenike*, 175–94; Salles, "Traveling to India," 163–64; Bowersock, "Review." For the oasis settlement at Dumata, see now Charloux and Loreto, *Dûma*.

various physical and social pathways to lowland Parthian and Sasanian space that bypassed Antioch.[7]

Accordingly, the hubs and distribution centers of the Levantine network were numerous and dispersed, and social bonds of various types moved information, products, credit, trust, and culture among them. The network also contained various civically, ethnically, or religiously oriented segments (Antiochenes, Palmyrenes, Nabataeans, Jews, and Edessenes, for example) that intersected, overlapped, or shared the same commercial players. Despite its dynamic qualities, most links of the network (except the Palmyrenes) only extended into lowland Parthian/Sasanian territories, and this determined where the network carried and anchored Christianity by or during the second and third centuries CE.

The members of the Levantine network frequently maintained contacts with merchants and commercial figures who were themselves embedded in a lowland Parthian/Sasanian network. This specific network maintained its hub at the city of Seleucia-Ctesiphon. Located near the confluence of the Tigris and Euphrates rivers and just upstream of Mesene and the Persian Gulf, investors and merchants in the city attracted and distributed the flows of eastern commodities and information that had moved westward across the Iranian plateau or northward through the Persian Gulf. But the regional orientation of the network included more than its lower Mesopotamian hub and its hinterland; it also integrated the merchants and commercial players of Nisibis and its environs, classical Assyria, the Zab River region, and lowland Khuzistan. As we will see, this network extended across the Iranian plateau and into central Asia, and it also reached across the Persian Gulf and to north India. It eventually established residential communities in south Asia. After the Levantine commercial network had transported and anchored Christianity in lowland Parthian territory, this network carried Christian culture into the Iranian plateau, central Asia, and the Persian Gulf during the late fourth century.

Since it is widely surmised that the merchant Maes Titianos had traveled from the Roman Levant to central Asia, his activity is seemingly inconsistent with the generic features of the Levantine and Parthian/Sasanian networks outlined above. Indeed, his movements would have far exceeded the social pathways that the Levantine network generated. But as we will see, the source material for Maes' movements is in fact ambiguous, and Maes' movements were in fact far more modest than has sometimes been

---

[7] Hezser, *Jewish Travel*, esp. 311–65 and 409–40; Young, *Rome's Eastern Trade*.

suggested. The following sections accordingly examine the evidence for the extension of the two socio-commercial networks that connected the Roman Levant and central Asia: the Levantine and the lowland Parthian/Sasanian. It also establishes how Maes' activity in fact conformed to the dispositions of their social pathways and residential anchor points.

Maes Titianos and Social Connectivity between the Roman Levant and Central Asia

According to a passage from the Babylonian Talmud, a Babylonian Jew traveled to "Marguan," which represents either the central Asian city of Merv (Antioch Margiana) or the region in which it was located (Margiana). His purpose for journeying there is unknown, but he may have been purchasing silk from central Asian merchants. While in "Marguan," his contacts offered him wine, which he refused on grounds of purity. Undeterred, they offered him beer, which he likewise refused.[8] It is difficult to date this episode, but it bears general implications for the nature of travel between the Roman Near East and central Asia during the periods of Roman, Parthian, and early Sasanian rule. It also has bearing on a notable episode recounted by the second-century CE geographer Claudius Ptolemy. In his *Geography* (1.11.6–7), Ptolemy provides a brief description of a merchant named Maes Titianos who had acquired measurements for the distance from the Syrian city of Hierapolis (Manbog) on the Euphrates River to the Tarim Basin of the Xinjiang region of western China and perhaps even beyond.[9] Ptolemy claims that he had obtained the testimony of Maes from the work of a geographer named Marinos. Ptolemy's passage is of unique importance for scholarly analysis of the connectivity of the Roman Levant and central Asia, which is otherwise poorly documented. But the significance of Ptolemy's account for the issue of trans-imperial and trans-continental connectivity poses issues of ambiguity.

Ptolemy's discussion of Maes Titianos, a merchant who was most probably active in north Syria c. 100 CE, is invaluable testimony for the commercial routes that touched the farthest reaches of the Asian continent.[10] When

---

[8] Bab. Talmud (ed. Epstein) *AZ* 31b.   [9] On Maes, see the entry of Anca Dan in *FGrH* 2213.
[10] Despite past controversies regarding Maes' origins and date, the most plausible explanation supported by recent scholarship is that Maes' family was of Anatolian origin, that he was an inhabitant of north Syria, and that he was active c. 100 CE, when the later Han dynasty had control of the Tarim Basin and facilitated commercial movement (and about half a century before Ptolemy wrote). Bernard, "De l'Euphrate à la Chine," 929–69, and Anca Dan in *FGrH* 2213 illuminate the debate regarding background and date. For a recent dissenting view that places Maes' activity in the

combined with various Roman imperial and Chinese sources, it helps illuminate the primary conduits, stopovers, and webs of intercontinental travel that connected later Han China, central Asia, Parthian Iran, and the Roman Levant. Accordingly, the route that Ptolemy traces has received detailed treatment and reconstruction.[11] In many respects, Ptolemy's discussion has informed how the commercial segments that inhabitants of the Roman Levant traversed have been perceived. It has even been posited that traces of Maes' trip are borne out by Chinese accounts that describe how an embassy reached Luoyang from places transcribed in English as "Meng-Qi and Doule" (or as alternatively rendered: "Meng-chie and Toule"). Certain scholars have suggested that these are in fact references to Macedonia or Maes Titianos specifically, and they thereby treat the embassy as the work of Maes himself.[12] Furthermore, since Maes is often understood to have voyaged to central Asia, the Tarim Basin, or even farther east, some have construed his activity as normative for the farthest extent that traders from Roman territory reached.[13] Others have posited that it is a unique aberration greatly exceeding how far most merchants and travelers went.[14] In either case, it is often surmised that Maes penetrated central Asia and sent close associates across the Pamir Mountains and into the Tarim Basin, thereby obtaining measurements for the distance from the Euphrates River to the Xinjiang region of China.

But as we will see, the source material for Maes' work can be interpreted differently. According to such a perspective, Maes Titianos never traveled to central Asia, nor did he even enter the Iranian plateau. In this sense, Maes' itinerary conformed to those of most Roman merchants who trekked from the Roman Levant into lowland Parthian or Sasanian territory either to engage in interregional commerce or to enrich themselves by acquiring the coveted commodities of long-distance transit trade,

---

late first century BCE but that largely agrees with this chapter regarding the movements of Roman and Parthian merchants, see Pyankov, "Romano-Parthian Merchants," 145–48.

[11] Bernard, "De l'Euphrate à la Chine," 929–69 and now Tupikova, Schemmel, and Geus, *Traveling along the Silk Road* are recent valuable examples.

[12] *Hou Hanshu* 88 in Hill, *Through the Jade Gate*, 5; and in Leslie and Gardiner, *Roman Empire in Chinese Sources*, 43. McLaughlin, *Rome and the Distant East*, 126–28 and *Roman Empire and the Silk Routes*, 188–92 discusses possible links to Maes and reconstructs Maes' activity on the assumption that *Hou Hanshu* in fact refers to him. "Meng-Qi/Meng-chie and Doule/Toule" must, however, remain unknown. See Hill, *Through the Jade Gate*, 132–34 and Leslie and Gardiner, *Roman Empire in Chinese Sources*, 148–50 for discussion of hypotheses regarding these locations, for difficulties with establishing them, and for emphasis that these place names do not refer to Maes Titianos in any meaningful way.

[13] Young, *Rome's Eastern Trade*, 196–97; Bernard, "De l'Euphrate à la Chine," 929–69. Previously, Raschke, "New Studies in Roman Commerce," 641–43 (with notes) and 846.

[14] McLaughlin, *Rome and the Distant East*, 106–9 and 126–28.

especially silk. The notion that Maes Titianos journeyed to central Asia and sent immediate associates even farther afield is based on the ambiguous description provided by Ptolemy's *Geography* (1.11.6–7). While analyzing this passage, the discussion to follow situates Maes' activity within a broader context of interregional and long-distance commerce that spanned from the Roman Levant to the Xinjiang region of China between the first century BCE and the third century CE. Based on the testimony of various ancient sources, it maintains that Maes obtained measurements for the distance between the Euphrates River and the Tarim Basin principally by consulting contacts within the Parthian empire, who themselves traveled to central Asia, corresponded with eastern merchants there, and conveyed information to him.[15] It also asserts that Maes' activity coheres with relatively consistent and longstanding commercial trends that connected such a geographical span, even as the regions located within it experienced socio-political shifts and periodic turbulences during the centuries that this chapter covers. Due to the following sections' emphasis on enduring trends, it is not essential for present purposes to establish the exact date of Maes' career. We will nonetheless proceed according to the premise that Maes was active c. 100 CE, which, as noted previously, is a widely (but not universally) accepted view.[16]

According to Ptolemy (1.11.6–7), Maes Titianos and his associates were responsible for obtaining the measurements for the distance from the Euphrates River (at Syrian Hierapolis) to "Sera," the principal city of the land of the "Seres."[17] After making this statement, Ptolemy (1.12.1–10) then proceeds to describe the route between Syrian Hierapolis and "Sera" based on his account. As a result of Ptolemy's testimony (in 1.11–12 generally), this merchant, named "Maes, who is also Titianos," is often reckoned to have traveled to central Asia, including Kushan territory, and to have sent his direct associates to the Xinjiang region of west China.[18] If so, his example reflects the possibilities of movement for a merchant willing to incur great risk and expense to bring large loads over a vast distance; such

---

[15] For a similar viewpoint (with different dating for Maes' activity), Pyankov, "Romano-Parthian Merchants," 145–58.
[16] Pyankov, "Romano-Parthian Merchants," 145–48.
[17] Ptolemy (ed. Stückelberger and Graßhoff) 1.11.6–7. In addition to scholars cited so far, key discussion about the measurements of Maes and Marinos are in Berggren and Jones, *Ptolemy's Geography*, 150–52 (Appendix C); Tupikova, Schemmel, and Geus, *Travelling the Silk Road*, 19–20. The Hellenistic foundations that speckled the expanse from Parthian Mesopotamia to central Asia before or by Maes' lifetime have recently been compiled by Cohen, *Hellenistic Settlements in the East*.
[18] Ptolemy (ed. Stückelberger and Graßhoff) 1.11–12; McLaughlin, *Rome and the Distant East*, 106–9 and 126–28 and *Roman Empire and the Silk Routes*, 188–92 discusses this episode.

activity likely required caravan travel consisting of many animals and people necessary for transport and defense. But Ptolemy (1.11.6–7) is quite vague regarding the figure of Maes, his associates or contacts, and his trek to the east. The key passage reads:

> Καὶ γὰρ δι' ἐμπορίας ἀφορμὴν ἐγνώσθη. Μάην γάρ φησί τινα τὸν καὶ Τιτιανόν, ἄνδρα Μακεδόνα καὶ ἐκ πατρὸς ἔμπορον, συγγράψασθαι τὴν ἀναμέτρησιν οὐδ' αὐτὸν ἐπελθόντα, διαπεμψάμενον δέ τινας πρὸς τοὺς Σῆρας.

> For it (the route from the Stone Tower to the Seres) has become known through the initiation (*aphormēn*) of commerce. For he (Marinos) says that a certain Maes, also called Titianos, a Macedonian man and a merchant from his father, compiled the distance. And he did not do so by traversing it, but by sending certain people (or: having certain people sent) across to the Seres.

In tandem with Ptolemy's treatment of central Asian territories, this passage is often interpreted as indicating that Maes had personally traveled across the Iranian plateau and deep into central Asia, where he reached the Stone Tower.[19] Being a city near the Pamir Mountains on the threshold of east Bactria and west China, the Stone Tower was perhaps Tashkurgan or Daraut-Kurgan in modern Kyrgyzstan, but its location is uncertain.[20] According to the prevailing interpretation, Maes had journeyed to the Stone Tower personally, and from there he had sent his agents to the "land of the Seres" or "Serike."[21] "Serike" putatively refers to the region of the Tarim Basin that now forms part of the Xinjiang region of west China, even if Ptolemy treats "Sera," its metropolis, as the end of the known world.[22] Nonetheless, the identity of "Sera" is still undetermined, and Ptolemy does not indicate where exactly Maes had personally traveled or whom he had dispatched into the Tarim Basin. Likewise, the extent to which he calculated distance through his own movement or by means of mobile contacts and informants is decidedly ambiguous.

---

[19] Ptolemy (ed. Stückelberger and Graßhoff) 6.10–13 and 17 treats (for example) regions that he labels Margiana, Bactria, the land of the Sogdians, the land of the Sakas, and Areia. Ptolemy does not mention the Kushan empire by name, but assuming that Maes was active c. 100 CE, it would have controlled certain central Asian territories at the time. Pyankov, "Romano-Parthian Merchants," 147–48.

[20] Hill, *Through the Jade Gate*, 2.21–28; Berggren and Jones, *Ptolemy's Geography*, 151; Bernard, "De l'Euphrate à la Chine," 953–56; Tupikova, Schemmel, and Geus, *Travelling the Silk Road*, 56.

[21] Young, *Rome's Eastern Trade*, 196–97; Bernard, "De l'Euphrate à la Chine," 929–69; McLaughlin, *Rome and the Distant East*, 106–9 and 126–28 and *Roman Empire and the Silk Routes*, 188–92.

[22] De la Vaissière, "Triple System," 527–36; Sergent, "Sères sont les soi-disant 'Tokhariens,'" 7–40.

It is evident that trade networks, court exchanges, and waves of religious ideas meaningfully connected the regions that Ptolemy associates with Maes' journey. The inhabitants of the Roman Mediterranean consumed products arriving from China, India, and even Indonesia, and people living in these regions had access to Mediterranean materials.[23] The study of the archaeology and cultural interactions of central Asia has enjoyed much recent activity.[24] But the segmentation of travel that facilitated the traffic of products is of vital importance for establishing how bodies carried Christianity from the Roman Levant and enabled it to find anchorage in various eastern regions. It is therefore worth analyzing who most probably had acquired measurements for Maes in the Iranian plateau and central Asia and how this issue relates to what is known about the interconnected yet discrete commercial networks that connected the Roman Levant, Parthian/Sasanian Mesopotamia and Iran, central Asia, and the Tarim Basin during the Roman, Parthian, and early Sasanian imperial periods. The disposition of such networks, combined with Ptolemy's treatment of Maes, in fact suggests that Maes did not calculate the distance between the Euphrates and the Tarim Basin by traveling or dispatching subordinate agents. The north Syrian segment of the Levantine network in which he participated facilitated his and his subordinates' movement into lowland Parthian territory, but not farther. Accordingly, his knowledge of the Iranian plateau, central Asia, and the Tarim Basin was generated by his contact with a commercial network of lowland Parthians that extended into central Asia.

---

[23] An exhaustive list is impossible without adding massive girth. Some recent works on such topics are: Young, *Rome's Eastern Trade*; McLaughlin, *Rome and the Distant East* and *Roman Empire and the Silk Routes*; Sidebotham, *Berenike*; Hoppal, "Roman Empire," 263–306; Rauh, *Merchants, Sailors, and Pirates*, esp. 93–134; Hill, *Through the Jade Gate*; Neelis, *Early Buddhist Transmission*; Fitzpatrick, "Provincializing Rome," 27–54; Dilley, "Religious Intercrossing"; Hansen, *Silk Road*; Gregoratti, "Parthian Empire;" Żuchowska, "Palmyra (Far Eastern)" and "Palmyra (Chinese Silk)," 29–38; Roller, *Ancient Geography*, 193–205; Hübner, "Palestine, Syria, and the Silk Road," and Lieu and Mikkelson, *Between Rome and China*. The works on Manichaeism cited in this book also constitute contributions to this phenomenon. The publications of the *Silk Road Journal* certainly bear relevance.

[24] Again, an exhaustive list is impossible, but some examples are de la Vaissière, *Sogdian Traders*; Holt, *Lost World of the Golden King*; Hiebert and Cambon, *Afghanistan*; Leriche et al., *Bactriane au carrefour des routes et des civilisations de l'Asie centrale*; Bopearachchi and Boussac, *Afghanistan*; Coloru, *Alessandro a Menadro*; Mairs, *The Archaeology of the Far East: A Survey*, "Waiting for the Barbarians," 9–30, and *Hellenistic Far East*; Burstein, "New Light," 181–92; the recent find of a notable Greek acrostic by a merchant named Sophytus, in Bernard, Pinault, and Rougemont, "Deux nouvelles inscriptions," 227–356. The notable excavations at Ai Khanoum can be found in Bernard et al., *Fouilles d'Aï Khanoum*, but see now Martinez-Sève, "Spatial Organization of Ai Khanoum," 267–84; and Mairs, *Hellenistic Far East*, 57–101. For a synthesis of material remains at Merv, see Simpson, "Merv." For later Roman coins in China, Li, "Roman Coins."

In regards to the distance between the Euphrates and the Tarim Basin, Ptolemy credits Maes with providing the measurements that Marinos replicated in his geography, and he critiques their flaws. But his brief citation of Marinos' description of Maes' measurements is vague regarding exactly what Maes or his direct associates measured. This issue can be in part resolved by Ptolemy's broader discussion of the distance between Hierapolis, the Stone Tower, and "Sera." While commonly speculated and presumably located in Xinjiang, the site for "Sera" remains unknown, and various postulates have in fact placed it in diverse locations on the stretch of Chinese territory from the Tarim Basin to Luoyang.[25] In his discussion, Ptolemy describes how the distance to "Sera" had previously been measured, divides the distance into two meaningful segments whose measurements are rendered in entirely different units, and suggests adjustments that need to be made. His discussion in fact indicates that neither Maes nor his immediate contacts had traveled into the Tarim Basin (the land of the Seres) or beyond.

In 1.11–12 of his geography, Ptolemy claims that Marinos, working through Maes, calculated the distance between the Euphrates (at Syrian Hierapolis) and the Stone Tower to be 876 *schoinoi*, which converts to 26,280 stades.[26] Due to his engagement with Marinos' consultation of Maes, Ptolemy also provides substantial information for commercial stopovers extending from the Euphrates, across lowland Parthian territory, into the Iranian plateau, and to the site of Bactra in central Asia. But Ptolemy expresses disagreement with Marinos' measurement for several reasons, and he avers that the distance between the Euphrates and the Stone Tower was 800 *schoinoi*, or 24,000 stades.[27] Ptolemy's critiques and accuracy need not be addressed for present purposes. What must be stressed is that for the segment between the Euphrates and the Stone Tower, Ptolemy indicates

---

[25] Sometimes associated with Luoyang, Bernard, "De l'Euphrate à la Chine," 957–62 suggests that it is Liangzhou (modern Wuwei), a site located due east of Dunhuang, from where many central routes from China to western regions stretched, and on the route extending eastward to Luoyang. Tupikova, Schemmel, and Geus, *Travelling the Silk Road*, 53 notes that it could be Liangzhou, Ganzhou, or Xi'an. See *Weilue* (trans. John Hill) at *Silk Road Seattle Project*,
http://depts.washington.edu/silkroad/texts/weilue/weilue.html#section4;
http://depts.washington.edu/silkroad/texts/weilue/weilue.html#section5;
http://depts.washington.edu/silkroad/texts/weilue/weilue.html#section9;
http://depts.washington.edu/silkroad/texts/weilue/weilue.html#section23.
Some of these relevant passages are also in Leslie and Gardiner, *Roman Empire in Chinese Sources*, 65–66. It is nonetheless possible that "Sera" was in Xinjiang. De la Vaissière, "Triple System," 33–35 discusses the different theories.

[26] Ptolemy (ed. Stückelberger and Graßhoff) 1.11.2 and 4.

[27] Ptolemy (ed. Stückelberger and Graßhoff) 1.11.2 and 8 and 1.12.1 and 3–10.

that either Maes or his direct associates had obtained actual physical measurements for intervals between major cities and stopovers by traveling and consulting local authorities. Ptolemy accordingly provides measurements for many intervals within the Parthian lowlands and the Iranian plateau. He also discloses distances between central Asian stopovers located from Merv to the Stone Tower, even if he provides a less detailed itinerary east of Bactra.

By contrast, Ptolemy's treatment of the land of the "Seres" (the Tarim Basin) in 1.11–12 indicates that neither Maes nor his direct associates had voyaged beyond central Asia at all. Instead of physical measurements, Ptolemy suggests that Maes had merely provided the time required for travel between the Stone Tower and "Sera."[28] Through his consultation of Marinos, Ptolemy indicates that Maes had measured the travel time between these sites to be seven months, and he converts this measurement into 36,200 stades.[29] Yet again, Ptolemy does not agree with this measurement, and one of his principal critiques is that due to variations in weather and diversions, the time that merchants needed to traverse a geographic span was a poor indication of physical distance covered. In his estimation, the latitude of the Stone Tower and "Sera" also suggested less distance than Maes had conveyed. As a result, Ptolemy surmises that the distance between the Stone Tower and "Sera" was a mere 18,100 stades.[30] But he provides no details of the itinerary.

It is in fact only in Book 6 of his geography (6.16) that Ptolemy finally provides a list of putative cities and sites roughly between the Stone Tower and "Sera" and plots coordinates.[31] Yet, Maes does not appear to have been a source for this information. While some toponyms located east of the Stone Tower bear a general aura of plausibility and could be legitimate names of cities of Tibet and the Tarim Basin that are loosely translated into Greek from Chinese, Iranian, or Indian languages, Ptolemy's coordinates for them do not coincide with primary trade arteries. Most important, Ptolemy arranges the cities of the Tarim Basin according to a north-south trajectory and sometimes confusedly lists the same place twice (which suggests his conflation of multiple sources).[32] His treatment indicates

---

[28] As emphasized by Lerner, "Ptolemy and the Silk Road," 9.
[29] Ptolemy (ed. Stückelberger and Graβhoff) 1.11.4.
[30] Ptolemy (ed. Stückelberger and Graβhoff) 1.11.6 and 1.12.1 and 10.
[31] Ptolemy (ed. Stückelberger and Graβhoff) 1.12.12 and 6.13–16 generally.
[32] Ptolemy (ed. Stückelberger and Graβhoff) 6.14–16 generally; Bernard, "De l'Euphrate à la Chine," 960–61, with n. 86–88; de la Vaissière, "Triple System," 527–36; and now the important Tupikova, Schemmel, and Geus, *Travelling the Silk Road*, 49–50 and 54.

that his source(s) for the land of the "Seres" in this instance was not Maes, who was measuring a west-to-east itinerary.[33] Again, the accuracy and method of Ptolemy's critique are not the primary issue. What must be stressed is that the information imparted by Maes and therefore replicated by Marinos was apparently not derived from any physical measurements acquired through the actual movement of Maes or his direct associates. Ptolemy's complete lack of toponymical information, city names, or commercial stopovers for Maes' putative route into the Tarim Basin suggest as much, and his north-south presentation of the Tarim Basin indicates that he was using sources other than Maes for the cities of the Seres. Perhaps Maes' silence can be attributed to the fact that Chinese authorities would have prevented him from documenting trade routes, their stages, and distances.[34] Yet, it is more reasonable all told to conclude that neither Maes nor his direct contacts had actually traveled the segment between the Stone Tower and "Sera," and they therefore had not obtained an explicit itinerary, any toponymical data, or any measurements, not even in Chinese *li*.[35] Maes or otherwise his direct associates had merely learned from merchants at the Stone Tower how long it took for people to journey from the Stone Tower to "Sera," and Maes had provided the time of a trip on an eastward trajectory from the Stone Tower, but little else. In this case, Ptolemy found Maes' information to be grossly misleading.

In short, Ptolemy divided the trek from the Euphrates to "Sera" into two segments whose distances were measured by two entirely different methods, and this has profound implications for how exactly Maes acquired his information. For the swath of territory between the Euphrates and the Stone Tower, Ptolemy's division and measurements are apparently derived from those of Marinos' consultation of Maes' description. Maes and therefore Marinos had provided measurements in *schoinoi* for the distance between the Euphrates and the Stone Tower. Likewise, even if Ptolemy's treatment of eastern parts of central Asia (in 1.11–12) displays a deficit of toponyms and specificity, he still at least provides physical measurements for the distances between Bactra and west China. This suggests that either Maes or his direct contacts had voyaged across the Parthian and Kushan

---

[33] De la Vaissière, "Triple System," 527–36.
[34] Bernard, "De l'Euphrate à la Chine," 961–62; McLaughlin, *Rome and the Distant East*, 127.
[35] Such itineraries exist in Chinese sources of the period, such as *Weilue* (trans. John Hill) at *Silk Road Seattle Project*, http://depts.washington.edu/silkroad/texts/weilue/weilue.html#section5.
  Also, Leslie and Gardiner, *Roman Empire in Chinese Sources*, 65. Calculations in *li* are provided, for example, in *Hou Hanshu* 88 (trans. John Hill) in *Through the Jade Gate*, 23–29; Leslie and Gardiner, *Roman Empire in Chinese Sources*, 45–53; and Hackl, Jacobs, and Weber, *Quellen*, 3.498–501.

empires, had obtained measurements as far as the Stone Tower, and had acquired a relatively accurate itinerary that Marinos had integrated into his composition. Otherwise, for the trek from central Asia to the "Seres," they had consulted other parties who were familiar with the trip and who provided a general calculation for time of travel.[36]

Such segmentation is supported by further observations that Ptolemy makes in Book 6 of his geography (6.13–14) regarding the dynamics of trade between central Asia and the Tarim Basin. He noticeably indicates that somewhat farther east of the Stone Tower, at the foot of the "Imaon Mountain" (the Pamir mountains), a substantial caravan station for merchants traveling to "Sera" was located. Ptolemy calls this site the *Hormeterion*.[37] In other words, Ptolemy indicates that the Stone Tower and the *Hormeterion* east of it were important transit points for commerce moving through central Asia toward China and a key organizational locus for traders of central Asia and the Tarim Basin. Ptolemy provides every indication that neither Maes nor his direct contacts had moved farther east of that caravan station. Accordingly, even if Chinese sources refer to embassies from "Mengqi and Doule" (or "Meng-chie and Toule") that occurred c. 100 CE, these almost certainly do not refer to Maes Titianos by name or his Macedonian background. The meanings of these terms are ultimately unknown, and Ptolemy's account in fact suggests that neither Maes nor his direct contacts traveled into the Tarim Basin to compile distance measurements. Instead, they had simply acquired from merchants of central Asia or the Tarim Basin the amount of time needed to voyage from the Stone Tower to "Sera." In this vein, the next two sections endeavor to clarify how far east Maes actually did journey and to what extent he relied on intermediaries for information. They thereby establish the dispositions of the Levantine and lowland Parthian/Sasanian socio-commercial networks that created the social pathways for Maes' movements and acquisition of knowledge.

Where Did Maes Titianos Travel?

As noted above, the movements of Maes Titianos are more ambiguous than often surmised. Strictly speaking, Ptolemy does not indicate that Maes voyaged to central Asia or China at all. He simply claims that

---

[36] Lerner, "Ptolemy and the Silk Road," 13–14 likewise doubts that Maes' direct contacts actually traveled to "Sera." Żuchowska, "Palmyra (Chinese Silk)," 34 notes similar issues.
[37] Ptolemy (ed. Stückelberger and Graßhoff) 6.13.1 and 14.1.

Maes did not traverse (οὐδ' αὐτὸν ἐπελθόντα) the expanse for which he had acquired measurements. By doing so, Ptolemy clarifies that Maes did not trek from the Stone Tower to "Sera" himself. But he also does not make explicit where Maes actually traveled or whether he reached central Asia, and for various reasons that this section will describe, it is in fact improbable that Maes entered the Iranian plateau.

Although Maes' ethnic background is uncertain, he was clearly based in north Syria and participated within a north Syrian segment of the Levantine commercial network that extended into Parthian territory. This segment, however, probably did not facilitate the movement of Roman Syrians beyond lowland Parthian space. Several interrelated factors that shaped commercial movement encourage this interpretation. First, the authorities of the Parthian empire implemented endeavors to disrupt the movement of Roman imperial inhabitants into the Iranian plateau and central Asia, and profits from the silk trade were a principal reason. Second, Roman sources that comment on trade routes or commercial movement imply that Roman Levantine segments terminated in lowland Parthia, and from there Parthian subjects undertook the trek to central Asia. Third, the trade routes that traversed the Persian Gulf and the Indian Ocean provided equally serviceable, if not superior, social and physical pathways that Roman merchants could pursue. They did not need to travel overland to central Asia. Finally, it is probable that most merchants who voyaged from the Roman Levant into Parthian and Sasanian territory were principally involved in forms of interregional trade by which they transported commodities produced in Roman Syria to markets in lowland Parthia and then moved commodities routinely produced in lowland Parthia to the Roman Levant. Since the acquisition of eastern transit commodities was by this logic of secondary concern, merchants acquired them opportunistically in lowland Parthian territory but did not endeavor to acquire them potentially at higher volumes, at lower prices, and with increased predictability in regions farther east.

The evidence for Parthian interference is not abundant and does not facilitate detailed knowledge, but it is sufficient to establish that interference did occur in regions governed directly by Parthian administrators. Even if Roman merchants could cross through many of the independent kingdoms or client realms that speckled the Parthian sphere of influence, they still would have needed to traverse territory directly governed by Parthia in order to enter and cross the Iranian plateau. The Parthians' activity is more obscure than that of the Sasanians, whose merchants notably acquired silk in central Asia and India and then sold it to

Romans at higher prices. But it was consistent with the Sasanian example, and the Parthian administration had many reasons to restrict the movement of people from the Roman Levant. By admitting them, it facilitated the extraction of tariffs from Roman merchants, who were permitted to enter and depart the Parthian empire with taxable wares. But while it perhaps never resulted in a "monopoly," their interference in movement amplified the ability of Parthian merchants to benefit from acquiring products from central Asia and selling them to Romans at higher prices. More provisionally, if the Parthian empire had the type of banking and investment presence that Roman elites (including senators and equestrians) exploited, then Parthian royals, magistrates, and loyal client dynasts would have been inclined to intervene. If they were participating in commercial enterprises, providing loans to merchants, or investing in bankers or creditors (who fronted merchants), then they had incentive to protect their investments by disrupting the Romans' direct acquisition of eastern transit products.[38]

Two Chinese sources with intimate links to the second and third centuries CE make explicit that Parthians disrupted Romans from traveling eastward. These stress that profits from the silk trade were a principal reason; Parthian authorities did not want traders from the Roman Levant to make direct contact with central Asian merchants.[39] In addition to the Chinese sources, Philostratus' *Life of Apollonius* suggests similarly. Admittedly, its treatment of Apollonius largely consisted of invented tradition and the author's imagination, and it is not an accurate source regarding Parthian geography. It also dates roughly at the period of transition between Parthian and Sasanian rule. But it nonetheless conveys what Romans normatively expected to encounter upon entering Parthian territory, and the expectations were twofold. First, they expected to register with either Roman or Parthian authorities at the border the commodities that they were exporting into Parthian space. According to Philostratus,

---

[38] For the relationship between merchants, bankers, and elite investors in the Roman empire, see Rauh, *Merchants, Sailors, and Pirates*, 135–45; and Fitzpatrick, "Provincializing Rome," 27–54. For overview of Roman finance, see now Reden, "Money and Finance," esp. 279–81; and Morley, "Early Roman Empire: Distribution," 587–88. For the political activity of Parthian aristocrats, see now Dąbrowa, "Parthian Aristocracy," 53–62.

[39] For *Hou Hanshu* 88 (compiled in the fifth century but based on earlier contemporary sources), consult Hill, *Through the Jade Gate*, 27; Leslie and Gardiner, *Roman Empire in Chinese Sources*, 51; Hackl, Jacobs, and Weber, *Quellen*, 3.501. But see the objections of Raschke, "New Studies in Roman Commerce," 641–43 and Young, *Rome's Eastern Trade*, 196. For *Weilue* (mid-third century), see *Silk Road Seattle Project* (trans. John Hill) http://depts.washington.edu/silkroad/texts/weilue/weilue.html#section11; and Leslie and Gardiner, *Roman Empire in Chinese Sources*, 67–71.

upon being approached by a tax collector at Zeugma, the sage Apollonius in fact announced the names of the noble qualities that he was bringing to Parthian territory. All being nouns of the female gender, these were moderation (σωφροσύνη), virtue (ἀρετή), self-control (ἐγκράτεια), manliness (ἀνδρεία), and rigor (ἄσκησις). Misinterpreting him, the tax collector then asked him to register in writing the names of these female slaves that he had just proclaimed.[40] Second, Philostratus significantly indicates that beyond Seleucia-Ctesiphon, guard posts (*phrourai*) regulated eastward movement. Travelers were asked their identities, their home cities, and the purpose of their itinerary, and such posts putatively prevented substantial caravans or even modest groups from moving into the Iranian plateau.[41] According to the *Life*, Apollonius was admitted to Babylon, which Philostratus erroneously places on the way to Iran in the region east of Seleucia-Ctesiphon and the Tigris, because his reputation had already reached Parthia. Although Philostratus ascribes such intervention to the anxieties of the current Parthian king regarding potential usurpation, his testimony arguably reflects (and distorts) conventional wisdom among Roman merchants regarding what travel in Parthia entailed, and such conventional wisdom was plausibly the product of the Levantine socio-commercial network that had established anchor points in lowland Parthian/Sasanian territory. Despite the substantial geographical inaccuracies in Philostratus' treatment of places east of lower Mesopotamia and his confused interpretation of Parthian guard stations, it is possible that his account, given its consistency with the Chinese sources, reflects his creative adaptation of the interference that Parthian magistrates posed for Romans at lowland emporia.[42]

Accordingly, Parthian magistrates both admitted and restricted the movement of Roman merchants so that Parthian traders could purchase silk and other goods from central Asians and then sell them to Roman merchants at a higher price. In this sense, Parthian interference in many ways cohered with the Sasanian activity that succeeded it; Procopius clarifies that in the sixth century CE, Roman traders, not able to buy silk directly from central Asian merchants by crossing Sasanian territory, endeavored to have Aksumite sailors acquire it for them in India.[43] But in accordance with such intervention, sources that discuss commerce in the

---

[40] Philostr. *VA* (ed. Jones) 1.20.
[41] Philostr. *VA* (ed. Jones) 1.21. Jones, "Apollonius of Tyana's Passage to India," 185–99.
[42] Jones, "Apollonius of Tyana's Passage to India," 185–99. Philostratus places Babylon east of Ctesiphon and conflates the Zagros mountains and the Hindu Kush.
[43] Procopius, *Bell. Pers.* (ed. Haury) 1.20.

Roman Near East and Parthia suggest that traders from Roman territory typically did not travel into the Iranian plateau and central Asia. Along with Ptolemy, Strabo of Amasea and Isidore of Charax, who both wrote during the reign of Augustus (31 BCE to 14 CE), describe major trade routes that extended from Roman Syria to central Asia. The value of these works is not so much in that they state explicitly where merchants trekked or commercial networks extended. They are significant because both authors seem to make implicit assumptions about such phenomena. They in fact assume that merchants and travelers from the Roman Levant voyaged little farther than Seleucia-Ctesiphon and that a north Syrian commercial segment of the Levantine network extended from Syrian Antioch and Zeugma to Parthian lower Mesopotamia but not into the Iranian plateau.

Strabo treats Seleucia-Ctesiphon and Babylon as natural terminal points for merchants journeying from Roman Syria. These needed to travel to Seleucia-Ctesiphon via the Upper Mesopotamian region that was inhabited by the Scenitae and therefore known as "Scenae." There various halting stations and cisterns were located.[44] Strabo does not indicate that Syrians were intent on moving farther or divulge any information regarding what such an itinerary would have entailed. In fact, he suggests that travelers into the Iranian plateau and toward the Caspian gates had their points of origin in Babylonia.[45] Moreover, by specifying that Medes acquired Indian and Babylonian goods and moved them northward into the Caspian Sea region, he indicates that materials that arrived in the Iranian plateau were being transported by lower Mesopotamians or by highlanders of Iran who did commerce there.[46] Offhand, it may seem that Strabo was simply presenting regionally based directions. After all, anyone traveling east into the Iranian plateau would at some point have to move from Babylonia or another lowland area. But it is just as reasonable to conclude that Strabo in fact presents the normative itineraries and terminal points for the primary commercial networks connecting the Roman Levant and central Asia. Significantly, his segmentation of commercial movement is supported by other articles of evidence, such as the work of Isidore of Charax.

In his description of Parthian commercial stopovers (which may have been part of a longer work on Parthia), Isidore of Charax treats Seleucia-Ctesiphon as the normative destination for merchants from Roman Syria.

---

[44] Strabo (ed. Radt) 16.1.27: ἡ ὁδὸς τοῖς ἐκ τῆς Συρίας εἰς Σελεύκειαν καὶ Βαβυλῶνα ἐμπορευομένοις.
[45] Strabo (ed. Radt) 11.13.7: οἱ ἐκ τῆς Περσίδος καὶ Βαβυλῶνος εἰς Κασπίους πύλας ὁδεύοντες.
[46] Strabo (ed. Radt) 11.5.8. See Rtveladze, "Studies on the Historical Geography," 137–39.

He notes that Phaliga, a village on the Euphrates whose name meant "halfway," was so called because it was roughly halfway between Antioch and Seleucia-Ctesiphon. His statement suggests that north Syrians who traveled into Parthian territory reckoned Seleucia-Ctesiphon to be the terminal point of their trek. Indeed, after measuring the distance from Antioch to Phaliga (at 120 *schoinoi*) and then from Phaliga to Seleucia-Ctesiphon (at 100 *schoinoi*), he guides his readers along the route to Seleucia-Ctesiphon in great detail and specifies its distance from Zeugma (171 *schoinoi*), yet again indicating that the distance to Seleucia-Ctesiphon was a measurement of special importance for merchants from Roman territory.[47] Moreover, while calculating the total distance from Antioch and Zeugma to Seleucia-Ctesiphon, Isidore does not do the same for the 687 *schoinoi* between Babylonia and Alexandria Arachosia (Kandahar), the last Parthian city before an entry into north India. It is possible that the discrepancy between Isidore's detailed description of the route from Zeugma to Seleucia-Ctesiphon and his more general treatment of the trip from Seleucia-Ctesiphon to Alexandria Arachosia reflects his integration of two different source traditions and not only his own determination.[48] But in either case, Isidore or his sources appear to have assumed that a trek from the upper Euphrates River to Parthian Babylonia (but no farther) was routine for merchants from Seleucid or Roman Syria. By contrast, traders working between Babylonia and central Asia could cover any assortment of distances and itineraries. All told, Isidore's emphasis on Phaliga as a notable equidistant point between Antioch and Seleucia-Ctesiphon and his preeminently detailed description of the trade stations between these two vast emporia indicate that Roman merchants from north Syria most frequently operated between Antioch or Zeugma and Seleucia-Ctesiphon and did not often travel farther east. This was surely in part because Seleucia-Ctesiphon was a significant epicenter of trade, but Parthian intervention also played a role.

In other words, both Strabo and Isidore map two distinct but interconnected commercial networks. One network consisted of Roman Syrians and other inhabitants of the Levant traveling to south Mesopotamia to acquire goods from merchants of Parthian territory; certain links of this network

---

[47] Isidore of Charax, *Mansiones Parthicae* (ed. Müller) 1. The text, with Isidore's fragments, can also be found in Isidore, *FGrH/BNJ* 781 (esp. F. 2).

[48] Isidore of Charax, *Mansiones Parthicae* (ed. Müller) 2–19. See the commentary of Duane Roller in *BNJ* 781, F2, who treats this issue, suggests that Isidore's text on stopovers may have been part of a general work on Parthia, and notes that Isidore may have been updating sources dating from as early as 100 BCE.

passed through Dura-Europos, whose Greek-speaking Christian community has been described in the previous chapter. The other network stretched from south Mesopotamia and other lowland Parthian locations into central Asia, with Parthian merchants covering the entire distance or a mere portion thereof. While an unlikely source, a patristic text known as the *Refutation of All Heresies*, often attributed (although spuriously) to Hippolytus of Rome (active in the early third century CE),[49] provides further evidence for such commercial segmentation, movement, and exchange. According to this work, a Syrian merchant living in Apamea known as Alcibiades had acquired a "heretical" text originally possessed by a religious leader named Elchasai. Upon acquisition, Alcibiades had then transported this text, alleged to be the revelation of a giant angel, to Rome during the episcopate of Callistus (217–222 CE).[50] The *Refutation* unfortunately does not provide many specifics regarding the Apamene figure's activity, but some of its statements are quite compelling.

As the *Refutation* describes, the Syrian Alcibiades had alleged that Elchasai himself had acquired the text from certain "Seres of Parthia" (ἀπὸ Σηρῶν τῆς Παρθίας). In this case, the "Seres" in question apparently were merchants of central Asia or the Tarim Basin who routinely transported silk to Merv, which was located in Margiana at the eastern rim of Parthia proper, was apparently ruled periodically by autonomous dynasts, and was often deemed "little Parthia" or "lesser Parthia" by Chinese sources. As the *Refutation*'s citation of prophecies from Elchasai's text indicates, the transaction occurred while the legions of the Roman emperor Trajan had occupied Parthian Mesopotamia (116–117 CE), and this indicates that Elchasai resided in Parthian Mesopotamia and had transported the text from Parthia proper or Margiana to his home region during its occupation by the Romans.[51] The *Refutation* additionally claims that

---

[49] Litwa, *Refutation*, xxxii–xlii, with Van der Horst "Review."
[50] *Refutation of All Heresies* (ed. Marcovich/ed. Litwa) 9.13.1 and 4. Much is uncertain regarding the figure of Elchasai, the nature of the sect with which Alcibiades was affiliated, and whether Mani in fact belonged to this sect. See Luttikhuizen, "Elchasaites," 335–64. My focus will accordingly be on the perceptions of Alcibiades' activity aired by the *Refutation*. Luttikhuizen maintains that Elchasai should be distinguished from the figure named Alchasaios who is the leader of the "baptist" sect to which Mani belonged in his youth, as is described in the *CMC* (ed. Koenen and Römer) 94–97. A different perspective on Elchasai and "baptists" is presented by Jullien and Jullien, *Apôtres des confins*, 141–45 and Lieu, *Manichaeism*, 35–51, with 42–43 treating this passage and maintaining that Elchasai was the founder of the sect to which Mani belonged. Also, Gardner and Lieu, *Manichaean Texts*, 31–35.
[51] *Refutation of All Heresies* (ed. Marcovich/ed. Litwa) 9.13.1 and 4, with 9.16.4 (for date). Luttikhuizen, "Elchasaites," discusses date and context. My interpretation of "Seres" is suggested by Lieu, *Manichaeism*, 40–41. For a different perspective on the identity of the Seres, see Conte, "'Seri' e 'Sini,'" 64–65. For "little/lesser Parthia," see *Hou Hanshu* 88 in Leslie and Gardiner, *Roman Empire*

according to Alcibiades, Elchasai had then given the text to his religious associate Sobiai (or alternatively, to "baptists").[52] In the early third century CE, the Syrian Alcibiades had acquired what was apparently a Greek translation of the original Aramaic text and brought it to Rome, where north Syrians maintained residential communities and commercial ties.[53]

Whether or not its claims are true or its dating accurate, the discussion contained in the *Refutation*, purportedly informed by the activity of a Syrian Apamene and information that had circulated at third-century CE Rome, reflects normative expectations for the dynamics of commercial movement in the Roman Levant and Parthian Mesopotamia. First, it accepts the premise that a religious leader located in Parthian Mesopotamia (while it was under Roman occupation) maintained commercial contacts with "Seres" who frequented Margiana and had obtained a text from them. Through his activity, he or his associates had the text transported westward across the Zagros Mountains to Parthian Mesopotamia. Second, the *Refutation* apparently delineates that it was only long after Elchasai had brought the text to Parthian Mesopotamia that the Syrian Alcibiades had obtained a copy or translation of it. This suggests that the north Syrian segment of the Levantine commercial network connecting the Roman Levant and Parthian Mesopotamia, or otherwise travelers who followed its social pathways, was responsible for transporting the contents of Elchasai's text to north Syria. The *Refutation*'s discussion of Elchasai's text accordingly reflects a normative understanding of the primary commercial networks and segments that moved goods from central Asia to the Mediterranean. North Syrian merchants traveled eastward into lower Mesopotamia or other lowland Parthian territories. They, however, did not enter the Iranian plateau. If they wanted goods from the Iranian plateau or central or east Asia, they worked through contacts in Parthia who had or could acquire them. While such Parthian contacts could move westward into the Roman Levant, they also trekked east into the Iranian highlands, where they interacted with merchants of central Asia or the Tarim Basin ("Seres").

An additional reason why Roman traders did not travel into highland Iran is because of the accessibility of the Persian Gulf. Parthian intervention likely

---

in *Chinese Sources*, 45; in Hill, *Through the Jade Gate*, 23; and in Hackl, Jacobs, and Weber, *Quellen*, 3.498, with Kaim, "Serakhs Oasis," 153–55. Seres probably refers to the people, not a region. Litwa, *Refutation*, 659–60, n. 94.

[52] This same figure also appears in the *CMC* (ed. Koenen and Römer) 97 as Sabbaios, the baptist. His name is suggestive of an Aramaic/Syriac root for bathing or washing. Gardner and Lieu, *Manichaean Texts*, 65. Luttikhuizen, "Elchasaites," 363 and Lieu, *Manichaeism*, 40 treat Sobiai/baptists.

[53] For merchants or travelers from the Levant in such locations, see Noy, *Foreigners at Rome*, 318–21 and Terpstra, *Trading Communities*, 152–63.

made it desirable for Roman Syrian traders to gain access to the Persian Gulf littoral, where the kingdom of Mesene apparently permitted unrestricted movement during substantial portions of the second century CE. Even when the Parthians intervened in the affairs of Mesene or exerted greater influence, as they did variously in the first and second centuries CE, it seems that the kingdom maintained a certain measure of autonomy and control over its commercial affairs, to the benefit of traders in the Roman empire, Parthian territory, and the Persian Gulf.[54] At the Persian Gulf, north Syrians could accordingly acquire eastern goods that had been carried through north India or even sail to India to make contact with central and south Asians.

The notable example of Palmyra and its vast commercial segment extending into the Indian Ocean illustrates this phenomenon. While their city was located in the dry Syrian steppe at the threshold of the Roman and Parthian empires, the Palmyrenes clearly opted to acquire silk and other transit commodities from the east by traveling in caravans to south Babylonia and Mesene, by maintaining residential communities in cities such as Vologasias, Phorat, and Charax Spasinou, and even by sailing to India.[55] So long as Mesene or even south Babylonia was controlled by the court at Charax Spasinou, and even amid varied degrees of effective Parthian royal intervention, the Palmyrenes crafted a robust segment of the Levantine commercial network that extended to the Persian Gulf and beyond. Inscriptions show that Palmyrenes maintained connections to an administrator of Mesene who governed Bahrain and to the royal court of Elymais (Khuzistan), and attestations of the Babylonian Talmud demonstrate the intensive activity of Palmyrene merchants in lower Mesopotamia.[56] While the Palmyrenes certainly maintained direct commercial lines to Rome itself, inscriptions at Red Sea Egypt (especially Berenike and Koptos) and south Arabia (at Shabwa and on a ceramic vessel of Qani), demonstrate the activity of

---

[54] On Mesene and its relations with Parthia, see Schuol, *Charakene*. Gregoratti, "Parthian Port," 209–229; and Dąbrowa, "Arsacid Empire," 175–78. For Mesene in the Babylonian Talmud, see Oppenheimer, *Babylonia Judaica*, 241–56.

[55] *IGLS* 17.1.16, 23–24, 150, 243, and 245; *PAT* 1062=Milik, *Dédicaces*, 13=*SEG* 7.135=Delplace and Yon, "Inscriptions," 284, An 30: contacts and residential communities in lower Mesopotamia or Mesene. *IGLS* 17.1.26 and 250: travel to India. For Chinese silk and Indian dye finds, Schmidt-Colinet and Stauffer, *Textilien aus Palmyra*; Stauffer, "Kleider, Kissen, bunte Tücher," 67–82. For Palmyra's interregional connections in the Hellenistic and early Roman periods, see now Schmidt-Colinet and al-As'ad, *Palmyras Reichtum*; Żuchowska, "Palmyra (Far Eastern)" and "Palmyra (Chinese Silk)."

[56] *IGLS* 17.1.227 and 245; Bab. Talmud (ed. Epstein) *Shab.* 21b and 31a, *Yeb.* 16a–17a, *Naz.* 47a, *Gitt.* 38a, and *Nidd.* 56b, for example. On Palmyra/Tadmor in the Talmudim (often reconstituted as "Tarmod"), see Hartmann, *Palmyrenische Teilreich*, 40–42 and 329–331 and Oppenheimer, *Babylonia Judaica*, 442–45. For the Palmyrenes and Parthia, Gregoratti, "Palmyrenes."

Palmyrene merchants and ambassadors in such regions.[57] The Palmyrene who dedicated an inscribed wooden table in the cave Hoq on Socotra in 258 CE was perhaps part of a link that connected the Palmyrenes of the Red Sea to those working the Persian Gulf and north India, even if Palmyrenes had increasingly opted to reach north India from Red Sea Egypt by this time.[58] But aside from two funerary *stelai* that may have been brought to Turkmenistan and Uzbekistan in modern times, no reliable evidence places Palmyrenes in the Iranian highlands or central Asia.[59] Palmyrenes apparently journeyed almost everywhere, but like most Roman Syrians, they did not move overland into the Iranian plateau or central Asia.[60]

Finally, it must be stressed that most Roman merchants who traveled into Parthian or Sasanian territory were not necessarily concerned primarily with long-distance transit trade. The appeal of long-distance transit luxuries exhibited in ancient sources and among modern scholars has arguably drawn much attention to how Roman traders of the Near East trafficked in eastern products. But it should be noted that the bulk of commerce in the premodern world, including the Roman and Parthian Near East, was of a regional or interregional character and involving the sale and acquisition of regionally produced goods, and it did not necessarily pertain to the movement of long-distance transit products transported by large caravans. In fact, recent work has discredited the notion that the regions along the "steppe frontier" between Rome and Parthia had mostly "caravan cities." Likewise, the *Palmyrene Tax Law* demonstrates that even at Palmyra, a city that invested heavily in the acquisition and sale of eastern goods, merchants trafficked in local and regional commodities or sought markets for them.[61]

---

[57] Dijkstra and Verhoogt, "Greek–Palmyrene Inscription," 207–18; Bernand, *Portes du Désert*, 39 (=*PAT* 0256), 62(?), 85, and 103; Robin, "Palmyréniens en Arabie du Sud," 490–92. Also, Arbach, "Visiteurs de Shabwa"; Sedov, "New Archaeological and Epigraphical Material," 318–20, with Briquel-Chatonnet, "*Graffiti* en langues nord-sémitiques," 387–88. South Arabians visited Palmyra by traveling overland. See Schiettecatte and Arbach, "Political Map."

[58] Gorea, "Palmyrene Tablette," 449–57 (449–51) contains text and photos and "Sea and Inland Trade," 463–85 discusses Palmyrene trade. Smith, *Roman Palmyra*, 68–80 and 150–74 treats Palmyra's economy and expatriates (160–63 on merchants). Seland, "Networks and Social Cohesion," 381–84 and *Ships of the Desert*, explores the Palmyrene commercial network. For Palmyrenes at Rome, see Terpstra, *Trading Communities*, 152–60.

[59] Palmyrene funerary inscriptions and reliefs have surfaced in the Merv oasis and are now in Tashkent. But they were most probably transported there by Russians in the nineteenth century. See Cussini, Review of *Palmyra*, 142–43 and Hübner, "Palestine, Syria, and the Silk Road," 45 on *PAT* 1123–24=Masson, "Two Palmyrene Stelae," 239–47.

[60] See now Gawlikowski, "Trade," 23.

[61] See Kaizer, "Questions and Problems," 62–66. *PAT* 0259=*CIS* 2.3, 3913. The decree is now accessible in Greek (partially), Palmyrenean, and English, with commentary. Healey, *Aramaic Inscriptions*, no. 37.

The reason for the primacy of such regional and interregional commerce that trafficked in Near Eastern goods is that participation in long-distance transit trade could be very profitable, but it was also prone to instability and heavy risk. Merchants could not easily be certain that they would have access to a steady stream of goods produced thousands of miles away or that they could acquire them at sufficiently low costs.[62] Accordingly, if traders wanted to ensure product availability, to obviate the need for "middle men," or to acquire transit goods at lower expense, they typically had to travel or extend their immediate commercial segments over substantial distances. For this reason, certain Palmyrenes resided at the Persian Gulf and voyaged to India instead of waiting for products to arrive at the Persian Gulf ports or Seleucia-Ctesiphon. From their Persian Gulf residences, they transferred goods to caravans of fellow Palmyrenes that moved them northwest to Palmyra and then the Roman Mediterranean.

But due to the risks of long-distance transit trade, it is reasonable to suspect that most Roman Syrian traders invested primarily in the known stability of regionally produced goods that could be transported for relatively predictable sale and profit at nearby, identifiable markets. In the Roman empire, major cities and areas of military concentration constituted the organizational hubs of distribution and acquisition for regional commodities within commercial networks, and merchants typically converged upon the major cities of their home territories, of adjacent regions, or of those connected to their home locality by the Mediterranean Sea.[63] As a result, late antique Syrian merchants are notable for having trafficked in such regional products, including various grains, grape wine, and olive oil, and for distributing them in local or regional contexts, or even westward to Italy and Gaul.[64] By contrast, the nature of the regional commodities that Roman Syrian merchants transported to Parthia or acquired there for distribution and sale in their home regions has not received definitive study, and such a topic is beyond the scope of this present discussion. It is nonetheless noticeable that residents of Parthian lower Mesopotamia produced wine from dates (and less so from grapes) and oil from sesame

---

[62] Local, regional, and interregional forms of trade too were certainly affected by volatile fluctuations in production, supply, and costs, but for obvious reasons, long-distance transit trade (whose commodities were often produced well beyond the immediate network of Roman merchants) posed even greater risks. For "volatile and opaque markets," see Bang, *Roman Bazaar*, 136–53 (and broadly, 131–201), as well as Morley, "Early Roman Empire: Distribution."

[63] Terpstra, *Trading Communities*; and Morley, "Early Roman Empire: Distribution," 571–80 with Peterson, "Trade and Traders in the Roman World: Scale, Structure, and Organisation," 149–167 and Alston, "Trade and the City in Roman Egypt," 168–202 inform my analysis.

[64] Decker, "Export Wine Trade" and *Tilling the Hateful Earth*, generally; Pieri, *Commerce du vin*.

(not olives), and Roman Syrian traders may have (for instance) exploited such disparities in their calculations of acquisition and distribution.[65] Whatever Syrians may have been trafficking to and from lower Mesopotamia, recent work on Roman Syrian commerce, agriculture, and economy indicates that Syrian merchants primarily profited by transporting goods produced in Syria to nearby regions, targeting stable and identifiable markets there, and acquiring regionally produced commodities to be brought back and sold in their native lands.[66] Roman Syrian commerce with an eastward orientation was probably little different.

Accordingly, Romans who ventured into lowland Parthian or Sasanian territory were typically engaged in the traffic of regionally produced commodities and converged on major cities, which constituted hubs of distribution. This is not to say that Roman Syrians did not acquire transit commodities. They, of course, did. But with the exception of the Palmyrenes, they usually did so within the purview of their normalized travels to the urban hubs of lowland Parthia to sell and acquire regionally produced goods and obtain whatever eastern transit commodities, such as silk, were accessible in such lowland markets. The sheer size of Seleucia-Ctesiphon, for instance, certainly would have attracted Roman Syrians in search of markets to distribute goods produced in Syria and to purchase items generated in south Mesopotamia. There, the opportunistic, if frequent, acquisition of eastern transit goods could occur.[67]

All told, Roman merchants, including Palmyrenes, did not travel overland to central Asia. Insubstantial as it may be, sufficient evidence indicates that Parthians prevented Roman traders from moving into the Iranian highlands. Roman geographers and patristic authors convey the fact that two primary commercial networks connected the Roman Levant to central Asia. The first consisted of merchants who moved from the Roman Levant

---

[65] Strabo (ed. Radt) 16.1.14 and, before him, Herodotus, 1.193–94 describe Babylonia as a place traditionally void of grapes and olives (and indeed affirm the importation of grape wine), even if vines had been introduced to Babylonia and Elymais by the Parthian period (Strabo [ed. Radt] 15.3.11). Also note Pliny, *NH* (ed. Jahn and Mayhoff) 14.102 regarding date and fig wine production among Parthians. Some parts of Babylonia (especially Neharpanya) were notable for vineyards, but they appear to be exceptional. Imported wine was apparently common. See the sources and discussion of Oppenheimer, *Babylonia Judaica*, 180–83, 294–300, 368–73, and 401–5. For dates and date wine trade in the late antique Persian gulf, refer to Payne, "Monks, Dinars, and Date Palms," 105–8. For production of grape wine in the late antique Roman Levant, Schachner, "'I Greet You and Thy Brethren'," 157–84; and Decker, *Tilling the Hateful Earth*, 121–48.

[66] Decker, *Tilling the Hateful Earth*, 228–56; Pieri, *Commerce du vin*. Likewise, for trade in the medieval Mediterranean, Goldberg, *Trade and Institutions*, 211–46.

[67] Strabo (ed. Radt) 16.1.16 in fact notes that saleable and refined items could be found at Seleucia-Ctesiphon especially. McLaughlin, *Rome and the Distant East*, 94–95.

(often from or through north Syria) to Seleucia-Ctesiphon or other lowland hubs, with the primary purpose of selling and buying regionally produced goods. The second comprised Parthian subjects who moved to central Asia, traded directly with central Asians, and provided merchants from the Roman Levant with wares. As the dominant patterns of Palmyrene commerce indicate, merchants from the Roman Levant who endeavored to amplify the profits of transit trade could extend their commercial lines eastward, but they did so by establishing direct links to the Persian Gulf and the Indian Ocean world. They did not move into the Iranian plateau and central Asia. Finally, the stability of regional or inter-regional production, acquisition, and distribution most probably informed the movements of merchants from the Roman Near East; eastern transit goods usually elicited only secondary concern or opportunistic purchases and sales. Roman Syrian merchants therefore limited their mobility to lowland Parthian or Sasanian territory. Ptolemy's account in fact describes various stopovers in upper Mesopotamia, classical Assyria, and the Zab River region, and Maes, whose reporting is the ultimate source of Ptolemy's information, apparently frequented these instead of sites in lower Mesopotamia.[68] But these also represent the farthest extent that Maes traveled. All told, the contemporary evidence indicates that if Maes Titianos did journey into Parthian territory, he would not have moved into the Iranian plateau or beyond.

Whom Did Maes Titianos Send to Central Asia?

As suggested above, Maes Titianos did not travel to central Asia. Yet, according to Ptolemy, he sent or arranged that certain people be sent to the "Seres" (διαπεμψάμενον δέ τινας πρὸς τοὺς Σῆρας) in the Tarim Basin. In regards to these people that Maes Titianos dispatched into the Iranian plateau toward China, however, Ptolemy is vague. The first point of ambiguity is the aorist participle διαπεμψάμενον. Typically translated by scholars as "he sent," the verbal adjective, being in the middle voice, could also be causative and denote a process by which Maes accomplished an action through others' work. The phrase διαπεμψάμενον ... τινας could

---

[68] Ptolemy (ed. Stückelberger and Graßhoff) 1.11–12 claims that Maes' route led from the Euphrates, across Mesopotamia to the Tigris river, then to the land of the "Garamaioi" in Assyria and Media (the Zab River region). Ptolemy's treatment of Asia in Book 6 and his list of important cities in Book 8 suggests that the following were some examples of important stopovers for Maes in lowland upper Mesopotamia: Edessa (5.18.10; 8.20.22), Nisibis (5.18.11; 8.22.23), Nineveh (6.1.3; 8.21.3), and Arbela (6.1.5; 8.21.3).

therefore describe how Maes had made arrangements for the dispatch of "τινες" to China and be translated as "he had certain people sent" or "he arranged to have certain people sent."[69] This nuance is perhaps significant. Maes may not have known or conversed personally with the people whose activity he had coordinated. He may have made arrangements through intermediaries. The second point regards the identity of the people who trekked eastward. Ptolemy identifies them as "certain people" (τινες). Scholarship has often treated these figures as agents or subordinates directly linked to Maes, whether these were his employees, companions, or contacts that he dispatched eastward. They are sometimes even treated as members of a caravan or embassy that Maes organized and sent across Asia.[70]

But ultimately, the identity of the people whom Ptolemy calls τινες is uncertain. They were not necessarily members of Maes' immediately personal circle or even from Roman territory. Based on the issues raised so far in this chapter, it is reasonable to suspect that some of them were inhabitants of Parthian territory with whom Maes had formed relationships of reciprocity. Likewise, others could have been merchants of central Asia or the Tarim Basin to whom Maes' direct contacts from Parthian territory had access. In other words, the "τινες" that Ptolemy describes can be divided into two discrete categories. The first were direct contacts in Parthian Mesopotamia who at Maes' behest had acquired measurements as they crossed the Iranian plateau and advanced to the Stone Tower. The second were central Asian merchants whom Maes arranged to have sent to China through his direct contacts in Parthian territory and who provided the time necessary for travel between the Stone Tower and "Sera." Since Maes relied on these distinct segments for information regarding the distance between the Euphrates and the Tarim Basin, Ptolemy's use of the participle διαπεμψάμενον should be understood as causative: "he had certain people sent" or "arranged to have certain people sent" to "Sera." In this sense, Maes' Parthian contacts had consulted merchants of central Asia or the Tarim Basin regarding their itinerary between the Stone Tower and "Sera."

As noted previously, the *Refutation* suggests that Parthian members of a lower Mesopotamian segment of the lowland Parthian/Sasanian commercial network traveled to central Asia, acquired goods from "Seres," and transported them to Roman merchants either in the Parthian lowlands or Roman

---

[69] Smyth, *Greek Grammar*, no. 1725.
[70] Young, *Rome's Eastern Trade*, 196–97; McLaughlin, *Rome and the Distant East*, 106–9 and 126–28. Bernard, "De l'Euphrate à la Chine," generally.

Syria itself. Sufficient evidence indicates that the Parthians maintained contact with the peoples of central Asia and China.[71] Another arguably significant but sparing source for trade segments across the Iranian plateau is the *Hymn of the Pearl*. Found in one Greek and one Syriac manuscript of the *Acts of the Apostle Thomas*, the *Hymn of the Pearl* is a mysterious text, and with varied opinions regarding its date, place of origin, and religious orientation.[72]

The *Hymn* was certainly popular among Manichaeans in late antiquity, even if its origin, date, and religious background have stirred substantial debate.[73] According to most (but not all) interpretations, it existed independently of the *Acts of Thomas* before eventually being interpolated into it, perhaps during the third or fourth centuries.[74] Syriac is generally understood to be the language of the surviving version's written composition, and at certain parts the Greek text appears to be dependent on the Syriac, especially in regards to toponyms.[75] Various scholars have theorized its

---

[71] Posch, "Chinesische Quellen zu den Parthern," 355–65; Hackl, Jacobs, and Weber, *Quellen*, 3.482–511; Tao, "Parthia in China," 87–104; Wiesehöfer, "Greeks, Iranians, and Chinese," 11–17.

[72] Poirier, *Hymne de la Perle* represents the foundational study, and 330–36 and 350–56 presents Syriac and Greek text. Ferreira, *Hymn of the Pearl*, 39–65 and 82–95 also provides Syriac and Greek, along with an accessible introduction to the text and the scholarly tradition. Many parts of the text are controversial, but most such issues do not affect my discussion, save for those raised by Roig Lanzillotta, "Syriac Original?" 121–23, who doubts the hymn's later insertion into the *Acts*, its eastern origins, and its Syriac priority (see n. 75 for my thoughts). For links to Mesopotamian precedents and gnosis (and an argument for a pagan authorship), see Parpola, "Mesopotamian Precursors," 181–94.

[73] Ferreira, *Hymn of the Pearl*, 4–9 discusses the various theories.

[74] Such a date is suggested by the close correspondence between the *Hymn*'s narrator and the figure of Mani in the *CMC* (ed. Koenen and Römer), esp. 17–24, which suggests that the insertion of the *Hymn* and the composition of the original narrative reflected by the *CMC* were contemporaneous. Poirier, *Hymne de la Perle*, 171–84 and 310–17 outlines the argument, and he places the text in the third century CE. But since the *Acts of Thomas* was probably composed in the mid-to-late third century CE, and not the early third as has often been surmised, and since the *CMC* is often deemed a fourth-century CE text (but translated from a Syriac original), the fourth century is perhaps possible. For a later third-century CE dating of the *Acts of Thomas*, see Myers, *Spiritual Epicleses*, 29–55 (esp. 44–55). See Lieu, *Manichaeism in Mesopotamia*, 78–87 on the *Cologne Mani Codex*. Note that Roig Lanzillotta, "Syriac Original?" 121–23 deems the *Hymn* to be part of the *Acts of Thomas*' initial (second-century) composition in Greek within a general Mediterranean environment. The view that the *Hymn* had autonomous origins does not negate the possibility that it could have been included in the original text of the surviving *Acts*, however. For my views on the Syriac priority and suggestion of a lower Mesopotamian origin of the *Hymn*, see the pages and notes immediately following.

[75] Poirier, *Hymne de la Perle*, 185–97 argues for Syriac priority and represents the conventional standpoint. Roig Lanzillotta, "Syriac Original?" 120–23 suggests Greek priority (see previous footnote). But I find the place names to be significant evidence for Syriac priority in ways that Roig Lanzillotta does not. The Greek seems to reflect a literal dependence on Syriac names for eastern places, with a certain unfamiliarity with some of them. For instance, Syriac *bet Qušan* (line 7) is translated very literally in the Greek as Κοσάνων (line 7). Greeks typically referred to the Kushans as Bactrians and translated accordingly. See the *Book of the Laws of the Countries* (ed. Drijvers) 44 and

place of origin based on its composition in Syriac or its putative religious orientation, and the surviving Syriac text is typically deemed a product of the third century, even if it perhaps is the reconstituted variation of an earlier tradition.[76] Edessa or Upper Mesopotamia, the seat of early Syriac, are common suggestions for the place of the surviving text's composition, but its topographical and toponymical orientation indicates that it was produced somewhere between lower Mesopotamia and the eastern Iranian plateau. For example, as the royal protagonist of the *Hymn* embarks on a trip from "the East" in order to acquire a magnificent pearl, he is adorned with riches from various regions that are within the Parthians' trading orbit.[77] Some of these riches were from regions to the east: chalcedony from India and agates from the Kushan territory of central Asia.[78] Others were from the regions to the immediate west that adjoined the Caspian sea: gold from the *Gelāyē* and silver from the great city of Ganzak (perhaps in Media Atropatene).[79] Yet, the fact that the *Hymn* describes the Iranian plateau as "the East" also suggests that it was composed west of it. If not upper Mesopotamia, lower Mesopotamia or Mesene, which both appear in the text and harbored speakers of Syriac with connections to Edessa by the

60 and (ed. Ramelli) 180 and 198, with *Preparation for the Gospel (Praeparatio Evangelica)* (ed. Mras and des Places) 6.10.46, with *BNJ* 710, Fr. 3. Maišan (line 18 and 70 of the Syriac) appears in the Greek as Μοσάνων (line 18: referring to inhabitants) and, more oddly, Μέσον (line 70, referring to the place); these forms are irregular and not consistent with the most common Greek conventions, like Μεσηνή, or those used in trilingual Persian royal inscriptions. The Greek seems dependent on the Syriac here. See for instance Strabo (ed. Radt) 2.1.1.31 and 16.4.1 (though Radt corrects Μαικηνή here); Pliny, *NH* (ed. Jahn and Mayhoff) 6.129; Josephus, *AJ* (ed. Niese) 1.145; Ammianus (ed. Seyfarth) 23.6.23 and 24.3.12, with *Res Gestae of Shapur* (ed. Huyse) 2, 36, and 44. Schuol, *Charakene*, 90–149 and 151–64 compiles references from Greek and Latin literature and Persian inscriptions. Finally, the Greek of the *Hymn*, apparently dependent on the Syriac, misconstrues the Syriac reference to Ganzak (line 6) as "*gazā*" and thus translates as "treasures" (line 6: Poirier, *Hymne de la Perle*, 261), and it renders the ethnic Gelai/Gelāyē (ܓܠܝܐ / 'elāyē, line 6; see further thoughts at n. 79 and Poirier, *Hymne de la Perle*, 260) as "the people above" (τῶν ἄνω, line 6), for the Syriac lexical form could also denote "above" or "upper."

[76] Ferreira, *Hymn of the Pearl*, 4–9 treats scholarship.
[77] Poirier, *Hymne de la Perle*, 329–36 for Syriac, 352–56 for Greek; Ferreira, *Hymn of the Pearl*, 38–65 for Syriac, 82–95 for Greek. Line numbers are taken from the poems as contained in these editions.
[78] *Hymn of the Pearl* (ed. Poirier and ed. Ferreira), Syriac text, line 7. I cite the Syriac text, which is almost universally accepted as the language of original composition or at least preceding the surviving Greek text (see n. 72–75). But see Roig Lanzillotta, "Syriac Original?" 12–23.
[79] *Hymn of the Pearl* (ed. Poirier and ed. Ferreira), Syriac text, line 6. Here *'elāyē* (which appears in the text) can be reckoned *gelāyē* (to which it is sometimes emended), a people of the Caspian Sea. The single manuscript of the *Book of the Laws of the Countries* accordingly features both forms. See *The Book of the Laws of the Countries* (ed. Drijvers) 44 and 60 and (ed. Ramelli) 180 and 198 (with n. 179). Tubach, "Four World Empires," 145–54, contends that this is a miswritten word for China (the Seres/*Šelāyē*). For silver, see pp. 37–41, n. 37–49.

later third century CE, therefore constitute the most reasonable interpretation for its regional origins.

Due to the lack of Parthian and early Sasanian sources on the matter, the *Hymn of the Pearl*, insofar as it appears to be an eastern witness, is arguably of immense value for understanding the commercial network that connected lowland Parthian/Sasanian territory and the Iranian plateau before the fourth century CE. It ostensibly depicts the movement of a Parthian prince between the Iranian plateau and Egypt. This prince, who is both narrator and protagonist, describes how he has been sent on embassy from Hyrcania with many eastern riches to purchase a pearl in Egypt, where he suffers detainment and loss of memory among the Egyptians until his liberation and return. In this sense, it could be tempting to interpret the *Hymn* as representing the normative, concentrated movement of people from the Iranian highlands westward across the Near East. But such an interpretation would pose problems. First, the protagonist's movement to Egypt is part of the *Hymn*'s textual agenda; a voyage, stint of servitude in Egypt, and liberation had many biblical parallels and served as obvious metaphors for the labors of spiritual redemption. Second, and perhaps more important, its writer only displays accurate topographical or toponymical knowledge of places in lower Mesopotamia and the Iranian plateau.

After the *Hymn* embeds its protagonist, a Parthian royal, in the social and cultural context of the Iranian plateau, it narrates how he travels west. The itinerary that the prince follows is stated twice in the *Hymn*, first to depict his movement westward and again to describe his return to the east.[80] Amid his itinerary, the prince first journeys to Mesene (Maišan) in the north Persian Gulf littoral. There, traders with links to the Indian Ocean world convened, and the *Hymn* expresses an awareness of Mesene as a significant trade emporium by calling it an inn and a harbor for merchants.[81] It is also worth mentioning that the *Hymn*'s narrative even later notes the shift of elevation between the heights of Hyrcania and lowland coastal Mesene.[82] After departing Mesene, the prince then moves north to "Babylon" (Babel), perhaps an archaizing reference to Seleucia-Ctesiphon or Babylonia.[83]

To this point, the text is geographically and toponymically coherent. But then the protagonist reaches a place called "Sarbug" and quite suddenly,

---

[80] Hyrcania is ostensibly identified as the place of origin in *Hymn of the Pearl*, Syriac text, 73. Tubach, "Weg des Prinzen," 87–111.
[81] *Hymn of the Pearl* (ed. Poirier and ed. Ferreira), Syriac text, 18 and 70–71.
[82] *Hymn of the Pearl* (ed. Poirier and ed. Ferreira), Syriac text, 70–74.
[83] *Hymn of the Pearl* (ed. Poirier and ed. Ferreira), Syriac text, 19 and 69.

Egypt.⁸⁴ Sarbug has never been identified, and the text provides no other meaningful toponym in the prince's overland itinerary between Babylonia and Egypt. A poem very much centered on the stretch of territory between lower Mesopotamia and central Asia, the *Hymn* displays little concern with geographic specificities of the Roman Levant or Upper Mesopotamia. Just as the surviving *Acts of Thomas* betrays the scantiest knowledge of India and suggests that Upper Mesopotamians rarely (if ever) went there, the *Hymn*'s geography indicates in no way that its composer had ever traveled to the Roman Levant or Egypt or had reliable contacts within the commercial networks that extended there. All told, the surviving *Hymn*'s composition in Syriac and its emphasis on the topography and toponymy between Babylonia and the Kushan empire suggest that its composer inhabited third-century CE Seleucia-Ctesiphon or Phorat and was affiliated with some Gnostic or Christian community, perhaps "baptists" or Manichaeans.⁸⁵ By the later third century CE, these cities significantly included populations that spoke Syriac (alongside other Aramaic dialects) and sported both religious and commercial populations that cohere with the *Hymn*'s textual disposition.⁸⁶ They were also embedded in a specifically eastward segment of the lowland Parthian/Sasanian commercial network extending into the Iranian plateau and central Asia.

In other words, the geographic orientation of the *Hymn* can be most plausibly explained by the existence in the Parthian and early Sasanian empires of a substantial commercial network of lowland Parthian subjects that extended from Seleucia-Ctesiphon, Mesene, and other lowland sites, across the Iranian plateau, and into central Asia. It thereby facilitated decent toponymical information for people inhabiting the stretch of territory between lowland Parthian/Sasanian territory and the Tarim Basin. Inhabitants of lower Mesopotamia or Mesene who participated or maintained connections within the network, such as the *Hymn*'s author, were better informed about the Iranian plateau than about the Roman Near East. As noted previously, the *Refutation* assumes that Elchasai, a religious leader located in Parthian Mesopotamia, was in contact with central Asian merchants and thereby implicated in the human movement that this commercial network shaped. This same commercial network and

---

⁸⁴ *Hymn of the Pearl* (ed. Poirier and ed. Ferreira), Syriac text, 19–20 and 69.
⁸⁵ Ferreira, *Hymn of the Pearl*, 4–9 on this and other theories.
⁸⁶ For this lower Mesopotamian context, see Lieu, *Manichaeism*, 33–59; Jullien and Jullien, *Apôtres des confins* generally, but esp. 137–52 (for "baptists" and Manichaeans); Van Rompay, "East: Syria and Mesopotamia," 365–70; Walker, "From Nisibis to Xi'an," 997–1000; Brock, *Hidden Pearl*, 2.72 and 89–95.

the toponymic knowledge that it afforded to inhabitants of the regions that it meaningfully connected also informed the geographic orientation of the *Hymn*'s author. But the text demonstrates no knowledge of the Roman Near East, and it further indicates that the Parthian and Sasanian merchants and travelers who exclusively focused their movement and activity on the Iranian plateau had little knowledge of Roman territory, even if they transferred goods and knowledge directly or by proxy to Roman merchants. Of course, not all lowland merchants had such a stark eastward orientation. A Jewish merchant of Mesene is represented by Josephus as frequenting Adiabene, and the *Teaching of Addai* discusses how "Assyrians" could travel to Edessa while disguised as merchants.[87] We have seen how the *Acts of Mar Mari* conceives of merchants from Iran as maintaining a residential presence at Edessa.[88] The lowland Parthian/Sasanian network certainly stretched to the Roman Levant and maintained residential anchor points there. But the *Hymn of the Pearl* reflects a much stronger anchorage in the segment of the network directly connecting lower Mesopotamia/Mesene and central Asia.

Whatever its religious orientation, the *Hymn of the Pearl* coheres intriguingly with the movements of Mani, a member of a "baptist" sect who founded the culturally eclectic and cosmopolitan religion of Manichaeism and wrote numerous of his works in Aramaic or Syriac.[89] Mani was notably born in Seleucia-Ctesiphon to a father named Patik (Pattikios) who had migrated there from Ecbatana/Hamadan. Shortly after his birth, Patik became a member of a "baptist" sect near Phorat in Mesene, and Mani joined him at the age of four. Upon reaching young adulthood, Mani then embarked on a mobile religious career that coheres with the concentrated, normative movement that the lowland Parthian/Sasanian network facilitated between Seleucia-Ctesiphon or Mesene and central Asia.[90] Just like the geographic orientation of the *Hymn*'s protagonist, Mani's travels reflect a pattern of movement that coheres with the physical and social pathways into the Iranian plateau that characterized this commercial segment.

Space does not allow for a broader discussion of Manichaeism or the full geographic extent of Manichaean worship during Mani's lifetime or after his death. Also, given the dispersal and differing chronologies of sources, reconstructing Mani's early mission in its specifics is very challenging, and

---

[87] Josephus, *AJ* (ed. Niese) 20.34–37; *Teaching of Addai* (ed. Phillips) ܐ.
[88] *Acts of Mār Mārī* (ed. Jullien and Jullien; ed. Harrak) generally, with 31 representing the reference to merchants.
[89] Lieu, *Manichaeism*, 78–84 describes these works.
[90] For Mani's origins, see Lieu, *Manichaeism*, 36–37.

much remains uncertain. But the basic, general frame of his movement has been established by previous scholarship, and it is significant.[91] As noted above, Mani was a member of a "baptist" sect located near Phorat. When Mani famously broke from this sect and began the missionary activity through which he founded a new religion, he first visited the highlands of Media and the city of Ganzak, located either in Media proper or Media Atropatene.[92] Having trekked south through lower Mesopotamia and to Mesene, a maritime merchant, apparently a Palmyrene, transported him to north India and certain parts of coastal Fars.[93] Interestingly, Mani seems not to have trekked into the hinterland of India extensively; the island of Dev, a trade emporium perhaps located at the mouth of the Indus river, was thereafter the locus of Mani's followers.[94]

At this point, it is even more difficult to reconstruct Mani's movements. Still, upon his return to Fars either by sea or overland (and perhaps after visiting the dynast of Turan), it seems that Mani traveled through Elymais, Mesene, and lower Mesopotamia, and from these lowland areas he crossed into the Iranian plateau and central Asia.[95] Amid his journeys, Mani eventually earned the attention and patronage of Shapur II and followed the movements of his court to various places, including Parthia and Fars. Certainly Mani sent disciples across imperial frontiers and deep into Roman territory and central Asia so that they could spread their new religious beliefs and practices, and both his itinerary and that of his followers focused on the court sites of prominent monarchs or regional

---

[91] My discussion is in many ways an abbreviated summary of Lieu, *Manichaeism*, 70–78, and *Manichaeism in Mesopotamia*, 22–25; Gardner and Lieu, *Manichaean Texts*, 5–8 with some additions, nuances, omissions, or alterations (all minor). For the difficulties with reconstructing the precise order of Mani's itineraries, Jones, "Things Mani Learned," 390–95.

[92] *CMC* 121 (ed. Koenen and Römer), with further emendations suggested by Römer, *Manis frühe Missionsreisen*, 2–12, who also discusses Ganzak's location. Gardner and Lieu, *Manichaean Texts*, 69 provide translation.

[93] *CMC* 144–45 (ed. Koenen and Römer), with further emendations suggested by Römer, *Manis frühe Missionsreisen*, 132–46. Gardner and Lieu, *Manichaean Texts*, 73 provide translation.

[94] Sundermann, *Mitteliranische manichäische Texte*, 4a.1, 56–57 (654–59), from M 4575 R II I, with Lieu, *Manichaeism in Mesopotamia*, 22–25 providing clarification of the content. Jones, "Things Mani Learned," discusses the identity of Dev/Deb.

[95] The *CMC* becomes fragmentary and then eventually ends at this point, and the main testimony for Mani's travels at this juncture are the following: Keph. 1, 14–16 and Keph. 76, 183–88 in Polotsky and Böhlig, *Kephalaia*, Vol. 1; the testimony of al-Nadim, which perhaps comes from the same source from which the *CMC* is derived (Gardner and Lieu, *Manichaean Texts*, 75–76), and Sundermann, *Mitteliranische manichäische Texte*, 2.2, 19–24 and 10–11.1, 101–3. Gardner and Lieu, *Manichaean Texts*, 6 and 73–79 translate the passages from the *Kephalaia*, al-Nadim, and the *CMC*, or otherwise explain the Iranian texts. For syntheses that integrate the sources just mentioned, see Lieu, *Manichaeism*, 70–78, and *Manichaeism in Mesopotamia*, 22–25. Recently studied material from the Beatty *Kephalaia* Codex is brought to bear by Dilley, "Mani's Wisdom"; and BeDuhn, "Parallels."

governors and dynasts.⁹⁶ Still, despite their courtly orientation, Mani's personal travels were both shaped and determined by the social pathways blazed by a lowland Parthian/Sasanian commercial network. While its varied segments extended north to the Caspian Sea region and south to India, Mani especially traversed the segment connecting lowland Sasanian territory to the Iranian plateau and central Asia.⁹⁷ Both the activity of Mani and the *Hymn of the Pearl* thereby reflect an intimacy with the human movement and geographic knowledge structured by the network of lower Parthian/Sasanian subjects who worked this segment.

In short, the geographic knowledge exhibited by the *Hymn of the Pearl* and the patterns of movement undertaken by Mani cohere with the existence of a durable commercial network that facilitated travel between lowland Parthian/Sasanian territory and central Asia. As such, the people who journeyed into central Asia on behalf of Maes Titianos were merchants of lowland Parthian territory whose commercial networking extended geographically to Merv and even beyond. These were also in the position to obtain information, however inexplicit and ambiguous, from central Asian merchants who traveled to and from China. As noted previously, Chinese sources describe embassies from "Mengqi and Doule" (or: "Meng-chie and Toule") that occurred c. 100 CE. These terms are ostensibly references to Maes Titianos by name or his Macedonian background. Their meanings, however, are ultimately unknown, and Ptolemy's account in fact suggests that neither Maes nor his immediate subordinates or companions traveled into the Tarim Basin to compile distances. Instead, Maes used his contacts in lowland Parthian territory, who voyaged to the Stone Tower and consulted central Asian merchants regarding how long a trip to "Sera" would have taken. Accordingly, Chinese sources in fact cannot have made reference to an embassy sent by Maes Titianos or by Macedonians. It never occurred.

Intermediaries in Parthian and Early Sasanian Space: Jewish and Palmyrene Evidence

So far, this chapter has analyzed evidence supporting the premise that a Levantine commercial network effectively terminated in the Parthian and

---

⁹⁶ As appropriately emphasized by Dilley, "Religious Intercrossing," 58–70, and "'Hell Exists'," 235–45, with Sundermann, "Manichaeism," 80.
⁹⁷ For Mani's disciples and subsequent spread, see Lieu, *Manichaeism*, 86–120, *Manichaeism in Mesopotamia*, 26–38, *Manichaeism in Central Asia and China*, and "Diffusion, Persecution, and Transformation of Manichaeism."

Sasanian lowlands. It also maintains that a network of Parthian or Sasanian subjects extending from these lowlands, across the Iranian plateau, and into central Asia acquired transit commodities for it. While often difficult to date the episodes that they depict, Jewish sources offer further support for such segmentation. As the materials indicate, Jews frequently traveled between Palestine or north Syria and Babylonia. But Jews of Palestine and north Syria apparently did not conduct commerce in central Asia or beyond themselves. These instead relied on Babylonian Jewish contacts, who themselves voyaged to or even settled in central Asia and acquired products for them.[98] Such Babylonian Jews also journeyed to Jerusalem and Palestine, as shown by the Jews who apparently trekked from lowland and highland Parthian territory to attend Passover at Jerusalem in the Acts of the Apostles.[99] Therein perhaps resides the significance of the Babylonian Jew who had reportedly traveled to "Marguan" and had to refuse impure beverages.[100] This passage is indicative of the tendency for Babylonian Jews to travel into the Iranian plateau and central Asia and even to establish a residential presence there in antiquity and late antiquity.[101] The Jew who traveled to "Marguan" was apparently interacting with non-Jews or with Jews whose frequent business with foreigners, such as Sogdians who transported silk to Merv from east Asia, encouraged them to sample prohibited potables.[102] Otherwise, Babylonian Jews are recorded as having been involved in the trade that passed through Mesene or as having connections to Media, Elymais (Khuzistan), the Persian Gulf, and India.[103] Jews from the Roman Levant, by contrast, did not travel to central Asia; like most Roman Syrians, they focused their endeavors on lowland Parthian and Sasanian territory and worked Jewish contacts there.

In the same way that Palestinian Jews could maintain Babylonian Jewish contacts in order to acquire transit commodities from central Asia, the Palmyrenes cultivated connections to kinsmen and fellow ethnics in Parthian and Sasanian territory. The wars between Rome and Parthia in the mid-second century CE; the fluctuating imposition of Parthian authority over south Babylonia and Mesene at various points in the first, second, and third centuries CE; and the rise of the Sasanian dynasty may have

---

[98] The primary study for this issue is Hezser, *Jewish Travel*, esp. 311–65 and 409–40.
[99] Acts 2:8–11. Similarly, *CIIP* 1.1.55.   [100] Bab. Talmud (ed. Epstein), *AZ* 31b.
[101] Jewish merchants apparently extended their travel much farther east during the Islamic period. Silverstein, "From Markets to Marvels," 91–104; and Hansen, *Silk Road*, 217–19.
[102] De la Vaissière, *Sogdian Traders*.
[103] Bab. Talmud (ed. Epstein,), *Bab. Bath.* 74b and *Qidd.* 22b (but see Van der Horst, "'India'," 578–79 and p. 72, n. 1); *Yom.* 77a; *Rosh Shan.* 23a; *Bab. Bath.* 73a and *Shabb.* 101a; *AZ* 7b. Also, Josephus, *AJ* (ed. Niese) 20.34–37.

prompted some disruption of Palmyrene trade with the Persian Gulf and Indian Ocean.[104] But such trade did not cease entirely.[105] The decline of the kingdom of Mesene and increased Parthian-Sasanian intervention in the Persian Gulf presumably hindered Levantine Palmyrenes from maintaining contacts with eastern merchants. But it must be remembered that the Parthians and Sasanians typically admitted and taxed merchants from the Levant and simply prevented them from crossing eastward. What this means is that Palmyrenes from Palmyra could not easily travel to India during various parts of the first through third centuries, but as noted above, Palmyrene residential communities had been established at Persian Gulf ports since the early second century CE. As these residential communities became Parthian or Sasanian subjects, they apparently remained in contact with their Levantine counterparts until the Roman conquest of Palmyra in 273 CE effectively severed it from the Indian Ocean.[106] Palmyrenes could thereby travel from Palmyra to the cities of Mesene on the Persian Gulf and acquire commodities from Palmyrenes who resided there, who were Parthian/Sasanian subjects, and who could sail to India due to their communities' long-standing presence in the region.

While not well documented, the persistence of Palmyrenes in the Persian Gulf region during the third century CE and thereafter has some basis in the sources. As noted above, the *Cologne Mani Codex* suggests that a Palmyrene sailor brought Mani to India c. 240 CE, and this figure would have been a resident of Phorat, not Palmyra.[107] Further evidence for the persistence of Palmyrene residential communities at the Persian Gulf may reside in a fourth-century CE bishop of Phorat who bore the common Palmyrene name of Bōlīdāʿ or Bōlīadāʿ and was martyred under Shapur II.[108] The Palmyrene who left a dedication in the cave Hoq on Socotra may also have been in contact with the Persian Gulf, even if his route

---

[104] It is widely accepted that wars between Roman and Parthia led to the disruption of Palmyrene trade and, as a consequence, the decline in caravan inscriptions between 160 and 190 CE. McLaughlin, *Rome and the Distant East*, 103–06; and Smith, *Roman Palmyra*, 79–80 (who adds the effects of the Antonine plague to the list). For Parthian interference, Dąbrowa, "Arsacid Empire," 175–78.

[105] Gregoratti, "Parthian Port," with "Palmyrenes" 30–33, in fact emphasizes continuity amid increased Parthian intervention in the second century CE.

[106] *IGLS* 17.1.67 and 74 date Palmyrene caravan activity to the 250s and 260s CE.

[107] *CMC* (ed. Koenen and Römer) 144–45; Tubach, "Mani und der Palmyrenische Kaufmann," 165–69.

[108] Tubach, "Palmyrener als Bischof," 137–44. He is attested by one of the martyr acts for Simeon bar Sabbaʿe in *Narration for the Blessed Simeon bar Sabbaʿe* (ed. Kmosko) 780–81 and 832, now translated in Smith, *Martyrdom*, 68 and 108, and a manuscript of 411 (from Edessa) that recounts the names of martyrs in Sasanian Persia, in Nau, "Martyrologes et ménologes," 23–26, with Brock, *History of the Holy Mar Maʿin*, 123–25.

reflected the itinerary of Palmyrenes sailing between Red Sea Egypt and India.[109] In this sense, the Palmyrenes, who had already established long-standing residential communities in the region, maintained their commercial links into the Indian Ocean world until the 260s and 270s CE, even if they did so presumably with increased intervention and a tendency to work seaborne segments between Red Sea Egypt and India. Above all, what must be stressed is that during the second and third centuries CE, Palmyrene caravans traveled overland from Syria to the Persian Gulf or south Babylonia, and Palmyrene residents of Mesene sailed into the Persian Gulf, Indian Ocean, and Red Sea.[110] Despite ample indication of their widespread movement, no reliable evidence indicates that any Palmyrenes crossed overland from the Levant, through Mesopotamia, and into the Iranian plateau or central Asia.[111]

While details regarding the activity of merchants living in the Parthian and early Sasanian empires are frustratingly few, the examples just described provide an impression of the contacts that merchants in the Roman Levant often needed to make if they were to participate in long-distance transit trade. They also sharpen focus on the "certain people" (τινες) whom Maes Titianos had arranged to trek eastward and collect travel information regarding the Iranian plateau, central Asia, and even the Tarim Basin/west China. A lowland Parthian/Sasanian socio-commercial network extended to east/south Arabia, north India, the Caspian Sea coast, and, of course, central Asia. Maes Titianos accordingly maintained contacts with merchants in lowland Parthian territory who voyaged frequently across the Iranian plateau to Merv, Bactra, or the Stone Tower. These were in the position to voyage to central Asia to collect information from central Asian contacts without the intervention of the Parthian administration. In turn, the central Asian contacts provided information on the time required for the journey from central Asia to "Sera" of west China. But they provided little else. Maes' direct contacts therefore gave him a relatively detailed itinerary for travel into the Iranian plateau and central Asia, but not for farther east.

---

[109] Gorea, "Palmyrene Tablette," 449–57 (449–51 contains text and photos) and "Sea and Inland Trade," 463–85 discusses developments in Palmyrene trade.

[110] *IGLS* 17.1.16, 23–24, 26, 150, 243, 245, and 250; *PAT* 1062=Milik, *Dédicaces*, 13=*SEG* 7.135=Delplace and Yon, "Inscriptions," 284, An 30. *IGLS* 17.1.67 and 74 date caravan activity to the 250s and 260s. See Gawlikowski, "Trade" and Gregoratti, "Palmyrenes," 35–36.

[111] As noted previously, Palmyrene funerary inscriptions and reliefs have surfaced at Merv and are now in Tashkent. But they were most probably transported there in modern times. See Cussini, Review of *Palmyra*, 142–43 and Hübner, "Palestine, Syria, and the Silk Road," 45. For inscribed reliefs, see *PAT* 1123–24=Masson, "Two Palmyrene Stelae," 239–47.

When Claudius Ptolemy claims that Maes Titianos compiled the distance from the Roman Levant to the Tarim Basin "not by traversing it, but by sending certain people (or: having certain people sent) through to the Seres" (οὐδ' αὐτὸν ἐπελθόντα, διαπεμψάμενον δέ τινας πρὸς τοὺς Σῆρας), the ambiguities of his statement should not be overlooked. No reliable evidence places Maes in Xinjiang or otherwise in China, and the premise that Maes himself traveled to central Asia or even organized a caravan in order to do so contravenes what Ptolemy, citing Marinos, specifically says. Moreover, while the evidence for specific commercial segments between the Roman Levant and Parthian or early Sasanian territory is not ample, the existing documentation indicates that for various reasons members of the Roman north Syrian segment of a Levantine network typically trekked only as far as Seleucia-Ctesiphon or some other lowland city farther north or south. It also suggests that merchants situated in Babylonia, classical Assyria, or the Zab River region and empowered by a commercial network extending across Iran in fact voyaged to central Asia, acquired transit goods and knowledge of central and east Asian commerce, and transferred them to merchants moving from Roman territory into the Parthian/Sasanian lowlands. Maes' trek to central Asia or even to the Tarim Basin of Xinjiang was therefore neither an aberration nor the rule. It simply did not occur. Like most merchants from the Roman Levant who were involved in the long-distance transit trade, Maes most probably traveled into the Parthian lowlands, namely classical Assyria/Adiabene or the Zab River region.[112] But he otherwise arranged to have lowland Parthian contacts journey eastward on his behalf, amass measurements of the routes that they traversed, and acquire both products and information from central Asian contacts. In this way, Maes' activity conformed to the long-standing dispositions of trans-imperial and trans-continental trade across Asia, and the segmentation that characterized it, in antiquity.

Commercial Segmentation, Christianity, and Culture

As this chapter has asserted, a Levantine socio-commercial network and its various segments connected the Levant directly to lowland Parthian/Sasanian space. From there, a lowland Parthian/Sasanian network stretched into the Iranian plateau, central Asia, the Persian Gulf, and even north India. The dispositions of these networks cohere with the evidence for the movement of Christianity offered in the previous chapter. The Levantine network

---

[112] As noted previously, Ptolemy, 1.12.5 indicates that Maes' itinerary passed through these regions.

carried Christianity to its residential anchor points in lowland Parthian/ Sasanian regions by c. 200 CE at the latest. There it took root in a variety of forms and sectarian communities, one of which included a youth named Mani, the founder of Manichaeism. From there, the lowland Parthian/ Sasanian network played a crucial role in transporting and anchoring Christian culture in regions farther east. Mani founded a cosmopolitan and inclusive religion, but even Mani's ministry followed the social pathways laid down by the lowland commercial network, and he accordingly traveled to and preached at its anchor points in lowland Sasanian territory, the Iranian plateau, north India, and central Asia. His disciples and converts carried Manichaean religious culture farther. Other forms of Christianity, however, had a longer gestation period, and the lowland network only began to carry Christian culture into the same regions in the late fourth century.

But certain additional observations regarding the importance of the Levantine and lowland Parthian/Sasanian networks for transmitting religious culture must be made. First, such networks did not merely bring religious culture eastward, but they also transported it westwards. Perhaps the best example of this is the movement of Manichaeism and the elements of Indian culture that it integrated. Within a generation of Mani's death, Manichaean culture had been firmly embedded in Roman imperial space. Various Iranian texts indicate that Manichaeans were preaching in Roman Syria, including Palmyra, late in Mani's life and after his death; these also accredit a figure named Adda specifically with missionary work in both Roman Syria and Egypt.[113] By c. 300, Manichaeism had become sufficiently widespread in Egypt and North Africa for the emperor Diocletian to condemn it in a rescript composed at Alexandria for his proconsul of Africa.[114] Egypt in particular became a Manichaean hotbed by the arrival of the fourth century CE. At this time, Alexander of Lycopolis, a resident of the Egyptian Thebaid, leveled an invective against Manichaeans there, and a pastoral letter that survives on papyrus denounced it too.[115] But the first generation of Mani's converts that carried the religious culture of Manichaeism into the Roman empire was following the social pathways created by the westward extensions of the lowland Parthian/Sasanian and Levantine networks. His disciples traveled to the residential anchor points

---

[113] Gardner and Lieu, *Manichaean Texts*, 111–14, who translate texts from Sundermann, *Mitteliranische manichäische Texte* 2.5, 26, 3.2, 36–41, and 3.3, 41–45, and from Andreas and Henning, *Mitteliranische Manichaica*, 10–11[301–302, along with other texts].

[114] In Riccobono et al., *Fontes iuris Romani*, 2.580–81. Manichaeism/Manichaeans appear to have been present at Rome in the early fourth century. *Liber Pontificalis* (ed. Duchesne) 1.168–69.

[115] Alexander of Lycopolis, *Disp.* (ed. Brinkmann) 2; *P. Rylands* 469.12–42.

that the lowland Parthian/Sasanian network had established in the Roman Levant and Upper Mesopotamia. From there, the Roman Levantine network maintained direct contact with eastern Mediterranean coastal cities, Rome, and even Gaul.[116] Once the mobile and cosmopolitan preachers of Mani's religion had a foothold in the Levant, they quickly moved to Egypt and other regions tied to the Levantine network.

As noted previously, Mani was famous for his travels to India, and his interest in Indian wisdom may have been inspired by the presence of Indians in Mesene. But the overlapping commercial networks that connected the Mediterranean world to India via the Persian Gulf certainly also amplified the tendency for Manichaeans of the Mediterranean to model Mani on Buddha and enabled the Indian traditions that Manichaeism had integrated to arrive among them.[117] They thereby contributed to the context in which the Christian composer(s) of the *Acts of Archelaus* could mockingly include a man who called himself "Buddha" among Mani's religious precursors.[118] Scholars now dismiss the possibility that the text was originally written in Syriac or in the Roman Near East (despites its narrative setting), and certain elements of it appear to reflect a context of rivalry between Manichaeans and Christians at home in Egypt, where the figure of Buddha had been known to Christians as early as the second century CE. But as we have seen (in Chapter 3), Roman Egyptians had lost direct contact with India during the initial generations in which Manichaeism had begun to circulate, and the articles of Indian wisdom that are attested among Manichaeans in Egypt were probably carried by interlinked socio-commercial networks from India to lower Mesopotamia, the Roman Levant, and then to Egypt. After Mani and his initial disciples had traveled to India and integrated Indian culture into their religious system, Manichaeans moved such culture along the social pathways that the Levantine and lowland Sasanian network had laid. This is most probably how Coptic-writing Manichaeans in late antique Egypt came to digest certain strands of Buddhism and even Jainism.[119]

---

[116] Terpstra, *Trading Communities*, 152–63; Decker, *Tilling the Hateful Earth* generally; Pieri, *Commerce du vin*.

[117] For the Manichaeans' debts to Indian religions, treatment of Buddha as Mani's forerunner, and the *Acta Archelai* as a parody of the Manichaeans' biography of Mani, which was itself indebted to a north Indian biography of Buddha, see Gardner, "Comments on Mani"; Klein, "Epic Buddhasarita"; Deeg and Gardner, "Indian Influence"; and Jones "Things Mani Learned." Ephrem, *Haer.* (ed. Beck) 3.7 associates Bardaisan with Greek learning and Mani with falsehood from India.

[118] *Acta Archelai* (ed. Beeson) 63.

[119] In *Acta Archelai* 62–63, the religious activity that served as the precursor to Mani's sect is depicted as having been undertaken by a Saracen merchant in Egypt, and from there a disciple named

But the rapid movement of Manichaeism throughout Afro-Eurasia was not paralleled by the similarly fast travel of other forms of Christianity eastward. Certainly, Christianity arrived in Mesopotamia fairly early. As we have seen, a Levantine socio-commercial network integrated commercial players from various regions of the Levant and of various religious persuasions (including Jews, Nabataeans, and Palmyrenes). The farthest extension of direct eastward contact for most of its segments was lowland Parthian/Sasanian space, to which it had transported Christianity by c. 200 CE. It could be deemed somewhat surprising that it did not transport Christianity farther east at an earlier date. After all, the Palmyrene segment was a vital and thriving one, and it maintained a potent presence in Mesene and extended into the Persian Gulf and north India. The Palmyrenes even may have transported "Palmyrene cursive" script into lower Mesopotamia and Mesene. Some surmise that the Manichaeans wrote with it, not the Syriac that it resembles.[120]

But in its uniqueness, the Palmyrene segment of the Levantine network does not appear to have integrated Christianity as quickly as its north Syrian or Upper Mesopotamia counterparts. Palmyrene merchants, of course, were connected to various parts of Syria. Once caravans had brought their goods to Palmyra from the Persian Gulf, tariffs were assessed, transactions occurred, and materials not consumed by locals were transported to the Mediterranean by way of Antioch or perhaps Emesa.[121] The Palmyrenes also had a residential settlement at Dura-Europos, the site of the earliest excavated Christian house church.[122] But due to their relatively isolated location in the dry Syrian steppe and the fact that movement eastward required camel transportation through roadless wilderness, most merchants from Levantine regions closer to the Mediterranean appear to have followed physical and social pathways through residential routing stations in north Syria and Upper Mesopotamia. Accordingly, all the epigraphic and archaeological evidence for Christianity at Palmyra dates after the city's late-third CE

Terebinthus traveled to Persia and called himself Buddha. Moreover, even if the text depicts a debate set in the Roman and Persian Near East, it does not appear to have been written there or in one of its languages. This episode informs the narration of Cyril of Jerusalem, *Cath.* (ed. Reischl and Rupp) 6.21–24. See Vermes and Lieu, *Hegemonius: Acta Archelai*, 6–16. For knowledge of "Boutta" among Alexandrian Christians, see Clement, *Strom.* (ed. Stählin and Früchtel) 1.15.71.3–6. For Jainism, Deeg and Gardner, "Indian Influence"; and Jones "Things Mani Learned."

[120] Pederson and Larsen, *Manichaean Texts*, 3–5 and 113–85 (esp. 132–37 and 164) discuss the debate regarding whether Manichaean script is derived from Syriac estrangelo or Palmyrene cursive.
[121] Seland, "Persian Gulf or the Red Sea?" 402–4.
[122] For Palmyrenes at Dura-Europos, see Dirven, "Palmyrenes."

century decline.[123] Even the Hebrew inscriptions raised by Jews there cannot be dated securely to the city's peak, although it is possible that the Palmyrene Jews buried at Beth Shearim were active at the time.[124] In other words, the Palmyrene segment had not yet integrated Christianity when it was maintaining direct and intensive contact with north India. This segment then endured disruption in the late third century, and the Palmyrenes who continued to live and trade in Mesene encountered and adopted the culture of Christianity through the activity of Levantines who had anchored it there and transmitted it to local converts. But after the Levantine network brought its various Christian strands to lowland Parthian territory, it took centuries for segments of a lowland network to absorb it and transport it eastward.

Conclusion

The socio-commercial networks that bound the Roman Levant to central Asia were both interconnected and segmented in ways that had a profound impact on how Christianity traveled and took root in eastern lands. A Roman Levantine network extended into lower Mesopotamia and other lowland Parthian/Sasanian territories and terminated there. This network included various subsets that possessed more specific regional, ethnic, or religious orientations, such as Palmyrenes and Palestinian Jews. It also included the Roman north Syrians among whom Maes Titianos operated and the Syriac-speaking Upper Mesopotamians whose language came to possesses an immeasurable vitality in the Persian Church of the East. As described previously (Chapter 4), the reliable textual evidence for Christianity in the Parthian/Sasanian empires indicates that it was anchored in lowland areas during the second century CE and had taken root in the form of established Christian communities thereafter. The communities of these lowland areas therefore suffered violence from Sasanian authorities during the fourth century CE, as demonstrated by the *Persian Martyr Acts*. But the movement of their Christian culture followed the well-laid social pathways of the Levantine socio-commercial network, whose circulation society channeled how bodies carried Christian culture into lowland Parthian/Sasanian areas and anchored it in expatriate residential settlements. Since the Levantine network maintained social

---

[123] Christian funerary inscriptions from the north necropolis at Palmyra do not predate the fifth century. *IGLS* 17.1.494–511. For church buildings, Delplace, "Palmyre," 225–35; and Majcherek, "More Churches" and "Excavating the Basilicas."

[124] *IJOr.* Syr. 44–49, with App. 1–10. Kaizer, "From Zenobia to Alexander the Sleepless," discusses Judaism in Palmyra.

presences in lower Mesopotamia, Assyria, Khuzistan, the Zab River region, and Mesene, Christianity first became well established in these places and among the bodies that inhabited it. The sole exception to the principles outlined here are the Palmyrenes, who did maintain a cohesive socio-commercial network that extended from Roman Syria to the Persian Gulf and India. But its members did not sufficiently embody Christian culture before the occupation of Palmyra in 273 CE and the disruption of its commercial network. Even if Palmyrenes in Sasanian territory did maintain connections to Roman Syria and continued to travel to India, they were effectively a subset of the lowland Sasanian network thereafter.

The Christian culture that was established in such lowland regions of the Parthian and Sasanian empires did not travel farther eastward immediately. It laid roots for centuries until processes of conversion transferred it to a lowland Sasanian network that maintained a central hub at Seleucia-Ctesiphon and diverse nodes in lowland territories, the Iranian plateau, and central Asia. This network too included various ethnic or religious subsets, such as the Babylonian Jews. Once members of the network had sufficiently adopted Christianity, they transported and transmitted it throughout their circulation society and embedded it in the expatriate residential settlements that they maintained in the Iranian plateau, Persian Gulf, central Asia, and subsequently India. This process was initiated in the later fourth century CE, but it was no doubt amplified by the institutional organization of the Church of the East and perhaps Sasanian persecutions, which could have encouraged migration away from intense areas of violence. Even the activities of Mani and the first generation of Manichaeans reflect such dispositions. Although Manichaeans carried their religious culture through Eurasia faster and earlier than most other Christians, it is noticeable that during his career of preaching, Mani carried his religious cultural along the social pathways established by a lowland Parthian/Sasanian socio-commercial network. He therefore trekked from lower Mesopotamia and Mesene to India and central Asia (and most places in between), where the commercial network terminated. Moreover, because the network maintained expatriate residential settlements eastward in central Asia and westward in the Roman Levant, his disciples and converts exploited such anchor points. From them, they initiated their missionary endeavors in regions farther afield and thereafter transformed the religious geography of Afro-Eurasia.

CHAPTER 6

The Late Antique Impact of the Acts of Thomas *and Christian Communities in India*

According to the surviving *Acts of Thomas*, Judas Thomas sailed from Jerusalem to India after being acquired by the Indian merchant Habban. Once there, king Gudnaphar paid him a substantial sum of money in exchange for his building a palace. Judas Thomas distributed the money to the poor and sick. When confronted by the angered Gudnaphar, Judas reported that he had built a palace that Gudnaphar could see only after having departed from the world. Gudnaphar contemplated a punishment, but in the meantime his brother Gad took ill and died. As his soul ascended to heaven, he discovered the palace that Judas Thomas had built. Having successfully petitioned the angels to release him, he informed his brother that the palace did in fact exist. Judas Thomas was spared, and he baptized many Indians into the Christian faith.[1] After many exploits, he was martyred by King Mazdai at an unnamed location. Even if this final martyr scene was written independently and added to the *Acts'* narrative, it circulated as part of the Thomas narrative quite early.[2]

The testimony of the written text of the *Acts of Thomas* bears an intriguing similarity to oral traditions maintained by Thomas Christians of south India. It is worth citing one notable example here, a poetic song often called the *Thomas Parvam* (or the *Thomas Ramban*). The *Thomas Parvam* was transcribed in Malayalam in 1601 by Thomas (Tomma) Ramban, who claimed to be the forty-eighth in line to have transmitted it and to be the descendent of a priest appointed "Ramban" by the apostle Thomas himself. As such, the oral tradition was recorded at the turn of the seventeenth century, but some treat it as quite ancient.[3] According to the *Thomas Parvam*, Thomas, after having preached at the cities of Kerala

---

[1] *Acts of Thomas* (ed. Wright) ܡܝܘ – ܡܗܘ of the Syriac; (ed. Bonnet) 17–24 of the Greek.
[2] *Acts of Thomas* (ed. Wright) ܪܠܐ of the Syriac; (ed. Bonnet) 168 of the Greek. Myers, *Spiritual Epicleses*, 33.
[3] This is according to one version that has been rendered in translation by T. K. Joseph and printed by Henry Hosten. See Menachery, *Nazranies*, 520–22.

in 50 CE ("in December of the year 50 of the Messiah") and thereafter, visited the site of Mylapore on the Coromandel coast. Upon his arrival at Mylapore, Thomas had a very intriguing and noteworthy encounter. There, the king entrusted him with the task of building his palace and paid him a substantial sum. But Thomas distributed the money to the poor and sick. The king was on the verge of putting him to death when his deceased brother, recently revived, informed him of the palace that he had built for him in heaven. The king then spared Thomas' life, and Thomas continued to preach in the region until he was killed by Brahmins for setting fire to Kali's shrine.[4] Clearly, many parallels between the *Acts of Thomas* and the *Thomas Parvam* can be discerned.

As we have explored in the Introduction, the obvious similarities between the written account of the *Acts of Thomas* and the oral tradition of the *Thomas Parvam* have often encouraged scholars and authors to accept the legitimacy or plausibility of the Thomas tradition.[5] After all, it could be surmised that the *Acts* and the oral *Thomas Parvam* constitute two distinct and ancient sources for the arrival of the apostle Thomas in south India. But one could just as easily maintain that these narratives do not constitute separate witnesses that lend credibility to the common episodes that they record.[6] Instead, the *Thomas Parvam* and similar oral traditions seem to have been derived from the written *Acts of Thomas* after it had begun to circulate among the Christian communities of India under the auspices of the Church of the East. Moreover, the lack of specific toponyms and topographic features in the narrative of the surviving *Acts* was in many ways an asset for south Indian Christians who reconstructed it so that it cohered with the formation of their sacred topographies. Since the *Acts* never named where Thomas died and was interred, Christians at the Kerala and Coromandel coasts of India encountered little threat of contradiction when they at some point before 1500 CE located Thomas' death at the hands of Brahmins in Mylapore and established his tomb there. In this way, Christians in medieval south India produced oral versions of the *Acts*

---

[4] Translated by T. K. Josephus and printed by Henry Hosten: see Menachery, *Nazranies*, 520–21 (quoted date is from 520). Also discussed by Frykenberg, *Christianity in India*, 99–100. Nedungatt, *Quest for the Historical Thomas*, 358–68 provides detailed discussion of this tradition. A similar plot is recorded in a Syriac summary written by a south Indian Christian in the eighteenth century. Land, *Anecdota Syriaca*, 1.24–30 (esp. 25–26). For other similar traditions that apparently circulated in the 16th century, Mundadan, *History of Christianity*, 29–30.

[5] Frykenberg, *Christianity in India*, 102; Tomber, "Bishops and Traders," 223–24; Seland, "Trade and Christianity," 78–79; Ramelli, "Tradizione su Tommaso," 75–76 and 80–82; Ellerbrock and Winkelmann, *Die Parther*, 273–75.

[6] As Brown, *Indian Christians*, 51–52 suggests.

that reflected their communal beliefs and that added layers of south Indian topographic and cultural specificity not to be found in the third-century CE Syriac text. In modern times, they have even produced "updated" written versions of these traditions, and thereby of the Thomas narrative.[7]

Yet, sources for Christianity composed in India before 1500 CE are lacking. One arguable reason for this is that during the council of Diamper (1599 CE), Roman Catholic authorities destroyed many manuscripts and texts of the Thomas Christians that they understood to have contained erroneous works. Few certainties can be established regarding the scope of destruction and the types of text that were lost. All told, due to the council of Diamper, it is difficult to reconstruct a history of Christianity in India from its inception to the sixteenth century CE. Many of the texts that might have constituted valuable sources did not survive it,[8] and it is thus virtually impossible to present a coherent history of Christianity in India before or after 500 CE.

Oral traditions, inscriptions on undated coppers plates, or legends in undated palm-leaf texts that are linked to the arrival of Thomas, another figure called Thomas Kinayi, or similarly early Christians in India ostensibly shed light on Christianity's early formation in the subcontinent. But these still have not been properly edited or dated by established philological criteria.[9] Transcribed after c. 1500 CE, several factors render the oral traditions particularly unreliable. One consideration is that comprehensive studies of these works need to be conducted before their reliability as evidence can be properly assessed. Until such issues receive clarification, they cannot be construed as meaningful evidence for the arrival of Thomas or early Christianity in India. Specialists in south Asian languages, history, and culture have not yet provided (to my knowledge) comprehensive analysis of all this material and its difficulties, and until they do, the reliability of such evidence does not merit unequivocal support.

---

[7] Compare Watts, *Riot in Alexandria*, 198–205.
[8] Briquel-Chatonnet, "Syriac Manuscripts," 289–99.
[9] Hosten, *Antiquities* assembles the objects, inscriptions, and texts that were accessible in the early twentieth century. Nedungatt, *Quest for the Historical Thomas*, 153–57 and 258–368, treats all the oral traditions and material items of north, central, and south India. Written or oral traditions composed by south Indians or otherwise related by priests of the Church of the East or south Indian Christians to Portuguese authorities are described by Tubach, "Veneration of the Apostle Thomas," 13–23; Mingana, "Spread of Early Christianity," 468–515; Land, *Anecdota Syriaca*, 1.24–30 (esp. 25–26); Menachery, *Nazranies* (generally). Kollaparambil, "Historical Sources," provides sources regarding Thomas Kinayi. Kollaparambil, *Babylonian Origins*, argues for the fourth-century origins of Thomas Kinayi based on the oral traditions and certain ninth-century CE copper plates. Frykenberg, *Christianity in India*, 92–110 also treats the oral traditions behind Thomas the apostle and Thomas Kinayi. The traditions regarding Thomas Kinayi may however be based on a seventh-century CE relocation to south India by people from south Arabia. Tubach, "Thomas Cannaneo," 404–7.

Another issue is that the oral traditions and legends, which are recorded in modern transcriptions or undated texts, bear numerous anachronisms suggesting that they were either composed or very heavily redacted after the eighth or ninth (if not the sixteenth) century CE. Many such anachronisms are detectable in the traditions regarding the apostle Thomas specifically. These sometimes indicate that the songs were composed or redacted to reflect intensifying interactions or even rivalries between Christians and Hindus/Brahmins in south India after the ninth century CE. In some instances, it appears that the songs were refined to meet the chronological expectations of a Portuguese and Latin Christian colonial gaze after 1500 CE.[10] Additional oral traditions or legends that ambiguously record the conversion of early kings or Brahmins to Christianity or Islam; that describe the pollution that Brahmins suffered at the hands of Christians; or that record persecutions allegedly conducted by the Cholas against Christians in 293 CE offer similar problems. These all exist in transcriptions dating after 1500 CE or texts without established dates.[11]

[10] The traditions often use *anno domini* years (and apparently the Gregorian calendar) to date Thomas' activity; such usage must be subsequent to 1500 CE, as the *anno domini* system and Gregorian calendar were introduced to India by the Portuguese. The oral traditions describe Thomas' encounters with Brahmins and other castes in south India and even attribute his martyrdom to the Brahmins on account of his confrontation with Kali. Yet, Brahmanic migration, landowning, and authority did not become preeminent at Kerala until c. the eighth-century CE, even if Brahmanic influences in south India are known for earlier periods. Menon, *Survey of Kerala History*, 145–54; Champakalakshmi, *Religion, Tradition, and Ideology*, 13–39 and 53–82; Veluthat, *Early Medieval*, 5–6, 61–68, and 295–306; Gurukkal, *Social Formations of Early South India*, 306–16; Thapar, *Early India*, 331–32; Singh, *History*, 573–80; Wink, *Al-Hind*, 311–12; Malekandathil, *Maritime India*, 47–48; Narayanan, *Perumals of Kerala*, 262–77. Intriguingly, a Syriac manuscript of the ninth century CE claims that Thomas was killed by Brahmins, which suggests that the oral traditions have some basis in the ninth century. Van Esbroeck, "Neuf listes," 141 and 188–89 (manuscript of 874).

[11] According to certain Hindu texts, written in a form of Malayalam dating to the sixteenth or seventeenth centuries, two "Buddhas" came from Baghdad at a date correlating to 317 CE to Mahadevar. They converted the seventh Perumal, who made his subjects adopt the new religion. Joseph, "An Indian Christian Date, 317 AD," 27–29. Another tradition recorded by Hindus describes how certain Brahmins were converted by Thomas at Palayur and how those who did not convert relocated due to the pollution of the place. Nedungatt, *Quest for the Historical Thomas*, 153–56 and 336–42. The fact that Hindu oral traditions record Thomas' travels in India would seem to support their authenticity, but obvious anachronisms are the reference to Baghdad, the landed and religious preeminence of Brahmins in south India before the eighth century CE (even if some Brahmanic influences are known for earlier periods), and the use of the title *Perumal* before the eighth century. Menon, *Survey of Kerala History*, 38–44, 103–4, 134–35, and 145–54; Champakalakshmi, *Religion, Tradition, and Ideology*, 13–39 and 53–82; Veluthat, *Early Medieval*, 5–6, 61–68, and 295–306; Gurukkal, *Social Formations of Early South India*, 306–16; Singh, *History*, 573–80; Wink, *Al-Hind*, 311–12; Malekandathil, *Maritime India*, 47–48; Narayanan, *Perumals of Kerala*, 262–77. Such traditions may reflect ongoing rivalries between Christians and Brahmins in south India. For a palm-leaf text recording an alleged third-century Chola persecution of Christians, see pp. 19–20, n. 58. This tradition

Other similar anachronisms are certainly present in the oral traditions for the arrival of Thomas Kinayi, who is reputed to have migrated from lower Mesopotamia to the Kerala coast with dozens of merchant families during the fourth century CE. Indeed, one oral tradition in fact uses *anno domini* dating to place his arrival in 345 CE.[12] Despite this issue, his fourth-century CE arrival receives ostensible corroboration from inscribed copper plates. These are now lost, but their contents were copied by Portuguese residents in India, and they bear witness to privileges that a local king gave to a figure named Thomas Kinayi and his followers. In one transcription of the Quilon copper plates, a final section apparently not on the actual plates mentions this figure as well.[13] Nonetheless, if such plates support the historical validity of Thomas Kinayi's activity, they point to a later date, like the eighth or ninth century CE. The copper plates that serve as points of comparison, including the Quilon copper plates, date to this period and thereafter.[14]

One could make similar observations for many material objects that some regard to be evidence of early Christianity in India. Whether inscribed or not, these have not been properly excavated or found in an archaeological context. Some objects that have been treated as early are in fact dubious in dating or are even indisputably later.[15] This premise has

---

was apparently transcribed c. 1800 CE (Farquhar, *Apostle Thomas in India*, 62, n. 4). For comments on late Hindu accounts, see Mundadan, *History of Christianity*, 30.

[12] Most, if not all, known material pertaining to this figure has been compiled in translation by Kollaparambil, "Historical Sources" (oral traditions at v–xiii). The oral traditions are also in Joseph, "Thomas Cana," 56.161–66 and 57.103–6. These oral traditions employ the *anno domini* measure for years and ostensibly the Gregorian calendar anachronistically. They render the residence of the *Katholikos* of the Church of the East as Baghdad. They describe how ships of Thomas Kinayi fire cannon salutes. They delineate how Thomas Kinayi was granted privileges by a *Perumal*, a title not attested until the eighth century CE. Menon, *Survey of Kerala History*, 38–44, 99–104, and 134–35. The privileges of Thomas were apparently inscribed on copper plates whose contents were copied by Portuguese authors and then were subsequently lost. But translations of the privileges use the twelve-month Jupiter dating cycle, a calendar not attested in Dravidian-speaking south India before the ninth century CE, even if used occasionally in north/central India in previous centuries. Salomon, *Indian Epigraphy*, 197–98; Sircar, *Indian Epigraphy*, 287–89; Dikshitar, *Selected South Indian Inscriptions*, 355–410. The form of dating does not appear in early Tamil inscriptions. See Mahadevan, *Early Tamil Epigraphy*. Veluthat, *Early Medieval*, 147–67 provides a useful synopsis of medieval epigraphy at Kerala.

[13] Kollaparambil, "Historical Sources," 13–20 and xiv–xxvi on these issues. The transcription of the Quilon plates with the reference to Thomas Kinayi in question, as recorded by Kollaparambil, is at the Bibliothèque Nationale de France (*Syr.* 186) and consists of Malayalam written in east Syriac script (xiv and xxvi). Since the reference to Thomas Kinayi does not appear in the actual surviving Quilon plates, it may be a later addition perhaps influenced by the now-lost copper plates of Thomas Kinayi.

[14] See pp. 219, n. 45.

[15] Hosten, *Antiquities* compiles many of these. Nedungatt, *Quest for the Historical Thomas*, 153–57 and 258–368 treats all the oral traditions and material items of north, central, and south India, with 153–57

bearing on the Pahlavi-inscribed stone crosses of south India. They are emblematic of Christianity activity in India during the seventh to tenth centuries CE or so.[16]

Finally, as we have seen, the oral traditions regarding the apostle Thomas and his evangelization of India bear signs of having been derived from the *Acts'* basic narrative template. The *Thomas Parvam* or similar oral traditions, like the *Margam Kali*, constitute its creative variations.[17] If anything, these traditions reflect how the written or oral narrative of the *Acts* circulated among Christians in south India some time after Christianity was anchored there. Amid its dissemination, it underwent reconstitution, adaptation, and transformation as south Indian Christians reworked it in ways that made it align with their physical topographies and social contexts. It was through this process that the unnamed burial place of the *Acts* became associated by such Christians with a site on the Coromandel coast. It was in this way that the killers of Judas Thomas in the *Acts*, being generic pagans with Zoroastrian traits, became Brahmins who worshipped the goddess Kali.

In fact, as this chapter argues, Christianity first arrived and became established in south India due to the fifth-century CE activity of Sasanian merchants. One element of Christian culture that these merchants or subsequent waves of migrants brought and transferred to local converts was the narrative of the *Acts of Thomas*. As the *Acts* became embedded in the lived experiences of Christians in south India, such Christians generated oral traditions that constituted variations on its narrative. As they did so, they located the episodes described by these traditions in the physical terrains that they had endowed with sacred value. Since the surviving *Acts* is completely void of toponyms and specific markers of Judas Thomas' itinerary in India, it offered diverse possibilities for south Indian audiences to embed its narrative in their local sacred topographies. The unnamed location at which king Mazdai had Thomas killed in the *Acts* was accordingly pegged to Mylapore of the Coromandel coast by Christians in the

---

(ostensibly Christian paraphernalia and oral traditions linked to a village of south India called Neelamperoor), 277–280 (Taxila Cross), and 281–304 (the Udayapur inscription of a medieval king in central India) discussing material objects.

[16] On St. Thomas crosses, for which much work remains to be done, see Cereti, Olivieri, and Vazhuthanapally, "Problem of the St. Thomas Crosses." Also, Malekandathil, *Maritime India*, 5–6; Hosten, *Antiquities*, 327–361.

[17] For a version of the song of *Margam Kali* relevant to the apostle Thomas, transcribed (or composed) in 1732 CE, see the translation of T. K. Joseph (printed by Henry Hosten) in Menachery, *Nazranies* 522–25. Nedungatt, *Quest for the Historical Thomas*, 357–58 and Vellian, "Margamkali," provide discussion.

region some time after the initial arrival of Christianity and the Thomas narrative. It is therefore treated as the site of Thomas' death and burial by existing south Indian traditions.

Soon after Christians began to inhabit south India, socio-commercial networks were responsible for transporting knowledge of their existence to Christians of the Mediterranean. As previously discussed, the invented traditions of the Parthian *Acts* (composed c. 150–200 CE or slightly later) and the Indian *Acts* (composed in the mid-to-late third century CE) had a huge impact on how Mediterranean and Upper Mesopotamian Christians experienced their Christian geographies. For centuries after their composition, they shaped what Mediterranean Christians believed regarding the formation of Christianity in the Indian subcontinent, and their beliefs were entirely divorced from any historical phenomena of Christianity there. But after c. 500 CE Christians in the Mediterranean world began to cultivate a knowledge of Christian brethren in India that had a valid historical basis. By then Sasanian Persians had anchored Christianity in south India and venerated what they identified as Thomas' burial site there. While this was happening, the Roman Egyptian network had re-established direct contact with south India and the Sasanian Persian Christian communities that populated it. It therefore transmitted knowledge about such Christians and their religious practices to the Mediterranean world. In turn, Mediterranean Christians began to conceive of Thomas as having been martyred and buried at Kalamene or Calamina, where an active cult site for Thomas' Indian tomb was located.

The Lowland Sasanian Network, the Persian Gulf, and India

A key catalyst for commercial movement between Sasanian Persia and India was the lowland Sasanian network that connected Mesopotamia and its environs to the Indian Ocean world. In the previous chapter, we examined the dispositions of this network and links to various locations in the Iranian plateau, central Asia, and the Persian Gulf. Long after the Levantine socio-commercial network had carried and anchored Christianity in lowland Parthian space (by 200 CE), the lowland Sasanian network transported it into the Iranian plateau, central Asia, and the Persian Gulf in the late fourth century CE. It even generated the social pathways and residential anchor points that Mani and his followers exploited to facilitate the rapid circulation of their religion during the third century. Ultimately, this lowland network transported and established Christianity in south India too.

For much of antiquity, the lowland Parthian and Sasanian network maintained direct contact and expatriate residential settlements in north India. While the central hub for the network was Seleucia-Ctesiphon, it had also established a variety of nodes in the region of Mesene, which was located at the confluence of the Persian Gulf, the Tigris River, and the Euphrates River. Being known as an "inn" and a "harbor" for merchants, Mesene constituted a valuable point of transfer for commodities and the site from which members of the lowland network could embark for India. The Palmyrenes established expatriate residential communities there during the second and third centuries CE for this very reason, but inhabitants of lowland Sasanian territory too maintained direct contact with India by cultivating a stable presence in Mesene's settlements. Their network facilitated the movement of people, information, credit, and commodities between lowland Sasanian territory and India, and ultimately the activity of lowland Sasanian merchants brought Christianity to coastal India and anchored it there.

In antiquity, merchants and diplomats traveled between Mesene and north India. Such activity is documented by various textual sources. In the *Cologne Mani Codex*, Mani found a boatman at Phorat who could transport him to India.[18] At least one Jew of the Babylonian Talmud bore the epithet Indian; he may have been an Indian or a lower Mesopotamian born in India.[19] A south Arabian inscription shows that two "Chaldeans" (residents of Mesene) were present at the coronation of a king of Hadramawt near Shabwa in the early third century CE. This indicates that the lowland Parthian/Sasanian network had a residential presence on the south Arabian coast, at Qane, but its members could engage in diplomatic endeavors in the interior.[20] While connected to the Levant, the Palmyrenes who lived in Mesene during the second and third centuries CE were exploiting the social pathways that the inhabitants of lower Mesopotamia and Mesene had created. These were certainly traveling to Barbarikon and Barygaza, which they conceived of as being located in "Scythia," with a frequent stopover at Bahrain.[21] Before Christianity took root there, the island of Kharg in the Persian Gulf certainly received

---

[18] *CMC* (ed. Koenen and Römer) 144–45; Tubach, "Mani und der palmyrenische Kaufmann," 165–69.
[19] Bab. Talmud (ed. Epstein) *Bab. Bath.* 74b and *Qidd.* 22b. As Van der Horst, "'India'," 578–79, significantly argues, Jews often described Ethiopia and Arabia as India, and this could be the case here. But since lower Mesopotamians had direct contact with India, Jews of Babylon were probably less likely to do this than counterparts farther west.
[20] Robin, "Palmyréniens en Arabie du Sud," 490–92. Also, Arbach, "Visiteurs de Shabwa."
[21] *IGLS* 17.1.26, 245, and 250.

Babylonian Jewish visitors and settlers and perhaps Palmyrene or even Nabataean ones too. One is tempted to conceive of Josephus' reference to a Jewish merchant at Mesene as part of this phenomenon.[22] In aggregate, the activity of Mani, Palmyrenes, and lower Mesopotamian Jews verify that the network extended to various parts of coastal India, and they indicate that it maintained residential anchor points on the island of Deb/Dev and the port of Barbarikon, both located at the mouth of the Indus River.[23]

But Indians were traveling into the Persian Gulf too. Through its treatment of the Indian merchant Habban, the surviving text of the *Acts* hints at this. It narrates how Habban travels to Jerusalem for the purpose of acquiring a craftsman to take to his king in India. But as previously argued, this episode was probably redacted from a prior textual tradition in which Habban brought Thomas from Mesene to India. This coheres more closely with the movements of ancient Indian merchants. Outside the narrative of the *Acts* and certain texts referring to Arabians or Ethiopians as "Indians," Indians are not documented as visiting Jerusalem in the period under consideration.[24] In fact, Alexandria was the most typical transit point for Indian and Kushan embassies traveling to Rome through the Indian Ocean and Red Sea, and Indian ambassadors visited other Roman or Greek cultural centers such as Antioch and Athens.[25] But otherwise, they cannot be firmly placed in the Roman Levant or Upper Mesopotamia. Even the treatment of Indians that appears in the Syriac works of Bardaisan or his students reflects literary borrowings or otherwise encounters that occurred at Rome, which periodically received Indian ambassadors. The most secure epigraphic evidence places Indian traders in the Arabian and Red Seas. They certainly frequented Socotra,[26] and a south Arabian inscription indicates that Indians attended the investiture of a king of Hadramawt in

---

[22] Steve, *Ile de Khārg*, 13–68; Josephus, *AJ* (ed. Niese) 20.34–37.
[23] Jones, "Things Mani Learned," 390–95 explores what Mani's Indian destinations may have been and the identity of "Deb/Dev."
[24] No Indians are mentioned in Acts of the Apostles (ed. Nestle-Aland) 9.2, in which diverse inhabitants of the Mediterranean and Asia (extending to Parthia) have traveled to Jerusalem and hear the apostles speaking their languages. For the composition of Jerusalem's population and visitors, see Di Segni and Tsafrir, "Ethnic Composition of Jerusalem's Population," 405–54.
[25] Strabo, *Geog.* (ed. Radt) 15.1.73 (Nicolaus of Damascus: *FGrH* 90, F. 100) and Cass. Dio (ed. Boissevain) 54.9 document a Saka embassy that attended Augustus' court in Samos, Antioch, Athens, and other eastern Mediterranean locations in 22 BCE. McLaughlin, *Roman Empire*, 157–58 has it coming overland to Antioch, but it could have simply accompanied Augustus to Samos and Antioch, having been transited through Alexandria. Also see Suet., *Aug.* (ed. Ihm) 21.3. Aug., *Res. Gest.* (ed. Scheid) 31. Schneider, *Die grossen Felsen-Edikte Aśokas*, 76–77 and 118–19 (13Q-R), for the embassies sent by the Buddhist king Asoka to Hellenistic Greeks.
[26] Strauch, "Indian Participants."

the early third century CE.[27] These were most certainly residents or visitors to Qane. Tamil graffiti on pottery fragments suggest that they traveled to Myos Hormos and Berenike in Egypt too.[28]

When merchants from the Roman Levant did encounter Indian traders, such encounters happened at or near the Persian Gulf. At Mesene, merchants departing for India from Phorat and Charax Spasinou and Indian merchants searching for commercial products were typical.[29] As the *Hymn of the Pearl* claims, the region of Mesene served as "an inn" or a "harbor" for merchants.[30] Indians, among others, frequented this "inn," this "harbor," where they engaged in transactions with travelers from the Levant or Upper Mesopotamia or with inhabitants of the Parthian/Sasanian lowlands. The presence of Indian household pottery at Sumhuram in Oman raises the possibility (but no certainty) that Indians were in direct contact with south Arabia and the Persian Gulf, and other archaeological evidence supports the existence of connectivity between inhabitants of the Persian Gulf region and India in antiquity.[31] Indians certainly reached the port of Apologos or the inland trading hubs located up the Tigris and Euphrates rivers; the *Periplus* places merchants of Barygaza there.[32] Sasanians and early

---

[27] Robin, "Palmyréniens en Arabie du Sud," 490–92. Also, Arbach, "Visiteurs de Shabwa."

[28] Thomas, "Port Communities," discusses, with Sidebotham, "Reflections of Ethnicity," 105–115. Salomon, "Epigraphic Remains."

[29] The route between India and the Persian Gulf, which Alexander's general Nearchus had sailed, is described by Arrian, *Indica* (ed. Roos) with 42–43 discussing the Persian Gulf destination. Also Cassius Dio (ed. Boissevain) 68.28–29 and the *Cologne Mani Codex* (ed. Koenen and Römer) 140–45. Chinese sources depict the reciprocal movement of traders between west India and both Rome (presumably Roman Egypt) and Parthia. See the passage of *Liang-shu* 54 in Leslie and Gardiner, *Roman Empire in Chinese Sources*, 100–1, which is a sixth century source that incorporates earlier material. For other (and earlier) Chinese sources for the Persian Gulf and Parthia, see *Hou Hanshu* 88 (trans. John Hill), in *Through the Jade Gate*, 21–27; Leslie and Gardiner, *Roman Empire in Chinese Sources*, 45–46. For links between the Persian Gulf and India, see Ray, *Winds of Change*, 12 and 52–57.

[30] The kingdom of Mesene/Maišan and its ports (Charax Spasinou, Phorat, and Apologos) have been examined by Schuol, *Charakene*, who treats the *Hymn of the Pearl* in the *Acts* and its depiction of Mesene as an inn or harbor for merchants (165–66). Also, Gregoratti, "Parthian Port" and Yon, "Ports."

[31] Pavan and Schenk, "Crossing the Indian Ocean"; Avanzini, "Notes for a History" and "Port of Sumhuram"; Pavan, "Trade and Commercial Routes." For the Persian Gulf's links to both Mesopotamia and the Red Sea region, as evidenced by both Roman and Mesopotamian finds at Ed-Dur (Omana?), see Rutten, "Roman Fine Wares," 8–24; Tomber, *Indo-Roman Trade*, 109–16. Mesopotamian torpedo vessels found at Indian sites may have taken a route through the Levant, the Red Sea, and into the Indian Ocean, but they also passed through the Persian Gulf. Dibba was also a meaningful transit point, as discussed by Jasim and Tousif, "Dibba." For the Indus region's connections to the pre-Hellenistic Near East, see Possehl, "India's Relations." Pottery found in late antique Sri Lanka can be traced to the vicinity of Susa in Iran. Stern et al., "From Susa to Anuradhapura."

[32] *PME* (ed. Casson) 35–36.

Islamic Arabs accordingly defined the Persian Gulf littoral as a region "of Indians" (*bēt hendwāyē* or *al-Hind*).³³ In his inscriptions of the late-third century CE, the Zoroastrian priest Kirdir boasts of his aggressive stance against Buddhists and Hindus. While these were present in the Sasanian Persian territories along the Hindu Kush, they also frequented ports of the north Persian Gulf littoral.³⁴

The opening narrative of the Indian *Acts* indicates that slaves were a common export of the Roman world to India. Judas Thomas was not the only Levantine slave depicted in the text; at the mysterious first port of disembarkation, a Hebrew woman is part of the musical entertainment for a wedding feast.³⁵ External evidence corroborates such a characterization. Indian societies did not have the kind of "slave economy" that the Roman empire fostered.³⁶ Slaves transported to India were treated as status commodities, not economic producers.³⁷ But a slave trade existed. When the *Palmyrene Tax Law* levies a tax on the transport of slaves, it is possible that merchants were moving some of these slaves southeastward toward the Persian Gulf.³⁸ In his *Life of Apollonius of Tyana*, Philostratus depicts Apollonius as announcing to a tax collector upon entering Parthian territory the names of the virtues that he was bringing to Parthia. As we have already witnessed, all his virtues were Greek feminine nouns, and so the tax collector then asks him to register with him the names of his female slaves.³⁹ Slaves, then, were a common export of Romans into Parthian and Sasanian imperial space, and many of these slaves certainly arrived in the Persian Gulf. If the opening episode of the Indian *Acts* was redacted from a narrative that depicted Habban as traveling to Mesene in search of a slave, it would align with such commercial trends.

For much of antiquity, the lowland Parthian and Sasanian network apparently maintained expatriate residential settlements in north India, especially at the mouth of the Indus river. Little evidence suggests that it maintained much direct contact with south India or Sri Lanka. But during the fifth century CE, the lowland Sasanian network began to extend its reach

---

³³ Brock, "Syriac Life," 166 and 187. Perhaps used in this way by the putative author of *The History of Mar Yaunan*, ed. Bedjan, *AMSS* 1.466 and the *Life of Mar Giwargis* (ed. Bedjan) 561.
³⁴ The edition/translation of Gignoux, *Quatre inscriptions du mage Kirdīr*, 60 and 69–70.
³⁵ *Acts of Thomas* (ed. Wright) ܡܗܪ – ܡܗܪ of the Syriac; (ed. Bonnet) 5 and 8–9 of the Greek.
³⁶ Harper, *Slavery in the Roman World* provides recent treatment of the later Roman "slave economy" and the interconnected markets and mode of production that underpinned it.
³⁷ *PME* (ed. Casson) 36 and 49.
³⁸ *PAT* 259=*CIS* 2.3, 3913=Healey, *Aramaic Inscriptions*, no. 37: iii. 1–8 of the Greek; ii. 2–7 of the Palmyrene.
³⁹ Philostr., *VA* (ed. Jones) 1.20.

to south India and Sri Lanka. At some point, a network from Fars maintaining a central hub at Rev-Ardashir apparently complemented its presence there. As these networks established residential anchor points in south India and Sri Lanka, they carried Christian culture there too. Writing c. 550 CE but commenting on travels that he undertook c. 515–525 CE, "Cosmas Indicopleustes" places congregations of the Church of the East at pepper-producing Malabar/Kerala (*Male*), the vicinity of Mumbai (*Kalliena*), Sri Lanka (Taprobane), and Socotra (*Dioskourides*).[40] He also states that these were administered by priests from the Sasanian Church of the East. His testimony explains how a fifth-century CE church history could claim anachronistically that a signatory bishop at the Council of Nicaea had represented the churches of "all Persia and India." As we have seen, medieval Syriac and Arabic texts, apparently citing earlier authors, indicate that Rev-Ardashir had begun to administer Christians in India during this period.[41] The lowland Sasanian network may have been vital in receiving Christianity from the Levantine network and in transmitting it to India, but the metropolitan see of Fars over time was responsible for ecclesiastical governance.

Various factors propelled the outward extension of the lowland Sasanian network and its counterpart from Fars. Writing in the sixth century CE, Procopius emphatically stresses that one reason that Persian merchants outdid their Roman or Aksumite rivals in acquiring silk was that they were able to linger in port cities. His statement indicates that by the reign of Justinian (527–565 CE), they had established residential communities in south India and Sri Lanka.[42] They had done so, it appears, for two interrelated reasons. The first is that Sasanian Persian traders were endeavoring to enhance their profits in the silk market, even if it is hard to discern whether they did so through coordination or the accumulation of uncoordinated activity. In addition to intervening in the movement of silk overland from central Asia to Roman territory, the Persians sought to ensure that they could overshadow the Romans and their proxies in acquiring it along the sea-lanes. Indeed, the Sasanian Persians eventually

---

[40] Cosmas Indicopleustes (ed. Wolska-Conus) 3.65, with 11.13–19 (on the authorship of Book 11, de Romanis, "Romanukharaṭṭha and Taprobane," 196, n. 133; and Darley, *Indo-Byzantine Exchange*, 108–24). Banaji, "'Regions that Look Seaward'," 114–19 discusses "Cosmas'" toponyms.
[41] On ps.-Gelasius, see Chapters 2 and 4, n. 59 and 22. According to the *Chronicle of Se'ert* (ed. and trans. Scher) 7.116–17, Maʿna, bishop of Rev-Ardashir and metropolitan of Fars, sent Syriac translations of the Greek works of Diodore of Tarsus and Theodore of Mopsuestia and other texts that he wrote in Persian to Persian Gulf locations and India. Ishoʿdad, *Commentaries* (ed. Gibson), Vol. 5, ܐ, with xiii–xiv, regarding a translation of a work of Theodore of Mopsuestia by "Daniel, the Indian." See Chapter 4, pp. 143–44, n. 15–16 for further discussion.
[42] Procopius, *Bell. Pers.* (ed. Haury) 1.20.

established settlements on the Malay peninsula and perhaps beyond,[43] and their movement made it easier to acquire silk far beyond the ability and reach of Roman or Aksumite merchants to do so.

A second reason represents the natural outcome of the efforts of Sasanian merchants to sail into the Bay of Bengal and southeast Asia.[44] Due to intensified commercial activity and maritime contact with southeast Asia and even China, Sasanian Persians established residential communities in south India and Sri Lanka in order to facilitate and profit from such movement. Through the stable presence of such anchor points in south India, the networks extending from lowland Sasanian territory and coastal Fars moved people, information, commodities, credit, and trust between Seleucia-Ctesiphon and Rev-Ardashir and southeast Asia. The presence of such merchants in south India has not left an overwhelming trail of evidence, but the Quilon copper plates, dating later to the ninth century CE, contain the privileges that south Indian kings extended to various merchants from south Mesopotamia, Khuzistan, or coastal Fars. Written in Tamil, at least one grant bears signatures of merchants in Arabic, Pahlavi, and Hebrew. The plates thereby reflect the enduring presence in south India of merchants of varied ethno-cultural and religious backgrounds, including those with points of origin in the north Persian Gulf littoral, during the Islamic period.[45] Other plates from Cochin inscribed in Tamil a little later also reflect a Jewish presence, and they constitute the earliest definitive proof of Jews in south India. Local traditions date these plates to 379 CE, but the king who issued them was probably active in the tenth or eleventh century CE.[46] On the basis of such plates, one can learn about Persian Christians

---

[43] See pp. 220–21, n. 52–54.

[44] Whitehouse and Williamson, "Sasanian Maritime Trade," 45–49; Daryaee, *Sasanian Persia*, 136–44; Beaujard, *Mondes*, 1.392–400. For Sasanians in India, as measured by Mesopotamian Torpedo jars, see Tomber, "Rome and Mesopotamia" and *Indo-Roman Trade*, 167.

[45] Cereti, "Pahlavi Signatures" for the signatures, with Narayanan, *Perumals of Kerala*, 277. Various studies on these plates as well as others of south India dating between the ninth and thirteenth centuries CE, are Joseph, "Malabar Miscellany," 13–16; Kollaparambil, "Historical Sources," 13–20 and xviii–xxvi; Gundert, "Translations and Analysis," 126–34, with the plates of 117–25; Dikshitar, *South Indian Inscriptions*, 350–55 and 357–63, with the plates of 348–50, 355–57, and 363–77; Pothan, *Syrian Christians*, 32–33 and 102–5. Menon, *Survey of Kerala History*, 38–44, 99–100, and 124–25 discusses such texts, as does Subbarayalu, *South India*, 176–79 and Veluthat, *Early Medieval*, 147–67, who provides a useful synopsis of medieval epigraphy at Kerala (esp. 154). Recent international collaboration on the Quilon copper plates, which is to result in publication, can be explored at http://849ce.org.uk/. See Lambourn, Veluthat, and Tomber, *Copper Plates from Kollam*.

[46] See Menon, *Survey of Kerala History*, 127–28, with scholarship from previous note. Otherwise, Wink, *Al-Hind*, 99–100; Fischel, "Exploration," 230–31, with n. 6; Katz, *Jews of India*, 13–15; Narayanan, *Perumals of Kerala*, 68–70. For plates, Dikshitar, *South Indian Inscriptions*, 345–48 (mistitled) and Gundert, "Translations and Analysis," 134–42. Oral traditions have created a greater antiquity for Jews in south India, but it is difficult to establish their veracity. See pp. 19–20, n. 57.

(*tarisapalli*), Jewish trade guilds (*anjuvannam*), and guilds that included Christians (*manigrammam*) and privileges conferred upon Christian figures like Sapir Iso and Iravi Kortthan.[47] Stone crosses that belonged to Christian communities in India at this time bear Pahlavi inscriptions. These suggest commercial links to Fars and the governing authority of the bishop of Rev-Ardashir.[48] They also coincide with the testimony of Timotheos I (c. 800 CE) regarding the routine movement of monks between the Persian Gulf and India and the increased emphasis on the stature of the apostle Thomas as founder within the diocese of Fars.[49] While it is unclear how and when exactly Syriac became a key ecclesiastical language of Christians in south India, their links to the Persian Church of the East were certainly vital.

Additional witnesses from the late Sasanian and early Islamic periods reflect the expanded trading horizons that Persians cultivated at the time. An author named Zādoi composed the *History of Mar Yaunan*, and while doing so, he identified himself as abbot of "the monastery of Mār Thomas in the land of India (*'atrā b-hendō*)" and located it "beneath the land of the Qaṭrāyē."[50] Since the term "India" could refer to territory as far north as the Persian Gulf, it is difficult to discern whether this monastery was located in India proper or farther north, among the islands or along the littoral of the Persian Gulf. The text also describes commercial activity between the Persian Gulf region and "Ṣin," a generic word for China that is nonetheless inclusive of southeast Asia.[51] Due to the increased extension of the lowland Sasanian network and its counterpart from Fars, residential communities were even established in southeast Asia, and they anchored Christianity there. By the eighth century CE, the bishop of Rev-Ardashir

---

[47] Sastri, *History of South India*, 164 and 200; Singh, *History*, 602; Menon, *Survey of Kerala History*, 100; Frykenberg, *Christianity in India*, 111–14 (111 specifying the titles of Christian/Jewish groups); Malekandathil, *Maritime India*, 38–61 (specifying titles of Christian/Jewish groups); Narayanan, *Perumals of Kerala*, 277–84 (for Jewish and Christian groups). For guilds, also Wink, *Al-Hind*, 71 and 101. For translations of the plates, see n. 45.

[48] Cereti, Olivieri, and Vazhuthanapally, "Problem of the St. Thomas Crosses": Brock, "Thomas Christians," 411; Malekandathil, *Maritime India*, 5–6. Also, Hosten, *Antiquities*, 327–61.

[49] Tubach, "Veneration of the Apostle Thomas," 21–22; Bar Hebraeus, *Ecclesiastical Chronicle* (ed. Abbeloos and Lamy), 3.172. For materials on Timotheos I and the significance of the references to letters of Timotheos made by Ibn al-Tayyib, see Baum and Winkler, *Church of the East*, 62. For texts/translations, see Ibn al-Tayyib (ed. Hoenerback and Spies), pt. 2, 119/121 and 149/152.

[50] *The History of Mar Yaunan*, in Bedjan, *AMSS* 1.466. Payne, "Monks, Dinars, and Date Palms," 99–101. The scholarly tradition had previously dated the text to c. 400 CE (its narrative is set in the fourth century), but certain elements, especially its interest in Qardagh, demonstrate a later date.

[51] *The History of Mar Yaunan*, in Bedjan, *AMSS* 1.494 reports the return of a ship from "Ṣin" to east Arabia. Ṣin (China) can here mean any place east of India, but it nonetheless shows that direct movement between the Persian Gulf and points east of India existed. Payne, "Monks, Dinars, and Date Palms," 106.

governed congregations in "Qalah" (Qalang) of Malaysia, along with those in India.[52]

The presence of Persian merchants in southeast Asia and even Canton receives further illustration by Chinese sources composed under the Tang dynasty.[53] While these sources often date to the Islamic period and after the collapse of the Sasanian Persian empire, they nonetheless correspond with "Cosmas Indicopleustes" in providing an indication of where Sasanian Persians were sailing by the sixth century CE. In 671, a Chinese pilgrim traveled from Canton to southeast Asia onboard a ship maintained by a Persian, and another who traveled to India in 727 CE described Persians as sailing through the "Western Sea" (the Persian Gulf), to Sri Lanka for precious objects, to the Malay peninsula for gold, and then to Canton for silk.[54] Tang sources also indicate that Persians had established fire temples on the Chinese mainland. They thus suggest that Persians were maintaining a residential presence in China and not just engaging in transitory exchanges of products.[55] Clearly, by the sixth century CE, Sasanian Persian merchants were sailing to southeast Asia (if not China) directly, and their residential establishments in south India were circumventing the ability of Roman merchants to acquire silk in Indian ports at that particular time. These same residential settlements enabled Christianity to find its anchorage in south India, where it still flourishes today.

Christians in India and Links to the Mediterranean and Upper Mesopotamia

As the previous section has emphasized, Sasanian Persian merchants transported their Christian culture to south India only in the fifth century CE. But before Christianity's arrival there, Mediterranean and Upper Mesopotamian Christians had for centuries believed that religious brethren lived there. Their views were based on textual traditions or variations thereof that narrated how Christianity had allegedly reached India. These traditions

---

[52] Isho'yabh III, *Liber epistularum* (ed. Duval) 247–55 (esp. 252) and 255–60. Whitehouse and Williamson, "Sasanian Maritime Trade," 45–49; Wink, *Al-Hind*, 48–51; Colless, "Persian Merchants."

[53] These are compiled by Schafer, "Iranian Merchants," 403–22; and So, "Middle Easterners," 259–75. For full discussion of seaborne connections links between the Islamic Middle East and East Asia, see Park, *Mapping the Chinese and Islamic Worlds* and Wink, *Al-Hind* (48–49: Tang sources).

[54] Schafer, "Iranian Merchants," 406; and Hansen, *Silk Road*, 164. Also, Park, *Mapping the Chinese and Islamic Worlds*, 5–7 and 29–34.

[55] Schafer, "Iranian Merchants," 407–8.

stemmed from the *Acts of Thomas*, and we have previously explored how it shaped Christian views regarding the presence of Christians in India.

It was only in the sixth century CE that truly autonomous and independent witnesses for Christianity in India apparently emerged. These witnesses were also noticeably active precisely when the lowland Sasanian network and its counterpart in coastal Fars had established Christian communities and culture in south Asia. Along with "Cosmas Indicopleustes," who places sixth-century CE Persian Christians in south India, Sri Lanka, and Socotra,[56] Greek and Latin authors began to associate Thomas' martyr and burial site with "Kalamene/Calamina." According to one theory, Kalamene/Calamina reflects a Greek and Latin filtering and reconstituting of *Cholamandalam*, the name locally used for the Coromandel coast of India.[57] Whether this is correct, we still have reason to surmise that references to Kalamene illustrate how Mediterranean Christians were responding to a burial site ascribed to Thomas in south India and the circulation of its reputation.

The Greek, Latin, and Syriac itineraries that record such a burial site exist in abundance. These are mostly anonymous, though some have circulated spuriously under the names of the third- and fourth-century CE authors Hippolytus, Epiphanius, and Dorotheus (and are sometimes erroneously ascribed to them by modern scholars). As a general rule, they provide an abbreviated summary informed by both the Parthian and Indian traditions of Thomas' career before noting his death and burial at "Kalamene/Calamina." Their celebrations of his deeds in Parthia describe how he evangelized the Parthians, Medes, Persians, Karmanians, Hyrcanians, Bactrians, and Margians.[58] Isidore of Seville is the earliest explicit witness, with a fixed date, for the tomb at "Kalamene/Calamina," though references also appear in traditions that can be dated somewhat

---

[56] Cosmas Indicopleustes (ed. Wolska-Conus) 3.65, with 11.13–19 (on the authorship of Book 11, see De Romanis, "Romanukharaṭṭha and Taprobane," 196, n. 133; and Darley, *Indo-Byzantine Exchange*, 108–24).

[57] Nedungatt, "Calamina, Kalamides, Cholamandalam," 181–99 and *Quest for the Historical Thomas*, 151–73. Nedungatt discusses various other theories too. Also, Tubach "Historische Elemente," 106–7. Nedungatt suggests that it was a Sankritized Tamil name. Monier-Williams, *A Sanskrit Dictionary*, 775 (maṇḍalam=territory); and Burrow and Emeneau, *A Dravidian Etymological Dictionary*, 413 (maṉ=land).

[58] The earliest apostolic itinerary that treats the Parthian ministry of Thomas (without a reference to India/Kalamene) is contained in the "*Anonymus* I" tradition associated with Vat. Gr. 1506 and the Verona fragment. This can be securely dated at latest to c. 500 but may extend earlier. Turner, "Primitive Edition," 63; Guignard, "Tradition grecque," and "Greek Lists," 480–87. Dolbeau, *Prophètes*, 184 adds spurious references to India/Kalamene in brackets in his translation. For further comments and bibliography on this tradition, see Jullien and Jullien, *Apôtres des confins*, 80–81.

earlier (see next paragraph).⁵⁹ Subsequently, a late insertion into a Greek translation of Jerome's *On Illustrious Men*⁶⁰ and anonymous itineraries of the eighth and ninth centuries CE spuriously ascribed to various late antique figures also invoked it.⁶¹ Among these sources, a few itineraries were conceivably influenced by a tradition (discussed in Chapter 1) in which Judas Thomas had preached to the Persian Magi of the Gospel of Matthew, and these therefore replaced the typical reference to Margians with one for "Magians." Initially, during the fourth and fifth centuries CE, citations of Thomas' Parthian ministry circulated independently of references to his Indian activity.⁶² But subsequently the two traditions were

---

⁵⁹ Isidore of Seville, *Births and Deaths of the Fathers* (ed. Gómez) 73. For full discussion, see Andrade, "Syriac Book."
⁶⁰ The tradition appears in a translation of Jerome's *Illustrious Men* attributed spuriously to a contemporary named Sophronius and therefore appears as an appendix to *Illustrious Men* in Fabricius, *Bibliotheca Ecclesiastica*, 214–17 and PL 23 col. 719–22 (as *de vitiis apostolorum* 5). But it is neither a part of Jerome's *Illustrious Men* nor authentically Jerome's. This instead constitutes the beginning of a translation of Jerome's *Illustrious Men* into Greek that cannot date before the seventh century CE. It includes passages inserted well after Jerome's initial composition, and this insertion regarding Thomas' Parthian itinerary was clearly produced to compensate for the absence of any activity of Thomas in Jerome's actual text (the Latin translation accompanying the Greek in *PL* 23 is apparently early modern, as J. P. Migne's comments in *PL* col. 600–1 indicate). The critical edition of Jerome's *Illustrious Men* (ed. Ceresa-Gastaldo) therefore rightly omits the passage. See Dolbeau, "Nouvelles recherches," 97 (now in *Prophètes*, 68–69); Tubach, "Historische Elemente," 105–10; and von Gebhardt, *Hieronymus de viris inlustribus*, vii–x and 2–13 (esp. 7–8) with Fabricius, *Bibliotheca Ecclesiastica*, 11–12 and 224, for text or argument for ps.-Sophronius' insertion of an apostolic itinerary. Nedungatt, *Quest for the Historical Thomas*, 160, and "Calamina, Kalamides, Cholamandalam," 185 treats the text as authentically Jerome's.
⁶¹ Greek texts are in Schermann, *Prophetarum vitae*, 111, 155–56, and 166, along with the Latin *Short Accounts of the Apostles* (*Breviarium apostolorum*) (207–12); the Latin text for pseudo-Epiphanius, which in certain instances is closer to the original, is from Dolbeau, "Une liste ancienne," 299–314 (text on 308–9); for the Latin of pseudo-Dorotheus, Dolbeau, "Une liste latine," 50–70 (68–70 for text). Both are now in Dolbeau, *Prophètes*, 227–62 (236–37 and 260–62). Likewise, *Births and Deaths of the Patriarchs* (ed. Fraga) 49.3, which dates to the late eighth century, claims that Thomas preached to "the Parthians and Medes" and died in "Calaminice, a city of India." Dolbeau, "Listes d'apôtres," 458–63 (updated in *Prophètes*, 73–79) provides synthetic treatment of the various traditions and dating. A Syriac manuscript dating to 874 CE claims that Thomas, from the tribe of Judah, preached among the Parthians and Medes and at Timor and inner India before dying at "Qalamaya"; this seems dependent on the Greek tradition and can be found in Van Esbroeck, "Neuf listes," 141 and 188–89. The same can be said for Thomas' association with Parthia in the tenth-century CE manuscript from Mt. Sinai of Lewis, *Catalogue*, 7. Barhebraeus, *Ecclesiastical Chronicle* (ed. Abbeloos and Lamy) 1.33–34 and 3.4–11 refers to both the Parthian and Indian traditions. Leloir, *Écrits apocryphes*, 2.740–42 and 755, with Bayan, *Synaxarion*, 421, conveys Thomas' Parthian tradition in Armenia.
⁶² The Latin *Births and Deaths of the Prophets and Apostles* (*de ortu et obitu prophetarum et apostolorum*), which probably dates to the fifth/sixth CE century and whose original Greek form may (but not certainly) date as early as the late fourth century and is best situated in the fifth century, and an early "Greco-Syrian" list (*Anonymus* II) from about the same time (in Schermann, *Prophetarum vitae*, 172, but corrected by Dolbeau, "Listes d'apôtres," 468, now in *Prophètes*, 187) associates Thomas with India and Calamina, but not Parthia. See Dolbeau, "Nouvelles recherches," 91–107 (esp. 101–2 and 106, now in *Prophètes*, 61–89, esp. 73–74 and 88) for text of *Births and Deaths* and "Listes d'apôtres,"

combined in the apostolic itineraries, and the tradition regarding Thomas' death and burial at a place called Kalamene/Calamina was introduced.[63]

While sometimes erroneously ascribed to Jerome's *Illustrious Men* (it is in fact inserted into a later Greek translation)[64] and certainly known by the time of Isidore of Seville, the status of Kalamene/Calamina as Thomas' burial site is apparently first attested in an anonymous Latin text recounting the deeds of the apostles. Known as the *Births and Deaths of the Prophets and Apostles* (*De ortu et obitu prophetarum et apostolorum*), the Latin text probably dates to the fifth or sixth century CE. It is based on an earlier (but now non-extant) Greek version that circulated some time before 500 CE and, as some scholars surmise, as early as 350 CE, but it cannot presently be confirmed that the reference to Kalamene/Calamina appears in these earlier versions. A burial site at Kalamene also appears in the manuscripts associated with the "*Anonymus* I" tradition (fifth-sixth centuries CE), but only in the later iterations. Most plausibly, the references to Kalamene/Calamina first circulated among Greek and Latin apostolic lists c. 500 CE or thereafter.[65] Subsequently, they were included in a litany of late antique and early medieval treatments of apostolic lists and itineraries. Alongside the *Births and Deaths of the Prophets and Apostles*, these included the anonymous *Short Accounts of the Apostles* (*Breviarium apostolorum*, probably

---

458–63 (now in *Prophètes*, 173–79) for synthesis and date of these traditions, with Schermann, *Propheten-und Apostellegenden*, 133–74 and 272–76. The recent work of Guignard, "Tradition grecque," esp. 175, 186, and 192–3 and "Greek Lists," 480–87, situates the tradition reflected by the Verona fragment ("*Anonymus* I") to the fifth century CE (perhaps stretching into the fourth) and notes that the oldest manuscripts (like Vat. Gr. 1506 and the Verona fragment) intriguingly only mention Thomas' Parthian itinerary, not his death and burial at Kalamene. See Turner, "Primitive Edition," 63; Dolbeau, *Prophètes*, 184, who adds spurious references to India/Kalamene in brackets.

[63] Isidore of Seville, *Births and Deaths of the Fathers* (ed. Gómez) 73 claims that Thomas preached among Parthians Medes, Persians, Hyrcanians, and Bactrians before dying at "Calaminia, a city of India." Similarly, *Births and Deaths of the Patriarchs* (ed. Fraga) 49.3, an emulation of Isidore's text, places Thomas among the Parthians but describes his death at "Calaminice."

[64] See n. 60.

[65] Even if some of the contents of *Births and Deaths* can be traced to the late-fourth century, it does not mean that the text in aggregate circulated so early, as it could have been compiling the itineraries of individual apostles that existed in earlier sources. See Dolbeau, "Nouvelles recherches," 91–107 (esp. 101–2 and 106, now in *Prophètes* 61–89, esp. 73–74 and 88, with revisions and addenda). The text integrates material from Jerome's corpus, and for the apostle Philip, mentions the province of Phrygia Pacatiana. This may situate the tradition for this specific apostle to the late fourth century CE, but these facts do not necessarily date the composition of the aggregate text. It could have included late-fourth century CE traditions and material from Jerome's corpus at a later date. Moreover, since the province of Phrygia Pacatiana existed for the duration of the later Roman empire, its mention merely provides a *terminus post quem* and does not secure an early date. In similar ways, the earliest manuscripts for the "*Anonymus* I" tradition do not mention where Thomas is buried; later manuscripts add it. Guignard, "Tradition grecque," 186 and 192–93, and "Greek Lists," 484–85.

sixth century CE), the work of Isidore of Seville (c. 600 CE), an Isidorean emulator, and lists spuriously attributed to Epiphanius, Dorotheus, and Hippolytus, as well as a Syriac manuscript that dates to 874 CE.[66]

But before the fifth century CE, no author who otherwise associates India with Thomas' preaching and death mentions the name of Kalamene/Calamina. In other words, it was only during the fifth or sixth centuries CE that Latin, Greek, or Syriac authors along the Mediterranean littoral began to associate Thomas' martyrdom with the Coromandel coast. It is not coincidental that sources of this period are the first to speak of pilgrims who traveled to India to visit Thomas' tomb.[67] The most reasonable explanation for such a chronology is that Sasanian Persians first carried and anchored both Christianity and the Thomas narrative in India during the fifth century CE. It was only subsequently that Christians in south India, inspired by the *Acts* and its ambiguous depiction of where Thomas died, venerated a tomb on the south Indian coast (probably at Mylapore but maybe elsewhere) as his initial resting place. At that juncture, the Roman Egyptian network, in which "Cosmas Indicopleustes" was active, re-established direct contact with India and began to transport knowledge regarding the Persian Christians residing in India to the Mediterranean world. As knowledge of Thomas' burial site circulated among authors in the Mediterranean, they called it Kalamene/Calamina. As we have seen, this perhaps constituted a variation on the local name for a south Indian region (*Cholamandalam*), without their being aware. But whatever its origin, they were using the name for a specific site in south India where local Christians boasted of Thomas' tomb.

Significantly, before Greek and Latin sources began locating Thomas' martyr and burial site at "Kalamene" or "Calamina," they overwhelmingly conceived of Edessa as his most prominent cult site. The *Acts of Thomas* provided the root for this tradition. At its end, the work reports that one of Thomas' followers collected his remains and escorted them out of India. The Syriac text claims they were brought to the "west"; the Greek indicates that they were taken to Mesopotamia.[68] Such statements clearly encouraged the belief that Thomas' relics had been acquired by Edessenes and were ultimately interred at Edessa. This view dominates the literature composed before 500 CE, even if accounts differ regarding how Thomas'

---

[66] For references, see preceding paragraphs and notes, esp. n. 61.
[67] Gregory of Tours, *Glor. Mart.* (ed. Arndt and Krusch) 31–32; *Anglo-Saxon Chronicle*, entry for 883/884 CE. Editions of the various manuscripts have been published in Dumvile and Keynes, *The Anglo-Saxon Chronicle*.
[68] *Acts of Thomas* (ed. Wright) ܓܪܒ of the Syriac text; (ed. Bonnet) 170 of the Greek text.

relics reached Edessa. One fourth-century Latin source makes the dubious claim that Syrians had persuaded Severus Alexander (222–235 CE) to request Thomas' relics from the rulers of India after having defeated the Persian king "Xerxes."[69] Likewise, in his *Nisibene Hymns*, Ephrem depicts the Devil as lamenting the arrival of Thomas' relics at Edessa due to a merchant's activity.[70] The pilgrim Egeria and various ecclesiastical histories placed them there as well during the fourth and fifth centuries CE, and a ninth-century CE Syriac chronicle locates them at Edessa during the fourth century CE too.[71] Eventually the tradition arose that Thomas' followers had absconded with his relics to Edessa immediately upon his death.[72]

The fame of Thomas' presence at Edessa continued through late antiquity. Gregory of Tours, even while displaying knowledge of the *Acts* and acknowledging that a church, monastery, and eternal flame were present at the site of Thomas' martyrdom in India, treated Edessa as the location of his relic cult.[73] Numerous Syriac poems, attributed (dubiously) to Ephrem in the past but probably dating significantly later, rendered India as Thomas' place of death and Edessa to be where his relics were located. The Syriac *Chronicle of 1234* clarifies that Thomas' body resided at Edessa deep into the Islamic period.[74] Even the sources that recorded Kalamene (or similar variants) of India to be the site of his martyrdom and burial could place his relics at Edessa.[75] In other words, the late antique tradition of Thomas' presence at Edessa, originating in the fourth century CE at latest, was promoted by Edessenes and became widespread among western European Christians, inhabitants of early Byzantium, and members of the Syrian Orthodox church living under Muslim rule. As such, Edessa is repeatedly attested as Thomas' resting place in Latin, Greek, and Syriac sources.

In fact, the references to a sacred site, resting place, or relic cult for Thomas in Latin, Greek, and Syriac sources before 500 CE overwhelmingly place these at Edessa. Some exceptions are testimonies that do not specify a location.[76] Occasionally, Christian authors claimed that lesser sites possessed relics of Thomas. C. 400 CE, Gaudentius of Brescia, for example,

---

[69] *Passion of the Holy Apostle Thomas* (ed. Zelzer) 61–62.   [70] Ephrem, *CN* (ed. Beck) 42.1–3.
[71] *Itinerary of Egeria* (ed. Maraval) 17.1 and 19.3; *Chron. 846* (ed. Brooks) 206. Socrates, *HE* (ed. Hansen) 4.18 and Sozomen, *HE* (ed. Bidez and Hansen) 6.18.
[72] For instance, *The Miracles of the Apostle Thomas* (ed. Zelzer) 76–77, dated to the sixth century (and found in the work of "ps.-Abdias").
[73] Gregory of Tours, *Glor. Mart.* (ed. Arndt and Krusch) 31–32.
[74] Lamy, *Sancti Ephraem*, 4.694–706; *Chronicle of 1234* (ed. Chabot) 2.133.
[75] Barhebraeus, *Ecclesiastical Chronicle* (ed. Abbeloos and Lamy) 1.33–34 and 3.4–11.
[76] For example John Chrys., *Ad Heb.* 26 (PG 63, col. 179) does not specify the location of Thomas' relics, but as an Antiochene Syrian, he was probably referring to Edessa.

claimed in a sermon that his church in Brescia possessed relics of Thomas, who had died in India.[77] A codex from Fulda dating to 546 CE, apparently for similar reasons, places Thomas' relics at "Iotabe," an island off the Sinai peninsula.[78] But significantly, no source explicitly places a tomb for Thomas in India before 500 CE. No one in the Mediterranean or Levant appears to have believed that he had an active cult or pilgrimage site there.

By contrast, it was only starting in the sixth century CE that Greek and Latin authors first began to specify a known burial site or tomb for Thomas in India or, apparently, the Coromandel coast. Intriguingly, while they recognized this site as containing Thomas' initial tomb, they did not necessarily deem his relics to be there; in some instances they explicitly noted that Thomas's relics were removed to Edessa after being buried in India.[79] It seems that Mediterranean Christians now accepted that a tomb in India was where Thomas was once buried but that his relics were in Edessa. Their attestations correspond with the settlement of Sasanian Christians in south India and the Roman Egyptian network's revitalized contact with the subcontinent. Due to these phenomena, Thomas' tomb in India subsequently enjoyed a far-reaching reputation on a par with that of Edessa. Gregory of Tours, of northern Gaul, describes Edessa as the current site of Thomas' relics, but he claims that a spot in India had previously held his body. His friend Theodore, having visited it, had told him that a monastery and church graced the site. An eternal flame, not fed by human efforts, marked the sanctity of Thomas' tomb. Although his perspective is based in part on his knowledge of the narrative of the *Acts*, which he invokes, he is clearly commenting on a site in India about which Roman and post-Roman Christians of the Mediterranean now knew.[80] It was indeed around this time that the *Births and Deaths of the Prophets and Apostles*, the later iterations of "*Anonymus* I," the *Short Accounts of the Apostles (Breviarium apostolorum)*, and Isidore of Seville were situating Thomas' first resting place at Calamina, Kalamene, or a variation thereof in accordance with a tradition that had begun c. 500 CE.[81]

---

[77] Gaudentius, *Sermo* 17 (PL 20, col. 963).   [78] Schermann, *Prophetarum vitae*, 216.
[79] For example, *Births and Deaths of the Prophets and Apostles* in Dolbeau, "Nouvelles recherches," 106 (now in *Prophètes*, 88); the later text at Schermann, *Prophetarum vitae*, 214 and the Syriac list of Van Esbroeck, "Neuf listes," 141 and 188–89 (manuscript of 874). Also Barhebraeus, *Ecclesiastical Chronicle* (ed. Abbeloos and Lamy) 1.33–34 and 3.4–11.
[80] Gregory of Tours, *Glor. Mart.* (ed. Arndt and Krusch) 31–32.
[81] Dolbeau, "Nouvelles recherches," 91–107 (esp. 101–2 and 106, now in *Prophètes*, 61–89, esp. 73–74 and 88, with revisions and addenda); Schermann, *Prophetarum vitae*, 207–12 for *Short Accounts of the Apostles (Breviarium apostolorum)*; Isidore of Seville, *Births and Deaths of the Fathers* (ed. Gómez) 73; Guignard, "Tradition grecque," esp. 175, 186, and 192–3 and "Greek Lists," 480–87. Also perhaps

In subsequent centuries, south India became increasingly famous for having the tomb of Thomas (but again, not necessarily his relics). An eighth-century CE codex, for instance, locates Thomas' tomb at "Aemina." This may have been an unfortunate rendering of Calamina, a name that scribes may have misunderstood. The codex perhaps clarifies that Calamina is meant when it locates "Aemina" in "India Saracinorum."[82] By doing so, it appears to indicate that Calamina was a spot at which commercial players in the Islamic world often convened and maintained residences, even if "India Saracinorum" could also be a reference to Arabia. If the codex is providing a distorted reference to Calamina and the Indian subcontinent, it coheres with the evidence for Arabian and Persian activity in south India and along the sea routes to east Asia. According to a ninth-century CE Arabic text, a merchant named Suleiman visited Quilon in 841 CE and reported that the *bethuma* (that is, *beth Thoma*, or the house of Thomas) could be reached there in ten days of sail from Quilon.[83] Due to such contact with the martyr site in south India, Alfred the Great sent pilgrims there a few decades later, and while the pilgrims' trip to India apparently included south Arabia (they visited a martyr site of the apostle Bartholomew), they seem to have brought alms to the monastery at the site of Thomas' martyrdom in India too.[84] Around the same time, a Syriac manuscript (of 874 CE) places the burial site of Thomas at "Qalamaya" and claims that Brahmins had martyred Thomas there.[85] This link between the death of Thomas and Brahmins is consistent in many respects with south Indian oral traditions regarding Thomas' ministry and, if anything, suggests that these oral traditions were at earliest products of the eighth or ninth century CE, when Brahmanic landowning and religious authority first became preeminent in the Kerala and Coromandel coasts.[86] Subsequently, religious rivalries gave rise to oral traditions among both Christians and Brahmins in which Thomas and other

---

ps.-Abdias' *Miracles of the Blessed Apostle Thomas* (ed. Zelzer) 90 (for the material of "ps.-Abdias," see Fabricius, *Codex* 2.687–736).

[82] Gaiffier, "Ancienne liste," 367–68.

[83] Contained in Reinaud, *Relations des voyages*, 2.19 for Arabic and 1.18 for French translation. Baum and Winkler, *Church of the East*, 56–57, treat this site as Thomas' tomb at Mylapore.

[84] *Anglo-Saxon Chronicle*, entry for 883/884 CE, in Dumvile and Keynes, *The Anglo-Saxon Chronicle*. The episode appears in most (but not all) manuscripts. Most indicate that the pilgrimage went to Rome and "India/Indea," but at least one outlier states "Iudea."

[85] Van Esbroeck, "Neuf listes," 141 and 188–89 (manuscript of 874).

[86] For Thomas' death in the *Thomas Parvam* and the *Margam Kali*, see Menachery, *Nazranies*, 520–25. For Brahmanic migration, landowning, and authority at Kerala, see Menon, *Survey of Kerala History*, 145–54; Champakalakshmi, *Religion, Tradition, and Ideology*, 13–39 and 53–82; Veluthat, *Early Medieval*, 5–6, 61–68, and 295–306; Gurukkal, *Social Formations of Early South India*, 306–16; Singh, *History*, 573–80; Malekandathil, *Maritime India*, 47–48; Narayanan, *Perumals of Kerala*, 262–77.

Christians had sought converts or died at Brahmin hands.[87] No written sources before that time indicate that Brahmins were specifically responsible for Thomas' death.

Attestations to Thomas' resting place in India continue thereafter, and it is only possible to summarize a few of them here. A tenth-century CE Syriac manuscript containing an apostolic itinerary likewise describes "Qalamina" as the site of Thomas' death but erroneously places the city in Parthia.[88] Emphasis on Thomas' south Indian tomb received the subsequent notice of numerous sources in diverse languages, especially as the frequency of Persian and Arabian trade in the Indian Ocean and with east Asia increased.[89] By the thirteenth century, the site of Mylapore on the Coromandel coast had by name begun to replace references to Kalamene/Calamina as the Indian site of Thomas' tomb, and a spate of writers from Europe or southwest Asia either specified Mylapore to be the site of Thomas' burial or, following previous traditions, referred generally to India or Kalamene. These include, to name some examples, an English monk named Ordericus Vitalis (twelfth century CE), the Syriac author Dionysius bar Salibi (twelfth century), Michael the Syrian (twelfth century), Solomon of Basra (who first specifies "Mahluph" in the thirteenth century), Barhebraeus (thirteenth century); Marco Polo (thirteenth), Jean de Mont Corvin (thirteenth), 'Amr ibn Mattai (fourteenth), Jean de Marignoli (fourteenth), and Nicolo de Conti (fifteenth). One can add to the list Awdisho' of Nisibis and the commentary of Mari ibn Sulayman (who briefly mentions Thomas in his broader discussion of work that Addai, Aggai, and Mari did in the east).[90] Since the authors just described were typically referring to contemporary circumstances or replicating earlier invented traditions, their value resides in their testimony regarding the existence of Thomas' tomb in medieval India. But their utility for

---

[87] See above, pp. 207–12, n. 3–4, 10, and 17.   [88] Lewis, *Catalogue*, 7.
[89] For this trade, Wink, *Al-Hind*; and Park, *Mapping the Chinese and Muslim Worlds*.
[90] In the second book of his *Historia ecclesiastica*, Ordericus (PL 188, col. 157–65 and ed. Prévost, 308–21 with 157 [306–7]) mentions the Parthian itinerary and Calaminea, cites the testimony of authors like Augustine and Gregory of Tours, and summarizes the late antique Latin variations of Thomas' *Acts*. His account seems to be informed especially by the *Passio sancti Thomae Apostoli* (ed. Zelzer). For other authors and texts mentioned, see Michael the Syrian (ed. Chabot) 4.92–93 (1.147–48) (Michael the Syrian and extract of Dionysius bar Salibi); Joseph Assemani, *Bibliotheca orientalis* 3.2.13, 19–20, and 34 ('Amr ibn Mattai); Solomon of Basra, *Book of the Bee* (ed. Budge) 119; Barhebraeus, *Ecclesiastical Chronicle* (ed. Abbeloos and Lamy) 1.33–34 and 3.4–11; Mai, *Scriptorum veterum nova collectio* 10.7 and 154 (Latin) 154 and 317 (Syriac) for Awdisho'; for Mari ibn Sulayman, see *Comm.* (ed. and tr. Gismondi) 128b–31b; 1–4 (esp. 1–2). For valuable discussion of relevant authors or manuscripts (including those for which references are not provided here), see Jullien and Jullien, *Apôtres des confins*, 85–87 and 107–110; Ramelli, "Tradizione su Tommaso," 78–82; Schermann, *Propheten- und Apostellegenden*, 272–76.

establishing the arrival of Christianity in India in antiquity is limited. The testimony of "Cosmas Indicopleustes" and Gregory of Tours and the references to Kalamene/Calamina in the apostolic itineraries are much more vital, and they indicate that Christianity did not enjoy anchorage in south India until sometime in the fifth century CE.

Traditions regarding Thomas' relics and burial may have varied in time and place, but in common they still reflect the potency of social networks in transporting across continents the culture of the Indian *Acts* and transforming it in the process. As we witnessed in Chapter 1, social networks carried the text and narrative of the *Acts* from Upper Mesopotamia and throughout the Roman Mediterranean merely decades after it was written. Mediterranean Christians therefore believed that coreligionists inhabited India. In similar ways, networks circulated knowledge regarding the presence of Thomas' putative relics at Edessa, thereby making Edessa a renown pilgrimage site for Roman Christians during the fourth century CE and thereafter. But as argued in the last few chapters, socio-commercial networks also transported Christianity eastward and anchored it in various sites of Mesopotamia, Iran, central Asia, the Persian Gulf, and India. These same networks brought with them the culture of the Thomas narrative, and as a result, Christians of south India embedded its basic tradition in their regional topography, thereby eventually transforming the anonymous location of Thomas' death in the *Acts* into the martyr and sacred site of Mylapore on the Coromandel coast. Even then socio-commercial networks continued to perform their task. During the sixth century CE, members of the Roman Egyptian socio-commercial network, such as "Cosmas Indicopleustes," had revived direct contact with south India and with the Christians who lived there by then. Some of them therefore transported to Mediterranean Christians the news that Thomas had died at "Kalamene" or "Calamina" and that his initial burial site could be found there. In such ways, socio-commercial networks of antiquity carried the constantly changing culture of Christianity, and the ceaselessly transforming narrative of the preaching of the apostle Thomas, from the Mediterranean to India and back again.

Conclusion

Over the fifth century CE, a lowland Parthian/Sasanian socio-commercial network, later aided by merchants from coastal Fars, transported Christianity to south India, and anchored it in ports there. Through its activity, the narrative tradition of Thomas' *Acts* and a tomb for

Thomas became rooted in south India. It was only thereafter that merchants, sailors, and churchmen from Red Sea Egypt and the Mediterranean world learned of a tomb for Thomas at "Kalamene," which perhaps referred to *Cholamandalam* and the site at Mylapore where Thomas Christians certainly celebrated Thomas' tomb in subsequent periods. These travelers transported their knowledge of his interment at this location to Greek-, Latin-, and Syriac-writing authors.

While the Thomas narrative continued to inform how Mediterranean Christians perceived the arrival of Christianity in India after c. 500 CE, their treatment of Thomas' martyr and burial site in India as being at a place called Kalamene, Calamina, or other variations reflected their understanding of an actual south Indian phenomenon. As "Cosmas Indicopleustes" demonstrates, Christians in the Mediterranean world and in Upper Mesopotamia were certainly in direct contact with members of the Church of the East who populated India. This situation differs drastically from what preceded it. On the basis of Thomas' *Acts* or variations of its basic narrative, Christians of the Mediterranean and Upper Mesopotamian regions had assumed, without any sound historical footing, that Christians dwelled in India. Their beliefs were informed by the invented traditions of the Parthian and Indian *Acts*, and they associated Thomas' relics with Edessa.

Accordingly, the unqualified references of Mediterranean Christians to Thomas' burial before c. 500 CE do not describe a tomb in India; they only refer to his relic cult at Edessa. In a similar vein, the statements that Mediterranean Christians made regarding coreligionists in India before 500 CE do not elucidate the situation on the subcontinent. They all were inspired by the invented traditions of the literary narrative of the *Acts* and the various written and oral variations that it fostered, and as we have seen, the Indian *Acts* was the product of a mid-to-late third-century CE Edessene literary agenda. Its inventions created among Christians a certain historical experience of Christianity in India, even before Christianity had arrived and found anchorage there.

The south Indian oral traditions regarding Thomas too should be seen in such a light. According to both the surviving *Acts of Thomas* and the *Thomas Parvam* (transcribed in 1601 CE), the apostle Thomas had promised to build a palace for a local or regional dynast. But this palace was a heavenly palace, one whose existence was verified only after the dynast's brother died and was miraculously revived. While these sources are ostensibly two separate witnesses for the same phenomenon, this is not likely the case. The antiquity of the *Thomas Parvam* has yet to be demonstrated, and it bears the hallmarks of being a variation on the narrative of the *Acts of Thomas*. But the *Acts* constituted an article of Christian culture that Sasanian Persians only brought to south India some time after they had carried and established Christianity there. After Christians of south India reconstituted and transformed such culture, interconnected socio-commercial networks enabled it to travel back to the Mediterranean, with the news that Thomas' body rested at "Kalamene," where he had died. But once it arrived in south India, the narrative of the *Acts* thereafter shaped how Christians there experienced the history of their religion, just as it had done for Christians of the Mediterranean and Middle East during earlier centuries.

Conclusion

In the surviving text of the *Acts of Thomas*, the apostle Judas Thomas is allotted India to evangelize. But he refuses to go on the grounds that he is Hebrew and weak. The recently resurrected Jesus, however, appears in a vision and urges him to proceed. When Judas Thomas again refuses, Jesus sells him to an Indian merchant named Habban. With the transaction completed, Habban and Judas Thomas sail from Jerusalem to a port city in the Persian Gulf and then to India proper. There Judas Thomas builds a heavenly palace for a king named Gudnaphar and is eventually killed by a king named Mazdai.

The *Acts of Thomas* and other anecdotal narratives like it have motivated ancients and moderns alike to conceive of the movement of Christianity across the Afro-Eurasian world system as unfettered and diffuse. The *Acts* even bears ostensible historical validity due to the oral traditions of Thomas Christians that cohere with its basic narrative. But the *Acts* has little value as a source for the activities of the apostle Judas Thomas, the early movement of Christianity across Afro-Eurasia, or social relations between inhabitants of the Roman Mediterranean and south Asia. The *Acts* is a composite accretion of invented and contrived episodes, and the earliest traditions regarding Thomas apparently did not have him travel across continents or suffer martyrdom at all. His reputation for evangelizing Parthia and then subsequently India can be linked to specific literary agendas of the late second and mid-to-late third centuries. Moreover, the narrative of the *Acts of Thomas* only traveled eastward as fast as Christianity and Manichaeism. It was one of the articles of culture that the Christian bodies of a Levantine socio-commercial network carried into lowland Sasanian space. There it was transferred to a lowland Sasanian network that bore its narrative to central Asia and eventually south India. Accordingly, oral or written traditions regarding Thomas that emerged among various Christian populations of Asia, including the Thomas Christians of south India, reflect their engagement with a literary tradition that traveled by means of the same socio-commercial networks that carried Christianity to remote places. They are not sources for any historical phenomenon of apostolic or early Christian evangelization. In fact, their significance does not reside in their testimonial value but in their status as articles of Christian culture that social networks transmitted between the ancient Mediterranean and India.

Ancient apostolic apocrypha, hagiographies, and ecclesiastical histories often make anecdotal references to merchants and associate them with the ability of Christianity to travel rapidly. They also depict solitary preachers as traversing geographic terrains in the manner of merchants. The *Acts*, for example, narrates how an Indian merchant transported Judas Thomas to India, and the *Acts of Mar Mari* accredits merchants from Khuzistan and Fars with bringing Christianity from Edessa to Iran. The holy man Mari encountered these merchants after he himself had trekked from Edessa, across Mesopotamia, and into the Iranian plateau. Traveling farther, he enjoyed the pleasant scent of the apostle Thomas. Ephrem indicates that a merchant was responsible for bringing Thomas' relics to Edessa from either India or an intermediary point. But such treatments of merchants and preachers typically reflect the literary demands of textual narratives that emulated the forms of movement depicted by the Acts of the Apostles, the ancient novel, the literary traditions regarding Mani and his disciples, and even one another. These factors frequently had a greater impact on late antique representations of movement than the social dynamics that actually carried Christian culture.

Christianity's trek to India and central Asia from the Roman Levant and Mediterranean required more time than such late antique representations would suggest. This is because culture in the ancient world did not simply travel by means of diffusion. People's bodies had to carry it. The bodies that carried it did not move in isolation; they engaged in forms of interrelation that determined the social pathways through which they moved. The social pathways through which culture traveled were not interminable; they had endpoints in which culture had to find anchorage, establish roots, and make the transfer to other bodies moving along different social pathways. In other words, trans-imperial social networks determined the mechanisms and timeline by which Christianity traveled outside the Roman empire, and in the period before 500 CE, these networks were foremost of a socio-commercial nature. A Levantine network (that included Jews, Palmyrenes, and Edessenes) was ultimately responsible for bringing Christianity to lowland Parthian and Sasanian territory. Only after Christianity had taken root in the various lowland residential settlements that this network maintained did a lowland Sasanian network transport it to central Asia and India. By contrast, a Roman Egyptian commercial network carried Christian culture to Aksumite Ethiopia and south Arabia during the fourth century CE and enabled it to take root at the residential settlements that the network had established in such regions. But by then it no longer extended to India and could not bring Christian culture there.

An exploration of the interconnected socio-commercial networks of ancient Afro-Eurasia affords a more reliable perspective on how and when Christianity traveled to various parts of the Red Sea and Indian Ocean worlds than the problematic narratives on which much modern scholarship has depended. The surviving Indian *Acts of Thomas* has no reliability as an historical source for Christianity's movement or interconnections between the Mediterranean and India. Thomas' Indian ministry was the invented tradition of a mid-to-late third-century Edessene textual agenda that sought to remove him from Parthia. Despite its invented origins, its narrative produced the belief that Christians inhabited India among subsequent generations of Mediterranean Christians, and it shaped Ephrem's treatment of Thomas' relics as having arrived from India (Chapters 1 and 6). Likewise, the late antique ecclesiastical historians and authors that describe the evangelization of places called "India" by preachers from Roman Egypt were in fact referring to Aksumite Ethiopia and south Arabia (Chapters 2–3). Even the Parthian *Acts of Thomas* was a purely contrived narrative that endowed Judas Thomas or Thomas, whom Christians had hitherto believed not to be a martyr, with the accomplishment of evangelizing Mesopotamia, Iran, central Asia, and north India (Chapter 1).

Due to the circulation of such invented narratives regarding Thomas, Christians of the late antique Mediterranean world had a perception of the state of Christianity in Iran, central Asia, and India that differed from its actual situation in these places. Such narratives coaxed them to believe that coreligionists inhabited these regions long before they actually had. They have even persuaded contemporary Christians and scholars of antiquity to cultivate similar beliefs. But the perceptions of ancient Christians regarding Thomas and the movement of Christianity through Asia reflect their historical experiences and how they construed their religious and ecclesiastical geographies. They do not reflect Christianity's actual movement and anchorage among the various societies of the Afro-Eurasian world system (Chapter 1). Such a process happened by other means.

Traders and merchants from the Red Sea coast of Roman Egypt did not carry Christianity to India and anchor it there. Direct contact and trade between Romans and Indians flourished during the first through third centuries CE. But the Roman Egyptian network that played a key role in facilitating it did not integrate merchants or other players who carried Christian culture at the time. Having suffered instability during the late third century CE, the network was only revitalized by the mid-fourth, at which point it had begun to carry and anchor Christian culture into the Red Sea littoral and south Arabia. But the network no longer extended directly to India, and it therefore did not carry Christian culture there. By the time that the Roman Egyptian network to India had been reestablished in the early sixth century CE, its participants discovered that Persian Christians with ties to lower Mesopotamia (and subsequently coastal Fars) were already populating the port cities of south India, Sri Lanka, and Socotra. These had begun to pass their Christian culture to south Indian converts and to establish a martyr site and tomb at the Coromandel coast (Chapters 2–3 and 6). At this point, the Roman Egypt network accordingly transported knowledge about Christians in south India to the Mediterranean world, including the existence of their tomb for Thomas at "Kalamene/ Calamina." But it did not anchor Christianity in the subcontinent itself.

The lowland Sasanian Persian network that transported Christianity to India only completed the final leg of a journey that involved varied stages of movement, anchorage, and transfer. The Levantine Roman socio-commercial network (and all of its subsets) did not extend much farther than lowland Sasanian Persian space. For many reasons, merchants who traveled from Roman Syria and Upper Mesopotamia typically terminated their trek in lowland Parthian/Sasanian territories, and their residential communities were situated in lower Mesopotamia, classical Assyria, the Zab River region, Khuzistan, and Mesene. These residential communities served as the anchor points in which Christians of the Levantine network were able to establish their Christian culture, and it was in these places that Christian culture took root until the lowland Sasanian network and its varied segments could carry it to the Iranian plateau, central Asia, the interior of the Persian Gulf, and India. Only thereafter did the lowland Sasanian network bear the Christianity of the Persian Church of the East to south India and Sri Lanka, with a network from coastal Fars carrying additional strands of Christian culture subsequently (Chapters 4–6).

The arrival of Christianity in south India from Sasanian Persian territory during the fifth century represents a significant shift in Mediterranean Christian knowledge of Christianity in eastern lands. It also represents another phase in the remarkable ability of the *Acts of Thomas* to shape Christians' experiences of the social pathways that their religion had taken through the Afro-Eurasian world system. After Persian Christians had begun to migrate to south India, they brought with them the narrative of the Indian *Acts of Thomas*, and both they and their south Indian converts eventually located the site of his death in the vicinity, where they identified a tomb in which he was believed to have first been buried. When the Roman Egyptian commercial network once again forged direct contact with India, its members encountered the presence of Persian Christian residential communities in south India and the veneration of Thomas' tomb (but not necessarily his body) at a site on the Coromandel coast. They began to conceive of Thomas' martyr site and burial place as Kalamene/Calamina, even if the belief that Thomas' actual relics were at Edessa persisted. Over time, the Christians of south India nurtured rich oral traditions regarding Thomas' evangelization of India, traditions derived from the basic template of his *Acts*. These oral traditions still survive among Thomas Christians today.

In the surviving text of the *Acts of Thomas*, the resurrected Jesus sold Judas Thomas to the Indian merchant Habban in Jerusalem. From there, Habban transported Judas Thomas to India. But the value of this text as a source for the historical phenomenon of early Christianity's movement does not lie in its anecdotal narrative. Being itself an article of Christian culture, the ways by which the narrative traveled, as opposed to its representation of travel, shed more light on how Christian culture moved from the Roman Mediterranean to India. From its origin point in late third-century Upper Mesopotamia, socio-commercial networks transmitted this narrative tradition westward throughout the Mediterranean, where a host of late antique Christians encountered it and accordingly began to believe that they had religious brethren in India. Such networks also transported it eastward into Sasanian Persia, central Asia, and India, where Christian converts and their descendants integrated the narrative into their beliefs regarding the arrival of Christianity in the Asian hinterland. As socio-commercial networks, with their discrete geographic segments, carried the tradition eastward and transferred it to new bodies and networks, Christian communities embraced the narrative in ways that forever transformed how they experienced their Christian past or their sacred topographies. The oral traditions of Thomas Christians in south India in fact reflect the work of such socio-commercial networks in bringing the narrative of Thomas to the Kerala coast. Therein resides the potency and value of the *Acts of Thomas* as an historical source for Christianity's trek to India.

APPENDIX I

Beginning of Syriac *Acts of Thomas* (Wright's Text)

Note: I checked and improved my translation against the translations and commentaries of Klijn and Attridge; some phrasings are theirs.

> Next, the "Act" of Judas Thomas, the apostle, when He sold him to the merchant Habban so that he would go down (and) convert India

When all the apostles had been in Jerusalem for some time – Simon Peter and Andrew; Jacob and John; Philip and Bartholomew; Thomas and Matthew the tax-collector; Jacob, the son of Halphai, and Simon the Qananite; and Judas, the son of Jacob – (they) apportioned the lands among one another, so that each of them would preach in the part that fell to him and in the land where his Lord sent him. By lot and portion, India fell to Judas Thomas, the apostle. But he was refusing to go, while saying, "I do not have the strength for this because I am weak, and I am a Hebrew man. How can I teach the Indians?" While Judas was reasoning in such ways, our Lord appeared to him in a nocturnal vision and said to him, "Thomas, do not be afraid, because my grace is with you." But he remained entirely disobedient, while saying, "My Lord, send me where you want. To India alone I will not go."

While Judas was reasoning in such ways, a certain merchant, an [Ind]ian, happened (to be) in the south land from [illegible name]. His name was Habban, and he was being sent by king Gudnaphar to bring to him a man, a skilled craftsman. Our Lord saw him while he was walking in the street and said to him, "Do you want to buy a craftsman?" He says to him, "Yes." Our Lord says to him, "I have a slave, a craftsman whom I will sell to you." He showed to him Thomas from afar and made an agreement with him for twenty (pieces) of silver as his price, and they wrote the following contract:

> I, Jesus the son of Joseph, craftsman from the village Bethlehem of Judah, declare that I have sold Judas Thomas, my slave, to Habban, the merchant of king Gudnaphar.

When they completed the contract for him, Jesus led Judas and went to Habban the merchant. Habban saw him and said to him, "Is this your master?" Judas says to him, "Yes, he is my master." Habban the merchant says to him, "He has in fact sold you to me." Judas was silent before him.

In the morning, he (Judas Thomas) rose and prayed. He addressed his Lord and said to him, "Behold, my Lord, however you want, may your will be done." He went unto Habban the merchant while taking nothing with him except his price, for our Lord had given it to him. Judas went and found Habban the merchant while he was bringing vessels aboard his ship. He began to bring (them) with him. When they had gone up (aboard) and sat, Habban the merchant says to Judas, "What is the skill that you are able to do?" Judas says to him, "Carpentry and masonry, the work of a craftsman." Habban the merchant says to him, "What do you know to make in wood and what in cut stone?" Judas says to him, "In wood, I have learned to make ploughs, yokes, goads, oars for river boats, and masts for ships; in stones: tombs, shrines, temples, and palaces for kings." Habban the merchant says to him, "And such is the skilled man for whom I was searching." They began to sail because a wind had risen. They were sailing steadily until they put in at Sanadrūk (or: Sandarūk, Sandrūk), the city (or: town, fortress).

APPENDIX 2

Beginning of Greek *Acts of Thomas* (Bonnet's text)

Note: I checked and improved my translation against the translations and commentaries of Attridge and Klijn; some phrasings are theirs.

Acts of the holy Apostle Thomas

1. During that time we, all the apostles, were in Jerusalem: Simon, the one called Peter, and Andrew, his brother; Jacob, the son of Zebedee and John, his brother; Philip and Bartholomew; Thomas and Matthew, the tax-collector; Jacob, the son of Alphaios and Simon the Kananite; and Judas, the son of Jacob. We divided all the regions of the world so that each one of us would travel in the region allotted to him and among the people in which the Lord sent him. India then fell by lot to Judas Thomas, the one who is also "Twin" (Didymos). But he was refusing to go forth, while saying that he could not go because of the weakness of his flesh, and "How am I, being a Hebrew man, able to travel among the Indians to proclaim the Truth?" When he was reasoning and speaking thus, the Savior appeared to him in the night and said to him, "Do not fear Thomas; go forth to India and preach the Word there. For my grace is with you." But he was not obedient and said, "Send me wherever else you want to send me. For I am not going forth to India."

2. While he (Judas Thomas) was speaking and had his heart set in this way, it happened that a certain merchant, who had come from India, was there. His name was Abbanes; he had been sent by king Goundaphores and had received a command from him to buy and bring a craftsman to him. The Lord, seeing him walking around the marketplace at noon, said to him, "Do you want to buy a craftsman?" And he said to him, "Yes." The Lord said to him, "I have a craftsman slave and I want to sell him." Having said this, he showed Thomas to him from a distance and settled with him for three litrai of (silver) bullion. He wrote a contract saying,

> I, Jesus son of the craftsman Joseph, declare that I have sold my slave named Judas to you, Abbanes the merchant of Goundaphores, king of India.

When the contract was completed, the Savior, taking with him Judas, the one who is also Thomas, led him off to Abbanes the merchant. When Abbanes saw him, he said to him, "Is this your master?" And the apostle said in response, "Yes, he is my master." He (Abbanes) says, "I purchased you from him." And the apostle kept his peace.

3. The next morning, while he prayed and beseeched the Lord, the apostle said, "I go wherever you want, Lord Jesus. May your will be done." He went off to Abbanes the merchant while carrying off nothing with him other than his price alone. For the Lord had given it to him while saying, "May also your price, along with my grace, be with you wherever you may go." The apostle overtook Abbanes just as he was bringing vessels aboard his ship. And so he began to bring them aboard with him too. When they had boarded the ship and had sat down, Abbanes questioned the apostle, while saying, "What sort of craft do you know?" And he (Judas Thomas) said, "In wood: ploughs, yokes, scales, ships, oars for ships, masts, and wheels; in stone: pillars, temples, and royal palaces." Abbanes the merchant said to him, "For I in fact need such a craftsman." So they began to sail. They had a favorable wind, and they sailed smoothly until they arrived at Andrapolis, a royal city (or: the city called Enadroch [or Enadoch, or Edron] of India).

Bibliography

Greek and Latin Sources (with Additional Sources in the Secondary Literature)

Acts of the Apostles and the New Testament Gospels. Ed. Eberhard Nestle, Erwin Nestle/Kurt Aland, Barbara Aland, *Novum Testamentum Graece et Latine*. 26th edn. Stuttgart: Deutsche Bibelgesellschaft, 1984.

Acts of Judas Thomas (Greek). Ed. Maximilian Bonnet, *Acta Apostolorum Apocrypha*, pt. 2, Vol. 2. Leipzig: H. Mendelsohn, 1903 (repr. Hildesheim: Olms, 1959), 99–291.

Acts of Philip. Ed. François Bovon, Bertrand Bouvier, and Frédéric Amsler, *Acta Philippi*. 2 vols. CCSA 11. Turnhout: Brepols, 1999.

Alexander of Lycopolis, *Disputation against the Manichaeans (Disp.)*. Ed. Augustus Brinkmann, *Alexandri Lycopolitani contra Manichaei opiniones disputatio*. Stuttgart: Teubner, 1885.

Ambrose, *Exposition on Twelve Psalms (in Ps.)*. Ed. Michael Petschenig, *Sancti Ambrosii Opera*, pars. 6: *Expositio Psalmorum XII*. CSEL 64. Vienna: Tempsky, 1962.

Arnobius, *Against the Pagans*. Ed. Augustus Reifferscheid, *Arnobii Adversus nationes libri VII*. CSEL 4. Vienna: C. Geroldi, 1875.

Arrian, *Anabasis*. Ed. A. G. Roos, *Flavii Arriani quae exstant omnia*, Vol. 1: *Alexandri Anabasis*. Edn. corr. Leipzig: Teubner, 1967.

Arrian, *Indica*. Ed. A. G. Roos, *Flavii Arriani quae exstant omnia*, Vol. 2: *Scripta minora et fragmenta*. Edn. corr. Leipzig: Teubner, 1967.

Athanasius, *Apology to Constantius*. Ed. H. C. Brennecke, Uta Heil, and Annette von Stockhausen, *Athanasius: Werke*, 2.8: *Die Apologien*. Berlin: De Gruyter, 2006.

Athanasius, *Letter to the Africans*. Ed. H. C. Brennecke, Uta Heil, and Annette von Stockhausen, *Athanasius: Werke*, 2.8: *Die Apologien*. Berlin: De Gruyter, 2006.

Augustine, *Against Adimantus*. Ed. Joseph Zycha, *Sancti Aureli Augustini de utilitate credenda; De duabus animabus; Contra Fortunatum; Contra Adimantum; Contra epistulam fundamenti; Contra Faustum*. CSEL 25. Vienna: Tempsky, 1891.

Augustine, *Against Faustus*. Ed. Joseph Zycha, *Sancti Aureli Augustini de utilitate credenda; De duabus animabus; Contra Fortunatum; Contra Adimantum; Contra epistulam fundamenti; Contra Faustum*. CSEL 25. Vienna: Tempsky, 1891.

Augustine, *City of God*. Ed. Bernard Dombart and Alphonse Kalb, *Aurelii Augustini opera*, pt. 14.1: *De Civitate Dei libri I–X*. CCSL 47. Turnhout: Brepols, 1955.

Augustine, *Confessions*. Ed. Lucas Verheijen, *Aurelii Augustini opera*, pt. 1: *Confessionum libri XIII*. CCSL 27. Turnhout: Brepols, 1981.

Augustus, *Res Gestae*. Ed. and trans. John Scheid, *Res Gestae divi Augusti: hauts faits du divin Auguste*. Paris: Les Belles Lettres, 2007.

Augustine, *Sermon on the Mount*. Ed. A. Mutzenbecher, *Aurelii Augustini opera*, pt. 7.2: *De sermone domini in monte, libros duos*. CCSL 35. Turnhout: Brepols, 1967.

Births and Deaths of the Patriarchs. Ed. J. C. Fraga, *Liber de ortu et obitu patriarcharum*. CCSL 108E. Turnhout: Brepols, 1996.

Cassius Dio. Ed. U. P. Boissevain, *Cassii Dionis Cocceiani Historiarum romanarum quae supersunt*. 5 vols. Berlin: Weidmann, 1895–1931.

Clement of Alexandria, *Stromateis*. Ed. Otto Stählin and Ludwig Früchtel, *Clemens Alexandrinus*, Vol. 2: *Stromata, Buch I–VI*. GCS 52. 4th edn. Berlin: Akademie Verlag, 2011.

Clementine Recognitions. Ed. Bernhard Rehm and Georg Streker, *Die Pseudoklementinen*, Vol. 2: *Rekognitionen in Rufins Übersetzung*. GCS 51. 2nd edn. Berlin: Akademie Verlag, 2011.

Cologne Mani Codex. Ed. and trans. Ludwig Koenen and Cornelia Römer, *Der Kölner Mani-Kodex: über das Werden seines Leibes*. Cologne: Westdeutscher Verlag, 1987.

Cosmas Indicopleustes, *Christian Topography*. Ed. and trans. Wanda Wolska-Conus, *Cosmas Indicopleustès: topographie chrétienne*. SC 141, 159, and 197. 3 vols. Paris: Cerf, 1968–1973.

Cyril of Jerusalem, *Catecheses*. Ed. W. C. Reischl and J. Rupp, *Cyrilli Hierosolymarum archiepiscopi opera quae supersunt omnia*. 2 vols. Munich: Sumtibus Librariae Lentnerianae, 1848–60; repr. Hildesheim: Olms, 1967.

Digesta. Ed. Theodor Mommsen and Paul Krueger (trans. Alan Watson), *The Digest of Justinian*. 4 vols. Philadelphia: University of Pennsylvania Press, 1985.

Dio Chrysostom. Ed. J. de Arnim, *Dionis Prusaensis, quem vocant Chrysostomum, quae exstant omnia*. 2nd edn. 2 vols. Berlin: Weidmann, 1962.

Epiphanius, *Panarion*. Ed. Karl Holl, *Epiphanius*. GCS, N. F. 13. 2nd edn. 5 vols. Berlin: Akademie Verlag, 1980–2013.

Epiphanius, *De gemmis*. PG 43, cols. 293–304; Ed. O. Günther, *Epistulae imperatorum pontificum aliorum*, Vol. 2. Vienna, Tempsky, 1898: 743–73. Ed. and trans. Robert Blake and Henri de Vis, *Epiphanius de Gemmis: The Old Georgian Version and the Fragments of the Armenian Version, and the Coptic-Sahidic Fragments*. London: Christophers, 1934; Ed. and trans. Felix Albrecht and Arthur Manukyan, *Epiphanius von Salamis: über die zwölf Steine im hohepriesterlichen Brustschild (de duodecim gemmis rationalis)*. Piscataway, NJ: Gorgias, 2014.

Eusebius, *Ecclesiastical History (HE)*. Ed. Eduard Schwartz and Theodor Mommsen, *Die Kirchengeschichte*. GCS, N. F. 6. 2nd edn. 3 vols. Berlin: Akademie Verlag, 1999.
Eusebius, *Life of Constantine (VC)*. Ed. Friedhelm Winkelmann, *Eusebius: Werke* 1.1: *Über das Leben des Kaisers Konstantin*. 2nd edn. Berlin: Akademie Verlag, 1975.
Eusebius, *Preparation for the Gospel*. Ed. Karl Mras and Édouard des Places, *Eusebius: Werke 8: Die Praeparatio evangelica*. GCS 43. 2nd edn. 2 vols. Berlin: de Gruyter, 2012.
Exposition of the Entire World. Ed. and trans. Jean Rougé, *Expositio totius mundi et gentium*. SC 124. Paris: Cerf, 1966.
Gaudentius of Brescia, *Tractates (Tract.)*. Ed. Ambruse Glück, *S. Gaudentii episcopi brixiensis tractatus*. CSEL 68. Vienna: Hoelder-Pichler-Tempsky, 1936.
Gregory of Nazianzus, *Orations (Or. 33)*. Ed. and trans. Claudio Moreschini, *Grégoire de Nazianze: Discours 32–37*. SC 318. Paris: Cerf, 1985.
Gregory of Nyssa, *Against Eunomius (Eun.)*. Ed. and trans. W. Jaeger, *Contre Eunome*. SC 521, 524, and 551. Paris: Cerf, 2007–2013.
Gregory of Tours, *Glory of the Martyrs*. Ed. Wilhelm Arndt and Bruno Krusch, *Monumenta Germaniae Historica: Scriptores Rerum Merovingicarum*, Vol. 1: *Gregorii Turonensis opera*. Hanover: Bibliopolii Hahniani, 1885.
Gregory the Great, *Homilia in Evangelia*. Ed. and trans. Raymond Étaix, Charles Morel, and Bruno Judic, *Homélies sur l'évangile*. SC 485 and 522. 2 vols. Paris: Cerf, 2005–2008.
Horace. *Q. Horati Flacci opera*. Ed. D. R. Shackleton-Bailey. Stuttgart: Teubner, 1985.
Incomplete Work on Matthew. Opus imperfectum in Matthaeum. PG 56: 611–946.
Isidore of Charax, *Mansiones Parthicae*. Ed Karl Müller, *Geographi Graeci Minores*. 2 vols. Paris: Firmin-Didot, 1861–1865: 1.244–56.
Isidore of Seville, *Births and Deaths of the Fathers*. Ed. and trans. César Casparro Gómez, *Isidoro de Sevilla: de ortu et obitu patrum*. Paris: Belles Lettres, 1985.
Itinerary from Eden (Hodoiporia apo Edem). Ed. and trans. Jean Rougé, *Expositio totius mundi et gentium*. SC. 124. Paris: Cerf, 1966: 350–55.
Itinerary of Antoninus Placentinus (Antonini Placentini Itinerarium). Ed. P. Geyer in *Itineraria et alia Geographica*. CCSL 175. Turnhout: Brepols, 1965: 127–74.
Itinerary of Egeria. Ed. and trans. Pierre Maraval, *Journal de voyage: itinéraire, Egérie*. SC 296. Paris: Cerf, 1997.
Jerome, *Letters (Ep.)*. Ed. Isidore Hilberg, *Sancti Eusebii Hieronymi epistulae*. CSEL 54. Edn. alt. 3 vols. in 4 pts. Vienna: VOAW, 1996.
Jerome, *On Illustrious Men*. Ed. Aldo Ceresa-Gestaldo, *Uomini illustri=De viris illustribus*. Florence: Nardini Editore, 1988.
John Chrysostom, *That Christ Is God: Quod Christus sit Deus*. PG 48, cols. 813–43.
John Chrysostom, *On Acts of the Apostles (Act. Apost.): In Acta Apostolorum*. PG 60, cols. 13–582.

John Chrysostom, *On John (Ioan.): In Ioannum*. PG 59, cols. 23–484.
John Chrysostom, *On the Letter to Hebrews (Ad Heb.): Ad Hebraeos*. PG 63, cols. 1–468.
John Malalas, *Chronicle*. Ed. John Thurn, *Chronographia*. Berlin: de Gruyter, 2000.
Juvenal. Ed. Jacob Willis, *Saturae sedecim: D. Iunii Iuvenalis*. Stuttgart: Teubner, 1997 and ed. Pierre de Labiolle and François Villeneuve, *Juvénal*. 12th edn. Paris: Belles Lettres, 1983.
Liber Pontificalis. Ed. L. Duchesne, *Le Liber Pontificalis: texte, introduction, et commentaire*. Paris: Boccard, 1955.
Liber Responsalis. PL 78, cols. 725–850.
Life of Alexius. Ed. Margarete Rösler, "Alexiusprobleme," *Zeitschrift für Romanische Philologie* 53 (1933): 508–28.
Marcian of Heraclea, *Periplus maris exteri*. Ed Karl Müller, *Geographi Graeci Minores*. 2 vols. Paris: Firmin-Didot, 1861–1865: 1.515–61.
Martial. Ed. D. R. Shackleton Bailey, *M. Valerii Martialis Epigrammata*. Stuttgart: Teubner, 1990.
Martyr Act of Arethas. Ed. and trans. Marina Detoraki and Joëlle Beaucamp, *Le martyre de Saint Aréthas et de ses compagnons (BHG 166)*. Paris: AACHCB, 2007.
Miracles of the Blessed Apostle Thomas (De miraculis beati Thomae apostoli). Ed. Klaus Zelzer, *Die alten lateinischen Thomasakten*. Berlin: Akademie Verlag, 1977: 45–77.
Names of the Fathers at Nicaea. Ed. Henry Gelzer, Henry Hilgenfeld, and Otto Cuntz, *Patrum Nicaenorum nomina*. Leipzig: Teubner, 1898.
Ordericus Vitalis, *Historia Ecclesiastica*. PL 188; Ed. Auguste le Prévost, *Orderici Vitalis Historiae Ecclesiasticae libri tredecim*. 5 vols. Paris: Julius Renouard et socios, 1838–55.
Origen, *Commentary on Matthew*, Latin translation. Ed. Erich Klostermann, *Origenes Werke* 11: *Origenes Matthäuserklärung* 2. GCS 38. 2nd edn. Berlin: Akademie Verlag, 2012.
Passion of the Holy Apostle Bartholomew. Ed. Maximilian Bonnet, *Acta Apostolorum Apocrypha*, pt. 2, Vol. 1. Leipzig: H. Mendelsohn, 1903 (repr. Hildesheim: Olms, 1959): 128–50.
Passion of the Holy Apostle Thomas (Passio sancti Thomae apostoli). Ed. Klaus Zelzer, *Die alten lateinischen Thomasakten*. Berlin: Akademie Verlag, 1977: 1–42.
Paulinus of Nola, *Carmina*. Ed. G. de Hartel, *S. Pontii Meropii Paulini Nolani opera*. CSEL 30. 2nd edn. Vienna: VOAW, 1999.
Peoples of India and the Brahmins. Ed. Wilhem Berghoff, *Palladius de Gentibus Indiae et Bragmanibus*. Meisenheim am Glan: Anton Hain, 1967; J. Duncan M. Derrett, "The History of Palladius on the Races of India and the Brahmans," *Classica et Mediaevalia* 21 (1960): 64–135 (text at 107–35).
Periplus Maris Erythraei (PME). Ed. and trans. Lionel Casson, *Periplus maris Erythraei: Text with Introduction, Translation, and Commentary*. Princeton: Princeton University Press, 1989.
Peter the Deacon, *On Holy Places*. Ed. R. Weber, *Itineraria et alia Geographica*. CCSL 175. Turnhout: Brepols, 1965: 91–103.

Philostorgius, *Ecclesiastical History*. Ed. Joseph Bidez and Friedhelm Winkelmann, *Philostorgius: Kirchengeschichte*. GCS 21. 3rd edn. Berlin: Akademie Verlag, 1981.
Philostratus, *Life of Apollonius*. Ed. and trans. Christopher Jones, *Apollonius of Tyana: Philostratus*. 2 vols. Cambridge, MA: Harvard University Press, 2006.
Philostratus, *Lives of the Sophists*. Ed. Carl Kayser, *Flavii Philostrati opera*, Vol. 2. Leipzig: Teubner, 1871.
Pliny the Elder, *Natural History*. Ed. Ludwig Jahn and Karl Mayoff, *C. Plini Secundi Naturalis historiae libri XXXVI*. 6 vols. Leipzig: Teubner, 1892–1909.
Porphyry, *De abstinentia*. Ed. Augustus Nauck, *Porphyrii Philosophi Platonici: opuscula selecta*. 2nd edn. Olms: Hildesheim, 1963.
Porphyry, *Fragments (De Styge)*. Ed. Andrew Smith, *Porphyrii Philosophi fragmenta*. Stuttgart: Teubner, 1993.
Pseudo-Gelasius of Cyzicus, *Ecclesiastical History*. Ed. G. C. Hansen, *Anonyme Kirchengeschichte (Gelasius Cyzicanus, CPG 6034)*. GCS, N.F. 9. Berlin: De Gruyter, 2002.
Ptolemy, *Geography*. Ed. and trans. Alfred Stückelberger and Gerd Graßhoff, *Klaudios Ptolemaios: Handbuch der Geographie*. 3 vols. Basel: Schwabe, 2006–2009.
Refutation of All Heresies. Ed. Miroslav Marcovich, *Hippolytus: Refutatio omnium haeresium*. Berlin: De Gruyter, 1986; Ed. M. David Litwa, *Refutation of All Heresies*. Atlanta. SBL Press, 2016.
Rufinus, *Ecclesiastical History (HE)*. Ed. Eduard Schwartz and Theodor Mommsen, *Die Kirchengeschichte*. GCS, N. F. 6. 2nd edn. 3 vols. Berlin: Akademie Verlag, 1999.
Septuagint. Ed. Alfred Rahlfs and Robert Hanhart, *Biblia graeca: septaginta id est vetus testamentum graece iuxta lxx interpretes*. 2nd edn. Stuttgart: Deutsche Bibelgesellschaft, 2006.
Socrates, *Ecclesiastical History (HE)*. Ed. G. C. Hansen, *Kirchengeschichte: Sokrates*. GCS, N. F. 1. Berlin: Akademie Verlag, 1995.
Sozomen, *Ecclesiastical History (HE)*. Ed. Joseph Bidez and G. C. Hansen, *Kirchengeschichte*. GCS, N.F. 4. 2nd. edn. Berlin: Akademie Verlag, 1995.
Strabo, *Geography*. Ed. Stefan Radt, *Strabons Geographika*. 10 vols. Gottingen: Vandenhoeck and Ruprecht, 2002–2011.
Theodoret, *Ecclesiastical History (HE)*. Ed. Leon Parmentier and G. C. Hansen, *Theodoret: Kirchengeschichte*. GCS, N.F. 5. 3rd edn. Berlin: Akademie Verlag, 1998.
Tibullus. Ed. Georg Luck, *Albii Tibulli aliorumque carmina*. Ed. alt. Stuttgart: Teubner, 1998.
Turribius of Asturica, *Letter to Leo*. PL 54, col. 693–94.

Sources in Near Eastern Languages (with Additional Sources in the Secondary Literature)

Acts of Judas Thomas (Syriac). Ed. and trans. William Wright, *Apocryphal Acts of the Apostles*. 2 vols. London: Williams and Norgate, 1871 (repr. Hildesheim: Olms, 1990), Vol. 1, ܡܚܬ-ܥܠܝ, Vol. 2, 146–298.

Bibliography

Acts of Mar Mari. Ed. and trans. C. and F. Jullien, *Les Actes de Mār Māri.* Louvain: Peeters, 2003; Ed. and trans. Amir Harrak, *The Acts of Mār Māri the Apostle.* Atlanta: SBL, 2005.

Aphrahat, *Demonstrations.* J. Parisot, *Patrologia Syriaca,* Vol. 1. Paris: Firmin-Didot, 1894.

Babylonian Talmud. Ed. and trans. Isidore Epstein. *Hebrew-English Edition of the Babylonian Talmud=Talmud Bavli.* 26 vols. London: Soncino, 1960–.

Barhebraeus, *Ecclesiastical Chronicle.* Ed. and trans. J.-B. Abbeloos and T. J. Lamy, *Gregorii Barhebraei Chronicon Ecclesiasticum: The Ecclesiastical Chronicle of Barhebraeus.* Leuven: Peeters, 1872–1877 (repr. Piscataway, NJ: Gorgias Press, 2012).

Book of the Laws of the Countries. Ed. and trans. H. J. W. Drijvers, *The Book of the Laws of the Countries: Dialogue on Fate of Bardaisan of Edessa.* Assen: Van Gorcum, 1964; Ed. and trans. Ilaria Ramelli, *Bardesane di Edessa: Contro il fato, κατὰ Εἱμαρμένης.* Bologna: Studio Domenicano, 2009.

Chronicle of 846. Ed. and trans. E. W. Brooks, *Chronica Minora,* Vol. 2. CSCO 3–4, Scriptores Syri 3–4. Paris: Typographeus Reipublicae, 1904.

Chronicle of 1234. Ed. J.-B. Chabot, *Anonymi auctoris Chronicon ad annum Christi 1234 pertinens.* CSCO, Scriptores Syri 36–37. Paris: Typographeus Reipublicae, 1916.

Chronicle of Arbela. Ed. and trans. Peter Kawerau, *Chronik von Arbela.* CSCO 467–68, Scriptores Syri 199–200. Leuven: Peeters, 1985.

Chronicle of Edessa. Ed. and trans. Ignazio Guidi, *Chronica minora,* Vol. 1. CSCO 1–2, Scriptores Syri 1–2. Paris: Typographeus Reipublicae, 1903.

Chronicle of pseudo-Dionysius of Tel-Mahre (or *Zuqnin Chronicle*). Ed. and trans. J.-B. Chabot, *Chronicon anonymum Pseudo-Dionysianum vulgo dictum.* CSCO 91, 104, and 121, Scriptores Syri 43, 53, and 66. Louvain: Durbecq, 1927–1949.

Chronicle of Se'ert (*Nestorian Chronicle*). Ed. and trans. Addai Scher, "Histoire nestorienne inédite: Chronique de Séert," *PO* 4–5, 7, and 13. Paris: Firmin-Didot, 1908–1919.

Cyrillona, *On the Scourges.* Ed. and trans. Carl Griffin, *The Works of Cyrillona.* Piscataway, NJ. Gorgias Press, 2016: 136–95.

Ephrem, *Against Heresies (Haer.).* Ed. and trans. Edmund Beck, *Des heiligen Ephraem des Syrers Hymnen contra Haereses.* CSCO 169–170, Scriptores Syri 76–77. Louvain: Durbecq, 1967.

Ephrem, *Nisibene Hymns (CN).* Ed. and trans. Edmund Beck, *Des heiligen Ephraem des Syrers Carmina Nisibena.* CSCO 218–19 and 240–41, Scriptores Syri 92–93 and 102–3. Louvain: Secretariat du CorpusSCO, 1961.

Gospel According to Thomas. Ed. Bentley Layton and trans. Thomas Lambdin, *Nag Hammadi Codex II, 2–7.* 2 vols. Leiden: Brill, 1989: 1.52–95.

History of Philip. Ed. and trans. William Wright, *Apocryphal Acts of the Apostles.* 2vols. London: Williams and Norgate, 1871 (repr. Hildesheim: Olms, 1990), Vol. 1, ܣ - ܒ, Vol. 2, 69–92.

Hymn of the Pearl. Ed. and trans. P.-H. Poirier, *L'Hymne de la Perle des Actes de Thomas: Introduction, Text-Traduction, Commentaire.* Louvain: Pierier, 1981: 330–36 and 350–56 (Syriac and Greek); Ed. and trans. Johan Ferreira, *The Hymn of the Pearl: The Syriac and Greek Texts with Introduction, Translation, and Notes*. Sydney: St. Paul Publications, 2002: 39–65 and 82–95 (Syriac and Greek).

Ibn al-Tayyib. Ed. and trans. W. Hoenerback and O. Spies, *Ibn aṭ-Ṭaiyib: Fiqh an-Naṣrānīya (Das Recht der Christenheit)*. 4 vols. CSCO 161–62 and 167–68, Scriptores Arabici 16–19. Louvain: Durbecq, 1956–57.

Ishoʻdad of Merv, *Commentaries*. Ed. and trans. Margaret Dunlop Gibson, *The Commentaries of Ishoʻdad of Merv, Bishop of Hadatha (c. 850 A.D.) in Syriac and English*. 5 vols. Cambridge: Cambridge University Press, 1911–1919.

Ishoʻdnah of Basra, *Book of Chastity (Liber Castitatis)*. Ed. Paul Bedjan, *Liber Superiorum*. Leipzig: Harrassowitz, 1901: 439–517 (under the title of *Liber Fundatorum Monasteriorum in regno Persarum et Arabum*).

Ishoʻyabh III, *Liber epistularum*. Ed. and trans. Rubens Duval, *Išoʻyahb Patriarchae III Liber epistularum*. CSCO 11–12, Scriptores Syri 11–12. Louvain, Secrétariat du CorpusSCO, 1962.

Jacob of Sarug, *Homilies on Thomas*. Ed. and trans. Werner Strothmann, *Drei Gedichte über den Apostel Thomas in Indien*. Wiesbaden: Harrassowitz, 1976.

John of Ephesus, *Ecclesiastical History (HE)*. Ed. and trans. E. W. Brooks, in *Iohannis Ephesini Historiae ecclesiasticae pars tertia*, 2 vols. CSCO 54–55, Scriptores Syri 54–55. Louvain: Durbecq, 1952.

John of Ephesus, *Lives of the Eastern Saints*. Ed. and trans. E. W. Brooks in *PO* 17–19. Paris: Firmin-Didot, 1923–1925.

Julian Romance. Ed. G. R. Hoffmann, *Iulianos der Abtruennige*. Leiden: Brill, 1880; Ed. and trans. Michael Sokoloff, *The Julian Romance: a New English Translation*. Piscataway, NJ: Gorgias, 2016.

Kephalaia. Ed. and trans. Hans Jakob Polotsky and Alexander Böhlig, *Kephalaia*, Vol. 1. Stuttgart: Kohlhammer, 1940.

Life of Mar Giwargis. Ed. Paul Bedjan, *Histoire de Mar-Jabalaha, de trois autres patriarches, d'un prêtre et de deux laïques, nestoriens*. Leipzig: Harrassowitz, 1895.

Manichaean Psalms. Ed. and trans. C. R. C. Allberry, *A Manichaean Psalm-Book*, pt. 2. Stuttgart: Kohlhammer, 1938; for the psalms of Heracleides, also Siegfried Richter, *Liber psalmorum [Psalm Book]*, pt. 2, fasc. 2: *die Herakleides-psalmen*. Turnhout: Brepols, 1996.

Mari ibn Sulayman. Ed. and trans. Enrico Gismondi, *Maris, Amri, et Slibae de patriarchis Nestorianorum commentaria*. 4 vols. in 2 pts. Rome: C. de Luigi, 1896–1899.

Martyr Act of the Blessed Simeon bar Sabbaʻe. Ed. M. Kmosko, "Martyrium de beato Simeone Bar Sabbaʻe," *Patrologia Syriaca* 2.1. Paris: Firmin-Didot, 1907: 715–79.

Martyr Act of Candida. Ed. and trans. Sebastian Brock, "A Martyr at the Sasanid Court under Vahran II: Candida," *AB* (1978): 167–81.

Michael the Syrian, *Chronicle*. Ed. and trans. J.-B. Chabot, *Chronique de Michel le Syrien Patriarche Jacobite d'Antioche (1166–1199)*. Paris: Leroux, 1899–1910.

Narration for the Blessed Simeon bar Sabbaʻe. Ed. M. Kmosko, "Narratio de beato Simeone Bar Sabbaʻe," *Patrologia Syriaca* 2.1. Paris: Firmin-Didot, 1907: 780–960.
Old Man of Edessa. Ed. Arthur Amiaud. *Le légende syriaque de Saint Alexis, l'homme de dieu.* Paris: F. Vieweg, 1889.
Old Syriac Gospels. Ed. Agnes Smith Lewis, *The Old Syriac Gospel, or, Evangelion da-Mepharreshē: Being the Text of the Sinai or Syro-Antiochene Palimpsest.* London: William and Norgate, 1910; F. Crawford Burkitt, *Evangelion da-Mepharreshe: The Curetonian Version of the Four Gospels.* Cambridge: Cambridge University Press, 1904; George Anton Kiraz, *Comparative Edition of the Syriac Gospels: Aligning the Sinaiticus, Curetonianus, Peshitta, and Harklean Versions.* Leiden: Brill, 1996.
Res Gestae of Shapur. Ed. and trans. Philip Huyse, *Die dreisprachige Inschrift Šabuhrs I. an der Kaʻba-i Zardušt (ŠKZ).* London: School of Oriental and African Studies, 1999.
Solomon of Basra, *Book of the Bee.* Ed. and trans. Earnest Wallis Budge, *Book of the Bee.* Oxford: Clarendon, 1886.
Synodicon orientale. Ed. and trans. J.-B. Chabot, *Synodicon orientale.* Paris: Librarie Klincksieck, 1902; repr. Piscataway, NJ: Gorgias Press, 2010.
Syriac Peshitta. Ed. P. E. Pusey and G. H. Gwilliam, *Tetraeuangelium Sanctum juxta simplicem Syrorum versionem ad fidem codicum, massorae, editionum denuo regcognitum.* Oxford: Clarendon Press, 1901; George Anton Kiraz, *Comparative Edition of the Syriac Gospels: Aligning the Sinaiticus, Curetonianus, Peshitta, and Harklean Versions.* Leiden: Brill, 1996.
Teaching of Addai. Ed. George Phillips, *The Doctrine of Addai, the Apostle, Now Edited in a Complete Form in the Original Syriac.* London: Trübner and Co., 1876. Repr. in George Howard, *The Teaching of Addai.* Chico, CA: Scholars Press, 1981.
Teaching of the Apostles (*Doctrina apostolorum*). Ed. and trans. William Cureton, *Ancient Syriac Documents.* London: William and Norgate, 1864: ܗܕ- ܠܡ; Arthur Vööbus, *The Synodicon in the West Syrian Tradition.* 4 vols. CSCO 367–70, Scriptores Syri 161–64. Louvain: CorpusSCO: 1.200–11.
Thomas the Contender. Ed. Bentley Layton and trans. John Turner, *Nag Hammadi Codex II, 2–7.* 2 vols. Leiden: Brill, 1989: 2.180–95.

Secondary Literature

Abdy, Richard. 2012. "Tetrarchy and the House of Constantine," in William Metcalf (ed.), 584–600. *The Oxford Handbook of Greek and Roman Coinage.* Oxford: Oxford University Press.
Adams, Colin. 2007. *Land Transport in Roman Egypt: A Study of Economics and Administration in a Roman Province.* Oxford: Oxford University Press.
Alston, Richard. 1998. "Trade and the City in Roman Egypt," in Helen Parkins and Christopher Smith (eds.), 168–202. *Trade, Traders, and the Ancient City.* London: Routledge.

Amar, Joseph. 2014. "A Shared Voice: When Jews and Christians Drank from the Same Wells," *TLS* (Oct. 2): 14–15.
Amidon, Philip. 2007. *Philostorgius: A Church History*. Atlanta, GA: Society of Biblical Literature.
Andrade, Nathanael. 2012 [2014]. "Inscribing the Citizen: Soados and the Civic Context of Palmyra," *Maarav* 19.1–2: 65–90.
Andrade, Nathanael. 2013. *Syrian Identity in the Greco-Roman World*. Cambridge: Cambridge University Press.
Andrade, Nathanael. 2015 [2016]. "The Voyage of Maes Titianos and the Dynamics of Social Connectivity between the Roman Levant and Central Asia/West China," *Mediterraneo antico* 16.2: 41–74.
Andrade, Nathanael. 2015. "The Syriac *Book of the Laws of the Countries*, Eusebius' *Preparation for the Gospel*, and *The Clementine Recognitions*: Early Witnesses for Christianity in Central Asia?" *Electrum* 22: 155–67.
Andrade, Nathanael. 2017. "Drops of Greek in a Multilingual Sea: The Egyptian Network and Its Residential Presences in the Indian Ocean," *Journal of Hellenic Studies* 137: 42–66.
Andreas, F. C. and Walter Henning. 1933. *Mitteliranische Manichaica aus Chinesisch-Turkestan*, Vol. 2. Berlin: Verlag der Akademie der Wissenschaften.
Anuja, Nama. 2016. "The British Museum Hariti: Toward Understanding Transculturalism in Gandhara," in Susan Alock, Mariana Egri, and James F. D. Frakes (eds.), 247–65. *Beyond Boundaries: Connecting Visual Cultures in the Provinces of Ancient Rome*. Los Angeles, CA: Getty Publications.
Arbach, Mounir. 2009. "Les visiteurs de Shabwa du VIIe s. av. J.-C. au IIIe s. ap. J.-C.," in Jean-François Breton (ed.), 289–93. *Shabwa et son context architectural et artistique du Ier siècle avant J.-C au IVe siècle après J.-C*. Beirut: IFPO.
Arnaud, Pascal. 2012. "*Le Periplus Maris Erythraei*: une œuvre de compilation aux préoccupations géographiques," in Boussac, Salles, and Yon (eds.), 27–61.
Aslanian, Sebouh David. 2011. *From the Indian Ocean to the Mediterranean: The Global Trade Networks of Armenian Merchants from New Julfa*. Berkeley: University of California Press.
Assemani, G. S. 1719–1728. *Bibliotheca orientalis clementino-vaticana*. 3 vols. in 4 pts. Rome.
Athikalam, James. 2002. "St. Thomas the Apostle and Thomas Christians," *Studia Missionalia* 51: 333–51.
Attridge, Harold. 1990. "The Original Language of the Acts of Thomas," in Harold Attridge, John Collins, and Thomas Tobin (eds.), 241–50. *Of Scribes and Scrolls: Studies on the Hebrew Bible, Intertestamental Judaism, and Christian Origins*. Lanham, MD: University Press of America.
Attridge, Harold. 2010. *The Acts of Thomas*. London: Polebridge.
Atwood, Christopher. 2012. "Huns and Xiongnu: New Thoughts on an Old Problem," in Brian Boeck (ed.), 27–52. *Dubitando: Studies in History and Culture in Honor of Donald Ostrowski*. Bloomington, IN: Slavica Publishers.
Aubert, Jean-Jacques. 2015. "Trajan's Canal: River Navigation from the Nile to the Red Sea," in de Romanis and Maiuro (eds.), 33–42.

Aubet, Maria Eugenia. 2013. *Commerce and Colonization in the Ancient Near East.* Trans. Mary Turton. Cambridge: Cambridge University Press.
Avanzini, Alessandra. 2008. "Notes for a History of Sumhuram and a New Inscription of Yashhur'il," in Alessandra Avanzini (ed.), 609–44. *A Port in Arabia between Rome and the Indian Ocean, 3rd c. BC-5th c. AD*: *Khor Rori, Report 2*. Rome: Bretschneider.
Avanzini, Alessandra. 2015. "The Port of Sumhuram (Khor Rori): New Data on Its History," in Mathew (ed.), 179–206.
Bagnall, Roger. 1985. *Currency and Inflation in Fourth Century Egypt.* Chico, CA: Scholars Press.
Bagnall, Roger, Christina Helms, Arthur M. F. W. Verhoogt et al. 2000–2005. *Documents from Berenike.* 2 vols. Brussels: Fondation Égyptologique Reine Élisabeth.
Bambourg, Gilles. 2015. "The Later Roman Empire," in Andrew Monson and Walter Scheidel (eds.), 258–81. *Fiscal Regimes and the Political Economy of Premodern States.* Cambridge: Cambridge University Press.
Banaji, Jairus. 2007. *Agrarian Change in Late Antiquity: Gold, Labour, and Aristocratic Dominance.* Updated edn. Oxford: Oxford University Press.
Banaji, Jairus. 2015. "'Regions that Look Seaward': Changing Fortunes, Submerged Histories, and the Slow Capitalism of the Sea," in de Romanis and Maiuro (eds.), 114–26.
Bang, Peter Fibiger. 2008. *The Roman Bazaar: A Comparative Study of Trade and Markets in a Tributary Empire.* Cambridge: Cambridge University Press.
Bang, Peter Fibiger and C. A. Bayly. 2011. *Tributary Empires in Global History.* New York: Palgrave Macmillan.
Bang, Peter Fibiger and C. A. Bayly. 2011. "Tributary Empires: Towards a Global Comparative History," in Bang and Bayly (eds.), 1–20.
Barabási, Albert-László. 2002. *Linked: The New Science of Networks.* Cambridge, MA: Perseus Pub.
Barabási, Albert-László. 2003. *Linked: How Everything Is Connected to Everything Else and What It Means for Business, Science, and Everyday Life.* New York: Plume.
Barnes, T. D. 1980. "The Editions of Eusebius' Ecclesiastical History," *GRBS* 21: 191–201.
Barnes, T. D. 1981. *Constantine and Eusebius.* Cambridge, MA: Harvard University Press.
Barton, Carlin and Daniel Boyarin. 2016. *Imagine No Religion: How Modern Abstractions Hide Ancient Realities.* New York: Fordham University Press.
Basset, René. 1907. "Le Synaxaire arabe jacobite (rédaction copte)," *PO* 1. Paris: Firmin-Didot: 219–379.
Baum, Wilhelm and Dietmar Winkler. 2003. *The Church of the East: A Concise History.* London: Routledge.
Baumer, Christoph. 2016. *The Church of the East: An Illustrated History of Assyrian Christianity.* New edn. London: Tauris.
Bayan, George. 1910. "Le Synaxaire Arménien de Ter Israël," *PO* 5. Paris: Firmin-Didot,: 344–556.

Beaujard, Philippe. 2010. "From Three Possible Iron-Age World-Systems to a Single Afro-Eurasian World-System," *JWH* 21.1: 1–43.
Beaujard, Philippe. 2012. *Les mondes de l'océan Indien*. 2 vols. Paris: Armand Colin.
Becker, Adam. 2002. "Anti-Judaism and Care for the Poor in Aphrahat's Demonstration 20," *JECS* 10.3: 305–27.
Becker, Adam and Annette Yoshiko Reed. 2003. *The Ways That Never Parted: Jews and Christians in Late Antiquity and the Early Middle Ages*. Tübingen: Mohr Siebeck.
Beckwith, Christopher. 2015. *Greek Buddha: Pyrrho's Encounter with Early Buddhism in Central Asia*. Princeton: Princeton University Press.
BeDuhn, Jason. 2010–2013. *Augustine's Manichaean Dilemma*. 2 vols. Philadelphia: University of Pennsylvania Press.
BeDuhn, Jason. 2013. "'Not to Depart from Christ'," in Van Oort (ed.), 1–18.
BeDuhn, Jason. 2015. "Parallels between Coptic and Iranian *Kephalaia:* Goundesh and the King of Touran," in Gardner, BeDuhn, and Dilley (eds.), 52–74.
BeDuhn, Jason. 2015. "Iranian Epic in the Chester Beatty *Kephalaia*," in Gardner, BeDuhn, and Dilley (eds.), 136–58.
BeDuhn, Jason. 2015. "Mani and the Crystallization of the Concept of 'Religion' in Third Century Iran," in Gardner, BeDuhn, and Dilley (eds.), 247–76.
BeDuhn, Jason and Paul Mirecki. 2007. *Frontiers of Faith: The Christian Encounter with Manichaeism in the Acts of Archelaus*. Leiden: Brill.
BeDuhn, Jason and Paul Mirecki. 2007. "Placing *the Acts of Archelaus*," in BeDuhn and Mirecki (eds.), 1–22.
Begley, Vimala. 1996. "Changing Perceptions of Arikamedu," in Begley et al. (eds.), 1.1–40.
Begley, Vimala et al. 1996–2004. *The Ancient Port of Arikamedu: New Excavations and Researches 1989–1992*. 2 vols. Paris: École Française d'Extrême-Orient.
Belfiore, Stefano. 2004. *Il periplo del Mare Eritreo di anonimo del I sec. d.C*. Rome: Società geografica italiana.
Bellina, Bérénice and Ian Glover. 2004. "The Archaeology of Early Contact with India and the Mediterranean World, from the Fourth Century BC to the Fourth Century AD," in Ian Glover and P. Bellwood (eds.), 68–88. *Southeast Asia, from the Prehistory to History*. London: Routledge.
Bentley, R. A. 2003. "Introduction to Complex Systems," in R. A. Bentley and H. D. G. Maschner (eds.), 9–23. *Complex Systems and Archaeology*. Salt Lake City: University of Utah Press.
Bentley. R. A. 2003. "Scale-Free Network Growth and Social Inequality," in R. A. Bently and H. D. G. Maschner (eds.), 27–45. *Complex Systems and Archaeology*. Salt Lake City: University of Utah Press.
Berggren, J. Lennart and Alexander Jones. 2000. *Ptolemy's Geography: An Annotated Translation of the Theoretical Chapters*. Princeton, NJ: Princeton University Press.
Bernand, André. 1972. *Le Paneion d'El-Kanaïs: les inscriptions grecques*. Leiden: Brill.
Bernand, André. 1984. *Les portes du désert: recueil des inscriptions grecques d'Antinooupolis, Tentyris, Koptos, Apollonopolis Parva et Apollonopolis Magna*. Paris: ECNRS.

Bernand, André and Olivier Masson. 1957. "Les inscriptions grecques d'Abou-Simbel," *REG* 70: 1–46.
Bernard, Paul. 2005. "De l'Euphrate à la Chine avec la caravane de Maès Titianos (c. 100 ap. n. è)," *CRAI* 149.3: 929–69.
Bernard, Paul et al. 1973–1992. *Fouilles d'Aï Khanoum*. 8 vols. Paris: Klinksieck.
Bernard, P, G.-J. Pinault, and G. Rougemont. 2004. "Deux nouvelles inscriptions grecques de l'Asie centrale," *Journal des savants*: 227–356.
Bertolino, Roberto. 2004. *Corpus des inscriptions semitiques de Doura-Europos*. Naples: Istituto Orientale.
Biffi, Nicola. 2005. *L'estremo oriente di Strabone: libro XV della Geografia*. Bari: Edipuglia.
Biffi, Nicola. 2011. "Ciò che Bardesane venne a sapere sull'India," *Classica et Christiana* 6.2: 305–35.
Bivar, A. D. H. 2007. "Gondophares and the Indo-Parthians," in Vesta S. Curtis and Sarah Stewart (eds.), 26–36. *The Age of the Parthians*. London: Tauris.
Blasi, Anthony, Jean Duhaime, and Paul-André Turcotte. 2002. *Handbook of Early Christianity: Social Science Approaches*. Walnut Creek, CA: Altamira, 2002.
Blue, Lucy. 2009. "Boats, Routes, and Sailing Conditions of Indo-Roman Trade," in Tomber, Blue, and Abraham (eds.), 3–13.
Blue, Lucy, J. D. Hill, and Ross Thomas. 2012. "New Light on the Nature of Indo-Roman Trade: Roman Period Shipwrecks in the Northern Red Sea," in Dionisius Agius et al. (eds.), 91–100. *Navigated Spaces, Connected Places: Proceedings of the Red Sea Project V*. Oxford: Archaeopress.
Boccaccini, Gabriele. 1991. *Middle Judaism: Jewish Thought, 300 B.C.E to 200 C.E.* Minneapolis, MN: Fortress Press.
Bonnet, Maximilian. 1903. See *Acts of Judas Thomas* (Greek).
Bopearachchi, Osmund. 1993. *Indo-Greek, Indo-Scythian, and Indo-Parthian Coins in the Smithsonian Institution*. Washington, DC: National Numismatic Collection, Smithsonian Institution.
Bopearachchi, Osmund. 1998. "Indo-Parthians," in Josef Wiesehöfer (ed.), 389–406. *Das Partherreich und seine Zeugnisse/The Arsacid Empire: Sources and Documentation*. Stuttgart: Steiner.
Bopearachchi, Osmund and M.-F. Boussac. 2005. *Afghanistan, ancien carrefour entre l'Est et l'Ouest*. Turnhout: Brepols.
Boussac, M.-F. 2014. "Revisiting the *Periplus Maris Erythraei*: Some Notes on Recent Studies," in Rila Mukherjee (ed.), 177–92. *Vanguards of Globalization: Port-cities from the Classical to the Modern*. Delhi: Primus.
Boussac, M.-F., J.-F. Salles, and J.-B Yon. 2012. *Autour du Périple de la mer Érythrée*. Lyon: MOM.
Boussac, M.-F., J.-F. Salles, and J.-B. Yon. 2016. *Ports of the Ancient Indian Ocean*. Delhi: Primus.
Bowersock, G. W. 2010. "New Greek Inscription from South Yemen," in J.-F. Salles and A. Sedov (eds.), 393–96.
Bowersock, G. W. 2013. Review of J.-B. Yon, "*Inscriptions grecques et latines de la Syrie* 17.1: *Palmyre*," *Syria* 90: 515–16.

Bowersock, G. W. 2013. *The Throne of Adulis: Red Sea Wars on the Eve of Islam.* Oxford: Oxford University Press.
Boyarin, Daniel. 2004. *Border Lines: The Partition of Judaeo-Christianity.* Philadelphia: University of Pennsylvania Press.
Brancaccio, Pia. 2013. *Living Rock: Buddhist, Hindu, and Jain Cave Temples in the Western Deccan.* Mumbai: Marg.
Bremmer, Jan. 2001. "The *Acts of Thomas*: Place, Date, Women," in Jan Bremmer (ed.), 74–90. *The Apocryphal Acts of Thomas.* Leuven: Peeters.
Briquel-Chattonnet, F. 2010. "L'expansion du christianisme en Arabie: l'apport des sources syriaques," *Semitica et Classica* 3: 177–81.
Briquel-Chattonnet, F. 2010. "Les *graffiti* en langues nord-sémitiques de Bir 'Ali (Qāni)," in Salles and Sedov (eds.), 387–88.
Briquel-Chattonnet, F. 2012. "Syriac Manuscripts in India, Syriac Manuscripts from India," *Hugoye* 15.2: 289–99.
Briquel-Chattonnet, F., A. Desreumeux, and J. Thekeparampil. 1998. "Découverte d'un manuscrit très important contenant des textes apocryphes dans la bibliothèque de la métropole de l'Église de l'Est à Trichus, Kérala, Inde," in René Lavenant (ed.), 587–97. *Symposium Syriacum VII.* Rome: Pontificio Istituto Orientale.
Brock, Sebastian. 1976. "Syriac Sources for Seventh-Century History," *BMGS* 2: 17–36.
Brock, Sebastian. 1979–1980. "Syriac Historical Writing: a Survey of the Main Sources," *Journal of the Iraq Academy, Syriac Corporation* 5: 1–30.
Brock, Sebastian. 1981–1982. "A Syriac Life of John of Dailam," *Parole de l'Orient* 10: 123–89.
Brock, Sebastian. 1992. "Eusebius and Syriac Christianity," in Harold Attridge and Gohei Hata (eds.), 212–34. *Eusebius, Christianity, and Judaism.* Leiden: Brill.
Brock. Sebastian. 1995. "Bar Shabba (Mar Shabbay), First Bishop of Merv," in Martin Tamcke, Wolfgang Schwaigert, and Egbert Schlarb (eds.), 190–201. *Syrisches Christentum weltweit: Studien zur syrischen Kirchengeschichte: Festschrift Prof. Wolfgang Hage.* Münster: LIT.
Brock, Sebastian. 1999–2000. "Syriac Writers from Beth Qatraye," *Aram* 11–12: 85–96.
Brock, Sebastian. 2007. "Syria and Mesopotamia: The Shared Term *Malka Mshiḥa*," in Markus Bockmuehl and James Carleton Paget (eds.), 171–82. *Redemption and Resistance: the Messianic Hopes of Jews and Christians in Antiquity.* London: T & T Clark.
Brock, Sebastian. 2008. *The History of the Holy Mar Ma'in with a Guide to the Persian Martyr Acts.* Piscataway, NJ: Gorgias.
Brock, Sebastian. 2008. "Saints in Syriac: A Little-Tapped Resource," *JECS* 16.2: 181–96.
Brock, Sebastian. 2011. "Thomas Christians," in Sebastian Brock et al. (eds.), 410–14. *Gorgias Encyclopedic History of the Syriac Heritage.* Piscataway, NJ: Gorgias Press.
Brock, Sebastian, with David G.K. Taylor. 2001. *The Hidden Pearl*, Vol. 2. Rome: Trans World.

Brock, Sebastian and Lukas Van Rompay. 2014. *Catalogue of Syriac Manuscripts and Fragments in the Library of Deir al-Surian, Wadi al-Natrun (Egypt)*. Leuven: Peeters.

Brockelmann, Carl and Michael Sokoloff. 2009. *A Syriac Lexicon*. Winona Lake, IN: Eisenbrauns.

Brodersen, Kai. 1995. *Terra cognita: Studien zur römischen Raumerfassung*. Hildesheim: Olms.

Brody, Lisa and Gail Hoffman. 2011. *Dura-Europos: Crossroads of Antiquity*. Chesnut Hill, MA: McMullen Museum of Art.

Brown, Leslie. 1956. *The Indian Christians of St. Thomas: An Account of the Ancient Syrian Church of Malabar*. Cambridge: Cambridge University Press.

Bukharin, Mikhail. 2012. "The Coastal Arabia and the Adjacent Sea-Basins in the *Periplus of the Erythrean Sea* (Trade, Geography, and Navigation)," in Boussac, Salles, and Yon (eds.), 177–236.

Bukharin, Mikhail. 2012. "The Greek Inscriptions at Hoq," in Strauch (ed.), 493–500.

Bukharin, Mikhail. 2012. "Greeks on Socotra: Commercial Contacts and Early Christian Missions," in Strauch (ed.), 501–39.

Burgess, J. A. S. 1883. *Report on the Buddhist Cave Temples and Their Inscriptions*. London: Trüber & Co.

Burgess, J. A. S. and Bhagvanlal Indraji. 1881. *Inscriptions from the Cave Temples of Western India*. Bombay: Government Central Press.

Burgess, R. W. 1997. "The Dates and Editions of Eusebius' *Chronici Canones* and *Historia Ecclesiastica*," *JThS* 47: 147–58.

Burrow, T. and M. B. Emeneau. 1984. *A Dravidian Etymological Dictionary*. 2nd edn. Oxford: Clarendon Press.

Burrus, Virginia. 2004. *The Sex Lives of the Saints: An Erotics of Ancient Hagiography*. Philadelphia: University of Pennsylvania Press.

Burstein, Stanley. 2010. "New Light on the Fate of Greek in Central and South Asia," *Ancient West and East* 8: 181–92.

Burt, R. S. 1999. "The Social Capital of Opinion Leaders," *The Annals of the American Academy of Political and Social Science* 566.1: 37–54.

Calvet, Yves. 1997. "Monuments paléo-chrétiens à Koweit et dans la region du Golfe," in R. Lavenant (ed.), 671–85. *Symposium Syriacum VII*. Rome: Pontificio Istituto orientale.

Cameron, Averil. 2015. "Christian Conversion in Late Antiquity: Some Issues," in Averil Cameron (ed.), 3–22. *Conversion in Late Antiquity: Christianity, Islam, and Beyond*. Burlington, VT: Ashgate.

Canepa, Matthew (ed.). 2010. *Theorizing Cross-Cultural Interaction among the Ancient and Early Medieval Mediterranean, Near East, and Asia*. Washington, DC: Smithsonian.

Carrington, Peter, John Scott, and Stanley Wasserman. 2005. *Models and Methods in Social Network Analysis*. Cambridge: Cambridge University Press.

Carter, R. A. 2008. "Christianity in the Gulf during the First Centuries of Islam," *Arabian Archaeology and Epigraphy* 19: 71–108.

Carter, R. A. 2013. "Christianity in the Gulf after the Coming of Islam: Redating the Churches and Monasteries of Bet Qatraye," in Christian Julien Robin and Jérémie Schiettecatte (eds.), 311–330. *Les préludes de l'Islam: ruptures et continuités dans les civilisations du Proche-Orient, de l'Afrique orientale, de l'Arabie et de l'Inde à la veille de l'Islam*. Paris: Boccard.

Cassis, M. 2002. "Kokhe, Cradle of the Church of the East: An Archaeological and Comparative Study," *Journal of the Canadian Society for Syriac Studies* 2: 62–78.

Casson, Lionel. 1986. "P. Vindob G 40822 and the Shipping of Goods from India," *Bulletin of the American Society of Papyrologists* 23.3–4: 73–79.

Casson, Lionel. 1989. *Periplus maris Erythraei: Text with Introduction, Translation, and Commentary*. Princeton: Princeton University Press.

Casson, Lionel. 1990. "New Light on Maritime Loans: P. Vindob G 40822," *ZPE* 84: 195–206.

Cereti, Carlo. 2009. "Pahlavi Signatures on the Quilon Copper Plates (Tabula Quilonensis)," in Werner Sundermann, Almut Hintze, and François de Blois (eds.), 31–50. *Exegisti monumenta: Festschrift in Honour of Nicholas Sims-Williams*. Wiesbaden: Harrassowitz.

Cereti, Carlo, Luca Olivieri, and Joseph Vazhuthanapally. 2002. "The Problem of the St. Thomas Crosses and Related Questions: Epigraphical Survey and Preliminary Research," *East and West* 52.1: 285–310.

Chakrabarti, Dilip. 2001. *Archaeological Geography of the Ganga Plain: the Lower and Middle Ganga*. Delhi: Permanent Black.

Chakrabarti, Dilip. 2006. "Relating History to the Land: Urban Centers, Geographical Units, and Trade Routes in the Gangetic and Central India of Circa 200 BCE," in Patrick Olivelle (ed.), 5-31. *Between the Empires: Society in India 300 BC to 400 CE*. Oxford: Oxford University Press.

Champakalakshmi, R. 2011. *Religion, Tradition, and Ideology: Pre-Colonial South India*. New Delhi: Oxford University Press.

Charloux, Guillaume and Romolo Loreto. 2014-2015. *Dûma: Report of the Saudi-Italian-French Archaeological Project at Dûmat al-Jandal*. 2 vols. Riyadh: Saudi Commission for Tourism and Antiquities. Available at https://hal.archives-ouvertes.fr/hal-00997906 and https://hal.archives-ouvertes.fr/hal-01509443/. Accessed December 1, 2017.

Cherian, P. J. 2011. *Pattanam Excavations 2011: Fifth Season Field Report*. Available at http://www.keralahistory.ac.in/pdf2014/ptm2011_field%2520Report.pdf. Accessed December 1, 2017.

Cherian, P. J. 2013. *Interim Report of the Pattanam Excavations/Explorations 2013*. Thiruvananthapuram: Kerala Council for Historical Research.

Cherian, P. J. 2014. *Unearthing Pattanam: Histories, Cultures, Crossings*. New Delhi: National Museum.

Chi, Jennifer and Sebastian Heath. 2011. *Edge of Empires: Pagans, Jews, and Christians at Roman Dura-Europos*. New York, NY: ISAW.

Chin, Catherine. 2006. "Rhetorical Practice in the Chreia Elaboration of Mara bar Serapion," *Hugoye* 9.2: 157–84 (pars. 1–23).

Ciancaglini, Claudia. 2008. *Iranian Loanwords in Syriac*. Wiesbaden: Reichert.

Clarke, Graeme. 2005. "Third-Century Christianity," in Alan Bowman, Averil Cameron, and Peter Garnsey (eds.), 589–671. *The Cambridge Ancient History*, Vol. 12: *The Crisis of Empire*. Cambridge: Cambridge University Press.
Cobb, Matthew Adam. 2014. "The Exchange of Goods from Italy to India during the Early Empire: The Range of Travel Times," *Ancient West and East* 13: 89–116.
Cobb, Matthew Adam. 2015. "Balancing the Trade: Roman Cargo Shipments to India," *Oxford Journal of Archaeology* 34.2: 185–203.
Cogan, Mordechai. 2000. *1 Kings: A New Translation with Introduction and Commentary*. New York: Doubleday.
Cohen, Getzel. 2006. *The Hellenistic Settlements in Syria, the Red Sea Basin, and North Africa*. Berkeley: University of California Press.
Cohen, Getzel. 2013. *The Hellenistic Settlements in the East from Armenia and Mesopotamia to Bactria and India*. Berkeley: University of California Press.
Collar, Anna. 2011. "Military Networks and the Cult of Jupiter Dolichenus," in Engelbert Winter (ed.), 217–46. *Von Kummuh nach Telouch: historische und archäologische Untersuchungen in Kommagene*. Bonn: Habelt.
Collar, Anna. 2012. "Commagene, Communication, and the Cult of Jupiter Dolichenus," in Michael Blömer and Engelbert Winter (eds.), 99–110. *Iuppiter Dolichenus*. Tübingen: Mohr Siebeck.
Collar, Anna. 2013. *Religious Networks in the Roman Empire: the Spread of New Ideas*. Cambridge: Cambridge University Press.
Colless, Brian. 1969. "Persian Merchants and Missionaries in Medieval Malaya," *Journal of the Malaysian Branch of the Royal Asiatic Society* 42.2: 10–47.
Coloru, Omar. 2009. *Da Alessandro a Menadro: il regno Greco di Battriana*. Pisa: Serra.
Comneno, Maria. 1998. "Nestorianism in Central Asia during the First Millennium: Archaeological Evidence," *Journal of the Assyrian Academic Society* 12.2: 20–67.
Conte, Rose. 2010. "'Seri' e 'Sini': fonti pagane e cristiane," *Linguistica Zero* 2: 56–93.
Corbier, Mireille. 2005. "Coinage and Taxation: The State's Point of View, A. D. 193–337," in Alan Bowman, Averil Cameron, and Peter Garnsey (eds.), 327–92. *The Cambridge Ancient History*, Vol. 12: *The Crisis of Empire*. Cambridge: Cambridge University Press.
Cracco Ruggini, Lellia. 1965. "Sulla cristianizzazione della cultura pagana: il mito Greco e Latino di Alessandro dall'età Antonina al Medioevo," *Athenaeum* 43: 3-80.
Cribb, Joe. 1985. "New Evidence for Indo-Parthian Political History," in Martin Price (ed.), 282–300. *Coin Hoards*, Vol. 7. New York, NY: ANS.
Cribb, Joe. 1992. "Numismatic Evidence for the Date of the 'Periplus'," in D. W. MacDowall, Savita Sharma, and Sanjay Garg (eds.), 131–45. *Indian Numismatics, History, Art, and Culture*, Vol. 1. Delhi: Agam Kala Prakashan.
Cribb, Joe. 1998. "Western Satraps and Satavahanas: Old and New Ideas of Chronology," in Amiteshwar Jha and S. Gerg (eds.), 167–82. *Ex Moneta: Essays on Numismatics, History, and Archaeology in Honour of Dr. David W. MacDowall*. New Delhi: Harman Publishing House.
Cribb, Joe. 1999. "The Early Kushan Kings: New Evidence for Chronology – Evidence from the Rabatak Inscription of Kanishka I," in Michael Alram and

Deborah E. Klimburg-Salter (eds.), 177–205. *Coins, Art, and Archaeology: Essays on the Pre-Islamic History of the Indo-Iranian Borderlands.* Vienna: OAW.

Crone, Patricia. 2012. *The Nativist Prophets of Early Islamic Iran: Rural Revolt and Local Zoroastrianism.* Cambridge: Cambridge University Press.

Cumont, Franz. 1926. *Fouilles de Doura-Europos (1922–1923).* 2 vols. Paris: Geuthner.

Cussini, Eleonora. 1998. Review of Andreas Schmidt-Colinet, "*Palmyra: Kulturbegegnung im Grenzbereich,*" *JAOS* 118.1: 142–43.

Dąbrowa, Edward. 2012. "The Arsacid Empire," in Touraj Daryaee (ed.), 164–87. *The Oxford Handbook of Iranian History.* Oxford: Oxford University Press.

Dąbrowa, Edward. 2013. "The Parthian Aristocracy: Its Social Position and Political Activity," *Parthica* 15: 53–62.

Dahlmann, Joseph. 1912. *Die Thomaslegende und die ältesten historischen Beziehungen des Christentums zum fernen Osten im Lichte der indischen Altertumskunde.* Freiburg: Herder.

Dan, Anca. "Maes Titianos," *FGrH* 2213.

Darley, Rebecca. 2014. "Indo-Byzantine Exchange, 4th to 7th Centuries: A Global History." PhD Diss: Birmingham University.

Darley, Rebecca. 2015. "Self, Other, and the Use and Appropriation of Late Roman Coins in Peninsular India (4th to 7th Centuries CE)," in H. P. Ray (ed.), 60–86. *Negotiating Cultural Identity: Landscapes in Early Medieval South Asian History.* London: Routledge.

Daryaee, Touraj. 2009. *Sasanian Persia: The Rise and Fall of an Empire.* London: Tauris.

D'Crux, F. A. 1929. *St. Thomas the Apostle in India: An Investigation Based on the Latest Research in Connection with the Time-Honoured Tradition Regarding St. Thomas in Southern India.* Madras: Premium Press.

De Jong, Albert. 2014. "The *Cologne Mani Codex* and the Life of Zarathushtra," in Geoffrey Herman (ed.), 129–48. *Jews, Christians, and Zoroastrians: Religious Dynamics in a Sasanian Context.* Piscataway, NJ: Gorgias Press.

De Romanis, Federico. 1997. "Rome and the *Notia* of India: Relations between Rome and Southern India from 30 BC to the Flavian Period," in Federico de Romanis and André Tchernia (eds.), 80–160. *Crossings: Early Mediterranean Contacts with India.* New Delhi: Manohar.

De Romanis, Federico. 1997. "Romanukharaṭṭha and Taprobane: Relations between Rome and Sri Lanka in the First Century CE," in Federico de Romanis and André Tchernia (eds.), 161–237. *Crossings: Early Mediterranean Contacts with India.* New Delhi: Manohar.

De Romanis, Federico. 2006. "*Aurei* after the Trade: Western Taxes and Eastern Gifts," in Federico de Romanis and Sara Sorda (eds.), 54–82. *Dal denarius al dinar: l'Oriente e la moneta romana.* Rome: Istituto Italiano di Numismatica.

De Romanis, Federico. 2010–2011. "Playing Sudoku on the Verso of the 'Muziris Papyrus': Malabathron and Tortoise Shell in the Cargo of the *Hermapollon*," *Journal of Ancient Indian History* 27: 75–101.

De Romanis, Federico. 2015. "Comparative Perspectives on the Pepper Trade," in de Romanis and Maiuro (eds.), 127–50.
De Romanis, Federico. 2015. "A Muziris Export: Schidai or Ivory Trimmings," in Mathew (ed.), 369–80.
De Romanis, Federico and Marco Maiuro. 2015. *Across the Ocean: Nine Essays on Indo-Mediterranean Trade*. Leiden: Brill.
Debié, Muriel, Michel-Yves Perrin, and Jean-Pierre Mahé. 2010. "L'Orient chrétien non byzantin," in Pascal Montaubin and Michel-Yves Perrin (eds.), 611–46. *Histoire générale du christianisme*, Vol. 1: *Des origines aux XVe siècle*. Paris: Presses Universitaires de France.
Decker, Michael. 2009. "Export Wine Trade to West and East," in M. M. Mango (ed.), 239–52. *Byzantine Trade, 4th–12th Centuries: The Archaeology of Local, Regional, and International Exchange*. Farnham: Ashgate.
Decker, Michael. 2009. *Tilling the Hateful Earth: Agricultural Production and Trade in the Late Antique East*. Oxford: Oxford University Press.
Decker, Michael. 2010. "Settlement and Trade in the Red Sea in Late Antiquity: An Archaeological Perspective," *Ancient West and East* 9: 193–220.
Deeg, Max and Iain Gardner. 2009. "Indian Influence on Mani Reconsidered: The Case of Jainism," *International Journal of Jaina Studies* 5.2: 1–30.
Delplace, Christiane. 2014. "Palmyre, de la ville – centre commercial international – à la ville – centre militaire et chrétien," in E. B. Aitken and J. M. Fossey (eds.), 225–35. *The Levant: Crossroads of Late Antiquity: History, Religion, and Archaeology*. Leiden: Brill.
Delplace, Christiane and J.-B. Yon. 2005. "Les inscriptions de l'agora," in Christiane Delplace and Jacqueline Dentzer-Feydy (eds.), *L'agora de Palmyre*. Bordeaux-Beirut: IFAPO.
Derrett, J. Duncan M. 1962. "The Theban Scholasticus and Malabar in c. 355–600," *JAOS* 82.1: 21–31.
Devadhar, C. R. 1981–1984. *Works of Kalidasa*. 2 vols. Delhi: Motilal Banarsidass.
Devos, P. 1966. "Les martyrs persans à travers leurs actes syriaques," in *Atti del convegno sul tema Persia e il mondo Greco-romano*, 213–25. Rome: Accademia Nazionale.
Devos, P. 1966. "Sozomène et les actes syriaques de S. Syméon Bar Ṣabbaʿe," *AB* 84.3-4: 443–56.
Di Segni, Leah and Yoram Tsafrir. 2012. "The Ethnic Composition of Jerusalem's Population in the Byzantine Period," *Liber Annuus* 62: 405–54.
Dijkstra, Jitse. 2013. "The Religious Transformation of Lower Nubia in Late Antiquity," in Jacques van der Vliet and J. L. Hagen (eds.) 111–22. *Qasr Ibrim, between Egypt and Africa: Studies in Cultural Exchange*. Leiden: Nederlands Instituut voor het Nabije Oosten.
Dijkstra, M. and A. M. F. W. Verhoogt. 1999. "The Greek-Palmyrene Inscription," in Steven Sidebotham and W. Wendrich (eds.), 207–18. *Berenike 1997*. Leiden: Research School CNWS.
Dikshitar, V. R. Ramachandra. 1952. *Selected South Indian Inscriptions: Tamil, Telugu, Malayalam, and Kannada*. Madras: University of Madras.

Dilley, Paul. 2013. "Religious Intercrossing in Late Antique Eurasia: Loss, Corruption, and Canon Formation," *JWH* 24.1: 25–70.
Dilley, Paul. 2015. "Also Schrieb Zarathustra? Mani as Interpreter of the 'Law of Zarades'," in Gardner, BeDuhn, and Dilley (eds.), 101–35.
Dilley, Paul. 2015. "'Hell Exists, and We have Seen the Place Where It Is': Rapture and Religious Competition in Sasanian Iran," in Gardner, BeDuhn, and Dilley (eds.), 211–246.
Dilley, Paul. 2015. "Mani's Wisdom at the Court of the Persian Kings: the Genre and Context of the Chester Beatty *Kephalaia*," in Gardner, BeDuhn, and Dilley (eds.), 15–51.
Dirven, Lucinda. 1999. *The Palmyrenes of Dura-Europos: A Study of Religious Interaction in Roman Syria.* Leiden: Brill.
Dognini, Cristiano. 2001. "La nascita di Krsna," in Dognini and Ramelli (eds.), 83–90.
Dognini, Cristiano. 2001. "I primi contatti fra il cristianesimo e il buddhismo," in Dognini and Ramelli (eds.), 91–102.
Dognini, Cristiano and Ilaria Ramelli. 2001. *Gli apostoli in India: nella patristica e nella letteratura sanscrita.* Milan: Medusa.
Dolbeau, François. 1986. "Une liste ancienne d'apôtres et de disciples, traduite du grec par Moïse de Bergame," *AB* 104: 299–314.
Dolbeau, François. 1990. "Une liste latine de disciples et d'apôtres," *AB* 108: 50–70.
Dolbeau, François. 1994. "Nouvelles recherches sur le *de ortu et obitu prophetarum et apostolorum*," *Augustinianum* 34: 91–107.
Dolbeau, François. 2005. "Listes d'apôtres et de disciples," in Pierre Geoltrain and Jean-Daniel Kaestli (eds.), 455–80. *Écrits apocryphes chrétiens*, Vol. 2. Paris: Gallimard.
Dolbeau, François. 2012. *Prophètes, apôtres et disciples dans les traditions chrétiennes d'Occident: vies brèves et listes en latin.* Brussels: Bollandistes.
Drake, H. A. 2005. "Models of Christian Expansion," in Harris (ed.), 1–14.
Dridi, Hédi. 2012. "Remarks on the Egyptian Branch of the Palmyrene Trade," in Strauch (ed.), 486–87.
Drijvers, H. J. W. 1975. "Bardaisan von Edessa als Repräsentant des syrischen Synkretismus im 2. Jahrhundert n. Chr.," in A. Dietrich (ed.), 109–22. *Synkretismus im syrisch-persischen Kulturgebiet.* Gottingen: Vandenhoeck und Ruprecht.
Drijvers, H. J. W. 1984. "Addai und Mani: Christentum und Manichäismus im dritten Jahrhundert in Syrien," in René Lavenant (ed.), 171–85. *Symposium Syriacum III: les contacts du monde syriaque avec les autres cultures.* Rome: Pontificio Istituto Orientale.
Drijvers, H. J. W. 1984. *East of Antioch: Studies in Early Syriac Christianity.* London: Variorum.
Drijvers, H. J. W. 1991. "*The Acts of Thomas*," in Wilhelm Schneemelcher and R. McL. Wilson (eds.), 322–411. *New Testament Apocrypha*, Vol. 2: *Writings Related to the Apostles: Apocalypses and Related Subjects.* Rev. edn. Cambridge: Clark and Co.

Drijvers, H. J. W. and J. F. Healey. 1999. *Old Syriac Inscriptions of Edessa and Osrhoene*. Leiden: Brill.
Dumvile, David and Simon Keynes (gen. eds.). 1983–. *The Anglo-Saxon Chronicle: A Collaborative Edition*. Cambridge: D.S. Brewer.
Dunn, James. 2013. "The Rise and Expansion of Christianity in the First Three Centuries C. E.: Why and How did Embryonic Christianity Expand Beyond the Jewish People?" in Rothschild and Schröter (eds.), 183–204.
Edward, James. 2009. *The Hebrew Gospel and the Development of the Synoptic Tradition*. Grand Rapids, MI: Eerdmans.
Ellerbrock, Uwe and Sylvia Winkelmann. 2012. *Die Parther: die vergessene Großmacht*. Mainz: Zabern.
Errington, Elizabeth and V. S. Curtis. 2014. *From Persia to Punjab: Exploring Ancient Iran, Afghanistan, and Pakistan*. Mumbai: Chatrapati Shivaji Maharaj Vastu Sangrahalaya.
Esler, Philip. 1996. *Modeling Early Christianity: Social-scientific Studies of the New Testament in Its Context*. London: Routledge.
Estiot, Sylviane. 2012. "The Later Third Century," in William Metcalf (ed.), 538–60. *The Oxford Handbook of Greek and Roman Coinage*. Oxford: Oxford University Press.
Fabricius, Johan. 1718. *Bibliotheca Ecclesiastica*. 4 pts. in 1 vol. Hamburg.
Fabricius, Johan. 1719. *Codex apocryphus Novi Testamenti*. 3 vols. in 2 pts. Hamburg.
Falk, Harry. 2004. "The Kaniska Era in Gupta Records," *Silk Road Art and Archaeology* 10: 167–76.
Falk, Harry. 2007. "Ancient Indian Eras: An Overview," *Bulletin of the Asia Institute* 21: 131–45.
Falk, Harry. 2015. "Indian Gold Crossing the Indian Ocean through the Millennia," in de Romanis and Maiuro (eds.), 97–113.
Faller, Stefan. 2000. *Taprobane im Wandel der Zeit: das Sri Lanka-Bild in griechischen und lateinischen Quellen zwischen Alexanderzug und Spätantike*. Stuttgart: Steiner.
Farquhar, John Nicol. 1926. "The Apostle Thomas in North India," *Bulletin of the John Rylands University Library* 10.1: 80–111.
Farquhar, John Nicol 1927. *The Apostle Thomas in North India*. Manchester: University of Manchester Press.
Farquhar, John Nicol. 1927. "The Apostle Thomas in South India," *Bulletin of the John Rylands University Library* 11.1: 20–50.
Farquhar, John Nicol. 1972. *The Apostle Thomas in India According to the Acts of Thomas*. Kottayam: Syrian Churches.
Fauconnier, Bram. 2012. "Graeco-Roman Merchants in the Indian Ocean: Revealing a Multicultural Trade," in Boussac, Salles, and Yon (eds.), 75–109.
Feissel, Denis, Jean Gascou, and Javier Teixidor. 1997. "Documents d'archives romains inédits du Moyen Euphrate (IIIe siècle après J-C)," *Journal des savants*: 3–57.
Fenn, Nina and Christiane Römer-Strehl. 2013. *Networks in the Mediterranean World: According to the Pottery in the Eastern Mediterranean and Beyond*. Oxford: Archaeopress.

Fenwick, J. 2009. *The Forgotten Bishops: The Malabar Independent Syrian Church and Its Place in the Story of the St. Thomas Christians of South India*. Piscataway, NJ: Gorgias Press.

Ferreira, Johan. 2002. *The Hymn of the Pearl: The Syriac and Greek Texts with Introduction, Translation, and Notes*. Sydney: St. Paul's Publications.

Fiaccadori, Gianfranco. 1983. "Teofilo Indiano: parte I, le origini," *Studi classici e orientali* 33: 295–331.

Fiaccadori, Gianfranco. 1984. "Teofilo Indiano: parte II, il viaggio," *Studi classici e orientali* 34: 271–308.

Fiey, J.-M. 1966. "Icho'dnah, métropolite de Basra, et son œuvre," *L'Orient Syrien* 11: 431–50.

Fiey, J.-M. *Saints syriaques*. 2004. Princeton: Darwin Press.

Fischel, Walter. 1967. "The Exploration of the Jewish Antiquities of Cochin on the Malabar Coast," *JAOS* 87.3: 230–47.

Fitzpatrick, Matthew. 2011. "Provincializing Rome: The Indian Trade Ocean Trade Network and Roman Imperialism," *JWH* 22.1: 27–54.

Fowden, Garth. 2013. *Before and After Muhammad: The First Millennium Refocused*. Princeton, NJ: Princeton University Press.

Francis, Emmanuel. 2013. *Le discours royal dans l'Inde du Sud ancienne: inscriptions et monuments pallava (IVème-IXème siècles)*, Vol. 1: *Introduction et sources*. Louvain-la-Neuve: Institut Orientaliste.

Frank, Andre Gunder and Barry Gills. 1993. "The 5000 Year World System," in Frank and Gills (eds.), 3–55.

Frank, Andre Gunder and Barry Gills. 1993. *The World System: Five Hundred Years or Five Thousand?* London: Routledge.

Frankfurter, David. 1998. *Religion in Roman Egypt: Assimilation and Resistance*. Princeton, NJ: Princeton University Press.

Frankopan, Peter. 2016. *The Silk Roads: A New History of the World*. New York, NY: Knopf.

Freyne, Seán. 2014. *The Jesus Movement and Its Expansion: Meaning and Mission*. Grand Rapids, MI: Eerdmans.

Frye, Richard. 1984. *The History of Ancient Iran*. Munich: C. H. Beck'sche Verlagsbuchhandlung.

Frykenberg, Robert. 1999. "India," in Adrian Hastings (ed.), 147–92. *A World History of Christianity*. Grand Rapids, MI: Eerdmans.

Frykenberg, Robert. 2003. "Christians in India: An Historical Overview of Their Complex Origins," in Robert Frykenberg (ed.), 33–61. *Christians and Missionaries in India: Cross-Cultural Communication since 1500*. Grand Rapids, MI: Eerdmans.

Frykenberg, Robert. 2008. *Christianity in India: From Beginnings to the Present*. Oxford: Oxford University Press.

Fuks, Alexander. 1951, "Notes on the Archives of Nicanor," *Journal of Juristic Papyrology*: 207–16.

Gaiffier, Baudouin de. 1963. "Une ancienne liste des localités où reposent les apôtres," in *Varii* (ed.), 365–71. *L'homme devant Dieu: mélanges offerts au père Henri de Lubac*, Vol. 1. Paris: Aubier.

Gardner, Iain. 2005. "Some Comments on Mani and Indian Religions According to the Coptic *Kephalaia*," in A. van Tongerloo (ed.), 123–36. *Il Manicheismo: nuove prospettive della richerca*. Turnhout: Brepols.
Gardner, Iain. 2015. "Mani's Last Days," in Gardner, BeDuhn, and Dilley (eds.), 159–208.
Gardner, Iain, Jason BeDuhn, and Paul Dilley. 2015. *Mani at the Court of the Persian Kings: Studies on the Chester Beatty* Kephalaia *Codex*. Leiden: Brill.
Gardner, Iain and Samuel Lieu. 2004. *Manichaean Texts from the Roman Empire*. Cambridge: Cambridge University Press.
Gawlikowski, Michal. 2016. "Trade across Frontiers: Foreign Relations of a Caravan City," in Jørgen Christian Meyer, Eivind Seland, and Nils Anfinset (eds.), 19–28. *Palmyrena: City, Hinterland, and Caravan Trade between Orient and Occident*. Oxford: Archaeopress.
Gebhardt, Oscar von. 1896. *Hieronymus de viris inlustribus in griechischer Übersetzung (der sogenannte Sophronius)*. Leipzig: Hinrichs.
Ghosh, A. 1956. "Museums and Exhibitions," *Indian Archaeology 1955–1956: a Review*, 59–64.
Ghosh, Suchandra. 2007. "Understanding Transitions at the Crossroads of Asia: Second Century B.C.E. to c. Third Century C.E.," *Studies in History* 23: 289–310.
Gibbs, Matt. 2012. "Manufacture, Trade, and the Economy," in Christina Riggs (ed.), 33–55. *The Oxford Handbook of Roman Egypt*. Oxford: Oxford University Press.
Gielen, Martin. 1990. *St. Thomas the Apostle of India*. Kottayam: Oriental Institute.
Gignoux, Philippe. 1983. "Titres et fonctions religieuses sassanides d'après les sources syriaques hagiographiques," *Acta Antiqua Academiae Scientiarum Hungaricae* 28: 191–203.
Gignoux, Philippe. 1986. *Iranisches Personennamenbuch*, Vol. 2.2: *Mitteliranische Personennamen*. Vienna: VOAW.
Gignoux, Philippe. 1991. *Les quatre inscriptions du mage Kirdīr: textes et concordances*. Leuven: Peeters.
Gignoux, Philippe, Christelle Jullien, and Florence Jullien. 2009. *Iranisches Personennamenbuch*, Vol. 7.5: *Noms propres syriaques d'origine iranienne*. Vienna: VOAW.
Glancy, Jennifer. 2012. "Slavery in *Acts of Thomas*," *Journal of Early Christian History* 2: 3–21.
Goitein, S. D. 1973. *Letters of Medieval Jewish Traders*. Princeton, NJ: Princeton University Press.
Goitein, S. D and Mordechai Akiva Friedman. 2008. *India Traders of the Middle Ages: Documents from the Cairo Geniza ("India Book")*. Leiden: Brill.
Goldberg, Jessica. 2012. "Choosing and Enforcing Business Relationships in the Eleventh-Century Mediterranean: Reassessing the 'Maghribī traders," *Past and Present* 215.1–2: 3–40.
Goldberg, Jessica. 2012. *Trade and Institutions in the Medieval Mediterranean: The Geniza Merchants and Their Business World*. Cambridge: Cambridge University Press.

Goldenberg, David. 2003. *The Curse of Ham: Race and Slavery in Early Judaism, Christianity, and Islam*. Princeton, NJ: Princeton University Press.
Gooren, Henri. 2010. *Religious Conversion and Disaffiliation: Tracing Patterns of Change in Faith Practices*. New York: Palgrave Macmillan.
Gorea, Maria. 2012. "The Palmyrene Tablette 'De Geest'," in Strauch (ed.), 449–57.
Gorea, Maria. 2012. "The Sea and Inland Trade of Palmyra," in Strauch (ed.), 463–85.
Green, Joel and Lee Martin MacDonald. 2013. *The World of the New Testament: Cultural, Social, and Historical Contexts*. Grand Rapids, MI: Baker.
Gregoratti, Leonardo. 2010. "The Palmyrenes and Arsacid Policy," *Vosprosy Epigrafiki* 4: 29–36.
Gregoratti, Leonardo. 2011. "A Parthian Port on the Persian Gulf: Characene and Its Trade," *Anabasis: Studia Classica et Orientalia* 2: 209–29.
Gregoratti, Leonardo. 2015. "Palmyra, City and Territory through Epigraphic Sources," in Giorgio Affanni et al. (eds.), 55–59. *Broadening Horizons*, Vol. 4. Oxford: Archaeopress.
Gregoratti, Leonardo. 2015. "The Parthian Empire: Romans, Jews, Greeks, Nomads, and Chinese on the Silk Road," in Mariko Namba Walter and James P. Ito-Adler (ed.), 43–70. *The Silk Road: Interwoven History*, Vol. 1: *Long-Distance Trade, Culture, and Society*. Cambridge, MA: Cambridge Institutes Press.
Griffin, Carl. 2016. *Cyrillona: A Critical Study and Commentary*. Piscataway, NJ: Gorgias.
Griffith, Sidney. 2003. "The *Doctrina Addai* as a Paradigm of Christian Thought in Edessa in the Fifth Century," *Hugoye* 6.2: 269–92.
Guignard, Christophe. 2015. "La tradition grecque de la liste d'apôtres 'Anonyme I' (*BHG* 153c), avec un appendice sur la liste *BHG* 152n," *Apocrypha* 26: 171–209.
Guignard, Christophe. 2016. "Greek Lists of the Apostles: New Findings and Questions," *Zeitschrift für Antikes Christentum* 20.3: 469–95.
Gundert, H. 1844. "Translations and Analysis of the Ancient Documents Engraved on Copper in Possession of the Syrian Christians and Jews of Malabar," *Madras Journal* 30: 115–47.
Gunther, J. J. 1980. "The Meaning and Origin of the Name 'Judas Thomas'," *Le Museon* 93: 113–48.
Gurukkal, Rajan. 2010. *Social Formations of Early South India*. New Delhi: Oxford University Press.
Gurukkal, Rajan. 2016. *Rethinking Classical Indo-Roman Trade: Political Economy of Eastern Mediterranean Exchange Relations*. New Delhi: Oxford University Press.
Gurukkal, Rajan and C. R. Whittaker. 2001. "In Search of Muziris," *JRA* 14.1: 334–50.
Gyselen, Rika. 1989. *La géographie administrative de l'empire sassanide: les témoignages sillographiques*. Paris: GECMO.
Haar Romeny, Bas ter. 2005. "The Syriac Versions of the Old Testament," in P. P. Khoury and P. G. Rahme (eds.), 58–83. *Nos sources: art et littérature syriaques*. Beirut: CERO.

Haas, Christopher. 1997. *Alexandria in Late Antiquity: Topography and Social Conflict*. Baltimore: Johns Hopkins University Press.
Haas, Christopher. 2008. "Mountain Constantines: The Christianization of Aksum and Iberia," *Journal of Late Antiquity* 1.1: 101–26.
Habicht, Christian. 2013. "Eudoxus of Cyzicus and Ptolemaic Exploration of the Sea Route to India," in Kostas Buraselis, Mary Stefanou, and Dorothy Thompson (eds.), 197–206. *The Ptolemies, the Sea, and the Nile*. Cambridge: Cambridge University Press.
Hackl, Ursula, Bruno Jacobs, and Dieter Weber. 2010. *Quellen zur Geschichte des Partherreiches: Textsammlung mit Übersetzungen und Kommentaren*. 3 vols. Gottingen: Vandenhoeck and Ruprecht.
Hage, Wolfgang. 2007. *Das orientalische Christentum*. Stuttgart: Kohlhammer.
Hall, Edith. 2012. *Adventures with Iphigenia in Tauris: A Cultural History of Euripides' Black Sea Tragedy*. Oxford: Oxford University Press.
Hansen, Valerie. 2012. *The Silk Road: A New History*. Oxford: Oxford University Press.
Harding, G. Lankester. 1971. *An Index and Concordance of Pre-Islamic Arabian Names and Inscriptions*. Toronto: University of Toronto Press.
Harmatta, J. 1999. *History of Civilizations of Central Asia*, Vol. 2: *The Development of Sedentary and Nomadic Civilizations, 700 BC to AD 250*. Paris: UNESCO.
Harper, Kyle. 2011. *Slavery in the Roman World, AD 275–425*. Cambridge: Cambridge University Press.
Harrak, Amir. 1999. *The Chronicle of Zuqnin, Parts III and IV: A.D. 488–775*. Toronto: Pontifical Institute of Mediaeval Studies.
Harrak, Amir. 2002. "Trade Routes and the Christianization of the Near East," *Journal of the Canadian Society for Syriac Studies* 2: 46–61.
Harrak, Amir. 2014. "Was Edessa or Adiabene the Gateway for the Christianization of Mesopotamia?" in E. B. Aitken and J. M. Fossey (eds.), 165–80. *The Levant: Crossroads of Late Antiquity: History, Religion, and Archaeology*. Leiden: Brill.
Harris, William. 2005. *The Spread of Christianity in the First Four Centuries*. Leiden: Brill.
Hart, George. 1975. *The Poems of Ancient Tamil*. Berkeley: University of California Press.
Hart, George. 2004. Review of *"Kavya in South India," JAOS* 124.1: 180–84.
Hart, George and Hank Heifetz. 1999. *The Four Hundred Songs of War and Wisdom: An Anthology of Poems from Classical Tamil, The Purananuru*. New York: Columbia University Press.
Hartmann, Udo. 2001. *Das palmyrenische Teilreich*. Stuttgart: Steiner.
Harvey, Susan Ashbrook. 2008. "Martyr Passions and Hagiography," in Susan Ashbrook Harvey and David Hunter (eds.), 603–27. *The Oxford Handbook of Early Christian Studies*. Oxford: Oxford University Press.
Hatke, George. 2013. *Aksum and Nubia: Warfare, Commerce, and Political Fictions in Ancient Northeast Africa*. New York: NYU Press.
Hauser, Stefan. 2007. "Christliche Archäologie im Sasanidenreich: Grundlagen der Interpretation und Bestandsaufnahme der Evidenz," in A. Mustafa,

J. Tubach, J. and G. S. Vashalomidze (eds.), 93–136. *Inkulturation des Christentums im Sasanidenreich*. Wiesbaden: Reichert Verlag.

Hauser, Stefan. 2008. "'Die Christen vermehrten sich in Persien und bauten Kirchen und Klöster': eine Archäologie des Christentums im Sasanidenreich," in Ulrike Koenen and Martina Müller-Wiener (eds.), 29–57. *Grenzgänge im östlichen Mittelmeerraum: Byzanz und die islamische Welt vom 9. bis 13. Jahrhundert*. Wiesbaden: Reichert.

Healey, J. F. 2007. "The Edessan Milieu and the Birth of Syriac," *Hugoye* 10.2: 115–27 (pars. 1–34).

Healey, J. F. 2008. "Variety in Early Syriac," in Holger Gzella and Margaretha Folmer (eds.), 221–30. *Aramaic in Its Historical and Linguistic Setting*. Wiesbaden: Harrassowitz.

Healey, J. F. 2009. *Aramaic Inscriptions and Documents of the Roman Period*. Oxford: Oxford University Press.

Hefner, Robert W. 1993. *Conversion to Christianity: Historical and Anthropological Perspectives on a Great Transformation*. Berkeley: University of California Press.

Herman, Geoffrey. 2013. "The Passion of Shabur, Martyred in the 18th Year of Yazdgird with a Fragment of the Life of Mar Aba Catholicos," *Journal of Semitic Studies* 58.1: 121–30.

Herman, Geoffrey. 2016. *Persian Martyr Acts under Yazdgird I*. Piscataway, NJ: Gorgias.

Hezser, Catherine. 1997. *The Social Structure of the Rabbinic Movement in Palestine*. Tübingen: Mohr Siebeck.

Hezser, Catherine. 2011. *Jewish Travel in Antiquity*. Tübingen: Mohr Siebeck.

Hiebert, Frederik and Pierre Cambon. 2008. *Afghanistan: Hidden Treasures from the National Museum, Kabul*. Washington, DC: National Geographic.

Hiley, David. 1993. *Western Plainchant: A Handbook*. Oxford: Clarendon.

Hill, John. 2015. *Through the Jade Gate to Rome: A Study of the Silk Routes during the Later Han Dynasty (1st to 2nd Centuries CE)*. Updated and expanded edn. 2 vols. Charleston, SC: Booksurge.

Ho, Engseng. 2006. *The Graves of Tarim: Genealogy and Mobility Across the Indian Ocean*. Berkeley: University of California Press.

Holt, Frank. 2012. *Lost World of the Golden King: In Search of Ancient Afghanistan*. Berkeley: University of California Press.

Hoppal, Krisztina. 2011. "The Roman Empire according to the Ancient Chinese Sources," *Acta Antiqua Academiae Scientiarum Hungaricae* 51: 263–306.

Horden, Peregrine and Nicholas Purcell. 2000. *The Corrupting Sea: A Study of Mediterranean History*. Malden, MA: Blackwell.

Hosten, Henry. 1936. *Antiquities from San Thomé and Mylapore*. Madras: Diocese of Mylapore.

Hoyland, Robert. 2001. *Arabia and the Arabs: From the Bronze Age to the Coming of Islam*. London: Routledge.

Hübner, Ulrich. 2016. "Palestine, Syria, and the Silk Road," in Lieu and Mikkelson (eds.), 19–73.

Humphries, Mark. 1998. "Trading Gods in Northern Italy," in Helen Parkins and Christopher Smith (eds.), 203–24. *Trade, Traders, and the Ancient City*. London: Routledge.
Huxley, George. 1983. "Geography in the *Acts of Thomas*," *GRBS* 24: 71–80.
Huyse, Philip. 1999. *Die dreisprachige Inschrift Šabuhrs I. an der Ka'ba-i Zardušt (ŠKZ)*. 2 vols. London: School of Oriental and African Studies.
Ingholt, Harald. 1954. *Palmyrene and Gandharan Sculpture: An Exhibition Illustrating the Cultural Interrelations between The Parthian Empire and Its Neighbors West and East, Palmyra and Gandhara*. New Haven, CT: Yale University Press.
Jacobsen, Anders-Christian, Jörg Ulrich, and David Brakke. 2009. *Critique and Apologetics: Jews, Christians, and Pagans in Antiquity*. Frankfurt: Peter Lang.
Jasim, Sabah and Eisa Yousif. 2014. "Dibba: An Ancient Port on the Gulf of Oman in the Early Roman Era," *Arabian Archaeology and Epigraphy* 25: 50–79.
Jayaswal, Vidula. 2012. *Glory of the Kushans: Recent Discoveries and Interpretations*. New Delhi: Aryan Books.
Johnson, Scott F. 2015. "Real and Imagined Geography," in Michael Maas (ed.), 394–413. *The Cambridge Companion to the Age of Attila*. Cambridge: Cambridge University Press.
Johnson, Scott F. 2016. *Literary Territories: Cartographical Thinking in Late Antiquity*. Oxford: Oxford University Press.
Jones, C. P. 2002. "Apollonius of Tyana's Passage to India," *GRBS* 42: 185–99.
Jones, C. P. 2007. "Procopius of Gaza and the Water of the Holy City," *GBRS* 47: 455–67.
Jones, F. Stanley. 2010. "Some Things Mani Learned from Jains," in Françoise Briquel-Chatonnet and Muriel Debié (eds.), 383–98. *Sur les pas des Araméens chrétiens: mélanges offerts à Alain Desreumaux*. Paris: Geuthner.
Jones, F. Stanley. 2012. *Pseudoclementina Elchasaiticaque inter Judaeochristiana: Collected Studies*. Leuven: Peeters.
Jongeward, David and Joe Cribb, with Peter Donovan. 2014. *Kushan, Kushano-Sasanian, and Kidarite Coins: a Catalogue of Coins from the American Numismatic Society*. New York, NY: the American Numismatic Society.
Joosten, Jan. 2003. "The Dura Parchment and the Diatessaron," *Vigiliae Christianae* 57.2: 159–75.
Joseph, T. K. 1927–1928. "Thomas Cana," *Indian Antiquary* 56: 161–66 and 57: 103–6, 160–65, and 209–214.
Joseph, T. K. 1928–1929. "Malabar Miscellany," *Indian Antiquary* 57: 24–30 and 58: 13–16.
Joseph, T. K. 1948. "An Indian Christian Date, 317 AD, from Hindu Documents," *Journal of Indian History* 28: 27–49.
Jouguet, Pierre. 1931. "Dédicace grecque de Médamoud," *Bulletin de l'institut français d'archéologie orientale* 31: 1–29.
Jullien, Christelle. 2004. "Contribution des Actes des martyrs perses à la géographie historique et à l'administration de l'empire sassanide," in Rika Gyselen (ed.), 141–69. *Contributions à l'histoire et à la géographie historique de l'empire sassanide*. Bures-sur-Yvette: GECMO.

Jullien, Christelle. 2006. "La minorité chrétienne 'grecque' en terre d'Iran à l'époque sassanide," in Rika Gyselen (ed.), 105–42. *Chrétiens en terre d'Iran: implantation et acculturation*. Paris: Association pour l'Avancement des Études Iraniennes.

Jullien, Christelle. 2007. "Contribution des Actes des martyrs perses à la géographie historique et à l'administration de l'empire sassanide (II)," in Rika Gyselen (ed.), 81–102. *Des Indo-Grecs aux Sassanides: données pour l'histoire et la géographie historique*. Bures-sur-Yvette: GECMO.

Jullien, Christelle. 2010. "Martyrs en Perse dans l'hagiographie syro-orientale: le tournant du VIe siècle," in Joëlle Beaucamp, Françoise Briquel-Chatonnet, and Christian Julien Robin (eds.), 279–90. *Juifs et chrétiens en Arabie: aux Ve et VIe siècles regards croisés sur les sources*. Paris: CNRS.

Jullien, Christelle. 2012. "Les Actes des martyrs perses: transmettre l'histoire," in André Binggeli (ed.), 127–40. *L'hagiographie syriaque*. Paris: Geuthner.

Jullien, Florence. 2005. "Figures fondatrices dans les apocryphes syriaques," in M. Debié et al. (eds.), 97–110. *Les apocryphes syriaques*. Paris: Geuthner.

Jullien, Florence. 2008. *Le monachisme en Perse: la réforme d'Abraham le Grand, père des moines de l'Orient*. Louvain: Peeters.

Jullien, Christelle and Florence Jullien. 2001. "La *Chronique d'Arbèles*: propositions pour la fin d'une controverse," *Oriens Christianus* 85: 41–83.

Jullien, Christelle and Florence Jullien. 2002. *Apôtres des confins: processus missionnaires chrétiens dans l'empire iranien*. Bures-sur-Yvette: GECMO.

Jullien, Christelle and Florence Jullien. 2003. *Aux origines de l'Église de Perse: les Actes de Mār Māri*. Leuven: Peeters.

Kaim, Barbara. 2012. "Serakhs Oasis at the Crossroads of Communication Routes," *Parthica* 14: 149–60.

Kaizer, Ted. 2006. "Capital Punishment at Hatra: Gods, Magistrates, and Laws in the Roman-Parthian Period," *Iraq* 68: 139–53.

Kaizer, Ted. 2010. "From Zenobia to Alexander the Sleepless: Paganism, Judaism, and Christianity at Later Roman Palmyra," in B. Bastl, V. Gassner, and U. Muss (eds.), 113–23. *Syrien-Palmyra-Rom: Festschrift für Andreas Schmidt-Colinet zum 65 Geburtstag*. Vienna: Phoibos.

Kaizer, Ted. 2013. "Questions and Problems concerning the Sudden Appearance of the Material Culture of Hatra in the First Centuries CE," in Lucinda Dirven (ed.), 57–72. *Hatra: Politics, Religion, and Culture between Roman and Parthia*. Stuttgart: Steiner.

Katz, Nathan. 2000. *Who Are the Jews of India?* Berkeley: University of California Press.

Keay, Frank Ernest. 1960. *A History of the Syrian Church in India*. 3rd edn. Delhi: I.S.P.C.K.

Kervran, Monique. 2005. *Qal'at al-Bahrain: A Trading and Military Outpost, 3rd Millennium BCE–17th Century AD*. Turnhout: Brepols.

Kervran, Monique. 2013. "Un siècle obscur de l'histoire de Tylos: 131–240 après J.-C.," in Christian Julien Robin et Jérémie Schiettecatte (eds.), 271–310. *Les préludes de l'Islam: ruptures et continuités dans les civilisations du Proche-Orient, de l'Afrique orientale, de l'Arabie et de l'Inde à la veille de l'Islam*. Paris: Boccard.

King, Karen L. 2008. "Which Early Christianity?" in Susan Ashbrook Harvey and David G. Hunter (eds.), 66–86. *The Oxford Handbook of Early Christian Studies*. Oxford: Oxford University Press.

Klauck, Hans-Josef. 2008. *The Apocryphal Acts of the Apostles: An Introduction*. Trans. Brian McNeil. Waco, TX: Baylor University Press.

Klein, W. 2005. "The Epic Buddhasarita by Aśvaghoṣa and Its Significance for the Life of Mani," in A. van Tongerloo (ed.), 223–32. *Il Manicheismo: nuove prospettive della richerca*. Turnhout: Brepols.

Klijn, A. F. J. 2003. *The Acts of Thomas: Introduction, Text, and Commentary*. Leiden: Brill.

Knappett, Carl. 2011. *An Archaeology of Interaction: Network Perspectives on Material Culture and Society*. Oxford: Oxford University Press.

Knappett, Carl. 2013. *Network Analysis in Archaeology: New Approaches to Regional Interaction*. Oxford: Oxford University Press.

Knappett, Carl. 2013. "Introduction: Why Networks?" in Knappett (ed.), 3–15.

Kolangadan, Joseph. 1995–1996. "The Historicity of Apostle Thomas Evangelization in Kerala," *The Harp* 8–9: 305–27.

Kollaparambil, Jacob. 1986. "Historical Sources on the Knanites," in Vellian (ed.), i–vi, 1–40, i–xxvi. *Symposium on Knanites*. Kottayam: Joythi Book House.

Kollaparambil, Jacob. 1992. *The Babylonian Origins of the Southists among the St. Thomas Christians*. Rome: Pontificum Istitutum.

Kollaparambil, Jacob. 1994. "The Identity of Mar John of Persia and Great India Who Attended the First Council of Nicaea," in R. Lavenant (ed.), 281–97. *Symposium Syriacum VI*. Rome: Pontificio Istituto Orientale.

Koltun-Fromm, Naomi. 2008. "Re-Imagining Tatian: The Damaging Effects of Polemical Rhetoric," *JECS* 16.1: 1–30.

König, Jason. 2009. "Novelistic and Anti-Novelistic Narrative in the *Acts of Thomas* and *Acts of Andrew and Matthias*," in Karla Grammatiki (ed.), 121–50. *Fiction on the Fringe: Novelistic Writing in the Post-Classical Age*. Leiden: Brill.

Koshelenko, G., A. Bader, and V. Gaibov. 1995. "The Beginnings of Christianity in Merv," *Iranica Antiqua* 30: 55–70.

Kosmin, Paul. 2013. "Rethinking the Hellenistic Gulf: The New Greek Inscription from Bahrain," *JHS* 133: 61–79.

Kraeling, Carl. 1956. *Excavations at Dura-Europos: Final Report*, 8.1: *The Synagogue*. New Haven, CT: Dura-Europos Publications.

Kraeling, Carl. 1967. *Excavations at Dura-Europos: Final Report*, 8.2: *The Christian Building*. New Haven, CT: Dura-Europos Publications.

Kreyenbroek, Philip. 2008. "How Pious Was Shapur I? Religion, Church, and Propaganda under the Early Sasanians," in V. S. Curtis and Sarah Stewart (eds.), 7–15. *The Sasanian Era: The Era of Iran*. London: Tauris.

Krishnamurthy, R. 2007. *Late Roman Copper Coins from South India: Karur, Madurai, and Tirukkoilur*. Chennai: Garnet.

Krueger, Derek. 2004. *Writing and Holiness: The Practice of Authorship in the Early Christian East.* Philadelphia: University of Pennsylvania Press.
Kurikilamkatt, James. 2004. "The First Port of Disembarkation of the Apostle Thomas in India According to the *Acts of Thomas,*" *Ephrem's Theological Journal* 8.1: 3–20.
Kurikilamkatt, James. 2007. *First Voyage of the Apostle Thomas to India: Ancient Christianity in Bharuch and Taxila.* Bombay: Asia Trading Company.
Lambourn, Elizabeth, Kesavan Veluthat, and Roberta Tomber. Forthcoming. *The Copper Plates from Kollam: Global and Local in Ninth Century South India.* Delhi: Primus.
Lamy, Thomas. 1882–1902. *Sancti Ephraem Syri hymni et sermones.* 4 vols. Mechliniae: Dessain.
Land, J. P. N. 1862–1875. *Anecdota syriaca.* 4 vols. Leiden: Brill.
Landau, Brent. 2008. "The Sages and the Star-Child: An Introduction to the Revelation of the Magi, an Ancient Christian Apocryphon." DTh diss: Harvard University.
Landau, Brent. 2010. *Revelation of the Magi: The Lost Tale of the Three Wise Men's Journey to Bethlehem.* New York: Harper.
Layton, Bentley. 1989. *Nag Hammadi Codex II, 2–7.* 2 vols. Leiden: Brill.
Leloir, Louis. 1992. *Écrits apocryphes sur les apôtres: traduction de l'édition arménienne de Venise.* 2 vols. Turnhout: Brepols.
Leriche, Pierre, Gaëlle Coqueugniot and Ségolène De Pontbriand. 2012. *Europos-Doura: Varia 1.* Beirut: IFPO.
Leriche, Pierre et al. 2001. *La Bactriane au carrefour des routes et des civilisations de l'Asie centrale: Termez et les villes de Bactriane-Tokharestan.* Paris: Maisonneuve and Larose.
Lerner, Jeffrey. 1998. "Ptolemy and the Silk Road: From Baktra Basileion to Sera Metropolis," *East and West* 48.1: 9–25.
Lerner, Jeffrey. 1999–2000. "The Greek Indians of Western India: A Study of the Yavana and Yonaka Buddhist Cave Temple Inscriptions," *International Indian Journal of Buddhist Studies* 1: 83–109.
Leslie, D. D. and K. H. J. Gardiner. 1996. *The Roman Empire in Chinese Sources.* Rome: Bardi.
Lewis, Agnes Smith. 1896. *Catalogue of the Syriac Mss. in the Convent of S. Catherine on Mount Sinai.* London: Clay and Sons.
Lewis, Agnes Smith. 1904. *Acta mythologica apostolorum.* London: Clay.
Lewis, Naphtali. 1989. *The Documents from the Bar Kokhba Period in the Cave of Letters,* Vol. 1: *Greek Papyri.* Jerusalem: Israel Exploration Society.
Li, Qiang. 2015. "Roman Coins Discovered in China and Their Research," *Eirene* 51: 279–299.
Lieberman, Victor. 1999. *Beyond Binary Histories: Re-Imagining Eurasia to c. 1830.* Ann Arbor: University of Michigan Press.
Lieu, Samuel. 1992. *Manichaeism in the Later Roman Empire and Medieval China: An Historical Survey.* 2nd edn. Tübingen: Mohr Siebeck.
Lieu, Samuel. 1994. *Manichaeism in Mesopotamia and the Roman East.* Leiden: Brill.

Lieu, Samuel. 1998. *Manichaeism in Central Asia and China*. Leiden: Brill.
Lieu, Samuel. 2008. "Manichaeism," in Susan Ashbrook Harvey and David G. Hunter (eds.), 221–36. *The Oxford Handbook of Early Christian Studies*. Oxford: Oxford University Press.
Lieu, Samuel. 2015. "The Diffusion, Persecution, and Transformation of Manichaeism in Late Antiquity and pre-Modern China," in Averil Cameron (ed.), 123–40. *Conversion in Late Antiquity: Christianity, Islam, and Beyond*. Burlington, VT: Ashgate.
Lieu, Samuel. 2016. "Da Qin and Fulin: The Chinese Names for Rome," in Lieu and Mikkelson (eds.), 123–46.
Lieu, Samuel and Gunner Mikkelson. 2016. *Between Rome and China: History, Religions, and Material Culture of the Silk Road*. Turnhout: Brepols.
Lieu, Samuel and Gunner Mikkelson. 2016. "Places and Peoples in Central Asia and in the Graeco-Roman Near East: A Multilingual Gazetteer from Select Pre-Islamic Sources," in Lieu and Mikkelson (eds.), 147–80.
Littmann, Enno and David Meredith. 1954. "An Old Ethiopic Inscription from the Berenice Road," *Journal of the Royal Asiatic Society* 3–4: 119–23.
Litwa, M. David. 2016. *Refutation of All Heresies*. Atlanta, GA: SBL Press.
Lizorkin, Eliyahu. 2012. *Aphrahat's Demonstrations: Conversations with the Jews of Mesopotamia*. Leuven: Peeters.
Long, Tracey. 2016. "Facing the Evidence: How to Approach the Portraits," in Andreas Kropp and Rubina Raja (eds.), 135–49. *The World of Palmyra*. Copenhagen: Det Kongelige Danske Videnskabernes Selskab.
Louth, A. 1990. "The Date of Eusebius' *Historia Ecclesiastica*," *JThS* 41: 111–23.
Luke, K. 1995–1996. "Gondopharnes," *The Harp* 8–9: 431–50.
Luttikhuizen, G. P. 2001. "The Hymn of Judas Thomas, the Apostle, in the Country of the Indians," in Jan Bremmer (ed.), 101–14. *The Apocryphal Acts of Thomas*. Leuven: Peeters.
Luttikhuizen, G. P. 2005. "The Elchasaites and Their Book," in Antti Marjanen and Petri Luomanen (eds.), 335–64. *A Companion to Second-Century Christian "Heretics."* Leiden: Brill.
MacDonald, M. C. A. 2001. "Arabi, Arabie, e Greci: forme di contatto e percezione," in Salvatore Settis (ed.), 231–66. *I Greci oltre la Grecia*. Turin: Giulio Einaudi. Published in English in MacDonald (2008).
MacDonald, M. C. A. 2003. "'Les Arabes en Syrie' or 'la pénétration des Arabes en Syrie': A Question of Perceptions?" in Maurice Sartre (ed.), 303–18. *La Syrie hellénistique*. Paris: Boccard.
MacDonald, M. C. A. 2008. *Literacy and Identity in Pre-Islamic Arabia*. Burlington, VT: Ashgate.
MacDonald, M. C. A. 2009. "Arabs, Arabias, and Arabic before Late Antiquity," *Topoi* 16: 277–332.
MacDonald, C. A. et al. 2015. "Arabs and Empires before the Sixth Century," in Greg Fisher (ed.), 11–89. *Arabs and Empires before Islam*. Oxford: Oxford University Press.

Mackenzie, G. T. 1901. *Christianity in Travancore*. Travancore: Travancore Govt. Press; Repr. Piscataway, NJ: Gorgias Press, 2011.

Mahadevan, Iravatham. 2003. *Early Tamil Epigraphs from the Earliest Times to the Sixth Century A.D.* Chennai, India, and Cambridge, MA: Cre-A and Harvard University Press.

Mahalingam, T. V. 1988. *Inscriptions of the Pallavas*. New Delhi: Indian Council of Historical Research.

Mai, Angelo. 1825–1838. *Scriptorum veterum nova collectio e vaticani codicibus*. 10 vols. Rome: Vatican.

Mairs, Rachel. 2011. *The Archaeology of the Far East: A Survey*. Oxford: Archaeopress.

Mairs, Rachel. 2012. "Glassware from Roman Egypt at Begram (Afghanistan) and the Red Sea Trade," *British Museum Studies in Ancient Egypt and the Sudan* 18: 61–74.

Mairs, Rachel. 2013. "*Sopha Gramma*: Acrostics in Greek and Latin Inscriptions from Arachosia, Nubia, and Libya," in Jan Kwapisz, David Petrain, and Mikolaj Szymanski (eds.), 279–308. *The Muse at Play: Riddles and Wordplay in Greek and Latin Poetry*. Berlin: Gruyter.

Mairs, Rachel. 2013. "Waiting for the Barbarians: the Fall of Greek Bactria," *Parthica* 15: 9–30.

Mairs, Rachel. 2014. *The Hellenistic Far East: Archaeology, Language, and Identity in Greek Central Asia*. Berkeley: University of California Press.

Majcherek, Grzegorz. 2005. "More Churches from Palmyra: An Inkling of the Late Antique City," in Piotr Bieliński and Franciszek Stępniowski (eds.), 141–50. *Aux pays d'Allat: mélanges offerts à Michal Gawlikowski*. Warsaw: Archeological Institute of Warsaw University.

Majcherek, Grzegorz. 2013. "Excavating the Basilicas," *Studia Palmyreńskie* 12: 251–68.

Malekandathil, Pius. 2010. *Maritime India: Trade, Religion, and Polity in the Indian Ocean*. Delhi: Primus Books.

Malkin, I., C. Constantakopoulou, and K. Panagopoulou. 2009. *Greek and Roman Networks in the Mediterranean*. London: Routledge.

Malkin, Irad. 2011. *A Small Greek World: Networks in the Ancient Mediterranean*. Oxford: Oxford University Press.

Marek, Christian. 2013. "A Roman Period Inscription in South Arabia," in Paul Yule (ed.), 163–65. *Late Antique Arabia: Ẓafār, Capital of Ḥimyar: Rehabilitation of a Decadent Society*. Wiesbaden: Harrassowitz.

Markovits, Claude. 2000. *The Global World of Indian Merchants, 1750–1947: Traders of Sind from Bukhara to Panama*. Cambridge: Cambridge University Press.

Martin, Victor. 1959. "Un recueil de diatribes cyniques: Pap. Genev. Inv. 271," *Museum Helveticum* 16.2: 77–115.

Martinez-Sève, Laurianne. 2014. "The Spatial Organization of Ai Khanoum, a Greek City in Afghanistan," *AJA* 118.2: 267–84.

Mason, Hugh. 1974. *Greek Terms for Roman Institutions: A Lexicon and Analysis*. Toronto: Hakkert.

Masson, M. E. 1967. "Two Palmyrene Stelae from the Merv Oasis," *East and West* 17: 239–47.

Mathew, K. S. 2015. *Imperial Rome, Indian Ocean Regions, and Muziris: New Perspectives on Maritime Trade*. New Delhi: Manohar.

Mayerson, P. 1993. "A Confusion of Indias: Asian India and African India in the Byzantine Sources," *JAOS* 113: 169–74.

McDowell, Sean. 2015. *The Fate of the Apostles: Examining the Martyrdom Accounts of the Closest Followers of Jesus*. Farnham: Ashgate.

McGrath, James. 2008. "History and Fiction in the *Acts of Thomas*: The State of the Question," *Journal for the Study of Pseudepigrapha* 17: 297–311.

McGuckin, John. 2004. "The Life of Origen," in John McGuckin (ed.), 1–24. *The Westminster Handbook to Origen*. Louisville, KY: Westminster John Knox Press.

McGuckin, John. 2004. "The Scholarly Works of Origen," in John McGuckin (ed.), 25–44. *The Westminster Handbook to Origen*. Louisville, KY: Westminster John Knox Press.

McLaughlin, Raoul. 2010. *Rome and the Distant East: Trade Routes to the Ancient Lands of Arabia, India, and China*. London: Continuum.

McLaughlin, Raoul. 2014. *The Roman Empire and the Indian Ocean: The Ancient World Economy and the Kingdoms of Africa, Arabia, and India*. South Yorkshire: Pen & Sword.

McLaughlin, Raoul. 2016. *The Roman Empire and the Silk Routes*. South Yorkshire: Pen & Sword.

McVey, Kathleen. 2015. "The *Letter of Mara Bar Serapion to his Son* and the Second Sophistic: Palamedes and the 'Wise King' of the Jews," in M. Doerfler, E. Fiano, and K. Smith (eds.), 305–27. *Syriac Encounters*. Leuven: Peeters.

Medlycott, Adolphus. 1905. *India and the Apostle Thomas: An Inquiry, with a Critical Analysis of the Acta Thomae*. London: David Nutt; repr. Piscataway, NJ; Gorgias Press, 2005.

Meeks, Wayne. 2003. *The First Urban Christians*. 2nd edn. New Haven: Yale University Press.

Meeks, Wayne. 2013. "From Jerusalem to Illyricum, Rome to Spain: the World of Paul's Missionary Imagination," in Rothschild and Schröter (eds.), 167–82.

Menachery, George. 1998. *The Nazranies*. Pallinada: SARAS.

Menachery, George. 2000. "Veracity of Parts of the *Acts of Judas Thomas* and the Song of Thomas Rambhan Corroborated by Advances in Indian Numismatic Studies," *The Harp* 13: 21–27.

Menon, A. Sreedhara. 1967. *A Survey of Kerala History*. Kottayam: Sahitya Pravarthaka.

Menon, K. P. Padmanabha. 1924–37. *A Historia of Kerala*. 4 vols. Ernkulam: Cochin Govt. Press. Repr. New Delhi: Asian Educational Services, 1983.

Meredith, David. 1953. "Two Inscriptions from the Berenice Road," *JRS* 43: 38–40.

Meredith, David. 1954. "Inscriptions from the Berenice Road," *Chronique d'Égypte* 29: 281–87.

Merkelbach, Reinhold and Josef Stauber. 2005. *Jenseits des Euphrat: griechische Inschriften: ein epigraphisches Lesebuch*. Munich: Saur.
Merz, Annette and Teun Tieleman. 2008. "The *Letter of Mara Bar Sarapion*: Some Comments on its Philosophical and Historical Context," in Alberdina Houtman, Albert de Jong, and Magda Misset-van de Weg (eds.), 107–34. *Empsychoi Logoi: Religious Innovations in Antiquity*. Leiden: Brill.
Merz, Annette and Teun Tieleman. 2012. *The Letter of Mara bar Sarapion in Context*. Leiden: Brill.
Milik, Jósef. 1972. *Dédicaces faites par des dieux (Palmyre, Hatra, Tyr) et des thiases sémitiques à l'époque romaine*. Paris: Geuthner.
Mingana, Alphonse. 1926. "The Spread of Early Christianity in India," *John Rylands Library* 10: 435–515. Reprinted as *The Spread of Early Christianity in India*. Piscataway, NJ: Gorgias Press, 2010.
Mirashi, Vasudev V. 1981. *The History and Inscriptions of the Sātavāhanas and the Western Kshatrapas*. 2 pts. in 1 Vol. Bombay: Maharashtra State Board.
Monier-Williams, Monier. 1899. *A Sanskrit-English Dictionary*. Oxford: Clarendon Press.
Monson, Andrew. 2012. *From the Ptolemies to the Romans: Political and Economic Change in Egypt*. Cambridge: Cambridge University Press.
Morelli, Federico. 2011. "Dal Mar Rosso ad Alessandria: il *verso* (ma anche il *recto*) del 'papiro di Muziris' (SB XVIII 13167)," *Tyche* 26: 199–234.
Morley, Neville. 2007. "The Early Roman Empire: Distribution," in Walter Scheidel, Ian Morris, and Peter Saller (eds.), 570–91. *The Cambridge Economic History of the Greco-Roman World*. Cambridge: Cambridge University Press.
Morony, Michael. 1984. *Iraq after the Muslim Conquest*. Princeton, NJ: Princeton University Press.
Morony, Michael. 2004. "Population Transfers between Sasanian Iran and the Byzantine Empire," in G. Gnoli and A. Panaino (eds.), 161–79. *Convegno internazionale: La Persia e Bisanzio*. Rome: Accademia nazionale dei Lincei.
Mosig-Walburg, Karin. 2010. "Deportationen römischer Christen in das Sasanidenreich durch Shapur I. und ihre Folgen: eine Neubewertung," *Klio* 92: 117–56.
Most, Glenn. 2005. *Doubting Thomas*. Cambridge, MA: Harvard University Press.
Muckensturm-Poulle, C. 1995. "Palladius' Brahmans," in M.-F. Boussac and J.-F. Salles (eds.), 157–66. *Athens, Aden, Arikamedu: Essays on the Interrelations between India, Arabia, and the Eastern Mediterranean*. New Delhi: Centre de Sciences Humaines.
Mundadan, A. Mathias. 1970. *Sixteenth Century Traditions of St. Thomas Christians*. Bangalore: Selbstverlag.
Mundadan, A. Mathias. 1989. *History of Christianity in India: From the Beginning up to the Middle of the Sixteenth Century (up to 1542)*. Bangalore: Church History Association of India.
Munro-Hay, Stuart. 1991. *Aksum: An African Civilisation of Late Antiquity*. Edinburgh: Edinburgh University Press.

Munro-Hay, Stuart and Bent Juel-Jensen. 1995. *Aksumite Coinage: A Revised and Enlarged Edition of the Coinage of Aksum*. London: Spink.
Muraviev, Alexey. 2015. "Reconstructed Colophon on the Text of the Syriac *Julian Romance* as a Clue to the Mystery of Its Author," *Hugoye* 18.2: 399–407.
Myers, Susan. 2010. *Spiritual Epicleses in the Acts of Thomas*. Tübingen: Mohr Siebeck.
Nappo, Dario. 2007. "The Impact of the Third-Century Crisis on the International Trade with the East," in Olivier Hekster et al. (eds.), 233–44. *Crises and the Roman Empire*. Leiden: Brill.
Nappo, Dario. 2015. "Roman Policy on the Red Sea in the Second Century CE," in de Romanis and Maiuro (eds.), 55–72.
Narayanan, M. G. S. 2013. *Perumals of Kerala: Brahmin Oligarchy and Ritual Monarchy*. Kerala: Cosmo Books.
Nasrallah, Laura. 2010. *Christian Responses to Roman Art and Architecture: The Second-Century Church amid the Spaces of Empire*. Cambridge: Cambridge University Press.
Nau, F. 1912. "Martyrologes et ménologes orientaux I-XIII: un martyrologe et douze ménologes syriaques," *PO* 10: 7–26.
Nebe, G. Wilhelm and Alexander Sima. 2004. "Die aramäisch/hebräisch-sabäische Grabinschrift der Lea," *Arabian Archaeology and Epigraphy* 15: 76–83.
Nedungatt, George. 2008. *A Quest for the Historical Thomas: A Re-Reading of the Evidence*. Bangalore: Theological Publications in India.
Nedungatt, George. 2010. "Calamina, Kalamides, Cholamandalam: Solution of a Riddle," *OCP* 76: 181–99.
Nedungatt, George. 2010. "India Confused with Other Countries in Antiquity?" *OCP* 76: 315–37.
Nedungatt, George. 2011. "The Apocryphal *Acts of Thomas* and Christian Origins in India," *Gregorianum* 92: 533–57.
Nedungatt, George. 2011. "Christian Origins in India According to the Alexandrian Tradition," *OCP* 77: 399–422.
Neelis, Jason. 2011. *Early Buddhist Transmission and Trade Networks: Mobility and Exchange within and beyond the Northwestern Borderlands of South Asia*. Leiden: Brill.
Neill, Stephen. 1984. *A History of Christianity in India*, Vol. 1: *The Beginnings to AD 1707*. Cambridge: Cambridge University Press.
Newman, Mark, Albert-László Barabási, and Duncan Watts. 2006. *The Structure and Dynamics of Networks*. Princeton, NJ: Princeton University Press.
Nickel, Lukas. 2013. "The First Emperor and Sculpture in China," *Bulletin of the SOAS* 76.3: 413–47.
Nongbri, Brent. 2013. *Before Religion: a History of the Modern Concept*. New Haven: Yale University Press.
Noy, David. 2000. *Foreigners at Rome: Citizens and Strangers*. London: Duckworth.
Ober, Josiah. 2008. *Democracy and Knowledge: Innovation and Learning in Classical Athens*. Princeton, NJ: Princeton University Press.
Oort, Johannes Van. 2013. *Augustine and Manichaean Christianity*. Leiden: Brill.

Oppenheimer, Aharon. 1983. *Babylonia Judaica in the Talmudic Period*. Wiesbaden: Reichert.
Parpola, Simo. 2001. "Mesopotamian Precursors of the *Hymn of the Pearl*," in R. M. Whiting (ed.), 181–94. *Mythology and Mythologies: Methodological Approaches to Intercultural Influences*. Helsinki: Neo-Assyrian Text Corpus Project.
Park, Hyunhee. 2013. *Mapping the Chinese and Islamic Worlds: Cross-Cultural Exchange and Premodern Asia*. Cambridge: Cambridge University Press.
Parker, D. C., D. G. K. Taylor, and M. S. Goodacre. 1999. "The Dura-Europos Gospel Harmony," in D. K. G. Taylor (ed.), 192–228. *Studies in the Early Text of the Gospels and Acts*. Atlanta: SBL.
Parker, Grant. 2008. *The Making of Roman India*. Cambridge: Cambridge University Press.
Parker, S. T. 2000. "The Roman 'Aqaba Project: The 1997 and 1998 Campaigns," *ADAJ* 44: 373–91.
Parker, S. T. 2002. "The Roman 'Aqaba Project: the 2000 Campaign," *ADAJ* 46: 409–28.
Parker, S. T. 2003. "The Roman 'Aqaba Project: the 2002 Campaign," *ADAJ* 47: 321–33.
Parthasarathy, R. 1993. *The Cilappatikaram of Ilanko Atikal: An Epic of South India*. New York: Columbia University Press.
Pavan, Alexia. 2015. "Trade and Commercial Routes along the Indian Ocean from the Early Centuries BC to the Beginning of the Christian Era: New Lights from the Indian Pottery Discovered at Sumhuram (Sultanate of Oman)," *Archäologische Berichte aus dem Yemen* 14: 123–33.
Pavan, Alexia and Heidrun Schenk. 2012. "Crossing the Indian Ocean before the *Periplus*: A Comparison of Pottery Assemblages at the Sites of Sumhuram (Oman) and Tissamaharama (Sri Lanka)," *Arabian Archaeology and Epigraphy* 23: 191–202.
Payne, Richard. 2011. "Monks, Dinars, and Date Palms: Hagiographical Production and the Expansion of Monastic Institutions in the Early Islamic Persian Gulf," *Arabian Archaeology and Epigraphy* 22: 97–111.
Payne, Richard. 2014. "An Archaeology of Sasanian Politics," *Journal of Ancient History* 2.2: 80–92.
Payne, Richard. 2015. *A State of Mixture: Christians, Zoroastrians, and Iranian Political Culture in Late Antiquity*. Berkeley: University of California Press.
Payne Smith, Robert. 1879–1901. *Thesaurus Syriacus*. 2 vols. Oxford: Clarendon.
Peacock, David and Lucy Blue. 2006–2011. *Myos Hormos-Quseir-al-Quadim: Roman and Islamic Ports on the Red Sea*. 2 vols. Oxford: Archaeopress.
Peacock, David, Lucy Blue, and Darren Glazier. 2007. "Review, Discussion, and Conclusion," in David Peacock, Lucy Blue, and Darren Glazier (eds.), 125–34. *The Ancient Red Sea Port of Adulis, Eritrea: Results of the Eritro-British Expedition, 2004–5*. Oxford: Oxbow.
Peacock, David and David Williams. 2007. "Introduction," in David Peacock and David Williams (eds.), 1–3. *Food for the Gods: New Light on the Ancient Incense Trade*. Oxford: Oxbow.

Peacock, David, David Williams, and Sarah James. 2007. "Basalt as Ships' Ballast and the Roman Incense Trade," in David Peacock and David Williams (eds.), 28–70. *Food for the Gods: New Light on the Ancient Incense Trade.* Oxford: Oxbow.

Pearson, Birger A. 2004. *Gnosticism and Christianity in Roman and Coptic Egypt.* New York: T&T Clark.

Pearson, Birger A. 2007. "Earliest Christianity in Egypt: Further Observations," in James Goehring and Janet Trimble, (eds.), 97–112. *The World of Egyptian Christianity: Language, Literature, and Social Context.* Washington, D.C.: Catholic University Press.

Pederson, Nils Arne. 2013. "Manichaean Self-Designations in the Western Tradition," in Van Oort (ed.), 155–76.

Pederson, N.A. and J. M. Larsen. 2013. *Manichaean Texts in Syriac: First Editions, New Editions, and Studies.* Turnhout: Brepols.

Peppard, Michael. 2012. "Illuminating the Dura-Europos Baptistery: Comparanda for the Female Figures," *JECS* 20.4: 543–74.

Peppard, Michael. 2016. *The World's Oldest Church: Bible, Art, and Ritual at Dura-Europos, Syria.* New Haven, CT: Yale University Press.

Perumalil, A. C. 1971. *The Apostles in India: Fact or Fiction.* 2nd edn. Patna: Catholic Book Crusade.

Peterson, Jeremy. 1998. "Trade and Traders in the Roman World: Scale, Structure, and Organisation," in Helen Parkins and Christopher Smith (eds.), 149–67. *Trade, Traders, and the Ancient City.* London: Routledge.

Phillips, Carl, François Villeneuve, and William Facey. 2004. "A Latin Inscription of South Arabia," *Proceedings of the Seminar of Arabian Studies* 34: 239–50.

Phillipson, David. 2012. *Foundations of an African Civilisation: Aksum & the Northern Horn.* Woodbridge, Suffolk: James Currey.

Phillipson, David. 2013. "Aksoum et le nord de la Corne de l'Afrique (ier–viie siècles)," in Christian Julien Robin et Jérémie Schiettecatte (eds.), 105–17. *Les préludes de l'Islam: ruptures et continuités dans les civilisations du Proche-Orient, de l'Afrique orientale, de l'Arabie et de l'Inde à la veille de l'Islam.* Paris: Boccard.

Photiadès, Pénélope. 1959. "Les diatribes cyniques du papyrus de Genève 271: leur traductions et élaborations successives," *Museum Helveticum* 16.2: 116–38.

Pieri, Dominique. 2005. *Le commerce du vin oriental à l'époque byzantine, Ve–VIIe siècles: le témoignage des amphores en Gaule.* Beirut: IFPO.

Piovanelli, Pierluigi. 2010. "Thomas in Edessa? Another Look at the Original Setting of the Gospel of Thomas," in Jitse Dijkstra, Justin Kroesen, and Yme Kuiper (eds.), 443–62. *Myths, Martyrs, and Modernity Studies in the History of Religions in Honor of Jan Bremmer.* Leiden: Brill.

Podipara, Placid. 1970. *The Thomas Christians.* Madras: Darton, Longman, and Todd.

Podipara, Placid. 1974. *Thomas Christians and Their Syriac Treasures.* Alleppey: Prakasam Publications.

Poirier, P.-H. 1981. *L'Hymne de la Perle des Actes de Thomas: Introduction, Text-Traduction, Commentaire.* Louvain: Pierier.

Poirier, P.-H. 1984. *La version copte de la Prédication et du Martyre de Thomas*. Brussels: Bollandistes.
Poirier, P.-H. 1996. "*Évangile de Thomas, Actes de Thomas, Livre de Thomas*: une tradition et ses transformations," *Apocrypha* 7: 9–26.
Poirier, P.-H. 1998. "*Les Actes de Thomas* et le Manichéisme," *Apocrypha* 9: 263–90.
Pollard, Elizabeth Ann. 2013. "Indian Spices and Roman 'Magic' in Imperial and Late Antique Indomediterranea," *JWH* 24.1: 1–23.
Pollock, Sheldon. 2006. *The Language of the Gods in the World of Men: Sanskrit, Culture, and Power in Premodern India*. Berkeley: University of California Press.
Possehl, Gregory L. 2012. "India's Relations with Western Empires, 2300–600 BC," in D. T. Potts (ed.), 758–69. *A Companion to the Archaeology of the Ancient Near East*, Vol. 2. Chichester: Wiley-Blackwell.
Posch, Walter. 1998. "Chinesische Quellen zu den Parthern," in Josef Wiesehöfer (ed.), 355–65. *Das Partherreich und seine Zeugnisse/The Arsacid Empire: Sources and Documentation*. Stuttgart: Steiner.
Pothan, S. G. 1962. *The Syrian Christians of Kerala*. Bombay: Asia Publishing House.
Potter, David. 2014. *The Roman Empire at Bay, AD 180–395*. 2nd edn. Milton Park: Routledge.
Potts, D. T. 1990. The *Arabian Gulf in Antiquity*. 2 vols. Oxford: Oxford University Press.
Potts, D. T. 2009. "The Archaeology and Early History of the Persian Gulf," in Lawrence Potter (ed.), 27–56. *The Persian Gulf in History*. New York: Palgrave Macmillan.
Power, Timothy. 2012. *The Red Sea from Byzantium to the Caliphate: AD 500–1000*. New York: American University in Cairo Press.
Puri, B. N. 1999. "The Kushans," in Harmatta (ed.), 247–64.
Puri, B. N. 1999. "The Sakas and the Indo-Parthians," in Harmatta (ed.), 191–209.
Puthiakunnel, Thomas. 1970. "Jewish Colonies of India Paved the Way for St. Thomas," in Jacob Vellian (ed.), 187–91. *The Malabar Church: Symposium in Honour of Rev. Placid J. Podipara C.M.I.* Rome: Pontificum Institutum Orientalium Studiorum.
Pyankov, Igor. 2012. "Romano-Parthian Merchants on the Silk Road Leading to the Crossing of the Oxus," *Parthica* 14: 145–48.
Ramelli, Ilaria. 1999. "Edessa e i Romani fra Augusto e i Severi: aspetti del regno di Abgar V e di Abgar IX," *Aevum* 73: 107–43.
Ramelli, Ilaria. 2000. "L'epitafio di Abercio: uno status quaestionis ed alcune osservazioni," *Aevum* 74: 191–206.
Ramelli, Ilaria. 2001. "Il cristianesimo in India dall'età costantiniana al V secolo," in Dognini and Ramelli (eds.), 103–20.
Ramelli, Ilaria. 2001. "La missione di Panteno e il "Matteo aramaico" recato secondo la tradizione da Bartolomeo," in Dognini and Ramelli (eds.), 45–58.
Ramelli, Ilaria. 2001. "La tradizione su Tommaso apostolo dell'India," in Dognini and Ramelli (eds.), 59–82.

Ramelli, Ilaria. 2002. *Il Chronicon di Arbela: presentazione, traduzione e note essenziali*. Madrid: Universidad Complutense Madrid.
Ramelli, Ilaria. 2003. "Un'iscrizione cristiana edessena del III sec. d. C.: contestualizzazione storica e tematiche," *'Ilu* 8: 119–26.
Ramelli, Ilaria. 2004. "La *Lettera di Mara Bar Serapion*," *Stylos* 13: 77–104.
Ramelli, Ilaria. 2005. "Gesù tra i sapienti greci perseguitati ingiustamente in un antico documento filosofico pagano di lingua siriaca," *Rivista di filosofia neoscolastica* 97: 545–70.
Ramelli, Ilaria. 2008. *Stoici romani minori*. Milan: Bompiani.
Ramelli, Ilaria. 2009. *Bardesane di Edessa: Contro il fato, κατὰ Εἱμαρμένης*. Bologna: Studio Domenicano.
Ramelli, Ilaria. 2009. *Bardaisan of Edessa: A Reassessment of the Evidence and a New Interpretation*. Piscataway: Gorgias Press.
Ramelli, Ilaria. 2009. *Possible Historical Traces in the Doctrina Addai*. Piscataway, NJ: Gorgias Press.
Ramelli, Ilaria. 2011. "Early Christian Missions from Alexandria to 'India': Institutional Transformations and Geographical Identifications," *Augustinianum* 51.1: 221–31.
Ramelli, Ilaria. 2015. "The Addai-Abgar Narrative: Its Development through Literary Genres and Religious Agendas," in Ilaria Ramelli and Judith Perkins (eds.), 205–46. *Early Christian and Jewish Narrative: the Role of Religion in Shaping Narrative Forms*. Tübingen: Mohr Siebeck
Raschke, M. G. 1978. "New Studies in Roman Commerce in the East," *ANRW* 2.9.2: 604–1361.
Rathbone, D. 2000. "The 'Muziris' Papyrus (SB XVIII 13167): Financing Roman Trade with India," *Bulletin de la Société Archéologique d'Alexandrie* 46: 39–50.
Rauh, Nicholas. 2003. *Merchants, Sailors, and Pirates in the Roman World*. Stroud, UK: Tempus.
Ray, H. P. 1994. *The Winds of Change: Buddhism and the Maritime Links of Early South Asia*. Delhi: Oxford University Press.
Ray, H. P. 2006. "Inscribed Pots, Emerging Identities: The Social Milieus of Trade," in Patrick Olivelle (ed.), 113–44. *Between the Empires: Society in India 300 BC to 400 CE*. Oxford: Oxford University Press.
Ray, H. P. 2013. "The King and the Monastery: The Pandu Lena at Nashik," in Brancaccio (ed.), 44–59.
Rebillard, Éric. 2012. *Christians and Their Many Identities in Late Antiquity, North Africa, 200–450 CE*. Ithaca, NY: Cornell University Press.
Reden, Sitta von. 2012. "Money and Finance," in Peter Fibiger Bang and Walter Scheidel (eds.), 266–86. *The Cambridge Companion to the Roman Economy*. Cambridge: Cambridge University Press.
Reed, Annette Yoshiko. 2009. "Beyond the Land of Nod: Syriac Images of Asia and the Historiography of 'the West'," *History of Religions* 49.1: 48–87.
Reed, Annette Yoshiko and L. Voung. 2013. "Christianity in Antioch: Partings in Roman Syria," in Shanks (ed.), 105–32.

Reger, Gary. 2009. "On the Road to India with Apollonios of Tyana and Thomas the Apostle," in Malkin, Constantakopoulou, and Panogopoulou (eds.), 249–63.
Reinaud, M. 1845. *Relations des voyages faits par les Arabes et les Persans dans l'Inde et à la Chine*. Paris: Imprimerie Royale.
Rensberger, David. 2010. "Reconsidering the *Letter of Mara bar Serapion*," in E. M. Meyers and P. V. M. Flesher (eds.), 3–21. *Aramaic in Postbiblical Judaism and Early Christianity*. Winona Lake, IN: Eisenbrauns.
Rezakhani, Khodadad. 2017. *ReOrienting the Sasanians: East Iran in Late Antiquity*. Edinburgh: Edinburgh University Press.
Riccobono, S. et al. 1968. *Fontes iuris Romani antejustiniani*. Ed. alt. 3 vols. Florence: S.A.G. Barbèra.
Richter, Siegfried. 2013. "The Beginnings of Christianity in Nubia," in Gawdat Gabra and Hany Takla (eds.), 47–54. *Christianity and Monasticism in Aswan and Nubia*. Cairo: The University of Cairo Press.
Rienjang, Wannaporn. 2011. "The Indo-Parthian Coins in the British Museum," *Oriental Numismatic Society* 207: 30–31.
Rivers, Ray, Carl Knappett, and Tim Evans. 2013. "What Makes a Site Important: Centrality, Gateways, and Gravity," in Knappett (ed.), 125–50.
Robin, Christian Julien. 1997. "The Date of the *Periplus of the Erythraean Sea* in Light of the South Arabian Evidence," in Federico de Romanis and André Tchernia (eds.), 41–65. *Crossings: Early Mediterranean Contacts with India*. New Delhi: Manohar.
Robin, Christian Julien. 2010. "Nagrān vers l'époque du massacre: notes sur l'histoire politique, économique, et institutionnelle et sur l'introduction du Christianisme (avec un réexamen du *Martyre d'Azqīr*)," in Joëlle Beaucamp, Françoise Briquel-Chatonnet, et Christian Julien Robin (eds.), 39–106. *Juifs et chrétiens en Arabie aux Ve et VIe siècles: regards croisés sur les sources*. Paris: CNRS.
Robin, Christian Julien. 2012. "Arabia and Ethiopia," in Scott Fitzgerald Johnson (ed.), 247–332. *Oxford Handbook of Late Antiquity*. Oxford: Oxford University Press.
Robin, Christian Julien. 2012. "Les Palmyréniens en Arabie du Sud," in Strauch (ed.), 488–92.
Robin, Christian Julien. 2012. "Sudarabiques et Aksūmites à Suquṭra d'après les inscriptions de Ḥōq," in Strauch (ed.) 438–42.
Robin, Christian Julien. 2012. "Suquṭra dans les inscriptions de l'Arabie du Sud," in Strauch (ed.), 443–45.
Rogers, E. M. 2003. *Diffusion of Innovations*. 5th edn. New York: Free Press.
Roig Lanzillotta, Lautaro. 2015. "A Syriac Original for the *Acts of Thomas?* The Hypothesis of Syriac Priority Revisited," in Ilaria Ramelli and Judith Perkins (eds.), 105–34. *Early Christian and Jewish Narrative: The Role of Religion in Shaping Narrative Forms*. Tübingen: Mohr Siebeck.
Roller, Duane. 2015. *Ancient Geography: The Discovery of the World in Classical Greece and Rome*. London: Tauris.
Römer, Cornelia. 1994. *Manis frühe Missionsreisen nach der Kölner Manibiographie*. Berlin: Westdeutscher Verlag.

Rothman, E. Natalie. 2012. *Brokering Empire: Trans-Imperial Subjects between Venice and Istanbul.* Ithaca, NY: Cornell University Press.

Rothschild, Clare and Jens Schröter. 2013. *The Rise and Expansion of Christianity in the First Three Centuries of the Common Era.* Tübingen: Mohr Siebeck.

Rtveladze, Edvard. 2012. "Studies on the Historical Geography of Southern Central Asia," *Parthica* 14: 137–43.

Rubin, Ze'ev. 2012. "Greek and Ge'ez in the Propaganda of King 'Ezana of Axum: Religion and Diplomacy in Late Antiquity," *Semitica et Classica* 5: 139–50.

Ruffing, Kai. 2013. "The Trade with India and the Problem of Agency in the Economy of the Roman Empire," in S. Bussi (ed.), 199–201. *Egitto dai Faraoni agli Arabi.* Pisa: Serra.

Rutten, K. 2007. "The Roman Fine Wares of ed-Dur (Umm al-Qaiwain, U.A.E) and Their Distribution in the Persian Gulf and the Indian Ocean," *Arabian Archaeology and Epigraphy* 19: 8–24.

Saint-Laurent, Jeanne-Nicole Mellon. 2015. *Missionary Stories and the Formation of the Syriac Churches.* Berkeley: University of California Press.

Salles, J.-F. 2005. "Bahrain, from Alexander the Great to the Sasanians," in Harriet Crawford and Michael Rice (eds.), 132–35. *Traces of Paradise: The Archaeology of Bahrain 2500 BC–300 AD.* London: Tauris.

Salles, J.-F. 2007. "Traveling to India without Alexander's Log-Books," in H. P. Ray and D. T. Potts (eds.), 157–69. *Memory as History: The Legacy of Alexander in Asia.* New Delhi: Aryan Books International.

Salles, J.-F. 2016. "Towards a Geography of the Harbours in the Persian Gulf in Antiquity (Sixth Century BC–Sixth Century AD)," in Boussac, Salles, and Yon (eds.), 137–64.

Salles, J.-F. and A. Sedov. 2010. *Qâni. Le port antique du Ḥaḍramawt entre la Méditerranée, l'Afrique, et l'Inde.* Turnhout: Brepols.

Salomon, Richard. 1991. "Epigraphic Remains of Indian Traders in Egypt," *JAOS* 111.4: 731–36.

Salomon, Richard. 1998. *Indian Epigraphy: A Guide to the Study of Inscriptions in Sanskrit, Prakrit, and the Other Indo-Aryan Languages.* New York, NY: Oxford University Press.

Samuel, G. John. 2010. *Heritage of Early Christian Communities in India: Some Landmarks.* Chennai: Institute of Asian Studies.

Samuel, G. J., J.B. Santiago, and P. Thiagarajan. 2008. *Early Christianity in India.* Chennai: Institute of Asian Studies.

Sandwell, Isabella. 2007. *Religious Identity in Late Antiquity: Greeks, Jews, and Christians in Antioch.* Cambridge: Cambridge University Press.

Sarre, F. P. T. and Ernst Herzfeld. 1911–1920. *Archäologische reise im Euphrat- und Tigris-begiet.* 4 vols. Berlin: Reimer.

Sastri, K. A. Nilakanta. 1976. *A History of South India from Prehistoric Times to the Fall of Vijayanagar.* 4th edn. Madras: Oxford University Press.

Sastry, T.S. Kuppanna. 1993. *Pancasiddhantika of Varahamihira.* Madras: Foundation Adyar.

Schachner, Lukas. 2005. "'I Greet You and Thy Brethren: Here Are Fifteen Shentasse of Wine': Wine as a Product in the Early Monasteries of Egypt and the Levant," *Aram* 17: 157–84.

Schafer, Edward. 1951. "Iranian Merchants in T'ang Dynasty Tales," *University of California Publications in Semitic Philology* 11: 403–22.

Schermann, Theodor. 1907. *Prophetarum vitae fabulosae: indices apostolorum discipulorumque Domini Dorotheo, Epiphanio, Hippolyto, aliisque vindicata*. Leipzig: Teubner.

Schermann, Theodor. 1907. *Propheten- und Apostellegenden nebst Jüngerkatalogen des Dorotheus und verwandter Texte*. Leipzig: Hinrichs'sche Buchhandlung.

Schiettecatte, J. 2012. "L'Arabie du Sud et la mer du IIIe siècle av. au VIe siècle apr. J.-C.," Boussac, Salles, and Yon (eds.), 237–73.

Schiettecatte, J. and M. Arbach. 2016. "The Political Map of Arabia and the Middle East in the Third Century Revealed by a Sabaean Inscription," *Arabian Archaeology and Epigraphy* 27: 176–196.

Schlumberger, Daniel. 2010. *L'Occident à la rencontre de l'Orient: choix de textes présentés par Mathilde Gelin*. Damascus: IFPO, 226–390. Originally published as "Descendants non-méditerranéens de l'art grec," *Syria* 37 (1960): 131–166 and 253–318.

Schmidt-Colinet, Andreas and Waleed al-As'ad. 2013. *Palmyras Reichtum durch weltweiten Handel: Archäologische Untersuchungen im Bereich der hellenistischen Stadt*. 2 vols. Vienna: Holzhausen.

Schmidt-Colinet, Andreas and Annemarie Stauffer. 2000. *Die Textilien aus Palmyra: neue und alte Funde*. Mainz: Zabern.

Schneider, Pierre. 2004. *L'Ethiopie et l'Inde: interférences et confusions aux extrémités du monde antique (VIIIe siècle avant J.-C.-VIe siècle après J.-C.)*. Rome: École Française.

Schneider, Pierre. 2016. "The So-Called Confusion between India and Ethiopia: The Eastern and Southern Edges of the Inhabited World from the Greco-Roman Perspective," in Serena Bianchetti, Michele Cataudella, and Hans-Joachim Gehrk (eds.), 184–202. *Brill's Companion to Ancient Geography: the Inhabited World in the Greek and Roman Tradition*. Leiden: Brill.

Schneider, Ulrich. 1978. *Die grossen Felsen-Edikte Aśokas: kritische Ausgabe, Übersetzung, und Analyse der Texte*. Wiesbaden: Harrassowtiz.

Schor, Adam. 2011. *Theodoret's People: Social Networks and Religious Conflict in Late Roman Syria*. Berkeley: University of California Press.

Schuol, Monika. 2000. *Die Charakene: Ein mesopotamisches Königreich in hellenistisch-parthischer Zeit*. Stuttgart: Steiner.

Schurhammer, Georg. 1970. "New Light about the Tomb at Mailapur," in Jacob Vellian (ed.), 99–101. *The Malabar Church: Symposium in Honour of Rev. Placid J. Podipara C.M.I.* Rome: Pontificum Institutum Orientalium Studiorum.

Schwabe, Moshe and Baruch Lifshitz. 1974. *Beth She'arim*, Vol. 2: *The Greek Inscriptions*. Jerusalem: Massada Press.

Schwemer, Anna Maria. 2011. "Die ersten Christen in Syrien," in Dmitrij Bumazhnov and Hans Reinhard Seeliger (eds.), 169–94. *Syrien im 1.-7. Jahrhundert nach Christus*. Tübingen: Mohr Siebeck.
Scott, John. 2012. *Social Network Analysis*. 3rd edn. London: SAGE.
Scott, John. 2012. *What Is Social Network Analysis?* New York: MacMillan.
Scott, Michael. 2016. *Ancient Worlds: An Epic History of the East & West*. London: Hutchinson.
Sedov, A. V. 1992. "New Archaeological and Epigraphical Material from Qana (South Arabia)," *Arabian Archaeology and Epigraphy* 3.2: 110–37.
Sedov, A. V. 2010. "Les fouilles du secteur 3: la synagogue," in Salles and Sedov (eds.), 87–122.
Sedov, A.V. and J.-F. Salles, 2010. "Place of Qâni' in the Rome-Indian Sea-Trade of the 1st-6th Centuries A.D.," in Salles and Sedov (eds.), 453–66.
Seland, Eivind. 2007. "Ports, Ptolemy, *Periplus*, and Poetry: Romans in Tamil South India and the Bay of Bengal," in E. H. Seland (ed.), 68–82. *The Indian Ocean in the Ancient Period: Definite Places, Translocal Exchange*. Oxford: Archaeopress.
Seland, Eivind. 2010. *Ports and Political Power in the Periplus: Complex Societies and Maritime Trade on the Indian Ocean in the First Century AD*. Oxford: Archaeopress.
Seland, Eivind H. 2011. "The Persian Gulf or the Red Sea? Two Axes in Ancient Indian Ocean Trade, Where to Go and Why," *World Archaeology* 43.3: 398–409.
Seland, Eivind H. 2012. "Trade and Christianity in the Indian Ocean during Late Antiquity," *Journal of Late Antiquity* 5.1: 72–86.
Seland, Eivind H. 2013. "The *Liber Pontificalis* and Red Sea Trade of the Early to Mid 4th Century," in Dionisius Agius et al. (eds.), 117–26. *Navigated Spaces, Connected Places: Proceedings of the Red Sea Project V*. Oxford: Archaeopress.
Seland, Eivind H. 2013. "Networks and Social Cohesion in Ancient Indian Ocean Trade: Geography, Ethnicity, Religion," *Journal of Global History* 8.3: 373–90.
Seland, Eivind H. 2014. "Archaeology of Trade in the Western Indian Ocean, 300BC-AD 700," *Journal of Archaeological Research*. Available at http://link.springer.com/article/10.1007%252Fs10814-014-9075-7. Accessed December 2, 2017.
Seland, Eivind H. 2014. "The Organisation of the Palmyrene Caravan Trade," *Ancient West and East* 13: 197–211.
Seland, Eivind H. 2015. "Palmyrene Long-distance Trade: Land, River, and Maritime Routes in the First Three Centuries CE," in Mariko Namba Walter and James P. Ito-Adler (eds.), 101–31. *The Silk Road: Interwoven History*, Vol. 1: *Long-distance Trade, Culture, and Society*. Cambridge, MA: Cambridge Institutes Press.
Seland, Eivind H. 2016. "*The Periplus of the Erythraean Sea*: a Network Approach," *Asian Review of World Histories* 4: 191–205.
Seland, Eivind H. 2016. *Ships of the Desert and Ships of the Sea: Palmyra in the World Trade of the First Three Centuries CE*. Wiesbaden: Harrassowitz.

Selby, Martha Ann. 2011. *Tamil Love Poetry: The Five Hundred Short Poems of Ainkurunuru, an Early Third-Century Anthology*. New York, NY: Columbia University Press.

Sellew, Ph. 2001. "Thomas Christianity: Scholars in Quest of a Community," in Jan Bremmer (ed.), 11–35. *The Apocryphal Acts of Thomas*. Leuven: Peeters.

Selvakumar, V., K.P. Shajan, and Roberta Tomber. 2009. "Archaeological Investigations at Pattanam, Kerala: New Evidence for the Location of Ancient Muziris," in Tomber, Blue, and Abraham (eds.), 29–41.

Senart, E. 1905–1906. "The Inscriptions in the Caves at Nasik," *Epigraphia Indica* 8: 59–96.

Senior, R. C. 2001–2006. *Indo-Scythian Coins and History*. 4 vols. Lancaster, PA: Classical Numismatic Group.

Sergent, Bernard. 1998. "Les Sères sont les soi-disant 'Tokhariens', c'est-à-dire les authentiques Arśi-Kuči," *Dialogues d'histoire ancienne* 24.1: 7–40.

Shanks, Hershel. 2013. *Partings: How Judaism and Christianity Became Two*. Washington, DC: Biblical Archaeology Society.

Shaw, Brent. 2011. *Sacred Violence: African Christians and Sectarian Hatred in the Age of Augustine*. Cambridge: Cambridge University Press.

Shepardson, Christine. 2007. "Controlling Contested Places: John Chrysostom's *Adversus Iudaeos* Homilies and the Spatial Politics of Religious Controversy," *JECS* 15.4: 483–516.

Shepardson, Christine. 2009. "Syria, Syriac, Syrian: Negotiating East and East," in Philip Rousseau (ed.), 455–66. *Companion to Late Antiquity*. London: Wiley-Blackwell.

Shepardson, Christine. 2014. *Controlling Contested Places: Late Antique Antioch and the Spatial Politics of Religious Controversy*. Berkeley: University of California.

Shinde, Vasant. 2013. "Early Historic Junnar: Archaeology and Art," in Brancaccio (ed.), 31–43.

Shinde, Vasant, Shreekant Jadhav, Abhijit Dandekar, and Shrikant Ganvir. 2007. "Junnar: An Early Historic Trading Emporium on the Deccan," *The Journal of Indian Ocean Archaeology* 4, 31–53.

Shoemaker, Stephen. 2008. "Early Christian Apocryphal Literature," in Susan Ashbrook Harvey and David Hunter (ed.), 521–48. *The Oxford Handbook of Early Christian Studies*. Oxford: Oxford University Press.

Shulman, David. 2016. *Tamil: A Biography*. Cambridge, MA: Belknap of Harvard University Press.

Sidebotham, Steven. 1986. *Roman Economic Policy in Erythra Thalassa, 30 B.C.–A.D. 217*. Leiden: Brill.

Sidebotham, Steven. 2004. "Reflections of Ethnicity in the Red Sea Commerce in Antiquity: Evidence of Trade Goods, Languages, and Religions from the Excavations at Berenike," in Paul Lunde and Alexandra Porter (eds.), 105–115. *Trade and Travel in the Red Sea Region*. Oxford: Archaeopress.

Sidebotham, Steven. 2011. *Berenike and the Ancient Maritime Spice Route*. Berkeley: University of California Press.

Sidebotham, Steven. 2012. "The Red Sea and Indian Ocean in the Age of Great Empires," in D. T. Potts (ed.) 1042–59. *A Companion to the Archeology of the Ancient Near East*. Malden, MA: Blackwell.

Sidebotham, Steven. 2015. "Roman Ports on the Red Sea and Their Contacts with Africa, Arabia, and South Arabia: Ancient Literacy and Recent Archaeological Evidence," in Mathew (ed.), 129–78.

Sidebotham, Steven and W. Z. Wendrich. 1999. *Berenike*, Vol. 4: *1997*. Leiden: Research School CNWS.

Silverstein, Adam. 2007. "From Markets to Marvels: Jews on the Maritime Route to China ca. 850–950 CE," *Journal of Jewish Studies* 58: 91–104.

Simmons, Michael B. 1995. *Arnobius of Sicca: Religious Conflict and Competition in the Age of Diocletian*. Oxford: Oxford University Press.

Simpson, St. John. 2014. "Merv, an Archaeological Case-study from the Northeastern Frontier of the Sasanian Empire," *Journal of Ancient History* 2.2: 116–43.

Sims-Williams, Nicholas. 2000. *Bactrian Documents from Northern Afghanistan*, Vol. 1: *Legal and Economic Documents*. Oxford: Oxford University Press.

Sims-Williams, N. and J. Cribb. 1995–1996. "A New Bactrian Inscription of Kanishka the Great," *Silk Road Art and Archaeology* 4: 75–142.

Singh, Upinder. 2008. *A History of Ancient and Medieval India: From the Stone Age to the 12th Century*. New Delhi: Pearson.

Sircar, D. C. 1965. *Indian Epigraphy*. Delhi: Motilal Banarsidass.

Sizgorich, Thomas. 2009. *Violence and Belief in Late Antiquity: Militant Devotion in Christianity and Islam*. Philadelphia: University of Pennsylvania Press.

Smith II, Andrew. 2013. *Roman Palmyra: Identity, Community, and State Formation*. Oxford: Oxford University Press.

Smith, Kyle. 2014. *The Martyrdom and History of Blessed Simeon Bar Ṣabbaʿe*. Piscataway, NJ: Gorgias Press.

Smith, Kyle. 2016. *Constantine and the Captive Christians of Persia: Martyrdom and Religious Identity in Late Antiquity*. Oakland: University of California Press.

Smith, Vincent. 1924. *The Early History of India from 600 B.C. to the Muhammadan Conquest, including the Invasion of Alexander the Great*. 4th edn. Oxford: Clarendon.

Smyth, Herbert Weir. 1956. *Greek Grammar*. Rev. ed. Cambridge, MA: Harvard University Press.

So, Francis K. H. 1987–1988. "Middle Easterners in the T'ang Tales," *Tamkang Review* 18.2: 259–76.

Sokoloff, Michael. 2015. See *The Julian Romance*.

Solin, Heikki. 1983. "Juden und Syrer im westlichen Teil der römischen Welt: eine ethnisch-demographische Studie mit besonderer Berücksichtigung der sprachlichen Zustände," *ANRW* 2.29.2: 587–789 and 1222–49.

Speidel, Michael. 2007. "Ausserhalb des Reiches? Zu neuen römischen Inschriften aus Saudi Arabien und zur Ausdehnung der römishen Herrschaft am Roten Meer," *ZPE* 163: 296–306. Reprinted in Michael Speidel, *Heer und Herrschaft im römischen Reich der hohen Kaizerzeit*. Stuttgart: Steiner: 633–49.

Speidel, Michael. 2015. "War, Trade, and Treaties: New, Revised, and Neglected Sources for the Political, Diplomatic, and Military Aspects of Imperial Rome's

Relations with the Red Sea Basin and India, from Augustus to Diocletian," in Mathew (ed.), 83–128.
Spittler, Janet. 2013. "Christianity at the Edges: Representations of the Ends of the Earth in the Apocryphal Acts of the Apostles," in Clare Rothschild and Jens Schröter (eds.), 353–75. *The Rise and Expansion of Christianity in the First Three Centuries of the Common Era*. Tübingen: Mohr Siebeck.
Stark, J. K. 1971. *Personal Names in Palmyrene Inscriptions*. Oxford: Clarendon.
Stark, Rodney. 1996. *The Rise of Christianity: A Sociologist Reconsiders History*. Princeton, NJ: Princeton University Press.
Stauffer, Annemaire. 2005. "Kleider, Kissen, bunte Tücher: einheimische Textilproduktion und weltweiter Handel," in Andreas Schmidt-Colinet (ed.), 67–82. *Kulturbegegnung im Grenzbereich*. Mainz: Zabern.
Stern, B. et al. 2008. "From Susa to Anuradhapura: Reconstructing Aspects of Trade and Exchange in Bitumen-Coated Ceramic Vessels between Iran and Sri Lanka from the Third to the Ninth Centuries AD," *Archaeometry* 50.3: 409–28.
Stern, Karen. 2010. "Mapping Devotion in Roman Dura-Europos: A Reconsideration of the Synagogue Ceiling," *AJA* 114.3: 473–504.
Steve, M.-J. (ed.). 2003. *L'Ile de Khārg: une page de l'histoire du Golfe persique et du monachisme oriental*. Neuchâtel: Recherches et publications.
Still, Todd and David Horrell. 2009. *After the First Urban Christians: The Social-Scientific Study of Pauline Christianity Twenty-Five Years Later*. New York, NY: T&T Clark.
Strauch, Ingo. 2012. "The Brahmi Scripts of Hoq: The Palaeographical Perspective," in Strauch (ed.), 286–342.
Strauch, Ingo et al. 2012. "Catalogue of Inscriptions and Drawings," in Strauch (ed.), 25–218.
Strauch, Ingo. 2012. *Foreign Sailors on Socotra: the Inscriptions and Drawings from the Cave Hoq*. Bremen: Ute Hempen Verlag.
Strauch, Ingo. 2012. "The Indian Participants of Trade: The Historical Perspective," in Strauch (ed.), 343–59.
Strauch, Ingo. 2012. "Socotra and the 'Indian Connection': Facts and Fictions," in Strauch (ed.), 366–403.
Subbarayalu, Y. 2012. *South India under the Cholas*. Oxford: Oxford University Press.
Subrahmanyam, Sanjay. 2005. *Explorations in Connected History*. 2 vols. New Delhi: Oxford University Press.
Sundermann, Werner. 1981. *Mitteliranische manichäische Texte kirchengeschichtlichen Inhalts*. Berlin: Akademie Verlag.
Sundermann, Werner. 2016. "Manichaeism on the Silk Road," in Lieu and Mikkelson (eds.), 75–90.
Suresh, S. 2004. *Symbols of Trade: Roman and Pseudo-Roman Objects Found in India*. New Delhi: Manohar.
Suresh, S. 2007. *Arikamedu: Its Place in the Ancient Rome-India Contacts*. New Delhi: Manohar.

Talbert, R. J. A. 2010. *Rome's World: The Peutinger Map Reconsidered.* Cambridge: Cambridge University Press.
Tao, Wang. 2007. "Parthia in China: A Re-examination of the Historical Records," in Vesta S. Curtis and Sarah Stewart (eds.), 87–104. *The Age of the Parthians.* London: Tauris.
Tardieu, Michel. 2008. *Manichaeism.* Trans. M. B. DeBevoise. Champagne-Urbana: University of Illinois Press.
Tchernia, André. 2016. *The Romans and Trade.* Oxford: Oxford University Press.
Teigen, H. F. and Eivind H. Seland. *Sinews of Empire: Networks in the Roman Near East and Beyond.* Oxford: Oxbow.
Terpstra, Taco. 2013. *Trading Communities in the Roman World: A Micro-Economic and Institutional Perspective.* Leiden: Brill.
Terpstra, Taco. 2015. "Roman Trade with the Far East: Evidence for Nabataean Middlemen in Puteoli," in de Romanis and Maiuro (ed.), 73–94.
Terpstra, Taco. 2016. "The Palmyrene Temple in Rome and Palmyra's Trade with the West," in Jørgen Christian Meyer, Eivind Seland, and Nils Anfinset (eds.), 39–48. *Palmyrena: City, Hinterland, and Caravan Trade between Orient and Occident.* Oxford: Archaeopress.
Thapar, Romila. 1997. "Early Mediterranean Contacts with India" in Federico de Romanis and André Tchernia (eds.), 11–40. *Crossings: Early Mediterranean Contacts with India.* New Delhi: Manohar.
Thapar, Romila. 2002. *Early India: From the Origins to A.D. 1300.* London: Allen Lane.
Thomas, Ross. 2012. "Port Communities and the Erythraean Trade," *British Museum Studies in Ancient Egypt and Sudan* 18: 170–99.
Thür, G. 1987. "Hypotheken-Urkunde eines Seedarlehens für eine Reise nach Muziris und Apographe für die Tetarte in Alexandria (zu P.Vindob. G. 40.822)," *Tyche* 2: 229–45.
Tieken, Herman. 2001. *Kavya in South India: Old Tamil Cankam Poetry.* Groningen: Egbert Forsten.
Tieken, Herman. 2003. "Old Tamil Cankam Literature and the So-Called Cankam Period," *Indian Economic and Social History Review* 40.3: 247–78.
Tisserant, Eugène. 1941. "Syro-Malabar Église," *Dictionnaire de Théologie Catholique* 14.2, cols. 3089–3162.
Tisserant, Eugène. 1957. *Eastern Christianity in India.* Trans. Edward Hambye. Bombay: Orient Longmans.
Tissot, Yves. 1981. "Les *Actes de Thomas*: exemple de recueil composite," in F. Bovon et al. (eds.), 223–32. *Les Actes apocryphes des Apôtres: Christianisme et monde païen.* Geneva: Labor et Fides.
Tobi, Yosef. 2013. "The Jews of Yemen in Light of the Excavation of the Jewish Synagogue of Qani'," *Proceedings of the Seminar for Arabian Studies* 43: 349–56.
Tomber, Roberta. 2007. "Bishops and Traders: The Role of Christianity in the Indian Ocean in the Roman Period," in Janet Starkey, Paul Starkey, and

Tony Wilkinson (eds.), 219–26. *Natural Resources and Cultural Connections of the Red Sea*. Oxford: Archaeopress.

Tomber, Roberta. 2007. "Rome and Mesopotamia: Importers into India in the First Millennium AD," *Antiquity* 81.4: 972–88

Tomber, Roberta. 2008. *Indo-Roman Trade: from Pots to Pepper*. London: Duckworth.

Tomber, Roberta. 2009. "Beyond Western India: the Evidence from Imported Amphorae," in Tomber, Blue, and Abraham (eds.), 41–52.

Tomber, Roberta. 2012. "From the Roman Red Sea to Beyond the Empire: Egyptian Ports and their Trading Partners," *British Museum Studies in Ancient Egypt and Sudan* 18: 201–15.

Tomber, Roberta. 2015. "The Roman Pottery from Pattanam," in Mathew (ed.), 381–94.

Tomber, Roberta, Lucy Blue, and Shinu Abraham. 2009. *Migration, Trade, and Peoples*, Part 1: *Indian Ocean Commerce and the Archaeology of Western India*. London: The British Academy.

Tomber, Roberta, David Graf, John Healey, Christiane Römer-Strehl, and Grzegorz Majcherek. 2011. "Pots with Writing," in Peacock and Blue (eds.), 2.5–10.

Tripati, Sila, Sunil Kumar Patnaik, and Gopal Charan Pradhan. 2015. "Maritime Trade Contacts of Odisha, East Coast of India, with the Roman World: An Appraisal," in Mathew (ed.) 215–30.

Trivellato, Francesca. 2009. *The Familiarity of Strangers: The Sephardic Diaspora, Livorno, and Cross-Cultural Trade in the Early Modern Period*. New Haven, CT: Yale University Press.

Trombley, Frank and John Watt. 2000. *The Chronicle of pseudo-Joshua the Stylite*. Liverpool: Liverpool University Press.

Trouillot, Michel-Rolph. 1995. *Silencing the Past: Power and the Production of History*. Boston: Beacon Press.

Tubach, Jürgen. 1993. "Ein Palmyrener als Bischof der Mesene," *Oriens Christianus* 77: 137–50.

Tubach, Jürgen. 1993. "Der Weg des Prinzen im Perlenlied," *Orientalia Lovaniensia Periodica* 24: 87–111.

Tubach, Jürgen. 1995. "Mani und der palmyrenische Kaufmann aus Forat," *ZPE* 106: 165–69.

Tubach, Jürgen. 1997. "Der Apostel Thomas in China: die Herkunft einer Tradition," *Zeitschrift für Kirchengeschichte* 108: 58–74.

Tubach, Jürgen. 2002. "Historische Elemente in den Thomasakten," *Hallesche Beiträge zur Orientwissenschaft* 33, *Studien zu den Thomas-Christen in Indien*: 49–116.

Tubach, Jürgen. 2002. "The Veneration of the Apostle Thomas in the Church Province of Persis," *The Harp* 15: 13–23.

Tubach, Jürgen. 2004. "The Four World Empires in the *Hymn of the Pearl*," *Journal of Eastern Christian Studies* 56.1–4: 145–54.

Tubach, Jürgen. 2006. "Thomas Cannaneo and the Thekkumbhagar (Southists)," *The Harp* 19: 399–412.

Tupikova, Irina, Matthias Schemmel, and Klaus Geus. 2014. *Traveling along the Silk Road: A New Interpretation of Ptolemy's Coordinates.* Berlin: Max Planck Institute.
Turner, C. H. 1913. "A Primitive Edition of the Apostolic Constitutions and Canons: An Early List of Apostles and Disciples," *JThS* 15: 53–65.
Turner, David. 2008. *Matthew.* Grand Rapids, MI: Baker.
Turner, Paula. 1989. *Roman Coins from India.* London: Royal Numismatic Society.
Ullendorf, E. 1955. "The Ethiopic Inscription from Egypt," *Journal of the Royal Asiatic Society*: 159–61.
Urban, Greg. 2001. *Metaculture: How Culture Moves through the World.* Minneapolis: University of Minnesota Press.
Vadakkekara, Benedict. 1995. *Origins of India's St. Thomas Christians.* Delhi: Media House.
Vadakkekara, Benedict. 2007. *Origin of Christianity in India: A Historiographical Critique.* Delhi: Media House.
Vashalomidize, Sophia. 2010. "The Apostle Thomas in Georgian Narratives," *The Harp* 25: 79–136.
Vaissière, Étienne de la. 2005. *Sogdian Traders: A History.* Leiden: Brill.
Vaissière, Étienne de la. 2009. "The Triple System of Orography in Ptolemy's Xinjiang," in W. Sunderman, A. Hintze, and F. de Blois (eds.), 527–36. *Exegisti monumenta: Festschrift in Honour of Nicholas Sims-Williams.* Wiesbaden: Harrassowitz.
Van den Bosch, L. P. 2001. "India and the Apostolate of St. Thomas," in Jan Bremmer (ed.), 125–48. *The Apocryphal Acts of Thomas.* Leuven: Peeters.
Van der Horst, Pieter W. 2015. "'India' in Early Jewish Literature," *JSJ* 46.4: 574–79.
Van der Horst, Pieter W. 2016. Review of M. David Litwa, *Refutation of All Heresies* (Atlanta: SBL, 2015). Available at http://bmcr.brynmawr.edu/2016/20 16/2016–12-05.html. Accessed December 3, 2017.
Van Esbroeck, Michael. 1994. "Neuf listes d'apôtres orientales," *Augustinianum* 34.1: 109–99.
Van Lantschoot, A. 1965. *Inventaire des manuscrits syriaques des fonds Vatican (490–631).* Vatican: Bibliotecs Apostolica Vaticana.
Van Rompay, Lukas. 2008. "The East: Syria and Mesopotamia," in Susan Ashbrook Harvey and David G. Hunter (eds.), 365–86. *The Oxford Handbook of Early Christian Studies.* Oxford: Oxford University Press.
Vellian, Jacob. 2012. "Margamkali: A Christian Folk Dance of Indian Christian Performing Arts," in Andrews Mekkattukunnel et al., 587–97. *Mar Thoma Margam: The Ecclesial Heritage of the St. Thomas Christians.* Kottayam: Oriental Institute of Religious Studies India.
Veluthat, Kesavan. 2009. *The Early Medieval in South India.* New Delhi: Oxford University Press.
Vermes, Mark and Samuel Lieu. 2001. *Hegemonius: Acta Archelai (The Acts of Archelaus).* Turnhout: Brepols.

Villeneuve, François. 2005–2006. "Farasan Inscriptions and Bukharin's Ideas: No *Pontifex Herculis* and Other Comments," *Arabia* 3: 289–96.
Vööbus, Arthur. 1958–1988. *History of Asceticism in the Syrian Orient: A Contribution to the History of Culture of the Near East*. 3 vols. Louvain: CorpusSCO.
Walburg, Reinhold. 2008. *Ancient Ruhuna: Sri Lankan-German Archaeological Project in the Southern Province*, Vol. 2: *Coins and Tokens from Ancient Ceylon*. Mainz: Zabern.
Walker, Joel. 2006. *The Legend of Mar Qardagh: Narrative and Christian Heroism in Late Antique Iraq*. Berkeley: University of California Press.
Walker, Joel. 2012. "From Nisibis to Xi'an: The Church of the East in Late Antique Eurasia," in Scott Fitzgerald Johnson (ed.), 994–1052. *Oxford Handbook of Late Antiquity*. Oxford: Oxford University Press.
Warmington, B. H. 1981. "Ammianus and the Lies of Metrodorus," *CQ* 31.2: 464–68.
Wasserman, Stanley and Katherine Faust. 1994. *Social Network Analysis: Methods and Applications*. Cambridge: Cambridge University Press.
Watts, Duncan. 2003. *Six Degrees: The Science of a Connected Age*. New York, NY: Norton.
Watts, Edward. 2010. *Riot in Alexandria: Tradition and Group Dynamics in Late Antique Pagan and Christian Communities*. Berkeley: University of California Press.
Watts, Edward. 2013. "Theodosius II and His Legacy in Anti-Chalcedonian Communal Memory," in Christopher Kelly (ed.), 269–284. *Theodosius II: Rethinking the Roman Empire in Late Antiquity*. Cambridge: Cambridge University Press.
Weerakkody, D. P. M. 1997. *Taprobane: Ancient Sri Lanka as Known to Greeks and Romans*. Turnhout: Brepols.
Weitzman, Michael. 1999. *The Syriac Version of the Old Testament: An Introduction*. Cambridge: Cambridge University Press.
Werner, Michael and Bénédicte Zimmermann. 2004. *De la comparaison à l'histoire croisée*. Paris: Seuil.
Werner, Michael and Bénédicte Zimmermann. 2006. "Beyond Comparison: Histoire Croisée and the Challenge of Reflexivity," *History and Theory* 45: 30–50.
Whitcomb, Donald. 2009. "The Gulf in the Early Islamic Period: The Contribution of Archaeology to Regional History," in Lawrence Potter (ed.), 71–89. *The Persian Gulf in History*. New York: Palgrave Macmillan.
White, L. Michael and O. Larry Yarbrough. 1995. *The Social World of the First Christians: Essays in Honor of Wayne A. Meeks*. Minneapolis, MN: Fortress.
Whitehouse, David and Andrew Williamson. 1973. "Sasanian Maritime Trade," *Iran* 11: 29–49.
Whitmarsh, Tim (ed.). 2007. *The Cambridge Companion to the Greek and Roman Novel*. Cambridge: Cambridge University Press.
Wiesehöfer, Josef. 2016. "Greeks, Iranians, and Chinese on the Silk Road," in Lieu and Mikkelson (eds.), 1–17.

Wilken, Robert. 2012. *The First Thousand Years: A Global History of Christianity*. New Haven, CT: Yale University Press.
Wilson, Andrew. 2015. "Red Sea Trade and the State," in de Romanis and Maiuro (eds.), 13–32.
Windstedt, E. O. 1909. "Some Coptic Legends about Roman Emperors," *CQ* 3.3: 218–22.
Wink, André. 1991. *Al-Hind: The Making of the Indo-Islamic World*, Vol. 1: *Early Medieval India and the Expansion of Islam, 7th–11th Centuries*. Leiden: Brill.
Wischmeyer, W. 1980. "Die Aberkiosinschrift als Grabepigramm," *Jahrbuch für Antike und Christentum* 23: 22–47.
Witakowski, Withold. 1987. "The Origin of the 'Teaching of the Apostles'," in H. J. W. Drijvers et al. (eds.), 161–71. *IV Symposium Syriacum 1984*. Rome: Pontificio Istituto Orientale.
Witakowski, Withold. 1996. *Chronicle, Known also as the Chronicle of Zuqnin, part III: Pseudo-Dionysius of Tel-Mahre*. Liverpool: Liverpool University Press.
Wood, Philip. 2010. *"We Have No King but Christ": Christian Political Thought in Greater Syria on the Eve of the Arab Conquest (C. 400–585)*. Oxford: Oxford University Press.
Wood, Philip. 2013. "The *Chronicle of Seert* and Roman Ecclesiastical History in the Sasanian World," in Philip Wood (ed.), 43–60. *History and Identity in the Late Antique Near East*. Oxford: Oxford University Press.
Wood, Philip. 2013. *The Chronicle of Seert: Christian Historical Imagination in Late Antique Iraq*. Oxford: Oxford University Press.
Yacoub III, Ignatius and Matti Moussa. 2009. *History of the Syrian Church of India*. Piscataway, NJ: Gorgias Press.
Yon, J.-B. 2002. *Les notables de Palmyre*. Beirut: IFAPO.
Yon, J.-B. 2016. "Ports of the Indian Ocean: the Port of Spasinu Charax," in Boussac, Salles, and Yon (eds.), 125–36.
Young, Gary. 2001. *Rome's Eastern Trade: International Policy, 31 BC–AD 305*. London: Routledge.
Youtie, Herbert. 1979. "P. Mich. Inv. 1759: ACHMON," *ZPE* 33: 206–8.
Zaleski, Ladislas. 1912. *The Apostle St. Thomas in India: History, Tradition, and Legend*. Mangalore: Codialbail Press.
Zaleski, Ladislas. 1915. *Les origines du christianisme aux Indes*. Mangalore: Codialbail.
Żuchowska, Marta. 2013. "Palmyra and the Far Eastern Trade," *Studia Palmyreńskie* 12: 381–87.
Żuchowska, Marta. 2016. "Palmyra and the Chinese Silk Trade," in Jørgen Christian Meyer, Eivind Seland, and Nils Anfinset (eds.), 29–38. *Palmyrena: City, Hinterland, and Caravan Trade between Orient and Occident*. Oxford: Archaeopress.
Zvelebil, K. V. 1956. "The Yavanas in Old Tamil literature," in F. Tauer, V. Kubickova, and I. Hrbek (eds.), 401–9. *Charisteria orientalia praecipue ad Persiam pertinentia*. Prague: Československé akademie věd.
Zvelebil, K. V. 1975. *Tamil Literature*. Leiden: Brill.

Index

Acts of Archelaus, x, 148, 203, 204
Acts of Mar Mari, 45, 148, 164, 165, 195, 234
Acts of the Apostle Thomas
  content, 1, 2, 4, 15, 21, 27, 28, 30, 31, 32, 35, 42, 43, 44, 45, 48, 49, 50, 53, 54, 57, 60, 61, 66, 69, 143, 148, 191, 194, 207, 208, 212, 215, 217, 230, 233, 234, 237
  date, location, and language, 27, 28, 32, 33, 34, 35, 36, 37, 38, 39, 40, 41, 42, 51, 55, 56, 57, 60, 61, 231
  impact, 2, 22, 27, 28, 30, 53, 59, 60, 61, 62, 63, 64, 65, 66, 87, 142, 143, 208, 212, 213, 222, 225, 226, 230, 231, 232, 233, 236, 237
  in scholarship, 2, 15, 16, 21, 64, 65, 111, 141
  Thomas Christians, 2, 18, 207, 208, 212, 225, 231, 233
  Thomasine literature, 28
Acts of the Apostle Thomas, Parthian, 52, 53, 56, 57, 59, 60, 61, 62, 63, 66, 139, 146, 148, 162, 163, 213, 231, 235
Acts of the Apostles, 14, 28, 35, 52, 62, 148, 198, 234
Addai/Thaddaeus, 14, 35, 49, 50, 54, 55, 56, 57, 60, 66, 111, 148, 149, 151, 164, 229
Adulis, 45, 80, 91, 118, 120, 132, 133
Aezanas, 133
Africa (east), 72, 73, 74, 78, 79, 81, 84, 88, 91, 92, 93, 112, 124, 129, 135
Aggai, 14, 49, 56, 57, 149, 229
Aila, 79, 92, 99, 126, 130
Aksum/Aksumites, 45, 78, 79, 80, 83, 86, 91, 92, 125, 132, 133
  as Indians, 72, 74, 78, 79, 81, 84, 85, 86, 87, 90, 91, 92
  Christianity, 22, 73, 79, 85, 86, 87, 91, 92, 93, 95, 112, 125, 127, 131, 132, 133, 134, 235
  commerce, 100, 121, 128, 132, 133
  diplomacy, 81, 126
Alexandria, 61, 64, 69, 74, 81, 85, 86, 87, 88, 91, 94, 95, 97, 98, 99, 100, 102, 109, 112, 113, 114, 115, 116, 117, 124, 126, 129, 130, 131, 132, 133, 159, 167, 182, 202, 209, 215

Anglo-Saxon Chronicle, 225, 228
Antioch, 110, 151, 153, 167, 181, 182, 204, 215
Anuradhapuras, 101
Aphrahat, 157
Arabia/Arabians, 73, 74, 76, 77, 78, 79, 88, 90, 91, 92, 93, 94, 97, 104, 118, 120, 124, 125, 129, 131, 185, 216, 228
  as Indians, 19, 72, 73, 74, 75, 76, 77, 78, 79, 82, 83, 84, 86, 87, 88, 90, 91, 93, 128, 129, 134, 135, 215
  Christianity, 22, 73, 75, 76, 77, 79, 88, 92, 93, 95, 112, 125, 127, 129, 130, 131, 132, 133, 134, 135, 162, 235, 236
  commerce, 73, 76, 100, 104, 105, 121, 127, 128, 131, 134, 166, 167, 200
  diplomacy, 73, 75, 81, 82
Arikamedu, 18, 19, 101, 103, 122
Arnobius, 59, 61, 62
Athanasius, 74, 85, 91, 130, 132, 242
Augustine, x, 12, 30, 62, 229

Bahrain, 5, 46, 49, 50, 185, 214
Bar Shabba (Mar Shabbay), 145, 146, 147, 254
Barbarikon, xi, 106, 120, 121, 122, 214
Bardaisan, 37, 52, 88, 141, 142, 146, 151, 203, 215
Bartholomew (apostle), 69, 77, 84, 85, 86, 88, 89, 90, 91, 92, 111, 228
Barygaza, 101, 104, 107, 109, 110, 120, 121, 122, 124, 214, 216
Berenike, 97, 99, 100, 101, 102, 103, 113, 114, 116, 121, 125, 126, 127, 130, 132, 167, 173, 185, 216
Births and Deaths of the Prophets and Apostles, 223, 224, 227
Book of the Laws of the Countries, 52, 54, 61, 62, 139, 141, 142, 146, 151, 162, 192
Brahmins, 18, 74, 79, 81, 88, 89, 93, 141, 208, 210, 212, 228

central Asia, 7, 31, 52, 61, 63, 66, 139, 163, 165, 166, 169, 173, 176, 177, 178, 188, 189, 192, 194, 196, 200, 201, 218, 233, 235

Index

Christianity, 1, 2, 3, 21, 22, 50, 139, 140, 146, 162, 230, 234, 236, 237
  commerce, 140, 155, 165, 166, 168, 170, 171, 172, 173, 174, 175, 177, 178, 181, 182, 183, 184, 186, 190, 194, 195, 197, 198, 201, 205, 206, 213
  Manichaeism, 156
Cheras, 19, 101, 108
Cholas, 101, 210
Christianity/Christians, ix, x, xi, 3, 13, 14, 15, 27, 30, 42, 45, 51, 58, 59, 61, 63, 66, 69, 141, 154, 205
  at Dura-Europos, 153, 183
  at Edessa, 55, 63, 66, 140, 142, 146, 148, 150, 151, 152, 153, 234
  at Palmyra, 204
  conversion, 12
  in Arabia, 22, 72, 76, 77, 88, 92, 93, 129, 131, 132, 135, 235
  in Asia, 1, 2, 3, 9, 10, 15, 21, 22, 50, 51, 54, 61, 64, 66, 140, 141, 143, 147, 148, 149, 156, 162, 163, 165, 166, 168, 173, 202, 204, 230, 233, 234, 235, 237
  in central Asia, 50, 52, 53, 61, 66, 139, 146, 162, 165, 202
  in Egypt, 130, 131, 132
  in Ethiopia, 22, 72, 85, 88, 90, 91, 92, 93, 129, 132, 133, 135, 235
  in India, 1, 2, 9, 10, 15, 16, 18, 20, 21, 22, 53, 54, 65, 66, 72, 95, 110, 111, 124, 125, 135, 140, 143, 144, 145, 147, 150, 208, 209, 211, 212, 213, 214, 220, 221, 222, 225, 230, 231, 232, 235, 236, 237
  in Iran, 50, 61, 139, 146, 149, 155, 156, 158, 161, 162, 165, 202
  in Parthian/Sasanian territory, 22, 140, 146, 147, 148, 149, 150, 154, 156, 157, 158, 161, 162, 166, 167, 202, 204, 205, 206, 234
  in the Indian Ocean, 3, 15, 16, 21, 69, 83, 93, 95, 100, 101, 125, 127, 130, 133, 134, 135, 136, 144, 220, 235, 236
  in the Persian Gulf, 144, 149
  in the Red Sea, 22, 69, 73, 92, 93, 95, 100, 125, 127, 129, 130, 134, 135, 236
  networks, 10, 11, 13, 15, 21, 22, 23, 29, 50, 100, 112, 125, 129, 130, 133, 134, 135, 140, 149, 162, 163, 165, 168, 201, 204, 205, 206, 213, 218, 233, 234, 236, 237
  Thomasine, 29
Chronicle of 1234, 226
Chronicle of 846, 226
Chronicle of Arbela, 147, 158
Chronicle of Edessa, 150
Chronicle of Se'ert, 143, 147, 154, 218
Clement of Alexandria, 51, 61, 129
Clementine Recognitions, 52, 61, 139
Clysma, 92, 99, 126

Codex of Fulda, 227
Cologne Mani Codex, 33, 154, 191
conversion, 11, 12, 13, 15, 22, 54, 55, 57, 88, 91, 133, 146, 206, 210
Coptos, 94, 97, 99, 100, 102, 114, 115, 116, 117, 120, 121, 122
Cosmas Indicopleustes, 72, 78, 83, 84, 132, 133, 134, 135, 140, 144, 218, 221, 222, 225, 230, 231
crosses (St. Thomas), 212, 220

Dura-Europos, 150, 153, 154, 157, 183

Edessa/Urhay, 14, 27, 29, 32, 33, 37, 45, 50, 52, 54, 55, 56, 57, 58, 59, 60, 66, 139, 141, 142, 143, 146, 148, 150, 151, 152, 157, 164, 167, 168, 189, 192, 195, 199, 225, 226, 227, 230, 231, 234, 237
Egeria, 58, 226
Egypt/Egyptians, 96, 103, 104, 106, 107, 109, 114, 123, 132, 155, 159, 185, 193, 194, 202, 203, 231
  Christianity from, 69, 77, 86, 91, 95, 111, 131, 132, 134, 135, 235
  Christianity in, 130
  commerce, 69, 72, 73, 76, 79, 81, 94, 95, 96, 97, 98, 99, 101, 102, 104, 105, 112, 115, 116, 118, 119, 120, 121, 122, 123, 124, 125, 126, 127, 128, 133, 186, 200, 216, 236
Ephrem, 58, 59, 62, 142, 203, 226, 234, 235
Epiphanius, 30, 62, 90, 91, 126, 128, 129, 223, 225
Ethiopia (Nubia), 85, 93, 95, 127
Ethiopia/Ethiopians (*see also* Aksum/Aksumites and Ethiopia (Nubia)), 59, 62, 74, 76, 78, 79, 89, 90, 91
  as Indians, 19, 72, 74, 75, 78, 79, 84, 85, 86, 89, 90, 91, 92, 128, 129
  Christianity, 79, 90, 91, 93, 125
  commerce, 120
Eusebius of Caesarea, 33, 37, 51, 52, 54, 55, 56, 57, 58, 60, 61, 88, 89, 92, 128, 129, 139, 142, 145, 147, 148, 151
Exposition of the Entire World, 76, 77, 78, 79, 81, 93, 128

Farasan islands, 107, 120
Fars, 22, 45, 143, 145, 148, 155, 160, 161, 164, 196, 218, 219, 220, 222, 230, 234, 236
Frumentius, 69, 74, 85, 86, 87, 91, 92, 132

Gospel of Thomas, 28, 29, 52
Gregory of Tours, 225, 226, 227, 229
Gudnaphar/Goundaphores (Gondophares), 16, 27, 31, 32, 38, 43, 44, 53, 55, 139, 207, 233

Hadramawt, 101, 214, 215
Himyar/Himyarites, 74, 75, 76, 77, 78, 81, 101, 125, 126, 131

Index

History of Mar Yaunan, 143, 144, 217, 220
Hou Hanshu, 110, 123, 170, 176, 179, 183, 216
Hymn of the Pearl, 33, 34, 36, 39, 191, 192, 193, 194, 195, 197, 216

India/Indians, x, xi, 1, 2, 4, 7, 11, 14, 16, 22, 27, 30, 31, 32, 34, 42, 43, 44, 45, 49, 50, 51, 52, 53, 54, 56, 57, 58, 59, 60, 61, 62, 63, 64, 65, 66, 69, 72, 73, 74, 80, 81, 82, 84, 86, 87, 88, 89, 92, 93, 101, 102, 103, 106, 107, 108, 109, 118, 120, 121, 123, 124, 126, 127, 129, 134, 139, 141, 142, 143, 145, 149, 150, 162, 163, 173, 182, 185, 192, 194, 198, 203, 207, 208, 209, 211, 212, 213, 214, 215, 216, 217, 219, 220, 221, 225, 226, 227, 228, 229, 230, 231, 233, 234, 235, 236, 237
    Christianity, 1, 2, 3, 9, 10, 11, 15, 16, 20, 21, 22, 53, 64, 65, 66, 95, 111, 125, 129, 135, 140, 141, 142, 143, 144, 145, 147, 208, 209, 210, 211, 212, 213, 218, 221, 222, 225, 230, 231, 232, 237
    commerce, 18, 22, 72, 73, 76, 83, 95, 97, 101, 102, 105, 106, 110, 120, 121, 125, 127, 128, 129, 133, 140, 141, 185, 217, 228
    definition, 96
    diplomacy, 110, 141
    Mani, 155, 196, 199, 202, 203, 206, 214
    Palmyrenes, 4, 5, 6, 104, 166, 167, 185, 186, 187, 199, 200, 204, 205, 206, 215
    Persians, 133, 140, 166, 168, 178, 180, 197, 199, 200, 201, 206, 212, 213, 214, 217, 218, 219, 221, 222, 225, 230, 232, 233, 235, 236, 237
    Roman Egyptians, 95, 99, 100, 101, 112, 116, 117, 118, 120, 124, 125, 128, 134, 135, 203, 213, 225, 235, 236, 237
    Thomas Christians, 2, 16, 27, 65, 207, 233, 237
    Thomas' tomb, 144, 145, 222, 225, 226, 227, 228, 229, 231
Indian Ocean, xi, 2, 21, 46, 51, 66, 69, 73, 75, 79, 80, 82, 83, 94, 99, 100, 105, 109, 115, 118, 121, 124, 126, 135, 178, 185, 189, 193, 199, 200, 213, 229
    Christianity, 3, 15, 21, 95, 100, 111, 134, 235
    commerce, 9, 22, 69, 95, 97, 112, 113, 120, 167
    diplomacy, 215
Indo-Greeks, 107
Indo-Parthians, 16, 31, 43, 52, 53, 65, 108, 139
Iran, 14, 52, 56, 61, 63, 78, 79, 155, 163, 164, 165, 175, 178, 181, 189, 190, 192, 193, 196, 197, 200, 202, 206, 213, 234, 235
    Christianity, 1, 21, 22, 50, 139, 146, 147, 149, 154, 157, 159, 161, 162, 230, 236
    commerce, 165, 166, 168, 170, 172, 173, 174, 180, 181, 184, 186, 189, 191, 193, 194, 195, 198, 201, 206, 213
    Manichaeism, 156, 162
Isidore of Charax, 181, 182

Isidore of Seville, 54, 63, 222, 223, 224, 227
Itinerary from Eden, 58, 76, 77, 78, 79, 81, 91, 93, 128, 129

Jerome, 59, 62, 88, 89, 90, 93, 128, 129, 223, 224
Jerusalem, 1, 4, 13, 27, 31, 42, 44, 45, 49, 50, 57, 64, 66, 90, 159, 198, 204, 207, 215, 233, 237, 243, 259, 273
Jesus of Nazareth, 1, 2, 13, 27, 28, 31, 33, 34, 48, 49, 50, 54, 55, 56, 57, 60, 63, 64, 139, 148, 151, 152, 233, 237
John Chrysostom, 62
Josephus, 18, 78, 152, 195, 198, 208, 215
Judaism/Jews, ix, 12, 19, 54, 63, 75, 98, 99, 115, 131, 152, 153, 157, 167, 168, 198, 204, 205, 206, 215, 219, 234
Jupiter Dolichenus, 9

Kalamene/Calamina, 144, 213, 222, 224, 225, 226, 227, 229, 230, 231, 232, 236, 237
Kharg, 47, 48, 149, 214
Khuzistan, 22, 45, 56, 148, 155, 157, 159, 164, 165, 168, 185, 198, 206, 219, 234, 236
Kushans, 52, 53, 62, 101, 139, 146

Letter of Mara bar Serapion, 152
Letter Regarding the Peoples of India and the Brahmins, 79, 80, 82, 93, 128, 129

Maes Titianos, 164, 165, 168, 169, 170, 171, 172, 173, 174, 175, 176, 177, 178, 189, 190, 197, 200, 201, 205
Mani, x, 11, 33, 34, 55, 111, 141, 148, 151, 154, 155, 156, 166, 183, 191, 195, 196, 197, 199, 202, 203, 206, 213, 214, 215, 216, 234, 269
Manichaeism/Manichaeans, x, xi, 8, 11, 12, 30, 33, 34, 111, 155, 156, 173, 183, 184, 191, 194, 195, 196, 197, 202, 203, 204, 206
Margam Kali, 212, 228
Martyr Act of Miles, 159, 160
Martyr Act of Pethion, 162
Martyr Act of Pusai, 155
Martyr Act of Saint Arethas, 75
Martyr Act of the Captives, 155, 159
Matthew (apostle), 58, 59, 69, 84, 85, 86, 88, 89, 90, 91, 223
Merv, 139, 144, 146, 147, 161, 162, 165, 169, 173, 175, 183, 186, 197, 198, 200
Mesene/Maišan/Charax Spasinou, 5, 8, 22, 46, 49, 69, 123, 143, 154, 157, 159, 161, 164, 168, 185, 192, 193, 194, 195, 196, 198, 203, 205, 206, 214, 215, 216
Miles, bishop of Susa, 159
Muziris, xi, 18, 82, 102, 103, 105, 106, 113, 114, 115, 117, 118, 120, 122, 123

Muziris papyrus, 102, 113, 114, 115, 116, 117, 123
Mylapore, 19, 103, 122, 208, 212, 225, 228, 229, 230, 231, 237, 266
Myos Hormos, 97, 99, 102, 103, 125, 127, 130, 216

Nabataeans, 10, 167, 168, 204
Names of the Fathers at Nicaea, 145
networks, 3, 7, 8, 9, 10, 11, 12, 13, 15, 21, 22, 29, 51, 62, 63, 64, 95, 100, 109, 124, 125, 131, 133, 140, 151, 152, 177, 201, 202, 218, 230, 234
   highland Persian, 218, 236
   Levantine, 22, 63, 156, 162, 166, 167, 168, 169, 178, 180, 181, 182, 184, 185, 197, 201, 202, 203, 204, 205, 213, 218, 233, 234, 235, 236
   lowland Parthian/Sasanian, 22, 155, 156, 162, 166, 168, 169, 183, 190, 193, 194, 195, 197, 200, 201, 202, 203, 206, 213, 214, 215, 217, 218, 219, 220, 222, 230, 233, 235, 236
   Palmyrene, 5, 6, 7, 8, 10, 206
   Roman Egyptian, 7, 9, 10, 12, 15, 22, 69, 72, 73, 83, 85, 93, 95, 96, 97, 98, 99, 100, 112, 113, 117, 118, 119, 120, 121, 123, 124, 125, 126, 127, 128, 129, 130, 131, 132, 133, 134, 135, 136, 163, 166, 167, 173, 184, 194, 198, 205, 213, 225, 227, 230, 235, 236, 237
   socio-commercial, 3, 4, 7, 9, 10, 11, 12, 13, 14, 15, 21, 23, 66, 72, 115, 119, 133, 135, 165, 166, 168, 173, 181, 182, 187, 188, 194, 203, 205, 213, 232, 234, 235, 237
Nisibis, 33, 54, 146, 147, 150, 151, 157, 159, 161, 168, 189, 194, 229

oral traditions, 15, 16, 19, 21, 60, 63, 65, 207, 208, 209, 210, 211, 212, 228, 231, 233, 237
Origen, 33, 34, 51, 53, 54, 61, 151
Palmyra/Palmyrenes, 4, 5, 6, 8, 10, 98, 99, 104, 116, 121, 122, 124, 166, 167, 168, 185, 186, 187, 188, 189, 196, 198, 199, 200, 202, 204, 205, 206, 214, 215, 217, 234
   India, 4, 5, 6, 104, 167, 185, 186, 187, 199, 206
   networks, 5, 6, 7, 8, 10, 205

Pandyas, 101
Pantaenus, 69, 88, 89, 90, 92
Parthians, 50, 54, 55, 56, 57, 59, 60, 65, 66, 87, 153, 171, 175, 179, 180, 182, 183, 184, 187, 193, 194, 198, 199, 201, 217, 222, 223
   Christianity, 139, 140, 146, 147, 148, 149, 150, 151, 152, 154, 156, 165, 166, 167, 168, 202, 205, 206, 213, 234
   commerce, 22, 153, 154, 162, 164, 165, 166, 168, 170, 173, 174, 176, 177, 178, 179, 180, 181, 182, 183, 184, 185, 186, 188, 189, 190, 191, 192, 193, 194, 195, 197, 198, 199, 200, 201, 202, 203, 204, 205, 214, 216, 217, 230, 236
   India, 214, 217

Passion of the Holy Apostle Thomas, 45, 226
Pattanam (*see also* Muziris), 103, 105, 115, 122
Periplus of the Erythraean Sea, 53, 72, 73, 94, 101, 102, 113, 117, 118, 119, 120, 121, 122, 128, 216, 217
Persian gulf, 4, 6, 8, 22, 45, 49, 50, 69, 76, 143, 162, 166, 167, 168, 184, 185, 187, 189, 193, 199, 201, 203, 204, 206, 213, 215, 216, 219, 220, 233
   Christianity, 144, 157
Persian martyrs, 159, 161, 162, 205
Peshitta, 152
Philostorgius, 74, 75, 76, 77, 78, 79, 92, 128, 129, 131
Pliny the Elder, 49, 72, 73, 81, 99, 101, 102, 120, 128, 188
Procopius, 91, 133, 134, 180, 218
ps.-Gelasius of Cyzicus, 62, 86, 87, 128, 145, 218
pseudepigraphon on the Magi, 58, 59, 62, 223
Ptolemy (Claudius), 53, 58, 62, 72, 73, 99, 102, 105, 106, 113, 120, 124, 128, 164, 165, 169, 170, 171, 172, 173, 174, 175, 176, 177, 178, 181, 189, 190, 197, 201

Qane, 120, 122, 131, 214, 216
Quilon copper plates, 20, 211, 219
Red Sea, xi, 2, 66, 73, 76, 78, 79, 83, 84, 85, 91, 93, 94, 103, 120, 129, 132, 133, 141, 142, 185
   Christianity, 21, 69, 100, 130, 235
   commerce, 9, 22, 69, 72, 94, 95, 97, 99, 100, 101, 104, 110, 112, 113, 115, 116, 117, 120, 123, 124, 125, 126, 127, 129, 134, 167, 235
   diplomacy, 215

Refutation of All Heresies, 62, 154, 183, 184, 190, 194
Rufinus, 52, 61, 74, 85, 86, 89, 91, 92, 128, 129, 132

Saba/Sabaeans, 101
Saka Kshatrapas, 101, 108, 109
Sangam poems (Tamil), 106
Sasanian Persians, xi, 46, 56, 78, 125, 144, 153, 154, 158, 160, 166, 179, 198, 199, 205, 206, 221
   Christianity, 22, 87, 139, 140, 143, 145, 146, 147, 148, 149, 150, 154, 156, 161, 165, 166, 167, 202, 205, 206, 213, 214, 217, 233, 234, 236, 237
   commerce, 22, 153, 154, 162, 163, 164, 165, 166, 168, 170, 173, 177, 178, 179, 180, 186, 188, 189, 190, 193, 194, 195, 197, 198, 199, 200, 201, 202, 203, 204, 205, 206, 212, 214, 216, 217, 218, 230, 235, 236
   India, 213, 214, 217, 218, 219, 221, 222, 225, 227, 232, 236
   Indian Ocean, 218, 219, 220, 221
   Manichaeism, 156, 206
   Zoroastrianism, 34
Satavahanas, 101, 108

Seleucia-Ctesiphon, 143, 144, 153, 157, 158, 159, 161, 166, 168, 180, 181, 182, 187, 188, 189, 193, 194, 195, 201, 206, 214, 219
Seres, 53, 58, 59, 61, 62, 164, 171, 172, 174, 175, 176, 177, 183, 184, 189, 190, 192, 201
Shapur II, 146, 155, 157, 158, 159, 160, 161, 196, 199
Short Accounts of the Apostles, 223, 224, 227
Socotra, 73, 75, 76, 77, 78, 79, 81, 82, 83, 93, 97, 100, 102, 104, 107, 109, 118, 119, 121, 124, 125, 126, 127, 129, 131, 133, 134, 135, 186, 199, 215, 218, 222, 236
Socrates, 61, 74, 85, 86, 89, 91, 92, 128, 129, 147, 226
Sophytus (inscription of), 7, 173
Sozomen, 74, 85, 86, 89, 91, 92, 128, 129, 158, 159, 160, 226
Sri Lanka, 22, 76, 79, 80, 82, 83, 84, 93, 101, 102, 120, 129, 133, 135, 217, 218, 219, 221, 222, 236
Stone Tower, 172, 174, 175, 176, 177, 178, 190, 197, 200
Strabo, 72, 73, 101, 102, 110, 128, 181, 182, 188, 215

Tarim basin, 58, 62, 169, 170, 171, 172, 173, 174, 175, 176, 177, 183, 184, 189, 190, 194, 197, 200, 201
Tatian, 153
Teaching of Addai, 37, 56, 57, 60, 148, 151, 195
Teaching of the Apostles, 49, 56, 57
Theodoret, 74, 85, 86, 88, 91, 128, 129, 147
Theophilus the "Indian", 69, 75, 76, 77, 78, 79, 81, 131, 132
Thomas (Judas Thomas), the apostle, 4, 21, 29, 44, 51, 55, 57, 60, 61, 63, 111, 140, 145, 148, 149, 208, 209, 220, 226, 227, 228, 230, 231, 233, 234, 235, 237, 240
Gondophares, 16, 27, 31, 32, 43, 53, 55, 207
India, 1, 2, 3, 14, 15, 27, 30, 31, 32, 35, 42, 43, 44, 45, 46, 49, 50, 51, 54, 55, 56, 57, 58, 59, 62, 63, 64, 65, 66, 87, 111, 143, 207, 208, 212, 217, 225, 226, 233, 234, 235
Magi, 58, 59, 62, 223
Mazdai, 32, 33, 34, 35, 212
name, 28
not a martyr, 50, 51, 61, 65
Parthia, 34, 44, 50, 51, 52, 53, 54, 56, 60, 61, 63, 64, 66, 139, 141, 146, 163, 223, 235
relic cult at Edessa, 58, 142, 143, 225, 226, 227, 230, 234, 235, 237
Thomas Christians, 16, 207, 208, 209, 210, 212, 231, 233, 237
tomb in India, 103, 122, 144, 145, 213, 222, 224, 225, 226, 227, 228, 229, 230, 231, 232, 236, 237
twin, 2, 28, 33, 34, 48
Thomas Christians, 2, 4, 27, 65, 140, 207, 209, 220, 233, 237
Thomas Kinayi, 19, 20, 209, 211
Thomas Parvam/Thomas Ramban, 207, 208, 212, 228, 231
Thomas the Contender, 28, 29, 52

Yavanas/Yonakas, 104, 106, 107, 108, 109, 123, 124

Zeugma, 180, 181, 182

Lightning Source UK Ltd.
Milton Keynes UK
UKHW020818051121
393294UK00021B/526